POLITICS IN THE AGE
OF AUSTERITY

To the memory of Peter Mair, friend and model scholar, who passed away on 15 August 2011, while this book, with his contribution, was being prepared for publication.

POLITICS IN THE AGE OF AUSTERITY

Edited by Armin Schäfer
and Wolfgang Streeck

polity

First published in 2013 by Polity Press

Polity Press
65 Bridge Street
Cambridge CB2 1UR, UK

Polity Press
350 Main Street
Malden, MA 02148, USA

ISBN-13: 978-0-7456-6168-1
ISBN-13: 978-0-7456-6169-8 (pb)

A catalogue record for this book is available from the British Library.

Typeset in 10 on 12 pt Adobe Sabon
by Servis Filmsetting Ltd, Stockport, Cheshire
Printed and bound by the MPG Printgroup, UK

For further information on Polity, visit our website: www.politybooks.com

Contents

Contributors

Mabel Berezin is Associate Professor and Chair of Sociology at Cornell University, Ithaca, New York.

Colin Crouch is Emeritus Professor at the University of Warwick and External Scientific Member of the Max Planck Institute for the Study of Societies, Cologne.

Philipp Genschel is Professor of Political Science at Jacobs University, Bremen.

Peter Mair was Professor of Comparative Politics at the European University Institute, Florence.

Daniel Mertens is a Researcher at the Max Planck Institute for the Study of Societies, Cologne.

Claus Offe is Emeritus Professor of Political Sociology at the Hertie School of Governance, Berlin, and of the Humboldt University, Berlin.

Armin Schäfer is a Researcher at the Max Planck Institute for the Study of Societies, Cologne.

Fritz W. Scharpf is Emeritus Director at the Max Planck Institute for the Studies of Societies, Cologne.

Peter Schwarz is Visiting Professor of Public Economics at the University of Göttingen and a former Research Associate at Jacobs University, Bremen.

Sven Steinmo is Professor of Political and Social Sciences at the European University Institute, Florence.

Wolfgang Streeck is Director at the Max Planck Institute for the Study of Societies, Cologne.

1

Introduction: Politics in the Age of Austerity

Armin Schäfer and Wolfgang Streeck

Democracy depends on choice. Citizens must be able to influence the course of government through elections. If a change in government cannot translate into different policies, democracy is incapacitated. Many mature democracies may well be approaching such a situation as they confront fiscal crisis. For almost three decades, OECD countries have – in fits and starts – run deficits and accumulated debt. Rising interest payments and welfare-state maturation have meant that an ever smaller part of government revenue is available today for discretionary spending and social investment. Whichever party comes into office will find its hands tied by past decisions. The current financial and fiscal crisis has only exacerbated the long-term shrinking of the room governments have to manoeuvre. As a consequence, projects for policy change have lost credibility – at least if they imply the redistribution of resources from old purposes to new ones. This is clearly the situation in those countries that were hit hardest by the 'Second Great Contraction' (Reinhart and Rogoff 2009). In Ireland, Italy, Portugal, Spain and of course Greece, governments of any colour will for decades be forced to cut and hold down spending.

In a number of farsighted articles, Pierson has outlined what he calls a 'fiscal regime of austerity' (Pierson 2001a, 2001b). Permanent austerity, according to Pierson, results when the ability to generate revenues is limited while at the same time spending needs to increase. In the 1990s, three causes came together that were not present in the decades immediately following the Second World War: diminished growth rates, the maturation of welfare states and an aging population. The diminished growth rates had their start in the mid-1970s, and since then rates have been lower on average than during the *trente glorieuses*. After the 'easy financing era' (Steuerle 1996: 416) had come to an end, revenues increased more slowly and, with few exceptions, public expenditure since then has exceeded government receipts (Streeck and Mertens, chapter 2 in this volume). In principle, governments could have counteracted this tendency through higher taxes. However, growing international tax competition has rendered it more difficult to raise taxes on companies and top income earners (see Genschel and Schwarz, chapter 3 in this volume). At the same time, taxing ordinary citizens more heavily through higher indirect taxes and social security contributions has become politically more costly, since real wages have also grown more slowly, if at all, than in the past (Pierson 2001b: 62).

On the expenditure side, Pierson emphasizes the 'maturation' of the welfare state and demographic change, both of which he suggests are bound to keep expenditure at high levels. Welfare-state maturation means that today a much larger share of the population is entitled to receive pensions than when public pension programmes were created. In the beginning, a very limited number of people qualified for benefits, while the working population financed the welfare state through (payroll) taxes. This favourable demographic profile changes, however, once the first generation of contributors retires (Pierson 2001b: 59). What is more, in an aging society people will receive benefits for a longer period of time, whereas the number of contributors will stagnate or even shrink. In combination, these long-term trends lead to a mismatch of spending obligations and public revenue.

The financial and subsequent economic crisis of recent years has resulted in a vast deterioration in public finances. In all OECD countries except Norway, Sweden and Switzerland, the need to save banks and jobs has meant a sharp rise in public debt (figure 1.1). In some countries, it has more than doubled since the onset of the crisis, surpassing 100 per cent of GDP in eight countries in 2012 (Obinger 2012).[1] High levels of public debt make it even more difficult to allocate resources from old to new purposes, since mandatory expenditures will tend to consume almost the entire budget. This puts pressure on governments to make unpopular choices. 'Responsible' or, for that matter, fiscally prudent choices may be at odds with citizens' needs and demands, in effect rendering governments less responsive to their constituencies (Mair, chapter 6 in this volume).

In parallel with the faltering capacity for discretionary spending, public fatigue with democratic practice and core institutions has grown. Turnout in parliamentary elections has been declining almost everywhere (Franklin 2004); electoral volatility is rising (Mair 2006); trust in politicians, parties and parliaments is on the decline (Putnam et al. 2000); party membership is collapsing (Van Biezen et al. 2012); and there is a noticeable gap between democratic aspirations and satisfaction with the way democracy actually works (Norris 2011). As opposition parties in heavily indebted countries can no longer promise not to cut expenditure

Figure 1.1: Increase in sovereign debt during the financial crisis, 2008–2012

Percentage of GDP

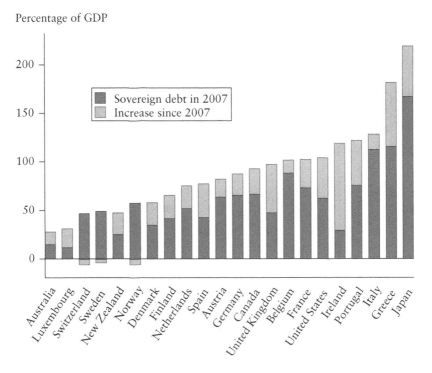

Source: OECD Economic Outlook No. 90.

in order to consolidate public finances, electoral choice becomes limited. At the same time, new anti-establishment parties have emerged or have gained new impetus in many countries (Norris 2005; Berezin, chapter 10 in this volume), and incumbent parties are finding it more difficult than in the past to stay in office. This book investigates what mechanisms may be at work to link rising debt and democratic disaffection. In this introduction, we focus more narrowly on the link between debt and falling turnout. After discussing each trend separately in the next two sections, we will discuss a number of direct and indirect pathways that seem to connect the two trends.

1 Rising debt

While the fiscal crisis of today's rich democracies became apparent only after 2008, it has long been in the making. Since the 1970s, almost all

Figure 1.2: Government debt as a percentage of GDP, seven countries, 1970–2010

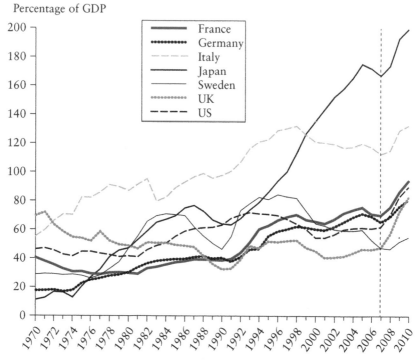

Source: OECD Economic Outlook No. 87.

OECD countries have had to borrow money to cover a chronic gap between public expenditure and public revenue, resulting in a steady increase in public debt. Like declining electoral participation, rising indebtedness was also observed throughout the OECD: in Social Democratic Sweden as well as in the Republican United States; in 'liberal market economies' such as the UK and in 'coordinated' ones such as Germany, Japan and Italy; in presidential as well as parliamentary democracies; under first-past-the-post systems and under proportional representation; and in competitive as much as in one-party democracies such as Japan.

Figure 1.2 shows the more or less steady rise of public debt as a percentage of GDP for seven selected countries over four decades, with the United States and the United Kingdom as the prototypical Anglo-American democracies, Japan as the leading capitalist democracy in Asia, France and Germany standing for the 'Rhineland capitalism' of continental Europe, Italy representing the Mediterranean pattern, and Sweden exemplifying the Scandinavian one. While there are differences between the seven curves,

Figure 1.3: Government debt as a percentage of GDP, OECD average, 1970–2010

Percentage of GDP

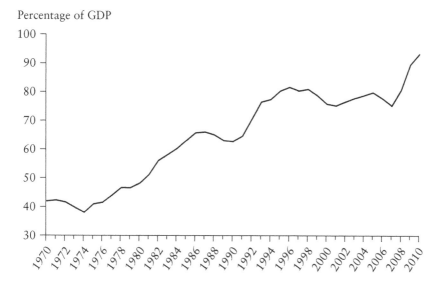

Note: Countries included in unweighted average: Austria, Belgium, Canada, France, Germany, Italy, Japan, Netherlands, Norway, Sweden, UK, US.

Source: OECD Economic Outlook No. 90.

the overall trend is the same for all of them, and indeed for the OECD as a whole (figure 1.3). Initial questions as to whether rising debt levels were 'sustainable' in the longer term came up as early as the late 1970s in several countries, and there were various attempts by economists to determine a maximum level of debt beyond which macro-economic performance would suffer. In the meantime debt continued to increase, however, falsifying successive claims that the debt build-up had hit a ceiling.

In the 1990s, led by the United States under the Clinton administration, an OECD-wide attempt was made to consolidate public budgets, mostly through privatization and cuts in social welfare spending, with the hope of using the post-1989 'peace dividend' towards fiscal relief. It was at this time that Pierson saw a new age of permanent austerity on the horizon, one in which public spending would be cut back to match stagnant or even declining tax revenue. Much hope was placed by economists and political leaders, increasingly including those on the left, in institutional reforms of national parliaments' budgeting procedures, as strongly propagated by international organizations. Apart from Sweden, however, which went through a dramatic financial-cum-fiscal crisis in the mid-1990s (see Steinmo, chapter 4 in this volume), and the United States, which by the end of the century was running a budget surplus, not

Figure 1.4: The causes of the fiscal crisis

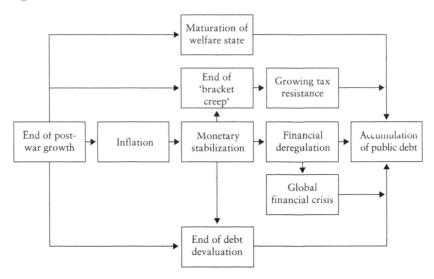

much was achieved. It is important to keep in mind that the latest jump in public debt (which wiped out the gains of the – politically very costly – consolidation efforts of the 1990s and early 2000s almost completely) was caused by the financial crisis of 2008 turning into a fiscal crisis when governments needed to rescue financial institutions that had been allowed to become 'too big to fail' and had to reinflate the 'real economy' through 'Keynesian' deficit spending.

Naturally there has been and continues to be discussion on the causes of the long-drawn build-up of public debt in an entire family of countries in the absence of major wars. On the surface, we may observe that indebtedness began to develop with the end of the postwar growth period in the late 1960s (figure 1.4). At this time public expenditure continued to increase, while the rising taxation that had accompanied it up to this point began to come to an end (figure 1.5). The 1970s was a period of high inflation throughout the industrialized capitalist world, which for a while served to devalue national debt burdens, just as growth had in the preceding period. When OECD countries, under the leadership of the Federal Reserve Bank of the United States, ended inflation in the early 1980s, however, three developments coincided to push up public debt. First, structural unemployment ensued almost everywhere, resulting in rising demand on the coffers of the welfare state. Second, the end of 'bracket creep' – the automatic advancement of taxpayers with nominally increasing incomes to higher tax rates under progressive taxation – made for rising tax resistance. And third, with lower nominal growth rates, in

Figure 1.5: Government expenditure and revenue, as a percentage of GDP, seven countries, 1970–2010

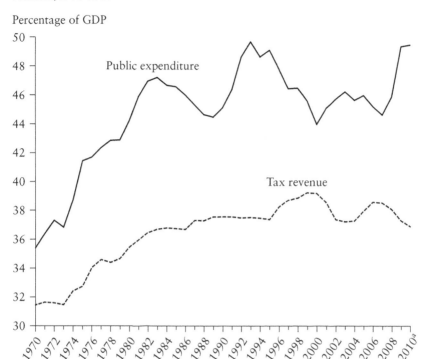

Percentage of GDP

Note: ᵃ Estimate.

Source: OECD Economic Outlook No. 87.

addition now to continuously lower real growth, past debt was no longer devalued with time. At this point, monetary stability encouraged holders of financial assets to lend money to governments, while governments felt encouraged to borrow by the low interest rates that followed the victory over inflation. Expanding asymmetries in international trade contributed as well. As surplus countries, first in the Middle East and later also in Asia, were seeking safe havens for their export earnings, the United States deregulated its financial industry to attract and absorb foreign capital, in an effort to finance the country's double deficit. Financial deregulation then resulted in the crash of 2008, which led to further accumulation of public debt and became the proximate cause of the current fiscal crisis in most advanced capitalist countries.

Expectations of an impending 'fiscal crisis of the state' have been around for some time (O'Connor 1973; Bell 1976). In the public finance theory tradition, the anticipated problem was that the revenue the 'tax state', or *Steuerstaat* (Goldscheid 1926; Schumpeter 1991 [1918]), would over time be able to raise ('confiscate') in a democratic-capitalist society whose assets were mostly privately owned would not be enough to cover the growing collective needs that social and economic progress were expected to generate. One can easily recognize the background to this argument in nineteenth-century debates on the future of capitalism and industrialism, where bourgeois-conservative *Kathedersozialisten* such as Adolph Wagner (with his 'law of expanding state activity') agreed with the Marxian diagnosis of a growing 'socialization of production' (*Vergesellschaftung der Produktion*) that required more and more collective regulation and support.[2] It was only in the 1970s and 1980s that the fiscal problem of capitalist political economy was redefined by the theory of 'public choice'. Rather than declaring that the fiscal means made available by society to the state were lagging behind growing collective needs, public-choice theorists now attributed the crisis appearing on the horizon to collective demands on the public purse having frivolously exceeded what was necessary and sustainable in a market economy, the ostensible result of pressures from competition between office-seeking politicians. Where public finance saw a potential fiscal crisis resulting from society being unwilling to pay for what it needed, public-choice theorists blamed society and its politics for excessively extracting resources from a private economy that would do much better if left in peace and to its own devices.[3]

The latest version of the public-choice account of the fiscal crisis of the state is the *common pool theory*, which has become established as the received opinion of the so-called new institutional economics. In essence it is just another version of the 'tragedy of the commons' story, which in turn is the riposte of standard economics to the Marxian analysis of primitive accumulation (Marx 1967 [1867, 1887]), in particular the 'enclosure' of the common land of English villages by the landed gentry, which is presented as prudent economic policy in pursuit of higher overall economic efficiency (North and Thomas 1973). Just as common ownership and the absence of private – i.e., capitalist – property allegedly resulted in irresponsible 'overgrazing' of common farmland, requiring a forcible modernization of the property regime, it is now being claimed that the public nature of government finance causes individually rational actors to take more out of the 'common pool' of state resources than they can sustain. In the popular version of the theory, democracy is the leading culprit, with its central actors – voters, interest groups and political parties – portrayed as being fundamentally irresponsible and unable to resist the temptations inherent in the free access to collectively owned resources. Vulnerable as its institutions are to popular pressure, so the story goes, democracy will inevitably result in irrational economic decisions, including commitments to public spending in excess of public revenues and resulting in ever rising indebtedness. Obviously the theory of the common pool has a strong Hayekian flavour in that it supports the conclusion that economic policy-making must be protected from electoral pressure and political opportunism and be vested in politically sterilized institutions such as independent central banks or regulatory authorities such as the European Commission. With respect to public finance and the fiscal crisis of the state, it was thinking along these lines that inspired the institutional reforms of the national budgeting procedures that were promoted in the 1990s, as well as the 'fiscal pact' that is currently being negotiated among European nations.

It is not our intention here to debate common pool theory in detail, as the main interest of this volume is to trace the impact of deteriorating public finances on democracy rather than vice versa. We may, however, note that the build-up of public debt since the 1970s did not exactly coincide with a parallel build-up in political participation and popular pressure on governments and markets. It was not only, as we have indicated, voter turnout that declined rather than increased during the period in question – and as we will see, disproportionately so among those at the bottom of our societies, who would be most likely to make demands on government spending. Trade union membership fell as well throughout the world of democratic capitalism, and often enough as a result of successful efforts at union-breaking by governments and employers (Visser 2006). Collective bargaining declined as a consequence, and with it the wages at the lower end of the labour market, while the earnings of shareholders and, even more so, managers improved dramatically, making for a stunning and sustained rise in inequality inside democratic-capitalist societies (Salverda and Mayhew 2009; OECD 2011; Schäfer, chapter 7 in this volume). Needs for 'restructuring' under alleged pressures of 'globalization' were and continue to be invoked to justify the retreat by governments from politically guaranteed full employment, the growing individualization of the employment contract, increasingly precarious employment, the renewal of managerial prerogative, the privatization of government services, and 'reformed' – i.e., recommodifying – social policy – all of which can be observed almost everywhere in rich democracies. Public debt, that is to say, accumulated alongside a long-drawn-out, pervasive process of economic *liberalization* rather than during a time of growing state intervention. The effective result of this was that capitalism withdrew from the commitments extracted from and entered into by it at the end of the Second World War. However this process may be interpreted or explained, it cannot possibly be conceived as having been driven by a rising influence over policy by democratically organized citizens.[4]

That the rise of public debt was not exactly due to a rise in the power of democracy may also be seen at present as governments, at the prodding of 'financial markets', jointly try to turn the tax and debt state that existed before 2008 into an *austerity* or *consolidation state* defined by balanced budgets and a (gradual) decline in public indebtedness. Everywhere the diagnosis is not that public revenue is too low relative to the functional needs of an advanced modern society, but that spending is too high on account of irrational collective or opportunistic individual behaviour. The cure, therefore, is more discipline in spending rather than in paying taxes – except perhaps for the taxes paid by ordinary people, such as social security or consumption taxes.[5] Consolidation is identified almost entirely with budget cuts. We know little as yet about how the austerity state of the future will work, and whether it will work at all – a few indications may be found in the following chapters. For example, according to Streeck and Mertens, chapter 2 in this volume, lower public spending will mean a higher proportion of it being devoted to more or less mandatory (non-discretionary) expenditure, resulting in less political choice and, probably, declining expectations in politics. Obviously spending cuts will affect mostly those who depend on public services and public assistance. They are also likely further to reduce public employment and depress the wages paid in the public sector, as a result of which the disparities in living conditions will continue to increase. Spending cuts will also set in motion further privatization and confirm the status of markets as the principal mechanism for the distribution of life chances.

In the next section we will look at the development of political participation, after which we will explore the possible influence that the determination of public finances and the rise of the austerity state may have had on the decline of citizen involvement in the public affairs of rich democracies.

2 Falling turnout

As debt has increased and the fiscal room for manoeuvre has diminished, electoral turnout has fallen. The declines have not always been dramatic, but they have occurred consistently across countries. With very few exceptions, electoral participation today is much lower than it was a few decades ago. As austerity has taken hold, it seems that many citizens now feel that electoral choices are limited and that turning out to vote is futile. This holds true for the less well-off in particular, as we will see. Average turnout rates rose for all Western democracies during the 1950s and 1960s. In the 1970s, a first slight decrease took place, which then accelerated considerably (figure 1.6). Each subsequent decade witnessed lower electoral participation. After 2000, voter turnout in parliamentary elec-

Figure 1.6: Electoral turnout in parliamentary elections, 1950–2011

Average percentage turnout
in parliamentary elections

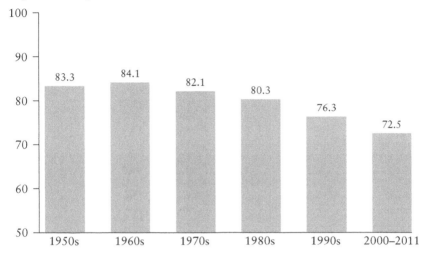

Countries: Australia, Austria, Belgium, Canada, Denmark, Finland, France, Germany, Greece, Ireland, Italy, Japan, Luxembourg, Netherlands, New Zealand, Norway, Portugal, Spain, Sweden, Switzerland, UK, US.

Source: www.idea.int/vt.

tions declined to 72 per cent on average – almost 12 points lower than in the 1960s.[6] What is remarkable about falling turnout is the universality of the trend throughout the Western world (Mair 2006). With the exception of Luxembourg – a country with strictly enforced compulsory voting – and Spain, turnout fell in all countries between 1970 and 2010 (table 1.1). Usually the decline ranges from 10 to 20 points, and there are no signs of a reversal. In fact, more than half of the elections with the lowest turnout rates since 1950 occurred in the 2000s. The more recent an election, the more likely is an all-time low in electoral participation.

Looking at general elections probably underestimates turnout decline. Nationwide elections are the most salient ones for most citizens, with participation rates that are much higher than those in 'second-order' – regional or local – elections (Reif and Schmitt 1980). Unfortunately there are few comparative studies of regional elections. One recent study has shown that regional elections tend to have lower turnout than general elections in eight out of nine countries, although there is considerable regional variation within states (Henderson and McEwen 2010). A number of studies also look at local elections. For example, Hajnal (2010:

Table 1.1: Turnout change and record low turnout in twenty-two democracies, 1970–2010

	Yearly change in turnout (1970–2010)	Cumulative change	Years of lowest turnout	Frequency of record low turnouts		
Australia	–.02	–0.8	1954, 1955, 2010	*Period*	*No.*	*%*
Austria	–.37	–14.8	1999, 2006, 2008	1950s	8	12.1
Belgium	–.08	–3.2	1968, 1974, 2010	1960s	1	1.5
Canada	–.41	–16.4	2000, 2004, 2008	1970s	2	3.0
Denmark	–.08	–3.2	1950, 1953, 1990	1980s	3	4.5
Finland	–.39	–15.6	1999, 2003, 2007	1990s	15	22.7
France	–.54	–21.6	1988, 2002, 2007	2000s	37	56.1
Germany	–.50	–20.0	1990, 2005, 2009			
Greece (1974–)	–.27	–9.7	1956, 2007, 2009			
Ireland	–.30	–12.0	1997, 2002, 2007			
Italy	–.35	–14.0	1996, 2001, 2008			
Japan	–.24	–9.6	1996, 2000, 2003			
Luxembourg	.03	1.2	1989, 1994, 1999			
Netherlands	–.19	–7.6	1994, 1998, 2010			
New Zealand	–.26	–10.4	2002, 2005, 2008			
Norway	–.20	–8	1993, 2001, 2009			
Portugal (1975–)	–.86	–30.1	1999, 2002, 2011			
Spain (1977–)	.04	1.3	1979, 1989, 2000			
Sweden	–.26	–10.4	1952, 1956, 1958			
Switzerland	–.26	–10.4	1995, 1999, 2003			
United Kingdom	–.36	–14.4	2001, 2005, 2010			
United States	–.49	–19.6	2002, 2006, 2010			

Source: www.idea.int/vt. This table updates and expands Mair (2006: 13).

36) reports of the United States that turnout in local contests declined from 62 per cent of registered voters in 1936 to 39 per cent in 1986. For a random sample of fifty-seven American cities, Wood (2002) finds an average turnout rate of 34 per cent for local elections held between 1993 and 2000. Taking Germany as an example, figure 1.7 shows turnout rates for three kinds of elections for each decade since 1950. Until the 1970s, electoral participation was generally growing, surpassing 90 per cent in the general elections of 1972 and 1976. Regional (*Landtagswahlen*) and local (*Kommunalwahlen*) elections never quite reached these levels but still recorded turnout rates well above 75 per cent. Then, from the 1980s onwards, turnout began to falter for all types of elections, most dramatically at the local level. In comparison with the 1970s, electoral participation declined by more than 20 percentage points in local and regional elections. Today, turnout rates of around 60 per cent in regional elections and around 50 per cent in municipal elections are the norm.

Figure 1.7: Turnout in Germany, 1950–2009

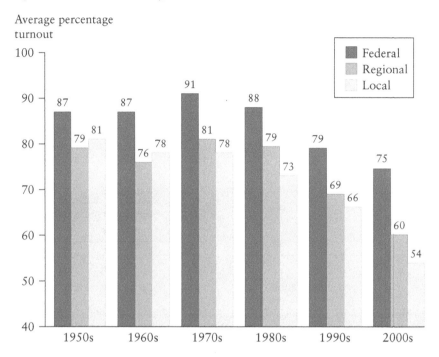

Average percentage
turnout

Source: Statistical office of Germany and of the federal states.

Although turnout decline is near universal *across* Western countries, it is by no means evenly distributed *within* them. Voters with more resources – education, income or social capital – participate much more frequently than the resource-poor. These differences tend to grow larger as turnout declines, because lower overall participation rates go along with more unequal participation. Given the regularity of this pattern, Tingsten (1975: 232) even speaks of a 'law of dispersion'. More recent studies have confirmed the basic pattern (Kohler 2006; Mahler 2008; Schäfer 2011). One way to show levels of dispersion is to compare countries with compulsory voting and those without. When the legal obligation to vote is strictly enforced, compulsory voting not only considerably increases electoral participation but also equalizes it. Figure 1.8 shows that, in four countries with mandatory voting (Australia, Belgium, Luxembourg and Greece), turnout rates are consistently higher across income and education groups. The effect is strongest at the lower end and less pronounced for those with high incomes or a high level of education. Without compulsory voting, the turnout of the less educated is more than

Figure 1.8: Voting probability of different social groups under voluntary and compulsory voting

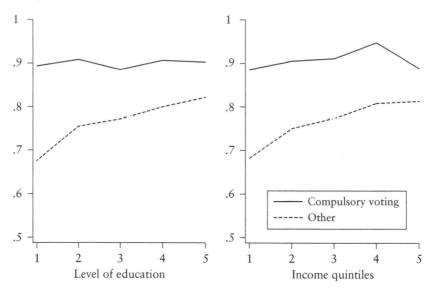

Note: For countries, see Figure 1.9. The figure shows predicted probabilities of voting calculated from a logistic regression (with robust standard errors) that controls for age, gender and political interest.

Source: International Social Survey Programme 2006 and European Social Survey, various years.

11 points lower than that of the highly educated. Exactly the same holds true for different income groups. Under mandatory voting, in contrast, nine out of ten people attend the polling booths across social groups.

In a more fine-grained analysis, figure 1.9 shows the difference in voting for different income and education groups in twenty-two countries that are ranked according to their overall turnout level. Not surprisingly, electoral participation is again highest in Australia, Luxembourg and Belgium, as these countries strictly enforce mandatory voting (which is not true for Greece). Turnout is particularly low in three Anglo-Saxon countries (the US, the UK and Canada) as well as in Switzerland. Almost without exception, people with higher levels of education or income have a higher probability of voting (controlling for age, gender and political interest). These differences are small in high-turnout countries, as we have seen before, and tend to be larger in low-turnout countries. Not all countries fit neatly into the overall pattern, however: Germany has a higher level of dispersion than one might expect, whereas Greece, Ireland and Japan have levels that are lower than expected.

Figure 1.9: Participatory gap between income and education groups

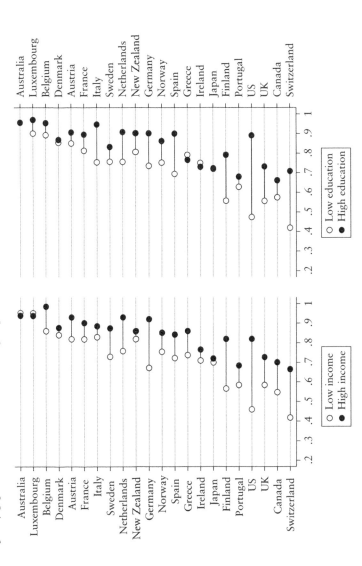

Note: The figure shows predicted probabilities of voting calculated from a logistic regression (with robust standard errors) that controls for age, gender and political interest. It contrasts the voting probability of the lower and highest quintile.

Source: International Social Survey Programme 2006 and European Social Survey, various years.

Figure 1.10: Constituency turnout in the 2005 British general election

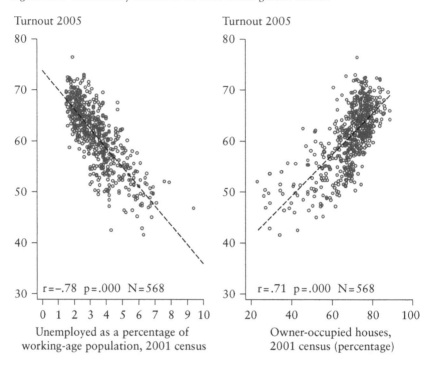

Turnout 2005   Turnout 2005

Unemployed as a percentage of   Owner-occupied houses,
working-age population, 2001 census   2001 census (percentage)

Source: Pippa Norris, The British Parliamentary Constituency Database, 1992–2005, Release 1.3.

Finally, there are large regional differences in turnout (Johnston and Pattie 2006). For example, in the British general election of 2010, turnout ranged from 44 to 77 per cent at the level of constituencies. High and low participation rates are by no means randomly distributed. Figure 1.10 shows a strongly negative correlation between the regional unemployment rate and electoral turnout in 2005 (census data for the 2010 constituencies are not yet available). In contrast, turnout rises with the number of people who live in their own houses. These patterns hold even if we control for the closeness of the electoral race in a constituency (a strong predictor of turnout), the number of pensioners and the proportion of manufacturing workers. Economic hardship clearly goes along with low participation rates. No matter what data source we look at, then, the basic pattern is clear: turnout is falling almost everywhere and at the same time is growing more unequal. As a result, the participatory gap between different social groups increases. To us, this suggests strongly that the less well-to-do have in the past two or three decades progressively lost faith in their political efficacy and have grown sceptical as to whether political participation serves their interests – and this view is not unfounded, as US studies show (Gilens 2005, 2012; Bartels 2008).

3 Debt and democracy

How could the deterioration of public finance in rich postwar democracies have undermined democratic participation and the democratic nature of politics in general? And how will the current transition from debt state to austerity state further affect democratic government? There is no simple answer to this, in particular because we have close to no historical precedents that could serve as guidelines.

Until the crisis, as Streeck argues in the concluding chapter to this volume, the build-up of debt, first public and then private, helped preserve liberal democracy by compensating citizens for low growth, structural unemployment, deregulation of labour markets, stagnant or declining wages, and rising inequality. The fiscal crisis of the state and the global economic crisis that followed it were the prices governments paid for their inability to prevent the advance of liberalization, or for their complicity with it. As governments increasingly gave up on democratic intervention in the capitalist economy, and the economy was extricated from the public duties it was promised it would perform when capitalist democracy was rebuilt after the war, it was through what came to be called the 'democratization of credit' that citizens were, temporarily, reconciled with the declining significance of democratic politics in their lives. This has now come to an end, as debt financing of public entitlements and private prosperity has reached a point where creditors are losing confidence that accumulated promises of repayment will ever actually be met.

With easy credit no longer available as a fix for liberalization and the associated democratic decline, the predominant theme of domestic as well as international politics in advanced capitalist democracies has become the consolidation of public finances through long-term institutionalized policies of austerity. How exactly the democratic austerity state of the future will work can only be guessed at. But some of its contours seem to be already visible. In the following we will summarize in nine short points what we regard to be the most likely future developments in the relationship between capitalism and democratic governance, and in particular between a tightening fiscal straightjacket for democratic politics, on the one hand, and the nature and extent of political participation, on the other.

1   Global liberalization, especially of capital markets, makes it highly unlikely that democratic countries will be able even partly to close the

gap between public expenditures and public revenues by setting higher taxes on corporate profits and high incomes. In the face of rampant tax competition, consolidation of public finances will have to be achieved overwhelmingly by spending cuts, apart from higher taxation of immobile assets – i.e., of consumers and low-income earners. As noted, spending cuts will tend to shift the structure of public expenditure in the direction of mandatory spending, at the expense of what has been called 'social investment' (Morel et al. 2012) in a more egalitarian distribution of the initial endowments of participants in market competition.

2   As liberalization-cum-fiscal discipline limits corrective intervention in the market, democracy will tend, even more than in the past two decades, towards 'post-democracy' (Crouch 2004), where public spectacles replace public action in pursuit of collective values and interests. With *panis* in increasingly short supply, more exciting *circenses* must be and will be provided in its place.

3   Institutionalized austerity will continue the privatization of government services that began in the 1980s and 1990s. Privatization forces or (as the case may be) allows citizens to rely on their own resources rather than on public provision, and to purchase in the market what they would otherwise have received from the state. The inevitable consequence is more inequality of access, for example to health care or education. Privatization should also reinforce tax resistance among the well-to-do, who are likely to be unwilling to pay both for the services they buy on their own for themselves and for the publicly funded services they do not use. It furthermore contributes to political apathy: among high-income earners, who, having effectively 'exited' from the community, no longer need 'voice' (Hirschman 1970), as well as among those at the lower end of the income distribution, who, in the presence of effective ceilings on public spending, cannot hope to get better services by voting for them.

4   Fiscal consolidation does not mean that democratic states will no longer need the confidence of financial investors, even under a regime of institutionalized austerity and with a primary budget that is balanced or in surplus. Given the huge amount of accumulated debt, governments will for a long time have to take up new debt to repay old debt. Buying sovereign debt will remain a lucrative investment for those with incomes high enough to allow them to save. As states finance public obligations by debt rather than taxes, therefore, they not only spare their well-to-do citizens from having their surplus funds confiscated but in addition offer them safe investment opportunities, paying them interest on assets that they continue to own rather than compelling them to contribute to the public purse. Since the financial capital invested in public debt can be passed on to the next generation, perhaps even with the interest it earns

in the meantime, the debt financing of democratic states contributes to preserving and reinforcing economic and social inequality in civil society.

5   As states will continue to need credit, financial markets will in turn continue to keep them under surveillance, even after the stable institutionalization of a firm political commitment to balanced budgets and debt reduction. The most important challenge for democratic theory in the coming years will be systematically to realize that the austerity state that has taken hold in democratic capitalism has two constituencies rather than just one: in addition to its people, it has to face 'the markets' and their specific demands on public policy (table 1.2). While it has long been known that the interests vested in a capitalist economy require special attention from governments if they are to be successful (Dahl 1969), the rise of financial markets in particular seems to have made market pressures equally if not more significant to citizen pressures when it comes to everyday political decision-making. Democratic theory may therefore be well advised to consider and experiment with a model of contemporary democratic-capitalist politics that provides for symmetry between peoples and markets as rivalling constituencies representing different 'logics' of action, perhaps best circumscribed provisionally as 'social justice' and 'market justice', respectively.[7]

People and markets are different in a number of respects, making it difficult and sometimes impossible for governments to do justice to both of them at the same time. Whereas a state's citizenry is nationally organized, financial markets are global (table 1.2). Citizens are resident in their country and typically cannot or will not switch their allegiance to a competing country, whereas investors can and do easily exit. Citizens 'give credit' to their government by voting in general elections, whereas creditors do or do not give money. Rights of citizenship are based in public law, whereas the claims of creditors are regulated in civil or commercial law. Citizens express approval or disapproval of their government in periodic elections, whereas 'markets' make themselves heard in auctions

difference between democratic + financial logic

Table 1.2: The two constituencies of the austerity state

The people	The markets
National	International
Citizens	Investors
Voters	Creditors
Rights of citizenship	Claims to assets
Elections (periodic)	Auctions (continual)
Public opinion	Interest rates
Loyalty	Confidence
Public services	Debt service

that are held almost continually. Whereas 'the people' articulate their views through public opinion, 'the markets' speak through the interest rates they charge. There is an expectation that citizens will be loyal to their country, in contrast to the mere hope that creditors will have 'confidence' in its government and the fear that they could withdraw this confidence if they were to become 'pessimistic' or to 'panic'. Finally, where citizens are expected to render public service and expect to receive public services, 'markets' want debt service.

The new kind of politics that is unfolding as states and governments try to reconcile the often conflicting demands of their two constituencies still awaits exploration. Faced with international investors who unrelentingly police sovereign commitments to austerity – and, if necessary, will make their discontent felt by raising the interest rate on new loans – states may perhaps best be compared to publicly traded firms in a world of 'shareholder value'. Like managers of joint stock companies, governments are under pressure to deliver what in their case one could call *bondholder* value to increasingly activist capital providers. For this to be possible, they have to turn their citizens into a disciplined quasi-workforce who willingly produce market-compatible returns on the capital that has been invested in them, both by moderating their demands on the 'social wage' accruing to them as citizens and by continuously improving their productivity, even as what they produce is a civic surplus to be turned over to those states providing the operational capital that their home government cannot extract from its more affluent citizens.

6 The new tensions between the social rights associated with citizenship and the commercial rights deriving from private ownership of financial assets evolve not just within national polities but also and increasingly at the international level. Here 'financial markets', globally organized as they are, are at a profound advantage compared to nationally constituted citizenries, not least because markets are much better able than citizens to capture international organizations and turn these into instruments of market interests. Foremost among these interests is to prevent individual governments from cutting their debt burden by unilateral restructuring or sovereign default. To this end creditors can enlist the help of the 'international community' of states with the credible threat that a 'credit event' in one country will, as a side effect, push up the interest rates to be paid by all others on their debt, not to mention potentially force them again to bail out affected financial firms that have remained 'too big to fail'. 'Financial markets' thus become the foremost proponents of 'international solidarity', in the sense of providing investors with the collective deposit insurance guaranteed by the family of capitalist states as a whole, called a 'firewall' or 'bazooka' by political PR specialists and reducing the *de facto* risk of lenders to zero.

Making the job of 'global governance' easier, international central banking has at its command an abundance of tools by which to make subsidies to financial speculators appear as assistance to poor states or their impoverished populations, if not to make them altogether invisible. Monetary policy remains a book with seven seals to the vast majority of people, in particular those who will ultimately have to pick up the bill. For example, hardly anyone understands the far-flung implications for European workers and taxpayers of the loans at 1 per cent interest dealt out to banks, and only banks, at the end of 2011 by the European Central Bank, whose president is the former Goldman Sachs executive Mario Draghi. The task of national governments, whose ministers are unlikely to understand what is going on either, is above all to sell their people on the machinations of international money technocrats and the compromises produced by financial diplomacy. If this is not certain to work, the preferred alternative is to enlist the help of financial 'experts' to hide, as much as possible, the extent of the potentially gigantic welfare losses that citizens are being asked to absorb for the benefit of capital owners and bonus-collecting money managers.

7   Popular agitation around the international politics of public debt tends to express itself in terms of nations versus nations, rather than people versus financial markets. In its leftist or, better said, its social-democratic version, the politics of public debt is framed as a debate over the duties of rich nations to come to the assistance of poorer ones – i.e., over solidaristic international redistribution. On the right, countries unable to service their debt are presented as collective sinners against economic reason and fiscal prudence, and as less hard-working than the deserving rich, making it necessary to teach them a lesson by letting them suffer. Both perspectives are fundamentally nationalist, in that countries are conceived as unitary communities with collective economic entitlements or obligations, regardless of differences and distributional conflicts between the sectors and classes within them. Moreover, the two perspectives converge in political practice in their demand for strict international controls over the domestic politics of debtor countries, in particular limitations on their economic and fiscal 'sovereignty', which is obviously in line with the demands of 'the markets'.

When the complexities of international fiscal and monetary policy are reduced to a conflict between more and less economically prudent nations, the stage is set for a rich repertoire of symbolic politics. Populist pseudo-debates on the relative economic and moral merits of 'the Greeks' and 'the Irish', not to mention 'the Germans', provide an opaque veil of sentiments and resentments behind which 'the markets' and their 'technocratic' henchmen, in central banks and public relations agencies, can do their work basically undisturbed by popular interference. Here as nowhere else, we may in the future be able to observe what it means when democratic politics runs dry and is replaced with more or less sophisticated social technologies for the procurement of mass acceptance of decisions for which 'There Is No Alternative', at least not under the auspices of the existing national and international distribution of power and privilege.

8   Further complications for the politics of consolidation result from the fact that some creditors are also citizens, especially since the 'reforms' of social security in the 2000s that introduced private pension insurance almost everywhere as a supplement to overburdened public pension systems. As insurance companies are heavily invested in public debt, those who now depend on them for part of their pensions have developed an interest in 'responsible' fiscal policies ensuring states' ability to live up to their financial obligations. At the same time, however, these citizen-creditors continue to need and insist on government services and citizen benefits, as well as low taxes on low or average incomes. More and more people thus find themselves on both sides of the defining front line of politics in the consolidation period of the debt state. On the one hand, this may expand the room of policy-makers to manoeuvre, potentially enabling them to mobilize support for austerity measures among citizens directly affected by them. On the other hand, paying for pension supplements with cuts to their pensions may not seem like too good a deal to a significant number of voters, and asking them to accept this may seriously detract from political support for privatization.

9   Perhaps most important of all, the interests not just of citizens but also of 'financial markets' seem to have deep internal contradictions. Holders of government bonds today require institutionalized austerity policies for reassurance that their claims to the assets of near-bankrupt, over-indebted states will enjoy priority over the claims of citizens. Austerity alone, however, is not likely to lower the public debt burden enough to make it reliably sustainable. There is wide agreement that what is also required is economic growth, although no one can say how this is to come about alongside deep cuts in public spending, higher taxes, a freeze on wages and rising unemployment, among other things. In fact, the fear is that austerity may drive countries under pressure to consolidate their public finances into a long-lasting recession or even depression, in effect increasing rather than reducing the size of their accumulated debt in relation to their economy, in spite and perhaps because of deep expenditure cuts.

How growth and austerity may be combined remains a mystery known only to the most faithful believers in supply-side economics, and clearly not to those social democratic politicians in Northern Europe who keep calling for 'a plan for growth', or even a 'Marshall Plan', for the

Mediterranean member states of European Monetary Union. Indications are, however, that a not insignificant number of those in 'the markets' and in international organizations subscribe to the Thatcherite belief that economic recovery requires two opposite sorts of 'work incentives': even higher profits and bonuses for the rich – investors and managers – and even lower wages and social security benefits for the poor. The far from unintended result will be a further increase in inequality between the top and the bottom in democratic societies. Whether this will be politically sustainable no one can say with any degree of certainty. We for our part refuse to rule out the possibility that the result will *not* be a further increase in political apathy, as in the last quarter century, but a reversal of this secular trend, in the direction of political radicalization.

We conclude this introduction by repeating that it is impossible to imagine what the politics of democracy-cum-austerity will be like – in (as yet still) rich democratic-capitalist countries co-governed by global capital markets – as there are no valid historical precedents. Balanced budgets have been or are presently being written into the fiscal constitutions of European democracies by international agreement or, as in the case of the UK, by national government policy. In a few years the United States may be the only country in the Western world that will still be adding to its national debt. What consequences this will have for international relations and the domestic politics and economics of both Europe and the US we cannot even speculate about at this point.

References

Bartels, L. M. (2008) *Unequal Democracy: The Political Economy of the New Gilded Age*. Princeton, NJ: Princeton University Press.

Bell, D. (1976) The public household: on 'fiscal sociology' and the liberal society, in D. Bell, *The Cultural Contradictions of Capitalism*. New York: Basic Books, pp. 220–82.

Crouch, C. (2004) *Post-Democracy*. Cambridge: Polity.

Dahl, R. A. (1969) *Pluralist Democracy in the United States*. Chicago: McNally.

Downs, A. (1960) Why the government budget is too small in a democracy, *World Politics* 12: 541–63.

Franklin, M. N. (2004) *Voter Turnout and the Dynamics of Electoral Competition in Established Democracies since 1945*. Cambridge: Cambridge University Press.

Gilens, M. (2005) Inequality and democratic responsiveness, *Public Opinion Quarterly* 69: 778–96.

Gilens, M. (2012) *Affluence and Influence. Economic Inequality and Political Power in America*. Princeton: Princeton University Press.

Goldscheid, R. (1926) Staat, öffentlicher Haushalt und Gesellschaft, in

W. Gerloff and F. Neumark (eds), *Handbuch der Finanzwissenschaft*. Tübingen: Mohr, pp. 146–84.

Hajnal, Z. L. (2010) *America's Uneven Democracy: Race, Turnout, and Representation in City Politics*. Cambridge: Cambridge University Press.

Henderson, A., and McEwen, N. (2010) A comparative analysis of voter turnout in regional elections, *Electoral Studies* 29: 405–16.

Hirschman, A. O. (1970) *Exit, Voice, and Loyalty: Responses to Decline in Firms, Organizations, and States*. Cambridge: Cambridge University Press.

Johnston, R., and Pattie, C. (2006) *Putting Voters in their Place: Geography and Elections in Britain*. Oxford: Oxford University Press.

Kohler, U. (2006) Die soziale Ungleichheit der Wahlabstinenz in Europa, in J. Alber and W. Merkel (eds), *Europas Osterweiterung: Das Ende der Vertiefung? WZB-Jahrbuch 2005*. Berlin: Sigma, pp. 159–79.

Mahler, V. A. (2008) Electoral turnout and income redistribution by the state: a cross-national analysis of the developed democracies, *European Journal of Political Research* 47: 161–83.

Mair, P. (2006) Ruling the void? The hollowing of Western democracy, *New Left Review* 42: 25–51.

Marx, K. (1967 [1867, 1887]) *Capital: A Critique of Political Economy*, Vol. 1. New York: International Publishers.

Morel, N., Palier, B., and Palme, J. (eds) (2012) *Towards a Social Investment Welfare State?* Bristol: Policy Press.

Norris, P. (2005) *Radical Right: Voters and Parties in the Electoral Market*. Cambridge: Cambridge University Press.

Norris, P. (2011) *Democratic Deficit: Critical Citizens Revisited*. Cambridge: Cambridge University Press.

North, D. C., and Thomas, R. P. (1973) *The Rise of the Western World: A New Economic History*. Cambridge: Cambridge University Press.

O'Connor, J. (1973) *The Fiscal Crisis of the State*. New York: St Martin's Press.

Obinger, H. (2012) Die Finanzkrise und die Zukunft des Wohlfahrtsstaates. *Leviathan*, 40: 441–61.

OECD (Organization for Economic Cooperation and Development) (2011) *Divided We Stand: Why Inequality Keeps Rising*. Paris: OECD; available at www.oecd-ilibrary.org/social-issues-migration-health/the-causes-of-growing-inequalities-in-oecd-countries_9789264119536-en (accessed 14 August 2012).

Pierson, P. (2001a) Coping with permanent austerity: welfare state restructuring in affluent democracies, in P. Pierson (ed.), *The New Politics of the Welfare State*. Oxford: Oxford University Press, pp. 410–56.

Pierson, P. (2001b) From expansion to austerity: the new politics of taxing and spending, in M. A. Levin, M. K. Landy and M. Shapiro (eds), *Seeking the Center: Politics and Policymaking at the New Century*. Washington, DC: Georgetown University Press, pp. 54–80.

Putnam, R. D., Pharr, S. J., and Dalton, R. J. (2000) Introduction: what's troubling the trilateral democracies?, in S. J. Pharr and R. D. Putnam (eds), *Disaffected Democracies: What's Troubling the Trilateral Countries?* Princeton, NJ: Princeton University Press, pp. 3–27.

Reif, K., and Schmitt, H. (1980) Nine second-order national elections: a conceptual framework for the analysis of European election results, *European Journal of Political Research* 8: 3–45.

Reinhart, C. M., and Rogoff, K. S. (2009) *This Time is Different: Eight Centuries of Financial Folly.* Princeton, NJ: Princeton University Press.

Salverda, W., and Mayhew, K. (2009) Capitalist economies and wage inequality, *Oxford Review of Economic Policy* 25: 126–54.

Schäfer, A. (2011) *Republican Liberty and Compulsory Voting*, MPIfG Discussion Paper 11/17. Cologne: Max Planck Institute for the Study of Societies.

Schmitter, P. C., and Streeck, W. (1999) *The Organization of Business Interests: Studying the Associative Action of Business in Advanced Industrial Societies*, MPIfG Discussion Paper 99/1. Cologne: Max Planck Institute for the Study of Societies.

Schumpeter, J. A. (1991 [1918]) The crisis of the tax state, in R. Swedberg (ed.), *The Economics and Sociology of Capitalism.* Princeton, NJ: Princeton University Press, pp. 99–141.

Steuerle, C. E. (1996) Financing the American state at the turn of the century, in W. E. Brownlee (ed.), *Funding the Modern American State, 1941–1995: The Rise and Fall of the Era of Easy Finance.* Cambridge: Cambridge University Press, pp. 409–44.

Tingsten, H. (1975) *Political Behavior: Studies in Election Statistics.* London: Arno Press.

Van Biezen, I., Mair, P., and Poguntke, T. (2012) Going, going, . . . gone? The decline of party membership in contemporary Europe, *European Journal of Political Research* 51: 24–56.

Visser, J. (2006) Union membership statistics in 24 countries, *Monthly Labour Review* 129: 38–49.

Wood, C. (2002) Voter turnout in city elections, *Urban Affairs Review* 38: 209–31.

2

Public Finance and the Decline of State Capacity in Democratic Capitalism

Wolfgang Streeck and Daniel Mertens

The relationship between public finance and democracy is a complex one, with many facets and a confusing multiplicity of diverse lines of causation and causal interdependence. For Schumpeter, who at the end of the First World War sketched out a programme of 'fiscal sociology' that he unfortunately never followed through (Schumpeter 1991 [1918]), the level and structure of taxation and public spending in a political jurisdiction was the most accurate reflection of the nature of political rule in that jurisdiction and the social order of which it was part, including the community's collective interests and objectives as well as its internal lines of conflict. Moreover, the extent to which a 'tax state' was able to extract material resources from its society appeared to be a powerful determinant of what its government could in practice do, and thus not just mirrored but also actively shaped social and political life.

The subject of how democracy in particular affects public finance and is in turn affected by it came to prominence in the decades after 1945 with the establishment of the mixed economy of democratic capitalism, an establishment that we now know was to be temporary. John Maynard Keynes had given the dignity of scientific theory to the use of public expenditure as an instrument to stabilize a crisis-prone market economy. Liberals, who continued to believe in the self-stabilizing capacity of markets free of state intervention, had argued early on that politically guaranteed full employment in particular was bound to generate what they considered severe economic distortions (Hayek 1967 [1950]). Their time was not to come until the 1970s and 1980s, however, when Western economies had become as highly and critically inflationary as neoliberal theory had predicted. Another attack on Keynesianism that became equally influential, especially in the 1990s, focused on the political process rather than on the economy as such. James Buchanan and others saw Keynesian doctrine as a welcome excuse for self-interested political leaders in an electoral democracy to spend more than they were able to raise in taxes, so as to serve the distributional demands of mass constituencies without provoking politically or economically dangerous resistance on the part of taxpayers (Downs 1960; Buchanan and Roback 1987; Buchanan 1985; Buchanan and Wagner 1978; Buchanan and Wagner 1977; Buchanan and Tullock 1977; Buchanan 1958). According to what would become the theory of 'public choice', Keynes was at a minimum guilty of reckless negligence when he failed to underline sufficiently the need to incur public debt in order to increase aggregate demand in times of unemployment. This debt would be repaid after recovery, thereby balancing public budgets over the economic cycle. As a result, argued adherents of the emerging public-choice school, Keynesianism was subject to being abused in democratic politics as a justification for continuous 'deficit spending', which was bound to give rise to continuously increasing public indebtedness.[1]

Whatever one may think of the causal mechanisms suggested by public-choice theory to account for fiscal imbalances, public deficits became the rule in almost all capitalist democracies during the 1970s and 1980s, with public debt increasing more or less steadily across the board (figure 2.1). Considered over time, that increase would seem to represent a process of profound if gradual historical change with respect to the balance between public revenues and expenditures as well as the structure and level of public spending. Richard Rose and his colleagues (Rose and Davies 1994; Rose 1990; Rose and Peters 1978) observed a tendency beginning in the 1970s for politicians to enact programmes, especially those entailing entitlements for citizens, that originally cost little but were bound to grow with time, binding future legislators in various legal or political ways and potentially crowding out spending for other, newly arising collective needs or objectives. Welfare-state programmes in particular were prone to 'mature', in the sense of growing incrementally over the years according to a logic of 'compound interest' and turning into immovable 'policy legacies' (Pierson 2001, 1998). This would ultimately result in a freezing of historical patterns of government spending, making state activities increasingly less responsive to changing interests among the citizenry. In the process, the share of mandatory spending in government expenditure would increase at the expense of discretionary spending, resulting in a condition of *fiscal sclerosis* pre-empting what could be called 'fiscal democracy'.

The slow maturation of historical spending programmes was not the only cause of the level and structure of public expenditure turning rigid.

Figure 2.1: OECD average of public debt, public spending and public revenue, as a percentage of GDP, 1970–1990

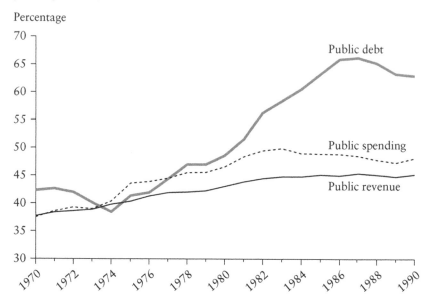

Note: Average includes: Austria, Belgium, Canada, France, Germany, Italy, Japan, Netherlands, Norway, Sweden, UK, US.

Source: Economic Outlook Database No. 90.

The Downsian effect for public spending continuously exceeding public revenues, which, as noted, must result in an accumulation of public debt, forced governments to set aside a growing share of their budgets to pay interest to their creditors. While interest rates may change over time, and indeed were at historical lows during the 1990s and early 2000s (figure 2.2), the entitlements of creditors are at least as fixed for governments as those of pensioners and other recipients of public transfers. Social policy and other domestic spending commitments may thus combine with growing expenditure on debt service to diminish governments' fiscal and political discretion, unless taxes can be raised to defend the state's room for political manoeuvre. Since it is reasonable to assume that there is an upper limit to taxation, although this may differ from country to country, one should then expect *a tendency in democratic polities for mandatory spending over time to crowd out discretionary spending*.

Declining fiscal discretion has distributional as well as functional consequences. To the extent that mandatory spending is welfare-state spending, it favours original beneficiaries who tend to be protected by 'grandfather clauses' over current contributors. As a result of cutbacks,

Figure 2.2: Long-term interest rate on government bonds, 1980–2010

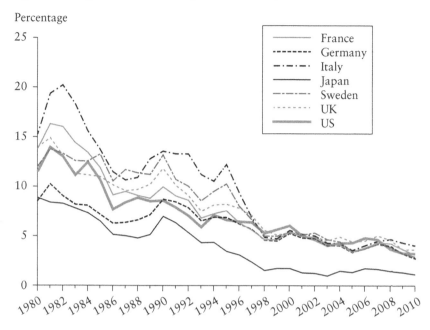

Source: Economic Outlook Database No. 90.

these current contributors will have to be content with lower benefits, at least in comparison with their lifetime contributions, but very likely also in absolute terms. Moreover, if they have previously unknown needs for public provision, for example childcare, they may be told that the resources these would require are already committed to other purposes. Similarly, when mandatory spending goes to debt service it favours those who can afford to save and invest in state bonds over citizens who have nothing left after having paid their taxes. As a growing share of public spending goes to pensioners (*Rentner*, in German), on the one hand, and *rentiers*, on the other, the space for democratic politics to serve competing claims by less well-protected groups must shrink. Over time, this may conceivably diminish the stake other groups see themselves as having in democratic participation.

In functional terms, discretionary spending in public budgets consists of a vast variety of different items. While certainly not all of these would be a loss to society and democracy if they were cut, included among them is what is called public investment, both in physical infrastructure and in human capital in the widest sense. If discretionary spending declines because mandatory spending must occupy a rising share of public

Figure 2.3: Total tax revenue, as a percentage of GDP, 1990–2007

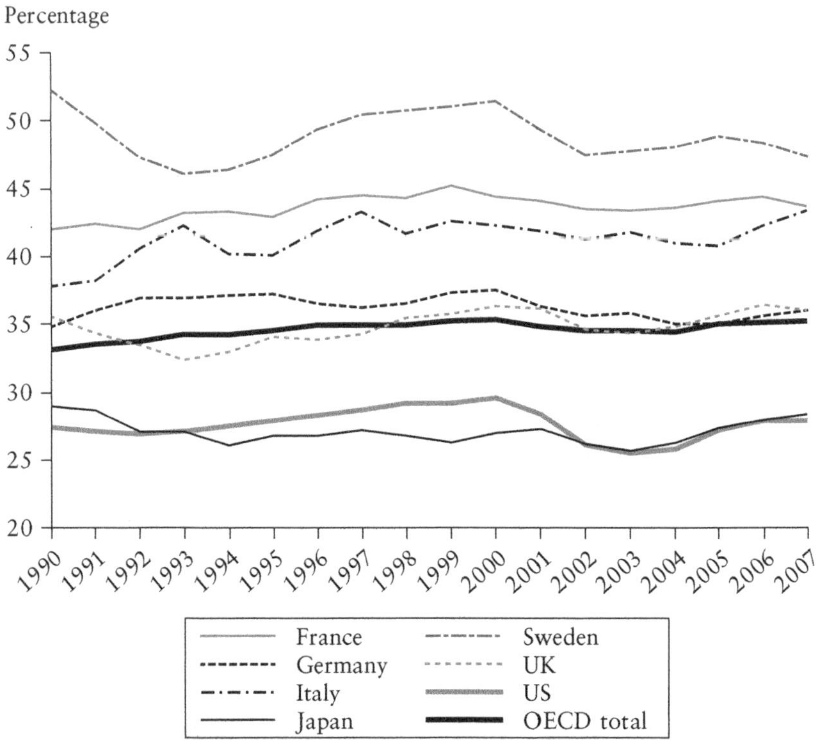

Percentage

—————— France	— ·· — ·· — Sweden	
- - - - - - - Germany	· · · · · · · · UK	
— · — · — · Italy	▨▨▨▨▨▨ US	
—————— Japan	━━━━━ OECD total	

Source: OECD Tax Revenue Statistics.

expenditure, public investment is also at risk of declining unless governments make special efforts to protect it. If public investment declines,
the capacity of states to provide for collective goods crucial to future
prosperity and social cohesion declines as well, and this diminishing
capacity is likely to be perceived as such by those groups of citizens who,
for whatever reason, depend on public as distinct from private provision
for their and their children's future well-being. Again, the result may be
indifference to democracy as we know it.

A decline in fiscal discretion is particularly likely in periods of fiscal
consolidation, to the extent that consolidation proceeds by reductions in
expenditure rather than increases in taxation. In the 1990s and 2000s, as
a matter of fact, before the 'Great Recession', fiscal consolidation efforts
not only relied overwhelmingly on spending cuts but also tended to be
associated with stagnant overall levels of taxation (figure 2.3). With
mandatory spending being by definition harder to cut than discretion-

ary spending, fiscal consolidation through expenditure cuts must further exacerbate the pressure from maturing policy legacies, and not just on discretionary spending as a whole but also on the public investment that is included in it. If fiscal consolidation under growing tax competition was the signature political trend of the period before the crisis of 2008, there is likely to be even more of it in the coming years, after the jump in public indebtedness that followed the collapse of the financial system. This makes it even more urgent to explore whether, and how, public spending became less discretionary in the past, thereby constraining democratic political choice and presumably, as a consequence, lowering the incentives for democratic political participation. It also raises the issue of whether, based on the experience of the first wave of consolidation efforts, one can expect that the current, and by necessity much more ambitious, drive for fiscal consolidation will significantly diminish the capacity of states to invest in the future well-being of their societies.

It is to these two issues that the present chapter is addressed: first, whether there is a tendency over time for 'fiscal democracy' to be constrained by a decline in the share of discretionary spending in public budgets; and, second, whether governments in periods of fiscal consolidation are able to protect their capacity to provide for collective goods by protecting public investment from expenditure cuts. In the terms suggested by Fritz Scharpf (1970, 2000), the first question relates to an important aspect of the 'input legitimacy' of democratic government – i.e., its capacity to be responsive to evolving demands of citizens. The second, then, concerns its 'output legitimacy' – the question of whether governments can effectively perform essential public functions on behalf of their society.

1 Fiscal democracy

Ever since the late 1970s, the problem of accumulating policy legacies has been a prominent theme in the literature on public finance. In addition to the high survival rate of political programmes and the quasi-automatic increases in social security and other entitlement spending, the apparently chronic budget deficits of most democratic states and the resulting rise in public debt have significantly limited the degrees of freedom left to governments in the deployment of their fiscal resources. As public debt increased, so did the interest due on it. Like the mounting costs of inherited programmes and maturing entitlements, debt service thus began to consume a rising share of tax revenue and gradually to fill the fiscal space for policy innovation and democratic choice.[2]

Accumulation of policy legacies may be conceived as a process of institutional sclerosis (Olson 1982) or institutional aging (Streeck 2009a). These concepts introduce time as a causal factor in the analysis of institutional change, raising the possibility that, the longer a democratic political system has existed, the less flexible it will be with respect to the allocation of its resources. From this perspective, it may for example be hypothesized that, the further the aging process has already progressed, the more difficult it will be in a democracy to achieve tax increases, which would temporarily suspend institutional aging; a tax increase that is used in full or in part to service or pay off public debt does not directly benefit those who must agree to it. Sclerotic foreclosure of policy innovation over time may in this way become self-reinforcing and eventually undermine the viability of democratic politics as such.[3]

1.1 Measuring fiscal democracy: the United States

From the perspective of a sitting government or legislature, accumulated policy legacies that occupy a large share of the state's tax revenues leave little room for decisions to be made in the present, because so much has already been decided in the past. Since fiscal democracy is essentially about the flexibility of fiscal resources, it is possible to measure it by the proportion of tax revenue that is not needed to cover obligations entered into in the past – that is, the proportion of tax revenue available in principle to be allocated to newly chosen purposes. This is roughly the way in which Eugene Steuerle and Timothy Roeper constructed their Steuerle–Roeper Fiscal Democracy Index (Steuerle 2010).[4] One advantage of the index is that it defines fiscal democracy in gradual-numerical terms – one can have more or less of it – and in a way that makes its development traceable over longer periods. In the following, we will briefly describe the construction of the Steuerle–Roeper Index for the United States and discuss what it tells us about the trajectory of fiscal democracy in the past four decades in this leading Western nation. We will then present a similar index for Germany and use it to compare the German and the American situations.

The basic distinction underlying the Steuerle–Roeper Index is between dedicated and disposable, or mandatory and discretionary, government spending. It is relatively straightforward to operationalize for the United States, where only discretionary budget allocations are voted upon by Congress and are easy to identify as such on this basis. Mandatory expenditure is not voted on because it is considered to be driven by events beyond the volition of legislators, in particular the incidence of social security or unemployment insurance claims or the costs of medical care under the federal health-care programmes of Medicare and Medicaid. Mandatory programmes create legal entitlements for citizens to benefits that cannot be refused or reduced as long as the entitlements exist. Of course Congress may cut entitlements, such as pensions, and thereby reduce mandatory spending. It must rewrite spending laws in order to do so, however, instead of being able simply to cut or place a ceiling on budgetary allocations. Like entitlement programmes, debt service is considered mandatory spending, since the interest due to creditors represents a legal entitlement that cannot unilaterally be reduced by Congress.[5] Defence spending, however, is considered discretionary, as it is voted on every year. Discretionary spending – what is left of government revenue after mandatory spending and debt service – is expressed as a percentage of government revenue rather than government spending, in order not to distort the measure of fiscal democracy by including new debt in its base.[6]

Fiscal democracy in the United States has been trending downwards since the beginning of the 1970s, from 60 per cent in 1970 to a little less than 0 per cent in 2009 (figure 2.4).[7] There were four cyclical upswings between 1970 and 2009; the strongest occurred in the boom period between 1992 and 2000, when revenue, now increasingly from a rapidly growing, deregulated financial sector, doubled while interest payments stagnated as a result of falling interest rates. Subsequent economic downturns, however, always ended with a new record low, except once (2000–3). The current crisis has critically exacerbated the problem, but essentially it has done nothing but accelerate a process that has long been under way. Projections by the Congressional Budget Office in 2012 for the current decade (included in figure 2.1) foresee an increase in fiscal discretion until 2015; the index is projected to fall again thereafter.

There is little ambiguity in this condition. 'As the amount we can spend on the new and unforeseen shrinks', writes Steuerle (2010),

> so does each generation's democratic control of social and economic priorities . . . .. For the first time in US history, in 2009 every single dollar of revenue was committed before Congress voted on any spending program. Meanwhile, most of government's basic functions – from justice to education to turning on the lights in the Capitol – are paid for out of swelling, unsustainable debts.

1.2 Measuring fiscal democracy: Germany

Applying the Steuerle–Roeper Index to Germany requires several adjustments where legal definitions, parliamentary procedures and political circumstances differ. First, a problem arises in applying the concept of 'mandatory spending' to the German situation. Unlike the situation in the US, the German legislature votes every year on the entire budget, and in this respect there is no formal distinction between discretionary and mandatory spending. However, there are at least four categories in

Figure 2.4: Steuerle–Roeper Fiscal Democracy Index, United States, 1970–2022: federal government revenue

Percentage

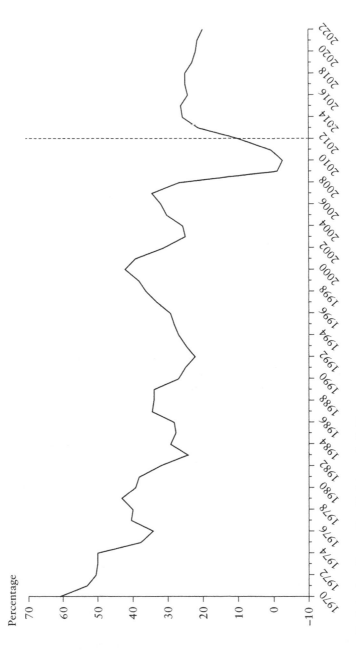

Note: Excludes Spending on Troubled Assets Relief Programme.

Source: Steuerle and Quakenbush 2012, Fiscal Democracy Index: An Update, based on earlier work with Timothy Roeper, see: http://blog.governmentwedeserve.org/2012/05/04/fiscal-democracy/.

the German federal budget, in addition to interest payments, that are *de facto* mandatory, in the sense that the government is in a variety of ways legally obligated to pay for them. Unlike in the US, the German Parliament has to write the respective amounts estimated by the Ministry of Finance into a comprehensive federal budget; its only alternative to doing so would be to change entitlement legislation with very strong political and constitutional support. For the period beginning in 1970, the four categories are:

- *Kriegsfolgelasten*: This refers to obligations resulting from the Second World War, including reparations and payments to victims of the Nazi regime. In 1970 this category still amounted to roughly 10 per cent of the federal budget. In subsequent decades it declined continuously and it has now almost disappeared.
- *Personnel*: Under German labour law it is extremely difficult for the legislature unilaterally to cut or withhold pay to government employees. Spending on personnel is essentially determined by collective agreements that bind the state as employer.
- *Subsidies to the (para-fiscal) social security funds*: Under German law, the federal government is obliged to cover whatever deficits may arise in the (pay-as-you-go) social security system, which is in principle funded by a payroll tax outside the federal budget. By now about one-third of federal spending is devoted to subsidizing the public pension system in particular.
- *Long-term unemployment benefits (Sozialhilfe, Grundsicherung)*: These are legal entitlements of individuals meant to guarantee them a minimum level of subsistence. The benefits are determined by the legislature, but its decisions are subject to review by the Constitutional Court.

We will treat all four of the above spending categories as mandatory in the American sense. Together with the costs of debt service, they constitute the dedicated part of government spending, as distinct from the discretionary part.

The second issue relates to defence. Formally, defence expenditures are discretionary in Germany, since no one is entitled to be paid out of the defence budget (except, of course, military personnel under valid contracts of employment). In substance, however, the German military is under the command of NATO, and the German defence budget is set up to complement spending by NATO; however, unlike the United States, Germany has no enemies, no client governments to protect, and no real strategic doctrine of its own. For this reason we have calculated the German index twice, in one case counting defence expenditures as

Figure 2.5: Steuerle–Roeper Fiscal Democracy Index, Germany, 1970–2011: federal government revenue

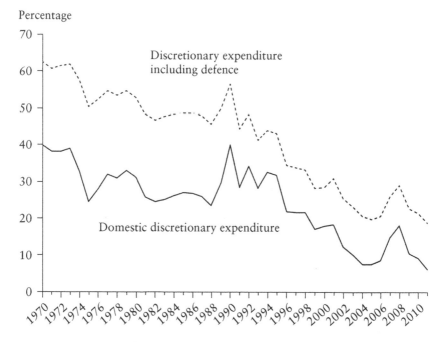

Note: For 2011 target values.

Source: Bundesfinanzberichte 1975–2012; authors' own calculations.

discretionary, in line with American practice, and in the other as being effectively outside of the control of the German legislature, and in this sense as mandatory.

Even more than in the US, fiscal democracy in Germany as measured by the index has been declining since the 1970s (figure 2.5). Over almost four decades, the more or less steadily growing spending on subsidies to the social security system, on social assistance for the long-term unemployed and, albeit less so, on interest has steadily narrowed the space available to German governments for political choice. It is true that spending on defence has declined, particularly in the years immediately after the end of the Cold War. In figure 2.5 this is reflected in the shrinking distance over time between the two lines – the upper, broken one treating defence as discretionary and the lower, solid one treating it as mandatory. The figure also shows that fiscal discretion with respect to domestic spending recovered for a few years in the early 1990s, when the largest part of the post-1989 'peace dividend' accrued, but that it

Figure 2.6: Mandatory and discretionary spending as a percentage of total federal government spending, Germany, 1970–2011

Percentage

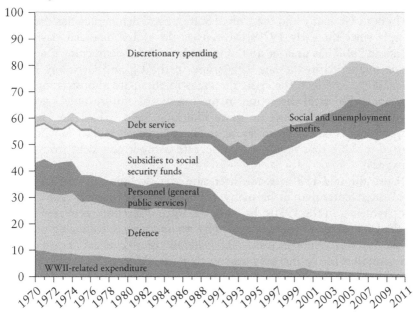

Note: The amounts for 2011 are target figures. The data for 1990 have been omitted due to the massive distortions caused by German reunification.

Source: Bundesfinanzberichte 1975–2012; author's own calculations.

continued its decline after 1995. The increase ten years later came from the consolidation efforts by the 'Grand Coalition' government (Merkel I), while the steep decline that followed after 2008 represents the fiscal effects of the current crisis of the global financial system.[8]

To show how dramatic the loss of fiscal democracy has been in the past four decades, it is useful to look at the dynamics underlying the historical change in the size of governments' discretionary fiscal space. For Germany (figure 2.6), we note that no fewer than two substantial peace dividends have been consumed since 1970, as expenditure on *Kriegsfolgelasten* petered out and the collapse of the communist bloc made it possible significantly to reduce defence spending in the 1990s. Yet the space for discretionary spending, and thus for fiscal democracy, has been cut nearly in half because of sharp increases in subsidies to the social security system (the worst of which occurred after reunification, though they began much earlier), spending on social assistance (for the growing segment of people confined to low-wage jobs or eliminated from the labour market altogether) and service on the debt, even though in the past two decades, as pointed out above, interest rates were particularly low.

In both Germany and the United States, fiscal democracy has declined steeply since the early 1970s. Moreover, the global financial crisis that began in 2008 has undone any of the gains in fiscal democracy that were made in the US in the late 1990s and in the US and Germany in the mid-2000s. In effect, the crisis threatens to eliminate almost completely any space for fiscal discretion in the foreseeable future unless governments are willing to take up new, additional debt (which the German government is barred from doing, under a balanced-budget amendment passed in 2008 that requires it to operate without new debt from 2016 onwards).

Until the mid-1980s, fiscal discretion was declining more sharply in the United States than in Germany, mainly because of rapidly rising interest payments. In the 1990s, by contrast, fiscal discretion recovered faster in the US because of the economic growth and budget-balancing policies of the Clinton administration. The generally more cyclical nature of the US economy is not the only reason that the US index is more volatile than that of Germany; the United States also places greater importance on defence spending as compared to social security spending. Still, over time both countries have suffered a severe decline in what we call fiscal democracy, which does not bode well for the input legitimacy of their political systems.

2 Public investment

If there is indeed a tendency for the share of public finance that is available for discretionary spending to shrink, this must raise the question of how long governments will continue to be able to fund future-oriented public investment that responds to changing social needs or aims to make societies more equitable and efficient. Pressures for fiscal consolidation are increasing, debt service is becoming more expensive, at least potentially, and the 'immovable objects' (Pierson 1998) of public policy are claiming a growing percentage of stagnant or even declining tax revenues; to maintain the same level of public investment, not to mention increasing it, would require shifting the resources available within the shrinking share of discretionary expenditure from old to new purposes. Here we will assess the relative capacity of governments to accomplish this shift.

2.1 Social investment

Public investment is not the only item left in public budgets after fixed obligations have been met. Discretionary spending includes a wide variety of rather idiosyncratic items that are difficult to classify and often impossible to compare cross-nationally. Moreover, as defined in standardized national account statistics, public investment is limited to a country's physical infrastructure, such as roads, railways, canals and bridges; to capital goods used by government, such as office machinery; and to improving and maintaining the existing capital stock – what is technically called 'gross fixed capital formation', or GFCF.[9]

There are indications that such spending has been in decline for several decades in most countries as a result of fiscal pressure. For example, de Haan and his colleagues (1996) reported a decline in government gross capital formation between 1980 and 1992 in the great majority of twenty-two OECD countries, in terms of both gross domestic product (GDP) and total government expenditure. The explanation offered is growing 'fiscal stringency', as indicated by a country's cyclically adjusted deficit. Keman (2010), looking at the relationship between public investment and total government outlays between 1992 and 2004, found a continuing decline for eleven out of eighteen OECD democracies, which he explains as 'collateral damage' resulting from a general downsizing of government spending. Similarly, Breunig and Busemeyer (2010), using data on twenty-one OECD countries from 1979 to 2003, reported a negative impact of fiscal austerity on the share of government spending devoted to public investment, which they account for as a result of a simultaneous increase in the share of non-discretionary entitlement spending, in particular on pensions.

Arguably, however, it is not exclusively or even primarily 'hard' public investment that should be looked at in the context of the social and political effects of fiscal austerity. Much of such spending is difficult to compare between countries because it depends on, and may be required by, both natural conditions and a country's economic development. There are also likely to be saturation points beyond which further construction is not needed or may even be undesirable for environmental or other reasons. For these and other reasons, we believe that primary attention should be paid to a different sort of public investment, one which seems to be of much greater importance for contemporary rich societies. By this we mean not physical but what we call 'social' investment, defined as a sort of public spending aimed at creating the conditions required for the prosperity and sustainability of 'post-industrial' or 'knowledge' societies.[10]

In particular, one may distinguish four categories of public spending that we consider social investment in this sense: spending on *educa-tion*, on *research and development*, on *families* and on *active labour market policy*. Spending on education and on research and development supports human capital formation and industrial innovation; it enhances economic prosperity and perhaps social equity. Education also serves to help integrate immigrants and their children into the national economy and society. Family policies are to enable women to have children while being gainfully employed and to improve the opportunities of children from less well-to-do families. They 'are defined as those policies that increase resources of households with dependent children; foster child development; reduce barriers to having children and combining work and family commitments; and, [*sic*] promote gender equity in employment opportunities' (OECD Directorate for Employment 2011). Active labour market policy, finally, is to improve the 'employability' of people at risk of becoming long-term unemployed, mostly by training but also by other measures that promote their social and economic inclusion.[11]

Can democratic government rededicate fiscal resources to social investment while policy legacies endure and the funds available for government activities are shrinking? It may matter in this context that in no country does social investment occupy a large share of government spending. For example, in Germany in 2007, the four items we have grouped in the category amounted together to roughly 15 per cent of total government spending, including the federal government, the *Länder* and the local communities. That the share of public spending devoted to social investment is relatively small is not necessarily bad news: it may mean that skilful governments with enough political willpower might be able to protect such spending from being cut under fiscal stress, or even gradually to increase it when other expenditures, among them those on physical infrastructure (see above), can or must be reduced.

2.2 *Method and case selection*

In the present chapter we trace the impact of fiscal stress – resulting from political and economic pressures for fiscal consolidation under domestic tax resistance and international tax competition – on social investment in three countries. Observations extend over a period of almost three decades, from 1981 (which is when comparable data are first available) to 2007, the year before the Great Recession. One reason we have opted for a three-country, longitudinal rather than a multi-country, cross-sectional design is that data on social investment are less than easy to compile and compare, since detailed information on national institutions and accounting practices can be acquired only for a limited number of cases.

Another is that a snapshot-style, cross-national comparison looking at a multitude of countries at a given moment misses the historical dynamics of countries and the interdependencies between them. While such a comparison promises to reveal general causal relations of an 'if A, then B' sort – a promise that is unlikely to be kept – it cannot detect how much countries' longer-term trajectories resemble one another. Nor can it determine whether differences between countries observed at the time of comparison are due merely to differences in the speed and timing of a parallel movement along a common path.

Static comparison fails to do justice to changing historical conditions that affect all country cases, such as the end of inflation in the OECD world and the associated general decline in interest rates in the 1980s. The defence of social investment against pressures for austerity, and even more the redirection of resources from old to new policy objectives, can only be a long-drawn-out process that must continue for more than a few years to produce stable results and must therefore be observed over a sufficiently long time span. Similar spending levels may mean different things if spending in one country has been declining for years while in the other it has been on a continuous increase. In fact, whether social investment is high or low at a given time may be indicative less of a country's capacity for fiscal innovation than whether investment is rising or declining. In light of this, we will focus on trends rather than conditions and on dynamic rather than static similarities and differences.

The three countries we have selected for study are Germany, Sweden and the United States. Germany is a country we know reasonably well, of course, which, given the institutional complexities of fiscal policy, is a good enough reason for including it. More importantly, Germany appears on many counts as a non-exceptional, intermediate, more or less average case: in 2007, before the advent of the Great Recession, the government share in its economy (at 44 per cent of GDP) and the level of taxation (at 40 per cent) were neither high nor low by OECD standards, and the same applied to its public debt (at 65 per cent). Still, as in most other countries, from the early 1970s onwards German public budgets were usually in deficit and accumulated debt rose steadily, provoking public concern and repeated attempts at fiscal consolidation, including the social security reforms of the second Schröder government (2002–5; see Streeck 2009b).

Sweden and the United States, by comparison, are extreme cases, each in the opposite direction. Sweden, representing the Scandinavian version of the postwar welfare state, was at least until 2007 the prototypical high-tax economy, with a government share of 51 per cent and a taxation rate of 49 per cent. In fact, although government spending was always very high, public deficits were rare, and in twenty-one of the thirty-nine years between 1970 and 2008 the Swedish state ran a budget surplus.[12] This did not protect the country from fiscal stress, however. Whereas fiscal problems in Germany accumulated slowly and steadily beginning in the 1970s, with budget deficits almost every year, Sweden suffered through two dramatic crises, one in 1982 and the other in 1992–3. Both crises instantly produced extremely high public deficits, but these were followed by aggressive and highly successful efforts at fiscal consolidation, especially in the 1990s. While the level of taxation has recently declined – in 1990 it was as high as 53 per cent of GDP and in 2000 it was 52 per cent – it is still higher than that in most other countries. Government indebtedness has returned to a relatively low level (48 per cent of GDP in 2007).

The United States is of course the prime example of a modern economy, with low government spending (37 per cent of GDP in 2007), low taxation (28 per cent) and a very small, 'liberal' welfare state. Unlike in Sweden, and more so than in Germany, tax resistance is high and government social intervention is not popular. Despite this, however, fiscal stress has been endemic since the end of inflation in the early 1980s, with huge deficits in the federal budget and high public debt as a result of stagnant growth, repeated tax cuts, and occasional invasions of faraway foreign countries. Renewed economic growth in the 1990s and a policy of austerity aimed at budget consolidation resulted in momentary surpluses, but these were soon to be wiped out by further tax cuts and the rising costs of the wars in Iraq and Afghanistan. In 2007, government debt was at 62 per cent of GDP, having been as low as 55 per cent in 2001.

Below we will analyse the development of social investment under fiscal stress in Germany, Sweden and the United States during the run-up to the financial and fiscal crisis that began in 2008. Part of the reason our analysis ends in 2007 is that the crisis has thrown public finances into deep disarray for the foreseeable future, so we have to wait for a new pattern to emerge. More importantly, the period that began in the mid-1990s was one of sustained endeavours throughout the OECD world to consolidate government finances. Under the leadership of the Clinton administration and international organizations such as the World Bank and the International Monetary Fund, major efforts were made to rein in the accumulation of public debt that had begun with the conquest of inflation in the early 1980s at the latest. As a matter of fact, public debt as a percentage of GDP fell by 17 percentage points in the United States between 1995 and 2001, by 18 percentage points between 1993 and 2007 in Sweden, and by almost 4 percentage points between 2004 and 2007 in post-reunification Germany. While the crisis undid most of the achievements of the consolidation policies of this period, we consider the fiscal experience of these years to be indicative of what we can inevitably expect in the era of incomparably stricter austerity policies that lies ahead, not least with respect to the fate of public investment under fiscal stress.

2.3 Variables and data: social investment

In this section we present and defend our aggregate measure of what we define as social investment. In contrast to some of the literature (e.g., Breunig and Busemeyer 2010; Keman 2010), we are not interested primarily in the size of public investment relative to total state expenditure; for our purposes, this is influenced too much by the overall state share in the national economy and makes substantive sense only where budgetary authority is centralized.[13] Instead we measure public investment in relation to GDP – i.e., in terms of its share in a country's yearly economic output. We believe that this is the method best suited to capture a state's real political effort, certainly comparatively but also over time.

- *Education*: A first inspection of the data on our three countries[14] reveals that public education expenditure in Sweden has declined sharply over past decades. Although spending is still by far the highest among the three countries, it fell from 8.5 per cent of GDP in 1980 to 6.1 per cent in 2007, with a strikingly continuous decline of 2 percentage points during the 1980s. Spending in the US has remained rather constant, fluctuating around 5 per cent until 2007. However, two exceptional highs are found in 1991 and 2003, when US spending rose to about 5.5 per cent. In both cases, the effect seems to be on account of low economic growth (1991 and 2001–3 were years when the US economy performed poorly) combined with institutional inertia regarding spending commitments.[15] Germany's spending has come down from a relatively high level in the 1970s, gradually decreasing from 4.6 per cent in 1980 to 3.9 per cent in 1988. After a slight upward movement in 1993, to 4.5 per cent, expenditure remained roughly constant before it fell to 4 per cent in the last observed year, 2007.
- *Research and development (R&D)*: Our data show how public spending on R&D has steadily decreased in Germany since the early 1980s, falling from 1.04 per cent of GDP in 1982 to 0.7 per cent in 2007. Developments in the US from the mid-1980s to the late 1990s show an even steeper downward trend. The increase after 2000 is driven mainly by a rise in spending on defence R&D (OECD 2007: 1). We note a renewed, albeit minor decline beginning in 2004. Swedish developments are more difficult to summarize, although public spending on R&D has also declined over time. After spending increases throughout the 1980s, growth-sensitive ups and downs in the early

1990s preceded a period of relatively constant expenditure. In recent years, however, spending has fallen to a low of 0.8 per cent of GDP, to some extent paralleling the other two countries. As absolute figures are small, and R&D activities institutionally inert, one may expect strong short-term effects of changes in economic growth, with increases producing a decline and decreases an increase in spending as a percentage of GDP.

- *Family support*: The development of public spending on family benefits has taken different paths in the three countries. While Sweden's spending level meandered around 4 per cent of GDP during the 1980s, it climbed to almost 5 per cent in 1992, only to fall sharply, to less than 3 per cent, at the end of the century. By 2007, family policy expenditure had again risen to 3.42 per cent of GDP. In Germany, spending declined in the 1980s, from 2 per cent to about 1.5 per cent, but after reunification it then returned to roughly 2 per cent. Without much variation in the 1990s and early 2000s, expenditure amounted to 1.83 per cent of GDP in 2007. In the US, the sum of cash and in-kind benefits never amounted to more than the 1980 level of 0.78 per cent. Spending levels went down to 0.44 per cent in the late 1980s and from then on fluctuated, with a peak value of 0.78 per cent in 2002, a year of low economic growth. Subsequently spending declined to 0.65 per cent in 2007.

- *Active labour market policy*: Active labour market policy (ALMP) is targeted at groups with handicaps on the labour market and aims to increase their employability. The three countries considered in this study have different spending profiles corresponding to different programme priorities. Still, there is a similar trend towards lower spending, although at different levels. The most dramatic decline has taken place in Sweden. After a decrease in spending in the late 1980s, expenditure bounced back in the 1990s to reach 2.5 per cent of GDP by the end of the decade. Thereafter, however, it declined sharply, to 1.12 per cent in 2007, which is the lowest level in the observed period.[16] Data on Germany first show a rise in spending that peaks at 1.49 per cent of GDP in 1992, which is followed by continuous decline, with minor ups and downs, to 0.72 per cent in 2007. Spending in the US has always been much lower than in the other two countries. It was comparatively constant for the first half of the observation period, until the late 1990s, after which it declined steadily, from 0.2 per cent to 0.13 per cent of GDP.

- *Social investment: aggregating education, R&D and family support*: A first inspection of the data for our four categories of social investment suggests a common tendency towards a historical decline in spending. As it turns out, at least some of the measures of social investment are highly correlated within countries over time.[17] We take this to indicate that it makes sense in principle to combine the different spending categories into an aggregate indicator. But, since changes in unemployment make ALMP spending heavily cyclical, we have decided not to include ALMP in our aggregate, although we will discuss it in the individual country sections.

Table 2.1 shows the three countries' aggregate spending on education, R&D and family support. In Sweden, social investment declined early in the 1980s and, after a short rebound, declined again from 1993 onwards. Having started at a level of 13 per cent of GDP, aggregate spending decreased to 10.3 per cent in 2007. Social investment in Germany developed in a similar way on a lower level, with some

Table 2.1: Social investment spending, as a percentage of GDP, 1981–2007

	Germany	Sweden	United States
1981	7.7	13.0	6.6
1982	7.5	12.6	6.7
1983	7.1	12.3	6.7
1984	6.7	12.0	6.5
1985	6.6	12.1	6.5
1986	6.6	12.1	6.5
1987	6.6	12.1	6.5
1988	6.4	11.7	6.5
1989	6.4	11.6	6.4
1990	6.5	11.9	6.5
1991	7.1	12.2	7.1
1992	7.0	12.5	6.9
1993	7.6	12.1	6.6
1994	7.5	11.9	6.4
1995	7.4	11.3	6.5
1996	7.4	11.1	6.5
1997	7.4	11.0	6.4
1998	7.2	10.8	6.4
1999	7.1	10.6	6.4
2000	7.1	10.2	6.2
2001	7.1	10.3	6.6
2002	7.3	10.8	6.8
2003	7.3	10.7	6.9
2004	7.2	10.7	6.6
2005	7.0	10.4	6.2
2006	6.6	10.5	6.4
2007	6.5	10.3	6.4

Sources: OECD Education at a Glance; OECD Public Educational Expenditure 1970–1988; OECD Research and Development Statistics; OECD Social Expenditure Database.

decline in the 1980s, a significant increase after reunification and, in the consolidation period before the crisis, another decline, from 7.6 per cent to 6.5 per cent of GDP. US social investment, as mentioned, was comparatively stable. Except for peaks in 1991 and 2003, which were associated with highs in educational spending, by and large it held constant at around 6.5 per cent throughout the period. In summary, social investment spending in Germany has gradually approximated US levels, while Swedish spending has continuously moved closer to the German level.

2.4 Excursus: social and physical investment

We now return briefly to public investment as defined in the bulk of the literature, in terms of physical investment, or GFCF. Combining our aggregate measure of public social investment with the standard indicator of public investment would raise highly complex issues of double-counting that cannot be resolved with the statistical sources at hand.[18] Still, by taking both measurements of public investment into account, we can derive a more detailed picture of fiscal developments during the last three decades.

Indeed, what emerges overall is a striking similarity in the development of social and physical investment (figure 2.7). Physical investment decreased in Germany and Sweden, whereas it remained largely constant in the United States, the country with the lowest level at the beginning of the period. The steepest decline took place in Germany, where physical investment fell from 3.4 per cent of GDP in 1981 to 1.4 per cent in 2007. The long-term trend, during which German physical investment sank below the American level, slowed only temporarily in the years immediately following reunification. In Sweden, expenditure on physical infrastructure dropped in the early 1980s, from 5 per cent to 3.3 per cent, and again in the mid-1990s, from 4 per cent to 3 per cent of GDP, strongly resembling the trend in social investment. Nevertheless, it remained clearly above American expenditure, where physical investment spending stayed at an average of more or less 2.4 per cent of GDP throughout the period.

2.5 Variables and data: fiscal stress

By fiscal stress we mean fiscal pressures for the consolidation of public finances. In a simplified model, we assume that stress starts with current, persistent, high and, in particular, *rising* public *deficits*. These result in, or add to, public *debt*. At a certain point, governments will face the need to *raise taxes* or *cut public spending*, or both. We suggest that this will apply

Figure 2.7: Social and physical public investment, three countries, as a percentage of GDP, 1981–2007

a) Social investment

Percentage

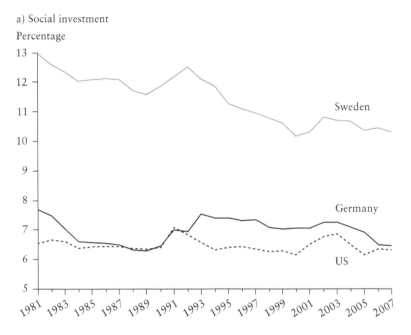

Sources: OECD Education at a Glance; OECD Public Educational Expenditure 1970–1988; OECD Research and Development Statistics; OECD Social Expenditure Database.

b) Physical investment

Percentage

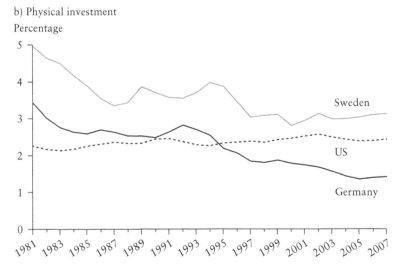

Source: OECD National Accounts.

Table 2.2: Indicators of fiscal stress, as a percentage of GDP, 1981–2007

	Germany			Sweden			United States		
	Deficit	Debt	Expenditure	Deficit	Debt	Expenditure	Deficit	Debt	Expenditure
1981	−3.4	33.6	47.5	−5.7	55.3	62.9	−3.3	40.9	34.7
1982	−3.4	36.5	47.5	−5.5	65.5	65.0	−4.3	45.8	37.0
1983	−2.8	38.2	46.6	−4.9	69.5	64.9	−5.2	48.8	37.1
1984	−2.0	39.0	45.8	−3.9	70.8	62.3	−5.2	50.5	36.2
1985	−1.4	39.5	45.1	−2.3	70.3	63.2	−5.1	55.3	36.9
1986	−1.4	39.6	44.4	−0.2	69.6	60.7	−5.0	58.8	37.4
1987	−1.6	40.9	45.0	2.1	61.9	58.5	−4.5	60.5	37.2
1988	−1.2	41.4	44.6	3.3	55.5	58.0	−3.8	61.2	36.3
1989	−1.3	39.8	43.1	3.3	50.4	60.0	−3.8	61.5	36.2
1990	−1.6	40.4	43.6	2.2	46.3	59.8	−4.2	63.0	37.2
1991	−2.4	37.7	46.1	−1.9	55.0	61.1	−5.1	67.8	38.0
1992	−2.8	40.9	47.3	−6.7	73.4	69.4	−5.3	70.2	38.6
1993	−2.6	46.2	48.3	−9.7	78.2	70.6	−4.9	71.8	38.1
1994	−5.0	46.5	47.9	−9.2	82.5	68.4	−4.0	71.0	37.1
1995	−5.1	55.7	54.8	−6.6	81.1	65.1	−3.1	70.6	37.1
1996	−5.2	58.8	49.3	−4.1	84.4	63.0	−2.2	69.8	36.6
1997	−2.7	60.3	48.3	−1.4	83.0	60.7	−1.0	67.4	35.4
1998	−2.1	62.2	48.1	0.0	82.0	58.8	0.0	64.1	34.6
1999	−0.8	61.5	48.2	1.8	73.2	58.6	0.8	60.4	34.2
2000	−1.0	60.4	45.1	2.0	64.3	55.4	0.5	54.5	33.9
2001	−1.7	59.7	47.5	1.2	62.7	55.2	−1.0	54.4	35.0
2002	−3.5	62.1	48.0	−0.4	60.2	56.4	−3.2	56.8	35.9
2003	−3.8	65.3	48.4	−0.8	59.3	56.5	−4.5	60.1	36.3
2004	−3.7	68.7	47.3	0.4	59.2	55.1	−4.2	61.1	36.0
2005	−2.9	71.1	46.9	1.5	59.9	54.7	−3.3	61.4	36.2
2006	−1.6	69.2	45.3	2.6	52.8	53.6	−2.7	60.9	36.0
2007	−0.7	65.3	43.6	2.9	47.4	51.8	−2.5	61.9	36.8

Notes: Deficit is the three-year moving average of annual budgetary balances, calculated as the mean of deficits occurring in t−1, t, and t+1. Debt reflects gross liabilities, and Expenditure is defined as total disbursements of general government.

Source: OECD Economic Outlook Database No. 87.

regardless of a country's existing level of debt, deficit, spending or taxation, and indeed this is borne out in the fiscal histories of our three countries over almost three decades. Moreover, we expect that, the less a government faced with high deficits and accumulating debt is able or willing to raise taxes, the stronger the fiscal pressure on discretionary public spending, including public investment. Since taxation levels in the three countries, while very different, remained by and large unchanged during the period of observation (although after 2000 they declined slightly; see figure 2.3), we have found it convenient to define fiscal stress as a combination of

increases in deficits and debt over time followed by a decline in overall government spending. Just as with our dependent variables, we then measure
all three components relative to GDP (table 2.2).

2.6 Results

We now present our results, first for each country separately and then for
the three countries in comparison.

- *Germany*: In the 1980s social investment declined, as did deficits and
  overall spending, while debt remained constant, at roughly 40 per cent
  (figure 2.8). After reunification, social investment increased sharply,
  together with deficits, spending and debt. Social investment was
  cut back again beginning in the mid-1990s, while deficits, spending
  and debt were reduced, sometimes significantly. Subsequently rising

Figure 2.8: Germany: social investment in relation to public deficit, public debt and
public expenditure, as a percentage of GDP

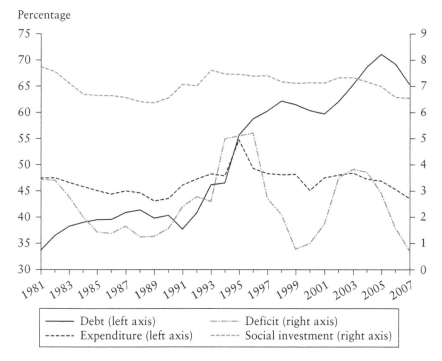

Percentage

| Debt (left axis) | Deficit (right axis) |
| Expenditure (left axis) | Social investment (right axis) |

Sources: OECD Education at a Glance, OECD Public Educational Expenditure 1970–
1988, OECD Research and Development Statistics, OECD Social Expenditure Database;
OECD Economic Outlook 87.

Figure 2.9: Sweden: social investment in relation to public deficit, public debt and public expenditure, as a percentage of GDP

Percentage

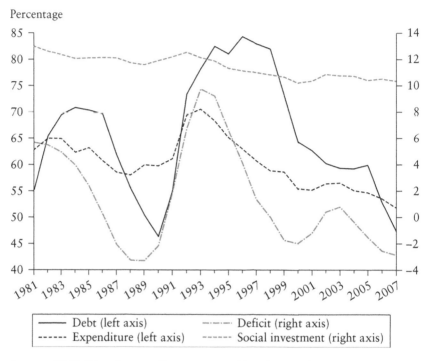

Debt (left axis) ──── Deficit (right axis) ──·──
Expenditure (left axis) ----- Social investment (right axis) ------

Sources: OECD Education at a Glance, OECD Public Educational Expenditure 1970–1988, OECD Research and Development Statistics, OECD Social Expenditure Database; OECD Economic Outlook 87.

deficits caused an increase in overall debt and allowed for a slight rise in public expenditure. Then the Schröder reforms and the austerity measures of the Grand Coalition of 2005–9 cut the deficit by cutting spending and, on the eve of the financial crisis, managed to lower the national debt by roughly 6 percentage points. By our aggregate measure, social investment during the same period declined from 7.3 per cent to 6.5 per cent of GDP – i.e., by about 10 per cent.

As mentioned above, spending on active labour market policy developed the same way; in fact, it was cut almost in half between 1999 and 2007. This was clearly *not* driven by a decline in policy demand, since between 1999 and 2005 the number of unemployed increased from about 3 million to 4.5 million. Spending on family support was also cut in the course of consolidation and declined faster than the population of children under fifteen, although the decline of the latter should arguably have called for an increase in policy effort.

Figure 2.10: US: social investment in relation to public deficit, public debt and public expenditure, as a percentage of GDP

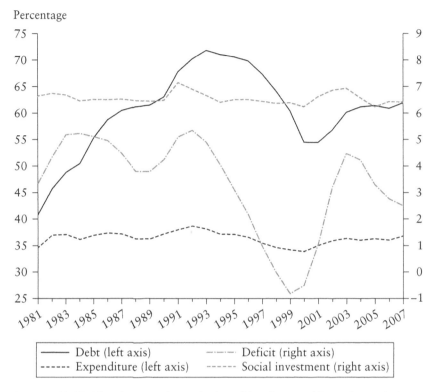

Sources: OECD Education at a Glance, OECD Public Educational Expenditure 1970–1988, OECD Research and Development Statistics, OECD Social Expenditure Database, OECD Economic Outlook 87.

- *Sweden*: Social investment declined steadily and dramatically during the entire period (figure 2.9). There were two phases of budget consolidation and debt reduction, from 1981 to 1989 and from 1995 to 2007. Overall public spending was sharply curtailed, especially in the latter period. Amid drastic spending cuts and a return to the Swedish tradition of running a budget surplus, social investment spending fell from 12.5 per cent of GDP in 1992 to 10.3 per cent in 2007, which amounts to a loss of no less than 18 per cent. At the same time, active labour market policy was cut in half between 1998 (2.46 per cent) and 2007 (1.12 per cent), remarkably in spite of the fact that, from the early 2000s onwards, unemployment increased from 190,000 to 300,000 and seems to have stabilized at that level. Spending on passive labour market policy followed the same pattern. Family support was also severely cut during the 1990s, while the number of children and the birth rate fell slightly, perhaps in part as a result of these cuts.

- *United States*: Social investment was low throughout the period, at between 6 per cent and 7 per cent of GDP (figure 2.10). Over time, there were two episodes in which it increased slightly, culminating in 1991 (7.1 per cent) and 2003 (6.9 per cent). Low social investment was associated with rising deficits and growing debt. There were also two periods of spending decline, from 1991 to 2000 (6.2 per cent) and from 2003 to 2007 (6.4 per cent); these were years of budget consolidation, in particular the late 1990s, when the US budget showed a surplus. Spending on active labour market policy, small as it always was in the United States, declined between 1997 and 2007, although the number of unemployed went up sharply between 2000 and 2003.

3 Conclusion: the decline of democratic state capacity

Public deficits generate cumulative public debt, which in turn gives rise to pressures for fiscal consolidation. Absent an increase in taxation, consolidation must be achieved by cuts in expenditure. Inevitably these cuts will affect discretionary more than mandatory spending. Since public investment is discretionary, it is highly likely to be cut if public expenditure is cut. Apparently this applies not just to traditional public investment in physical infrastructure but also to social investment, even though its magnitude may seem small in absolute terms. Contrary to what one might expect, moreover, there seems to be no substitution of social for physical investment, as apparently the two are equally and simultaneously affected by fiscal stress and political austerity. *If governments want or need to pursue fiscal consolidation, it appears to be impossible to protect – or, as is arguably necessary, to increase – social investment without raising taxes.*

Obviously the mechanism we have identified is not a logically necessary one. Because we have found it at work in three otherwise very different countries, however, we have become convinced that it does represent a powerful tendency inherent in mature democratic polities and their fiscal regimes. Still, it need not be true that fiscal consolidation without higher taxes depresses future-oriented public investment. To show that it could be otherwise requires no more, but also no fewer, than one or two examples of countries where a decline in overall public spending went together with constant or even increasing social investment. No such case has yet come to our attention.

In fact, our suspicion that fiscal consolidation and stable or increasing

Figure 2.11: UK: social investment in relation to public deficit, public debt and public expenditure, as a percentage of GDP

Percentage

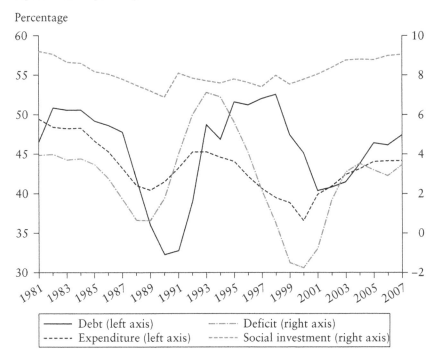

—— Debt (left axis)	··—··— Deficit (right axis)
- - - - - Expenditure (left axis)	- - - - - Social investment (right axis)

Sources: OECD Education at a Glance, OECD Public Educational Expenditure 1970–1988, OECD Research and Development Statistics, OECD Social Expenditure Database, OECD Economic Outlook 87.

social public investment are unlikely to be compatible is confirmed indirectly by the recent fiscal history of another rich democracy, the United Kingdom. The UK seems to be one of the very few major countries where social investment increased rather than declined in the years before 2008, more precisely after New Labour took office in 1997 (figure 2.11). However, this increase coincided with growing public expenditure funded by deficits and rising public debt. By comparison, public expenditure in the UK was cut between 1981 and 1989 in an effort to reduce public indebtedness without raising taxes, and, as we would expect, social investment declined by more than a fifth.

That our findings for our three countries are essentially the same makes them all the more alarming. In fact, comparison between them suggests that public investment may be likely to decline most where original spending levels were high and least where spending was already initially so low that it could not easily be lowered further. Thought through to the end, our results might even raise the question of a convergence at the lowest possible level of collective investment.

Traditional – 'hard' – public investment may be subject to saturation in advanced industrial countries. Clearly, the same cannot be said of social investment. Today research and development is a major source of economic progress and prosperity; education serves to enable a country's citizens to participate fully in the social life of an evolving 'knowledge society' and to compete successfully in the global economy; family policies are meant to counter the gaping demographic deficit typical of contemporary rich societies; and active labour market policy assists the weakest members of society in establishing and maintaining occupational competencies, thereby helping to equalize social and economic life chances. Education and labour market policy in particular are of special significance in countries with high levels of immigration, such as the three covered by this chapter. Rather than a *decline* in social investment spending, one would therefore have had good reason to expect an *increase*, in response to rising needs for public intervention and political problem-solving. This is actually what much of current political rhetoric, at least in Europe, continues to demand and indeed to promise. As fiscal stress increases, however, the opposite is happening – as we have shown – and not just in the United States but also in a country such as Sweden, the archetype of the 'Scandinavian model'.

The results of our analysis bear out our claim that comparing trajectories over time is at least as productive in social and political science as using cross-sectional snapshots. A cross-sectional approach would have revealed that, in 2007, Sweden spent a lot more on social investment than Germany, and Germany spent more than the US. This is undoubtedly the case, but in order to assess what the three spending levels really mean, and in what direction the three countries may be going, it is essential to understand that social investment has declined in all of them, especially in recent years, when public spending was cut after a period of public-sector deficits and an accompanying increase in public debt. As social and political change normally proceeds gradually, through trends rather than events, a longitudinal as opposed to a cross-sectional perspective suggests that we should search for underlying 'structural' causes of the developments we have found, rather than for one-time policy decisions, changes in government or momentary conjunctural circumstances. It also suggests that, for a country such as Sweden, where social investment has been descending to a 'normal' continental European and perhaps a German level for more than a decade now, defending its traditional social-democratic identity would require nothing short of a major political-economic turnaround, even though for another decade it may yet exhibit significantly higher public spending than, for example, Germany

– a country that, in the absence of major political change, will continue to descend towards the American level.

Another issue where the comparative analysis of trends over time yields important insights is taxation. Cross-sectional observation would suggest that the United States could easily solve its fiscal problems by raising its taxes by a few percentage points, to a level that would still remain far short of even the German one. But the fact that in the 2000s the level of taxation *declined* in all three countries, including the traditionally high-tax economy and society of Sweden, warns against analytical and political voluntarism. If taxation levels have changed in recent years, the change was obviously downwards rather than upwards. Resistance to tax increases has apparently been widespread in rich industrialized countries since the 1970s, when the end of the postwar growth period registered with citizens and 'bracket creep' could no longer be relied upon to provide states with a rising share of their societies' economic resources. Governments then began relying upon debt to close the endemic gaps between revenue and spending, until this was no longer feasible. Next, they sought consolidation, but did this through spending cuts rather than tax increases. This was the case not just in the US, but also in social-democratic Sweden and centrist continental European Germany.

If one considers the decade before 2008 as the trial run for a new wave of even more incisive consolidation of public finances in rich democracies, as we do, one cannot but arrive at dire predictions concerning the future capacities of governments to assist their societies in coping with changed conditions of prosperity and equality. If governments cannot protect public investment – especially what we call social investment – from fiscal pressures, then governmental impact on the structure and the performance of modern societies must decline. Citizens, responding to what appears to be another stage in the gradual demise of the governing capacities of democratic states, may continue to lose interest in democratic politics. Instead of contributing to the provision of collective goods, they will turn to private markets in growing numbers in order to supply themselves with what they need to survive and prosper in a situation of changing economic opportunities. But not everyone will be able to pay the price for the private as opposed to the public enhancement of his or her marketability, so there will be distributional consequences from lower public investment as well as from reduced welfare-state spending. For example, declining or stagnant family support will leave unchanged the next generation's initial distribution of life chances as determined by a family's social status. Declining investment in public education will force the increasingly large number of individuals from disadvantaged social groups to forgo opportunities for social advancement or will cause them to incur significant amounts of private debt[19] – provided they have access to credit in the first place.

None of this bodes well for the coming years, when the additional debt accumulated in the course of the financial crisis will have to be cut back under the watchful eyes of the very 'financial markets' that caused the global recession in the first place and thereby forced governments to sacrifice the gains of a decade of fiscal consolidation. Further reductions in public spending, following the pattern of the 1990s and 2000s, only on a much larger scale, have already been announced in all major industrial countries. On the basis of our findings, it seems very hard to believe that this would not include a continuation of the cuts in public investment that we have observed in the past two-and-a-half decades. The question this will raise – a question, we expect, that will be harder than ever before to ignore – is whether democratic states under capitalism, with their manifold public responsibilities, on the one hand, and the severe restrictions on how they may raise the means needed to discharge them, on the other, will still be able to do what is required for the future viability of their increasingly unstable, fragile and disorganized societies. Will what appears to be urgently needed also be possible? Will, in the coming years, the politically possible systematically fall short of the socially necessary? Will the political capacity of modern states be up to their increasing number of tasks, or will it atrophy under ever tightening conditions of fiscal austerity? As yet there is little to make us optimistic about the answers.

References

Auer, P., Efendioğlu, Ü., and Leschke, J. (2008) *Active Labour Market Policies around the World: Coping with the Consequences of Globalization*. Geneva: International Labour Organization.

Breunig, C., and Busemeyer, M. (2010) Fiscal austerity and the trade-off between public investment and social spending, *Journal of European Public Policy* 19(6); available at: www.tandfonline.com/doi/abs/10.1080/13501763.2011.6 14158 [article first published online 27 September 2011].

Buchanan, J. M. (1958) *Public Principles of Public Debt: A Defense and Restatement*. Homewood, IL: Richard R. Irwin.

Buchanan, J. M. (1985) The moral dimension of debt financing, *Economic Inquiry* 23: 1–6.

Buchanan, J. M., and Roback, J. (1987) The incidence and effects of public debt in the absence of fiscal illusion, *Public Finance Quarterly* 15: 5–25.

Buchanan, J. M., and Tullock, G. (1977) The expanding public sector: Wagner squared, *Public Choice* 31: 147–50.

Buchanan, J. M., and Wagner, R. E. (1977) *Democracy in Deficit: The Political Legacy of Lord Keynes*. New York: Academic Press.

Buchanan, J. M., and Wagner, R. E. (1978) The political biases of Keynesian economics, in J. M. Buchanan and R. E. Wagner (eds), *Fiscal Responsibility in Constitutional Democracy*. Leiden: Martinus Nijhoff, pp. 79–100.

De Haan, J., Sturm, J. E., and Sikken, B. J. (1996) Government capital formation: explaining the decline, *Weltwirtschaftliches Archiv* 132: 55–74.

Downs, A. (1960) Why the government budget is too small in a democracy, *World Politics* 12: 541–63.

Greif, A. (2006) *Institutions and the Path to the Modern Economy*. Cambridge: Cambridge University Press.

Greif, A., and Laitin, D. A. (2004) A theory of endogenous institutional change, *American Political Science Review* 98: 633–52.

Hayek, F. A. von (1967 [1950]) Full employment, planning and inflation, in F. A. von Hayek (ed.), *Studies in Philosophy, Politics, and Economics*. Chicago: University of Chicago Press, pp. 270–9.

Keman, H. (2010) Cutting back public investment after 1980: collateral damage, policy legacies and political adjustment, *Journal of Public Policy* 30: 163–82.

Lewin, T. (2011) Burden of college loans on graduates grows, *New York Times*, 11 April; available at: www.nytimes.com/2011/04/12/education/12college. html (accessed 1 March 2012).

Morel, N., Palier, B., and Palme, J. (eds) (2012) *Towards a Social Investment Welfare State?* Bristol: Policy Press.

OECD (Organization for Economic Cooperation and Development) (2007) *OECD Science, Technology and Industry Scoreboard: Briefing Note on the United States*. Paris: OECD.

OECD (Organization for Economic Cooperation and Development) (2009) *National Accounts at a Glance*. Paris: OECD.

OECD Directorate for Employment, Labour and Social Affairs (2011) *Families and Children*. <http://web.archive.org/web/20100116170439/http:/www.oecd. org/department/0,3355,en_2649_34819_1_1_1_1_1,00.html> (accessed 18 September 2012).

Olson, M. (1982) *The Rise and Decline of Nations*. New Haven, CT: Yale University Press.

Olson, M. (1983) Political economy of comparative growth rates, in D. C. Mueller (ed.), *The Political Economy of Growth*. New Haven, CT: Yale University Press, pp. 7–52.

Pierson, P. (1998) Irresistible forces, immovable objects: post-industrial welfare states confront permanent austerity, *Journal of European Public Policy* 5: 539–60.

Pierson, P. (2001) From expansion to austerity: the new politics of taxing and spending, in M. A. Levin, M. K. Landy and M. Shapiro (eds), *Seeking the Center: Politics and Policymaking at the New Century*. Washington, DC: Georgetown University Press, pp. 54–80.

Rose, R. (1990) Inheritance before choice in public policy, *Journal of Theoretical Politics* 2: 263–91.

Rose, R., and Davies, P. L. (1994) *Inheritance in Public Policy: Change without Choice in Britain*. New Haven, CT: Yale University Press.

Rose, R., and Peters, G. (1978) *Can Government Go Bankrupt?* New York: Basic Books.

Scharpf, F. W. (1970) *Demokratietheorie zwischen Utopie und Anpassung.* Konstanz: Universitätsverlag.

Scharpf, F. W. (2000) Interdependence and democratic legitimation, in S. J. Pharr and R. D. Putnam (eds), *Disaffected Democracies: What's Troubling the Trilateral Countries?* Princeton, NJ: Princeton University Press, pp. 101–20.

Schumpeter, J. A. (1991 [1918]) The crisis of the tax state, in R. Swedberg (ed.), *The Economics and Sociology of Capitalism.* Princeton, NJ: Princeton University Press, pp. 99–141.

Steuerle, C. E. (2010) The U.S. is broke. Here's why. *USA Today,* 26 January; available at: www.usatoday.com/NEWS/usaedition/2010-01-27-column27_ST_U.htm (accessed 1 March 2012).

Steuerle, C. E., and Rennane, S. (2010) The role of fiscal councils and budget offices: lessons from the United States, unpublished manuscript.

Stiglitz, J. E. (2003) *The Roaring Nineties: A New History of the World's Most Prosperous Decade.* New York: W. W. Norton.

Streeck, W. (2009a) *Institutions in History: Bringing Capitalism Back In,* MPIfG Discussion Paper 09/8. Cologne: Max Planck Institute for the Study of Societies.

Streeck, W. (2009b) *Re-Forming Capitalism: Institutional Change in the German Political Economy.* Oxford: Oxford University Press.

Streeck, W., and Mertens, D. (2011) *Fiscal Austerity and Public Investment: Is the Possible the Enemy of the Necessary?*, MPIfG Discussion Paper 11/12. Cologne: Max Planck Institute for the Study of Societies.

United Nations (2009) *System of National Accounts 2008.* New York: United Nations.

3

Tax Competition and Fiscal Democracy

Philipp Genschel and Peter Schwarz

1 Fiscal democracy constrained

What is 'fiscal democracy'? The term was coined by Eugene Steuerle but never properly defined. The meaning is quite intuitive, however. Democracy, according to Steuerle (2008), is fundamentally 'about equal rights to vote – and have your representatives vote – on the nation's current priorities'. Since a nation's current priorities usually have financial implications – they require the allocation of public money – democracy is at its core a fiscal affair. It concerns equal rights to vote on tax and expenditure policies. Yet voting confers democratic control only to the extent that votes can make a difference in policy terms. If 'there is no alternative' (what Margaret Thatcher dubbed TINA), voting is redundant. Fiscal democracy has not only formal prerequisites – equal voting rights – but also substantive prerequisites – policy choice and autonomy. True fiscal democracy occurs when voters have the power to change the government and the government has the power to change fiscal policies in light of voter preferences.

In his own work, Steuerle has focused on the substantive prerequisites of fiscal democracy and, more specifically, on the constraints that the policy obligations entered by 'yesterday's legislators' (Steuerle 2010: 876) impose on the fiscal choices of today's legislators. To measure these constraints he has developed the Fiscal Democracy Index, which measures the percentage of public revenue that remains available after expenditures on mandatory programmes (including interest payments on the public debt). Applied to the federal budget of the United States, the index shows a steady decline beginning in the 1960s (ibid.: 878). In 2010, it turns negative, indicating that, even before Congress voted on any spending programme for that year, more than the available revenue had already been allocated to mandatory expenditure programmes. Streeck and Mertens (2010) report a similar downward trend in fiscal discretion for Germany. Other empirical studies also point to the long-term accumulation of expenditure-side constraints on fiscal democracy (Pierson 1998). The recent sovereign debt crisis greatly exacerbates the problem.

Fiscal democracy faces threats not only from the expenditure side but also from the revenue side. New or mounting obstacles to raising public revenue can reduce the scope for fiscal policy discretion as well. Our concern in this chapter is with one particular revenue-side constraint: international tax competition. The political economy literature is split on whether such competition undermines fiscal democracy, and, if so, to what extent. Some scholars argue that tax competition harms fiscal democracy by constraining national tax autonomy. Others claim that tax competition fails to constrain national taxation and therefore cannot harm fiscal democracy. The first position became popular in the late 1980s and early 1990s, when radical tax reforms in the US and the UK and rapid advances in global and regional economic integration seemed to herald a new era of international competition (Sinn 1988; Steinmo 1994; Swank 2006). Many authors feared, and some hoped, that this would lock governments into a race to the bottom in taxation that would all but erase national tax autonomy (Edwards and Keen 1996). This concern was particularly widespread in Europe. Economists warned that the completion of the single market would turn the EU into 'a single large tax haven' (Giovannini and Hines 1991: 172) in which fiscal competition would wipe out redistributive taxes on mobile factors and turn the tax system into one of mere benefit taxation (Sinn 1994). The second position rose to prominence in the late 1990s and early 2000s, when scholars began submitting the predictions of the first position to empirical testing and failed to find clear-cut evidence of a dramatic race to the bottom. Some authors concluded that competitive constraints on national taxation were largely irrelevant: governments 'wishing to expand the public economy for political reasons may still do so (including increasing taxes on capital to pay for new spending)' (Garrett 1998: 823). The notable success of Denmark, a small, open, high-tax economy, seemed to vindicate this conclusion (Campbell 2009: 262).

Our findings indicate that both positions are wrong. The latter view, that tax competition is no threat to fiscal democracy because it does not constrain taxation, underrates the stringency of tax competition. As we will show for a sample of twenty-two OECD countries (OECD-22),[1] tax competition does constrain national taxation in important ways. The former view, that tax competition harms fiscal democracy because it constrains national tax autonomy, assumes that competitive constraints on national taxation translate directly into constraints on national fiscal democracy. This is not the case. Tax competition has ambiguous effects: while it undermines fiscal democracy in most countries, it expands the scope for fiscal democracy in some (mostly small, poor and peripheral) countries.

The rest of the chapter is structured into five sections. Section 2 briefly reviews the concept of tax competition and explains why it affects fiscal democracy differently in different countries. The next three sections investigate the extent of tax competition among OECD-22 countries: section 3 scrutinizes competitive constraints on tax rates, section 4 focuses on competitive effects on tax revenues, and section 5 analyses the redistributive consequences of tax competition, while section 6 summarizes the empirical findings and discusses implications for fiscal democracy.

2 Tax competition: symmetric and asymmetric

Tax competition refers to the process of national governments vying for an internationally mobile tax base by strategically undercutting their taxes. In order to analyse its implications for fiscal democracy, we start with a very simple conceptual model. In its starkest form, this baseline model features two identical countries sharing one international mobile tax base ('capital') (Zodrow and Mieszkowski 1986; Wilson 1999). The tax policies of both countries are interdependent: high taxes in country A swell country B's revenues by pushing a larger share of the mobile tax base towards B; low taxes in A depress B's revenues by poaching elements of the tax base from B. This policy interdependency triggers a 'race to the bottom' in taxation as each country tries to appropriate a disproportionate share of the mobile tax base by undercutting the other country's tax rate. In equilibrium, tax rates are lower in both countries than they would otherwise be, resulting in lower tax revenues and/or a shift of the tax burden to immobile tax bases. The effects on fiscal democracy are straightforward. Tax competition constrains the revenue-raising capacity both for competing countries as a group *and* for each country individually. The range of feasible fiscal policies shrinks; fiscal democracy is universally undermined. The obvious antidote is tax harmonization.[2]

> [I]f citizens are to retain the ability to choose the goods and services they would like to provide to themselves collectively through democratically elected institutions, and to use the tax system to achieve a more socially acceptable distribution of income, the forces of globalization . . . will have

to be neutralized. The most obvious way for that to happen is for countries to agree to coordinate and harmonize aspects of their tax systems, particularly as they relate to the taxation of income from capital. (Brooks and Hwong 2010: 819)

So far, our baseline model assumes both countries to be identical: tax competition is symmetric. Obviously, however, real-world countries are not identical but differ across various dimensions, including country size. The introduction of differences in country size (in terms of initial endowments of tax base) changes the results of the baseline model considerably: if countries differ in size, they no longer face similar competitive constraints and no longer suffer equal welfare losses. Instead, the smaller country has stronger incentives to cut tax rates than the larger country and suffers a smaller revenue loss in the competitive equilibrium (Bucovetsky 1991; Kanbur and Keen 1993). Indeed, if the difference in size is large enough, the smaller country generates more revenue under tax competition than in its absence. Intuitively, this is because, for the small country, the revenue loss from a tax cut – i.e., revenue forfeited from the (initially small) domestic tax base – is relatively minor compared with the major revenue gain from the inflow of part of the (initially large) foreign tax base of the other country. Hence the small country faces a more elastic supply of the mobile tax base than its large competitor. In equilibrium, it will undercut the rate of the large country and attract a disproportionately large share of the internationally mobile tax base. There is a clear 'advantage of "smallness"' in tax competition (Wilson 1999: 278). Tax competition is asymmetric.[3]

Asymmetric tax competition has ambiguous effects on fiscal democracy. The overall effect is negative, because the competitive dynamics constrain the taxing capacity of the group of competing countries as a whole. But the effect for the small country is positive: it gains in revenue-raising capacity and therefore has more policy options for democratic choice. What the small country gains, however, the large country more than loses. The effect of tax competition on national fiscal democracy is clearly negative for the larger country. As a consequence, tax harmonization to curb tax competition is likely to be contested between the large country (which would benefit) and the small country (which would lose). Asymmetric tax competition is a matter of common concern for voters and governments in all competing countries but does not lend itself easily to commonly acceptable solutions.

So much for the theory of tax competition; what about its reality? To the extent that tax competition exists, the baseline model leads us to expect three major tax policy trends:

- *race to the bottom*: a downward trend in tax rates and tax revenues as countries engage in competitive tax cutting
- *asymmetry*: a pronounced tendency of small countries to undercut the tax rates of large countries and raise more tax revenue from mobile bases
- *redistribution*: a shift of the mobile tax base from large to small countries (international redistribution) and a shift of the tax burden from mobile to immobile tax bases (domestic redistribution).

A lot of high-powered econometric research has gone into evaluating these predictions, most of this which is narrowly focused on corporate taxation. The findings have been mixed: results vary according to the prediction tested, time frame, sample selection, and measure of the corporate tax burden. In this chapter, we take a different approach. Based on simple indicators on all three predictions, we show that the existence of tax competition is more obvious and straightforward than much of the econometric research makes it appear. Our analysis starts in the 1980s (before the onset of deep economic integration) and ends in 2007 (the last year before the financial crash and for most variables also the last year for which data are available) and covers all major taxes.

3 Tax competition and tax rates

Does tax competition trigger a race to the bottom in tax rates? Does it cause asymmetries in tax-rate levels that correspond to the size of the country? In order to investigate these questions, it is important to distinguish two modes of tax competition: general and targeted (Keen 2001; Kemmerling and Seils 2009). Under *general tax competition*, governments vie for a mobile tax base by cutting *general* tax rates such as the standard corporate tax rate. Under *targeted tax competition*, by contrast, they compete for a mobile tax base by offering *preferential tax treatment* specifically for particularly mobile parts of the base. As an example, think of special corporate tax regimes, which reduce the level of taxation selectively on specific corporate forms and functions, such as foreign-held companies, companies located in special business zones, holding companies or captive insurance.

Figures 3.1a and 3.1b provide evidence on *general tax competition*. Figure 3.1a tracks historical trends in four general tax rates. It shows a dramatic fall in the corporate tax rate (down from an OECD-22 average of 46 per cent in 1985 to less than 30 per cent in 2007). The top personal income tax rate also fell by 16 percentage points, but from a higher initial

Figure 3.1: Tax rates, OECD-22 averages

a) Historical trends

Percentage

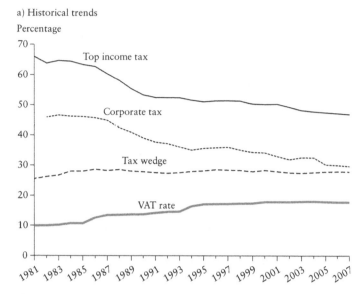

Sources for top income tax rates, VAT rate, and corporate tax: Bundesministerium der Finanzen, Die wichtigsten Steuern im internationalen Vergleich, several issues.
Sources for tax wedge figures: OECD, Taxing Wages.

b) Correlations with country size

Correlation coefficient

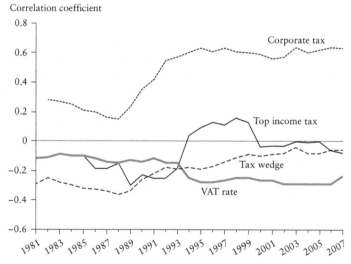

Sources: For top income tax rates, VAT rates, and corporate tax: Bundesministerium der Finanzen, *Die wichtigsten Steuern im internationalen Vergleich*, several issues; for tax wedge figures: OECD, *Taxing Wages*.

level (63 per cent in 1985 down to 47 per cent in 2007). The VAT rate increased (from roughly 11 per cent in 1985 to roughly 18 per cent in 2007). The tax wedge[4] of an average wage earner (single, no children) has been more or less stable since the mid-1980s (at around 28 per cent). In short, there is evidence of a pronounced race towards the bottom in general corporate tax rates and a relatively less pronounced downward trend in top personal income tax rates, but not in tax wedges or VAT rates.

Figure 3.1b tracks the correlation of the general tax rates and the size of OECD-22 countries over time.[5] If tax competition does have asymmetric effects on small and large countries, as the baseline model suggests, we should observe a positive correlation of tax rates and country size. The correlation should gain in strength over time, as the level of market integration, and hence competitive pressure, increases. This is indeed what we find for the corporate tax rate: its correlation with country size increased from 0.21 in 1985 to 0.63 in 2007, indicating a growing tendency of small states to undercut the corporate tax rates of large states. Much of the empirical literature takes this as strong evidence of increasing competitive pressure (Devereux et al. 2002; Ganghof 2006; Plümper et al. 2009; Genschel and Schwarz 2011). All other correlations are negative or show no clear trend. In sum, figure 3.1b suggests that general tax competition affects corporate tax rates but not top personal income rates, tax wedges, or VAT rates.

Table 3.1 presents evidence on *targeted tax competition*. The countries are arranged according to size of population (column 2). Column 3 provides information on targeted competition in corporate taxation. While there is strong anecdotal evidence that special corporate tax regimes have been spreading since the 1980s, systematic internationally comparative time-series data are lacking (Kemmerling and Seils 2009). The best we can do is to list the number of 'potentially harmful' corporate tax regimes identified by the OECD among its member states in 2000 (OECD 2006). The list shows that all OECD countries but four have adopted one or more special corporate tax regimes, suggesting that targeted competition is widespread in corporate taxation. The correlation between country size and the number of special corporate tax regimes is negative but small: large states are only slightly less likely to have such regimes than small states. Closer inspection suggests that domestic institutions may have more impact on the probability of special corporate tax regimes being adopted. The number of such regimes tends to be high among continental welfare states (Belgium, France, Germany, Luxembourg, the Netherlands, Switzerland) and Mediterranean states (Greece, Italy, Portugal, but not Spain) but low among Anglo-Saxon economies (Australia, New Zealand, the UK, the US, but not Canada

Table 3.1: Targeted tax rates

	Country size (millions)	Special corporate tax regimes	Top rate on personal interest income			
			Residents		Non-residents	
	2000	2000	1985	2007	1985	2007
Luxembourg	0.5	3	57	10[b]	0	0
NZ	3.8	0	–	–	–	–
Ireland	3.9	2	65	20[b]	35	0
Norway	4.5	1	64	0.40	0	–
Finland	5.2	1	–	28[b]	–	0
Denmark	5.4	0	73	59	0	0
Switzerland	7.3	2	39	40	35	15
Austria	8.1		67	25[b]	5	0
Sweden	8.9	1	80	30[b]	0	0
Portugal	10.4	3	60	20[b]	13.8	20
Belgium	10.3	5	25[b]	15[b]	25	15
Greece	10.6	4	63	10[b]	56.8	10
Netherlands	16.2	7	72	52	0	0
Australia	19.7	1	–	–	–	–
Canada	31.4	3	50	46	25	25
Spain	40.5	1	66	43	18	0
Italy	58.0	2	12.5[b]	27[b]	21.6	27
UK	59.2	0	60	40	30	0
France	59.5	2	65	48	25	16
Germany	82.6	2	56	47	0	0
Japan	127.6	0	75	20[b]	20	15
United States	283.0	1	50	42	30	30
OECD-22		1.95	57.87	33.10	17.91	9.11
Correlation[a]		–0.16	–0.13	0.38	0.25	0.49

Notes:
[a] Correlations are with the population logarithm.
[b] Schedular taxation.

Sources: Population: http://stats.oecd.org/index.aspx?queryid=254; Special corporate tax regimes; OECD 2006 top rate on personal interest income; Bundesministerium der Finanzen; *Die wichtigsten Steuern im internationalen Vergleich*, several issues.

and Ireland) and Nordic welfare states (Denmark, Finland, Norway, Sweden).

Targeted competition in personal income taxation focuses mainly on high-wage professionals and private investors. There is widespread anecdotal evidence of countries offering special tax regimes to foreign professionals ('expats') who are working temporarily in the domestic economy, so that these countries can attract human capital and the multinational companies employing it (PWC and CEER 2005). For example, Sweden provides tax incentives to foreign experts residing no longer than five years in the country; the Netherlands has tax incentives for foreign experts, artists and athletes; and Spain, until recently, offered a special rate of only 24 per cent to soccer players (the 'Lex Beckham'). Unfortunately, a lack of internationally comparative data prevents us from presenting systematic data for all OECD-22 countries. Data are available, by contrast, on targeted competition for private investment income. We focus on interest income. As a rule, interest income is fully taxable in the residence country of the investor, with a tax credit given for any withholding tax charged by the source country of the investment. In practice, however, the private investor may evade residence-country taxation by not reporting their foreign interest income. Governments can compete for interest income in two ways. First, they can selectively cut the top personal income tax rate on resident interest income so as to reduce the incentive for domestic investors to engage in outbound tax evasion (columns 4 and 5). Second, they can reduce their withholding taxes on the interest income of foreign investors so as to attract inbound investment of non-residents (columns 6 and 7).

The standard approach to cutting the tax burden on resident investors is to tax interest income outside the framework of the progressive personal income tax at a low proportional rate (known as 'schedular taxation'). As column 4 shows, only two of the OECD-22 countries applied a schedular approach in 1985. By 2007, however, ten did so (Column 5). The spread of schedular taxation has caused the top rate on resident personal interest income to fall faster than the top personal income tax rate. While between 1985 and 2007 the latter fell by only 16 percentage points on average for the OECD-22 (see figure 3.1a), the former went down by 25 percentage points, from 58 per cent (1985) to 33 per cent (2007). Personal interest income is now often taxed at substantially lower rates than personal income from other sources. In 2007, the rate gap between the (low) tax rate on resident personal interest income and the (high) top personal income tax rate was as wide as 14 percentage points, on OECD-22 average. The rate of interest income taxation is now positively correlated with country size (0.38 in 2007), as the baseline model would predict: small countries are more likely to have low interest income tax rates (and to adopt a schedular approach to interest income taxation) than large countries. At the same time, governments have also cut the withholding tax burden on non-resident interest income. As columns 6 and 7 show, the withholding tax rate dropped from an average of 18 per cent in 1985 to 9 per cent in 2007. There is also a positive association with country size (0.49 in 2007): small states are more likely to charge lower withholding taxes than large states. In conclusion, while governments tried to stem outbound tax evasion of domestic residents by making targeted cuts to resident interest income, they vied for inbound tax evasion of foreign investors by reducing the withholding taxes on non-resident interest income.

The evidence presented in this section suggests that tax rate competition has increased since the 1980s. Corporate taxation is now subject to strong general *and* targeted tax competition. Personal income taxation is subject to strong targeted competition for interest income and arguably some limited competition for highly qualified labour. But there is no indication that the drop in top personal income tax rates was caused by general tax competition. There is also no evidence of tax competition based on VAT or the tax wedge affecting the average production worker.

4 Tax competition and tax revenues

Does tax rate competition matter for tax revenues? Looking at figure 3.2a, it is far from obvious that it does. As the figure shows, the trend in total tax revenues is up, not down. On OECD-22 average, revenues increased from roughly 35 per cent of GDP in 1985 to roughly 37 per cent in 2007. The budget balance has also improved. While budget deficits oscillated around 4 per cent of GDP over the 1980s and early 1990s, budgets were close to balance, over the business cycle, for most of the 2000s.[6] Even if we focus on corporate taxation, arguably the 'most well-supported case' (Devereux and Sørensen 2006: 14) of tax competition, there is no clear-cut evidence of a race to the bottom in tax revenues. A huge empirical literature has tried to estimate the influence of economic openness on capital tax revenues – with mixed results. Some studies find a positive relationship: economic openness is associated with more capital taxation (e.g., Quinn 1997; Garrett and Mitchell 2001). Some find a negative relationship: openness is associated with less capital taxation (Rodrik 1997; Winner 2005; Schwarz 2007; Devereux et al. 2008). And some find essentially no relationship at all (e.g., Swank 2006; Slemrod 2004). On average, corporate tax revenues have increased in OECD-22 countries by almost a quarter, from roughly 3 per cent of GDP in 1981 to close to 4 per cent in 2007 (figure 3.2a).[7]

Yet a closer look at the reasons behind the increase in corporate tax revenues warns against denying the revenue effects of tax competition lightly. First, governments have partly compensated for the negative revenue effects of falling statutory tax rates by broadening the tax base – for example, by curtailing tax credits, depreciation allowances and deductions (Stewart and Webb 2006). As the tax base grows broader and broader, the scope for this compensation strategy shrinks. The probability that future tax cuts will have negative revenue effects increases. This suggests that the revenue effects of corporate tax competition may have a delayed impact. Second, rising corporate tax revenues

Figure 3.2: Revenues and deficits, OECD-22 averages

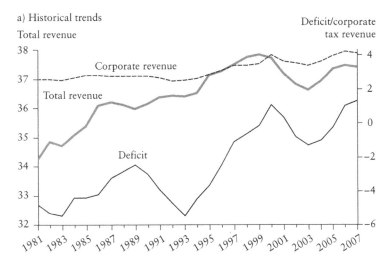

a) Historical trends

Total revenue

Deficit/corporate tax revenue

b) Correlations with country size

Correlation coefficient

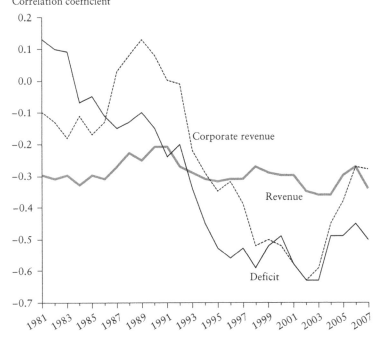

Sources: OECD, *Stat Extracts*, http://stats.oecd.org/index.aspx?; authors' own calculations.

are driven by a growth in the underlying macro-economic tax base. The share of corporate income (profits and capital gains) in national income has risen continuously since the 1980s (see table 3.3 below). The positive revenue effect of this has partly offset the negative effects of competitive rate cuts (Kramer 1998). Third, the upturn in corporate profitability is partly endogenous to corporate tax competition. To some extent, the endogeneity is purely statistical: tax competition increases foreign direct investment and profit shifting into small countries and thus the share of corporate profits in these countries (table 3.3 below). Since there are more small countries than large countries, this leads to an increase of (unweighted) average profitability. To some extent, the endogeneity is real: the competitive downward pressure on corporate tax rates creates a widening gap (in relative terms and sometimes even in absolute terms) between low corporate and high top personal income tax rates (see table 3.4 below). This gap encourages domestic income shifting from the personal to the corporate sector: corporations turn into onshore tax shelters for rich individuals (Ganghof and Genschel 2008). According to one estimate, a 1 percentage point increase in the gap between the top personal tax rate on interest income and the statutory corporate tax rate induces a 2.6 per cent increase in the share of private savings channelled through the corporate sector (Devereux and Sørensen 2006: 12). Another study suggests that reducing the corporate tax rate by 10 percentage points will raise the percentage of incorporated companies in the business sector as a whole, and hence will increase the corporate tax base by 7 per cent (de Mooij and Ederveen 2008: 682).

What do the correlation data reported in figure 3.2b add to this debate? As the figure shows, the level of total tax revenues is negatively associated with country size (−0.34 in 2007): large countries collect less tax revenue than small countries. While this is in line with the predictions of the baseline model, it is unlikely to be caused by tax competition. First, the negative correlation predates the onset of deep economic integration in the 1990s and does not increase discernibly thereafter. Second, small states have higher spending requirements than large states because the provision of public goods such as defence, monetary, financial and regulatory institutions, technical infrastructure and embassies is often subject to economies of scale. This forces small states to spend more in per capita terms on public goods provision than large states, and hence to tax more, all else being equal (e.g., Alesina and Spolaore 2003: 3).

The picture is different with respect to corporate tax revenues (figure 3.2b). While corporate revenues were essentially unrelated to country size during the 1980s (oscillating between −0.1 in 1981 and 0.13 in 1989), the correlation coefficient drops dramatically over the 1990s, reaches a low of –0.63 in 2002, and stays negative thereafter (–0.28 in 2007). During the 2000s, large OECD countries collected significantly less in corporate tax revenues than their smaller peers, as the baseline model would predict. To be sure, corporate tax is not a major revenue raiser in OECD countries, such that the absolute revenue effect may be small. Yet even marginal revenue losses (or gains foregone) are politically painful for governments constrained by high levels of mandatory expenditure. Also, the revenue losses (or gains foregone) from corporate taxation may be just the tip of the iceberg of hard-to-measure losses from other mobile capital tax bases, such as personal capital income. This view is supported by the data on budget deficits: while budget deficit tended to be slightly higher in small countries during the 1970s and early 1980s (0.13 in 1981), the correlation coefficient fell dramatically over the 1990s, largely in step with that of corporate tax rates. The correlation reached a low of –0.63 in 2002 and stayed negative for the rest of the 2000s (–0.5 in 2007): large states (France, Germany, Italy, Japan, the UK, the US) ran large budget deficits, while many small states recorded budget surpluses (Denmark, Finland, Ireland, Luxembourg, New Zealand, Norway, Sweden). This is consistent with the idea that tax competition helped small countries to reduce their reliance on debt by increasing revenues from corporate profits and other mobile forms of capital income, as well as through positive knock-on effects on labour taxation. To the extent that the influx of foreign capital drives up labour demand and wages, it tends to improve revenues from labour taxation as well.

To explore this idea further, we performed a simple regression analysis of budget deficits in OECD-22 countries (table 3.2). We expected high corporate tax revenues to be associated with low budget deficits: as tax competition enhances the capacity of small states (and restricts the capacity of large states) to collect revenues from corporate profits and other forms of mobile capital, the budget balance of small states should improve. We therefore expected corporate tax revenues to be positively associated with the budget balance. In order to assess this prediction, we controlled for two other variables which could potentially influence the budget balance. One is economic growth (in terms of GDP): high growth rates reduce deficits by decreasing outlays on unemployment benefits and other counter-cyclical social transfers and by increasing the yield of progressive taxes (Darby and Melitz 2008). The other is country size: as various authors have argued, tax competition is not the only way in which small states benefit from economic openness. They also benefit because their size allows them to specialize in developing a comparative advantage in exclusive niches of global product and services markets (Streeck 2000) and to profit handsomely from this advantage. Their high

Table 3.2: Explaining the size of budget deficits in OECD-22 countries, 1992–2007

	1992	1997	2002	2007
Corporate tax revenue	1.11	0.98	1.05	1.67
(% of GDP)	(1.57)	(2.42)**	(2.49)**	(5.63)***
GDP growth	0.28	0.29	−0.08	−0.43
	(0.82)	(1.14)	(−0.34)	(−0.73)
Population (logged)	−0.31	−0.53	−0.78	−1.10
	(−0.67)	(−1.36)	(−1.53)	(−2.31)**
Number of observations	21	21	21	21
Adjusted R²	15.7	42.3	47.7	68.2

Notes: t-values are shown in parentheses; three, two or one asterisk represents a corresponding significance of 1%-, 5%-, or 10%-level respectively. Dependent variable is overall government deficit scaled by GDP.

degree of economic openness also enables them to externalize part of the costs of fiscal adjustment onto foreign countries (Laurent and Cacheux 2007). Even at the same given level of corporate tax revenues, therefore, we still expected small open economies to have lower deficits than large countries.

The results presented in table 3.2 are in line with these expectations. The coefficients of corporate tax revenues and country size are sizeable and have the predicted positive or negative associations: corporate tax revenue is positively associated with the budgetary balance, and country size is negatively associated. The significance of both variables increases over time. The impact of growth, by contrast, is insignificant at all times. The model fit improves over time. In 2007, the model explains almost 70 per cent of the variance in budget deficits. With the exception of 2007, a 1 percentage point increase of corporate tax revenues as a share of GDP improves the budget balance by roughly 1 percentage point. The effect is larger in 2007, perhaps due to cyclical overheating in that year.

This section offers three lessons on the revenue effects of tax competition: first, tax competition has not reduced the level of total taxation in OECD-22 countries. Second, tax competition has revenue effects at the level of selected taxes. As we have shown for corporate tax, small states find their revenue-raising capacity enhanced by tax competition; large states find it constrained. Third, the tax competition-induced variance in revenue-raising capacity accounts partly for the significant improvement in the budgetary position of small OECD countries since the 1980s and the persistence of chronic deficits in large countries.

5 Tax competition and redistribution

According to the baseline model, tax competition redistributes the mobile tax base from large to small countries (international redistribution) and the tax burden from mobile to immobile tax bases – i.e., from capital to labour and consumption (domestic redistribution). We investigate both redistributive effects in turn.

5.1 International redistribution

According to the baseline model, small countries will attract a dis-proportionately large share of the mobile tax base under tax competition (the advantage of 'smallness'). We use two indicators to check this proposition: the share of corporate income (profits and capital gains) in GDP and employment created by inbound foreign direct investment as a share of the domestic labour force (table 3.3).[8] Both indicators are broadly in line with the baseline model, thus lending further support to the claim that tax competition accounts partly for different trends in the corporate tax revenues and deficits of large and small countries (section 4).

As table 3.3 shows, corporate income as a percentage of national income in OECD-22 countries has increased, on average, from roughly 30 per cent in 1995 to roughly 33 per cent in 2005. The correlation with country size is negative at both points in time (–0.56 and –0.54, respectively): corporate income tends to make up a large percentage of the national income in small countries because of the inflow of tax-sensitive corporate profits and investments (for a recent review of the tax sensitivity of corporate profits, see de Mooij and Ederveen 2008).

The picture is broadly similar if we turn to employment created by inward foreign investment (table 3.3). Manufacturing employment by foreign multinationals accounted for an average of 2.6 per cent of the total labour force of OECD-22 countries in 1997 and an average of 2.7 per cent in 2007. The employment percentage is negatively correlated with country size (–0.62 and –0.64, respectively): small countries attract relatively more job creation by foreign firms than do large countries. Data on services employment are more limited but suggest that the share of services employment in the total labour force has increased sig-nificantly. The negative correlation with country size is very strong for 2007 (–0.75). These data, limited as they may be, are in line with survey findings suggesting that the location of service activities is more sensi-tive to tax than the location of manufacturing activities (Ruding Report 1992: 102). Service establishments such as holding companies, financial

Table 3.3: International distribution of mobile tax base

	Gross operating surplus as percentage of national income		Employment by foreign multinational enterprises as percentage of the national labour force			
			Manufacturing		Services	
	1995	2005	1997	2007	1997	2007
Luxembourg	37	40	5.98	4.08	–	–
NZ	–	–	–	–	–	–
Ireland	–	44	7.47	4.60	–	6.55
Norway	36	48	1.84	2.43	2.38	–
Finland	34	34	2.03	2.75	–	5.01
Denmark	28	28	1.65	2.90	–	–
Switzerland	27	28	–	2.97	–	5.13
Austria	26	33	–	4.25	2.32	7.18
Sweden	32	28	3.05	4.59	3.01	6.68
Portugal	30	28	1.65	1.92	0.96	–
Belgium	29	31	–	–	5.77	4.09
Greece	–	40	–	–	–	–
Netherlands	32	34	2.10	2.03	2.11	–
Australia	30	33	–	–	–	–
Canada	32	35	–	–	–	–
Spain	–	28	2.25	1.74	–	3.34
Italy	37	35	–	1.87	–	3.09
UK	30	28	2.63	2.80	3.25	6.34
France						
Germany	27	32	1.10	2.74	–	–
Japan	–	31	0.14	0.28	0.08	0.42
United States	23	24	1.47	1.29	1.54	2.15
OECD-22	30	33	2.60	2.74	2.38	4.34
Correlation	–0.56	–0.54	–0.62	–0.64	–0.40	–0.75

Sources: Authors' own calculations, from OECD *Stat Extracts*, http://stats.oecd.org/index.aspx?.

services firms, coordination centres and headquarters often serve as receiving ends for profit-shifting operations out of high-tax jurisdictions. Companies are concerned particularly, therefore, with locating these service establishments in low-tax jurisdictions (see also Palan et al. 2010: 52–7).

As the baseline model suggests, small countries do indeed attract a disproportionate share of the mobile corporate tax base. This brings fiscal advantages in terms of improved revenues, as argued in section 4. It also has non-fiscal advantages such as better access to the technology of foreign firms (stimulating innovation and growth) and higher levels of employment, as well as upward pressure on wages. The influx of foreign investment increases the relative scarcity of labour and pushes up labour demand and the national average wage as a result (with positive knock-on effects on labour taxation). Multinational companies also usually pay wages above the national average: the mark-up is an average of 40 per cent in OECD countries (OECD 2006; authors' calculations). In fact, it was these positive employment effects, rather than narrow fiscal reasons, that motivated Ireland to embrace tax competition as a strategy of national economic development, and that motivated other countries, especially in Eastern Europe, to copy Ireland's apparent success (Laurent and Cacheux 2007).

5.2 Domestic redistribution

According to the baseline model, tax competition shifts the (relative) tax burden from mobile to immobile tax bases – i.e., from capital to labour and consumption. The ratio of capital to labour taxes should fall (the race to the bottom), and smaller countries should end up with lower ratios because they face stronger incentives to engage in competitive tax cutting than large countries (asymmetry). Various authors have tested these predictions by regressing different measures of the capital to labour tax ratio on batteries of independent variables, including economic openness and country size for different country samples (Garrett and Mitchell 2001; Schwarz 2007; Winner 2005; Krogstrup 2004; König and Wagener 2008; Garretsen and Peters 2007; Bretschger and Hettich 2002). The results are not completely conclusive. Many studies confirm the negative effect of economic openness on the capital to labour tax ratio: open borders are associated with relatively lower capital relative to labour taxes. Others find no such evidence (e.g., Garrett and Mitchell 2001). Some studies also find that small countries have lower capital to labour tax ratios than large countries (Winner 2005; Schwarz 2007; Garretsen and Peters 2007), while others do not (König and Wagener 2008; Haufler et al. 2009).

We see at least two reasons why a competition-induced shift in the tax burden may not unequivocally show up in lower capital to labour tax ratios. First, many studies cover the effect of country size (operationalized by either population size or GDP) in the fixed-effects estimators (Garretsen and Peters 2007; Haufler et al. 2009; Devereux et al. 2008). This is problematic because these estimators measure the coefficients of a country's deviations from its mean size only and cancel out cross-national differences in country size: they restrict the effect of country size to changes in one particular country's size over time and fail to capture the effects of differences in size across countries at a given point in time. This makes it very difficult to identify any effect of country size on capital to labour tax ratios, because cross-country variation is swept out of the data and within-country variation over time is very scarce. Second, those studies not using a fixed-effects estimator (e.g., Bretschger and Hettich 2002; Schwarz 2007) usually measure the average effect of country size on the capital to labour tax ratio over a certain period of time. This would be fine if the time period started in the 1990s – i.e., after the onset of deep market integration. Most studies range back to the 1970s, however, thus lumping together time periods in which country size is unlikely to matter because market integration was shallow (the 1970s and 1980s) and time periods in which country size should matter because markets were deeply integrated (the 1990s and 2000s).

We cope with both problems by comparing different measures of the capital to labour tax ratio at two different points (1985 and 2007) to determine whether the ratios have fallen over time and and/or whether the correlation with country size has increased. The ratios are computed from the nominal tax rates analysed in section 3. Recall that important tax rates on mobile capital (the corporate tax rate and the tax rate on the resident interest income of private investors) have fallen considerably since 1985, while tax rates on immobile labour and consumption have increased (VAT), stagnated (tax wedge) or decreased by relatively less (top personal income tax rate). As a consequence, the ratios of capital tax rates to labour tax rates have generally fallen, indicating a shift in the nominal tax burden from mobile to immobile bases (table 3.4). The fall has been most pronounced in the personal interest income tax-rate to tax-wedge ratio: while in 1985 the rate applied to resident personal interest income was 2.07 times higher than the tax wedge, in 2007 it was only 1.19 times higher.

As table 3.4 also shows, the race to the bottom in nominal tax rate ratios was accompanied by growing asymmetries between large and small countries. The correlations of tax ratios and country size generally increased between 1985 and 2007, except for the corporate tax rate to VAT ratio. All correlations for 2007 are positive, and most of them are quite sizeable, indicating that small countries impose relatively lighter nominal tax burdens on mobile capital than do large countries. To be sure, a shift in the nominal tax burden from capital to labour does not translate one-to-one into a shift in the effective tax burden. But, given that nominal tax rates are important determinants of effective burdens, such a shift is likely to have considerable impact. At the very least, therefore, our findings add credence to empirical studies reporting that economic openness and country size significantly reduce the effective capital to labour tax ratio (e.g., Schwarz 2007; Winner 2005).

Table 3.4: Tax rates and ratios, OECD-22 averages

Tax rates	OECD-22 average		Correlation with country size	
	1985	2007	1985	2007
Capital				
CTR[a]	46.1	29.7	0.21	0.63
TRRII[b]	57.6	33.8	–0.12	0.34
Labour				
VAT	10.7	17.7	–0.10	–0.24
Tax wedge	28.0	27.8	–0.32	–0.06
TPITR[c]	63.4	46.9	–0.10	–0.08
Tax ratios				
CTR/VAT	2.53	2.23	0.42	0.37
CTR/Tax wedge	1.65	1.07	0.33	0.50
CTR/TPITR	0.76	0.69	0.34	0.76
TRRII/VAT	3.16	2.30	–0.29	0.36
TRRII/Tax wedge	2.07	1.19	0.18	0.45
TRRII/TPITR	0.92	0.76	–0.08	0.25

Notes:
[a] CTR = corporate tax rate.
[b] TRRII = tax rate on resident interest income (private investors).
[c] TPITR = top personal income tax rate.

Sources: CTR, TRPII, TPITR and VAT rate: Bundesministerium der Finanzen; *Die wichtigsten Steuern im internationalen Vergleich*, several issues; Tax wedge: OECD, *Taxing Wages*.

6 Implications for fiscal democracy

The evidence presented in this chapter offers strong support for the view that tax competition exists. We note three key findings. First, general and targeted tax rates on real, financial and human capital have been racing to the bottom since the 1980s as small countries systematically undercut the tax rates of large countries (section 3). Second, the capital tax base is moving from large to small countries (international redistribution) and the nominal tax burden is shifting from capital to labour and consumption (domestic redistribution; section 5). Third, while the total level of tax revenues remains unaffected, small countries see their capacity to raise revenue from mobile capital increase, while large countries see their capacity decrease (section 4).

The implications for fiscal democracy are ambiguous. First, tax competition has a negative effect on national tax autonomy: all competing countries – large and small – see their ability to tax mobile capital constrained. Governments have to tax immobile labour and consumption comparatively more in order to meet mandatory spending requirements. The shift of the tax burden away from capital is borne out not only by the evidence presented here in section 4 but also by tax policy reactions to the recent financial crisis. Given the role of the financial sector in causing the crisis, policy-makers throughout the political spectrum called for additional taxes on this sector to pay for part of the fiscal damage. While the G-20 initially endorsed this position, and many governments introduced some new levies at the national level, competitive pressure prevented the coordinated introduction EU-wide (or worldwide) of financial transaction taxes (Brast 2011). Instead, policy-makers have addressed their fiscal woes mostly through spending cuts and tax increases on labour and consumption. As a close inspection of tax policy changes in EU member states for 2008–10 reveals, tax increases have been focused on excises, social security contributions and VAT (Lierse and Seelkopf 2011). Even if governments manage to maintain total tax levels, their ability to make rich capital owners contribute erodes. Tax competition may thus contribute to increased income inequality between the very rich and the rest of society.

Second, tax competition has positive effects on fiscal democracy in small, peripheral low-tax countries. Countries such as Ireland or Luxembourg have profited from the competition-induced inflow of mobile capital, both directly in terms of tax revenues and indirectly in terms of new jobs, upward pressure on wages and, as a consequence, higher labour tax revenues. As Hannes Winner has shown for a panel of OECD countries, small countries have lower corporate *and* labour taxes than large ones, all else being equal (Winner 2005). This explains why left-wing parties in small countries often support aggressive tax competition strategies. For example, take the insistence of the new Irish Fine Gael–Labour government on defending the low Irish corporate tax rate: in effect, the government is betting on international redistribution from other large countries rather than on domestic redistribution from capital to reach its economic and distributive goals. This may not be a bad bet; while Ireland was particularly hard hit by the financial crisis, it is recovering faster than other small victims of the crisis such as Greece, which never seized upon tax competition as a strategy of national economic development.

Third, even if we accept that tax competition expands the scope for fiscal democracy in small countries, it achieves this expansion by constraining fiscal democracy in large countries. According to the baseline model, large countries will accept exploitation by small countries because the fiscal costs of fighting back are too high. This cannot be relied upon in the real world, because the governments of large countries may wish

Table 3.5: Corporate tax rate changes

	Corporate tax rate		Change
	2007	2011	2007–2011
Luxembourg	29.6	28.8	–0.8
NZ	–	–	
Ireland	12.5	12.5	0
Norway	28	28	0
Finland	26	26	0
Denmark	25	25	0
Switzerland	21.3	21.3	0
Austria	25	25	0
Sweden	28	26.3	–1.7
Portugal	26.5	29	2.5
Belgium	34	34	0
Greece	25	20	–5
Netherlands	25.5	25	–0.5
Australia	30	30	0
Canada	36.1	32.5	–3.6
Spain	32.5	30	–2.5
Italy	37.3	31.4	–5.9
UK	30	27	–3
France	34.4	34.4	0
Germany	38.7	29.8	–8.9
Japan	39.5	42	2.5
United States	39	39	0
OECD-22	29.7	28.4	–1.3
Correlation	0.69	0.61	–0.26

Source: Eurostat 2011; authors' own calculations.

to cut their taxes for purely domestic reasons. Thus, as table 3.5 shows, many large countries, including Canada, Germany, Italy, Spain and the UK, have recently cut their corporate tax rate to reinvigorate their crisis-stricken economies. France and the US are also considering cuts.

The recent wave of corporate tax rate cuts in large countries increases the competitive pressure on all countries. While large countries suffer relatively more from tax competition than small countries, they also have more power to bring about tax competition. Intuitively, if a large country cuts its taxes, this will put much more pressure on other countries to do the same than if a small country were to enforce a similar cut. As various authors have argued, the United States tax reform of 1986 was what triggered the global downward competition in corporate taxation (Hallerberg and Basinger 1998; Swank 2006). An equally dramatic tax cut in, say, Norway would never have had such a dramatic effect. It follows that large countries also have more power to mitigate tax competition. It is not the likes of Luxembourg, Estonia and Ireland which hold the key to preventing a meltdown of capital taxation; it is the United States, Japan, Germany, France and other large countries. If the scope for democratic choice in capital taxation is to be retained – or enlarged – under conditions of tax competition, large countries have to take the lead. They have to keep their tax rates up in order to allow smaller states to cut their taxes less drastically. Such consideration would preserve more options for fiscal policy choice for all countries, but there would be significant cost for the large countries. Benevolent hegemony is not for free.

References

Alesina, A., and Spolaore, E. (2003) *The Size of Nations.* Cambridge, MA: MIT Press.

Baldwin, R. E., and Krugman, P. (2002) Agglomeration, integration and tax harmonisation, *European Economic Review* 48: 1–23.

Basinger, S., and Hallerberg, M. (2004) Remodeling the competition for capital: how domestic politics erases the race to the bottom, *American Political Science Review* 98: 261–76.

Brast, B. (2011) The European politics of financial sector taxation: why is it so difficult for EU member states to harmonize financial sector taxation? Unpublished MA thesis, Jacobs University, Bremen.

Bretschger, L., and Hettich, F. (2002) Globalization, capital mobility and tax competition: theory and evidence for OECD countries, *European Journal of Political Economy* 18: 695–716.

Brooks, N., and Hwong, T. (2010) Tax levels, structures, and reforms: convergence or persistence, *Theoretical Inquiries in Law* 11: 791–821.

Bucovetsky, S. (1991) Asymmetric tax competition, *Journal of Urban Economics* 30: 167–81.

Campbell, J. L. (2009) Epilogue: a renaissance for fiscal sociology, in W. Martin, A. K. Mehrotra and M. Prasad (eds), *The New Fiscal Sociology: Taxation in Comparative and Historical Perspective.* Cambridge: Cambridge University Press, pp. 256–65.

Darby, J., and Melitz, J. (2008) Social spending and automatic stabilizers in the OECD, *Economic Policy* 23: 715–56.

De Mooij, R. A., and Ederveen, S. (2008) Corporate tax elasticities: a reader's guide to empirical findings, *Oxford Review of Economic Policy* 24: 680–97.

Devereux, M. P., and Sørensen, P. B. (2006) *The Corporate Income Tax: International Trends and Options for Fundamental Reforms.* Brussels: European Commission Directorate-General for Economic and Financial Affairs.

Devereux, M. P., Griffith, R., and Klemm, A. (2002) Corporate income tax reforms and international tax competition, *Economic Policy* 17: 451–95.

Devereux, M. P., Lockwood, B., and Redoano, M. (2008) Do countries compete over corporate tax rates?, *Journal of Public Economics* 92: 1210–35.

Edwards, J., and Keen, M. (1996) Tax competition and Leviathan, *European Economic Review* 40: 113–34.

Ganghof, S. (2006) *The Politics of Income Taxation: A Comparative Analysis.* Colchester: ECPR Press.

Ganghof, S., and Genschel, P. (2008) Taxation and democracy in the EU, *Journal of European Public Policy* 15: 58–77.

Garretsen, H., and Peters, J. (2007) Capital mobility, agglomeration and corporate tax rates: is the race to the bottom for real?, *CESifo Economic Studies* 53(2): 263–93.

Garrett, G. (1998) Global markets and national politics: collision course or virtuous circle?, *International Organization* 52: 787–824.

Garrett, G., and Mitchell, D. (2001) Globalization, government spending and taxation in the OECD, *European Journal of Political Research* 39: 145–77.

Genschel, P., and Schwarz, P. (2011) Tax competition: a literature review, *Socio-Economic Review* 9: 339–70.

Giovannini, A., and Hines, J. R. (1991) Capital flight and tax competition: are there viable solutions to both problems?, in A. Giovannini and C. Mayer (eds), *European Financial Integration*. Cambridge: Cambridge University Press, pp. 172–220.

Hallerberg, M., and Basinger, S. (1998) Internationalization and changes in tax policy in OECD countries: the importance of domestic veto players, *Comparative Political Studies* 31: 321–52.

Haufler, A., Klemm, A., and Schjelderup, G. (2009) Economic integration and the relationship between profit and wage taxes, *Public Choice* 138: 423–46.

Hays, J. C. (2009) *Globalization and the New Politics of Embedded Liberalism.* Oxford: Oxford University Press.

Kanbur, R., and Keen, M. (1993) Jeux sans frontières: tax competition and tax coordination when countries differ in size, *American Economic Review* 83: 877–92.

Keen, M. (2001) Preferential regimes can make tax competition less harmful, *National Tax Journal* 54: 757–62.

Kemmerling, A., and Seils, E. (2009) The regulation of redistribution: managing conflict in corporate tax competition, *West European Politics* 32: 756–73.

König, T., and Wagener, A. (2008) *Post Materialist Attitudes and the Mix of Capital and Labour Taxation*, CESifo Working Paper Series No. 2366. Munich: CESifo.

Kramer, H. (1998) Economic aspects of tax co-ordination in the EU, in Austrian Federal Ministry of Finance (ed.), *Tax Competition and Co-ordination of Tax Policy in the European Union*. Vienna: Österreichisches Institut für Wirtschaftsforschung.

Krogstrup, S. (2004) *Are Corporate Tax Burdens Racing to the Bottom in the European Union?*, EPRU Working Paper 2004-04. Copenhagen: University of Copenhagen, Institute of Economics.

Laurent, É., and Cacheux, J. L. (2007) *The Irish Tiger and the German Frog: A Tale of Size and Growth in the Euro Area*, OFCE Working Paper No. 2007-31. Paris: Observatoire français des conjonctures économiques.

Lierse, H., and Seelkopf, L. (2011) Capital markets and tax politics: a comparative analysis of European tax reforms during the crisis. Unpublished manuscript, Jacobs University, Bremen.

OECD (Organization for Economic Cooperation and Development) (2006) *The OECD's Project on Harmful Tax Practices: The 2006 Progress Report*. Paris: OECD.

Palan, R., Murphy, R., and Chavagneux, C. (2010) *Tax Havens: How Globalization Really Works*. Ithaca, NY: Cornell University Press.

Pierson, P. (1998) Irresistible forces, immovable objects: post-industrial welfare states confront permanent austerity, *Journal of European Public Policy* 5: 539–60.

Plümper, T., Treoger, V. E., and Winner, H. (2009) Why is there no race to the bottom in capital taxation?, *International Studies Quarterly* 53: 761–86.

PWC (PriceWaterhouseCoopers) and CEER (Centre for European Economic Research) (2005) *International Taxation of Expatriates: Survey of 20 Tax and Social Security Regimes and Analysis of Effective Tax Burdens on International Assignments*. Frankfurt am Main: Fachverlag Moderne Wirtschaft.

Quinn, D. (1997) The correlates of change in international financial regulation, *American Political Science Review* 91: 531–51.

Rodrik, D. (1997) *Has Globalization Gone Too Far?* Washington, DC: Institute for International Economics.

Ruding Report (1992) *Report of the Committee of Independent Experts on Company Taxation*. Luxembourg: Amt für amtliche Veröffentlichungen der Europäischen Gemeinschaften.

Schwarz, P. (2007) Does capital mobility reduce the corporate–labour tax ratio?, *Public Choice* 130(3): 363–80.

Sinn, H.-W. (1988) U.S. tax reform 1981 and 1986: impact on international capital markets and capital flows, *National Tax Journal* 41: 327–40.

Sinn, H.-W. (1994) How much Europe? Subsidiarity, centralization and fiscal competition, *Scottish Journal of Political Economy* 41: 85–107.

Slemrod, J. (2004) Are corporate tax rates, or countries, converging?, *Journal of Public Economics* 88: 1169–86.

Steinmo, S. (1994) The end of redistribution? International pressures and domestic tax policy choices, *Challenge* 37: 9–17.

Steuerle, C. E. (2008) An issue of democracy, *The Government We Deserve*, 23 June; available at: www.urban.org/publications/901181.html (accessed 9 August 2011).

Steuerle, C. E. (2010) America's related fiscal problems, *Journal of Policy Analysis and Management* 29: 876–84.

Stewart, K., and Webb, M. C. (2006) International competition in corporate taxation: evidence from the OECD time series, *Economic Policy* 21(45): 153–201.

Streeck, W. (2000) Competitive solidarity: rethinking the 'European social model', in K. Hinrichs, H. Kitschelt and H. Wiesenthal (eds), *Kontingenz und Krise: Institutionenpolitik in kapitalistischen und postsozialistischen Gesellschaften*. Frankfurt am Main: Campus.

Streeck, W., and Mertens, D. (2010) *An Index of Fiscal Democracy*, MPIfG Working Paper 10/3. Cologne: Max Planck Institute for the Study of Societies.

Swank, D. (2006) Tax policy in an era of internationalization: explaining the spread of neoliberalism, *International Organization* 60: 847–82.

Wilson, J. D. (1999) Theories of tax competition, *National Tax Journal* 52: 269–304.

Winner, H. (2005) Has tax competition emerged in OECD countries? Evidence from panel data, *International Tax and Public Finance* 12: 667–87.

Zodrow, G. R., and Mieszkowski, P. (1986) Pigou, Tiebout, property taxation, and the underprovision of local public goods, *Journal of Urban Economics* 19: 356–70.

4

Governing as an Engineering Problem: The Political Economy of Swedish Success

Sven Steinmo

Sweden is once again attracting the attention of scholars and pundits from around the world because of its apparent ability to pull together high levels of economic growth and remarkably egalitarian outcomes. Indeed, in the context of the most recent economic crisis sweeping the globe, Sweden stands out as one of the most successful countries in Europe in terms of fiscal resilience and economic growth.[1] Swedes are clearly very satisfied with their system, one that many consider among the most 'democratic' in the world. Certainly fiscal stress, economic competition and demographic change are constraining the choices available to leaders in all rich democracies, but it appears that the straightjacket has a much looser fit in Sweden. The quetion is, why?

In this chapter I will argue that it is important to distinguish between Sweden's decision-making institutions and its egalitarian welfare state. While these two are related, they need to be understood separately – particularly if we want to appreciate the modern Swedish political economy. The first should be understood as a *decision-making model*, while the second is a set of *policy outcomes*. I argue that the 'Swedish model' rests on a particular decision-making regime that, first and foremost, has been highly centralized. I will describe how the system works more specifically below, but it is central to realize that the Swedish decision-making model gives enormous policy autonomy to political and administrative elites.

All democratic countries face what I call a 'democratic dilemma': the legitimacy of the system is based on two conflicting principles. On the one hand, a democratic system is a system in which the citizens or voters ultimately direct public policy. In a good democracy we believe the government will be responsive to the desires and demands of the citizens. At the same time, however, all governments' legitimacy is based on their efficacy. Can they get things done? These conflicting principles/ demands present rather difficult tensions in all democratic states. The more responsive the political elite is to the short-term preferences of the citizens, the less likely the government will be to make choices that are in the interest of the whole of society and/or in the system's long-term self-interest. It is my contention that, for particular contingent historical reasons, Sweden was able to find a balance between these competing goals of efficiency and efficacy.

In sum, if we step back from the particular choices and specific public policies pursued by Sweden and Swedish elites over the past decades, this country's success must be understood as a product of the fortuitous combination of the fact that (a) the institutional design has offered the elite enormous political and policy autonomy and (b) an elite political culture worked to build a largely egalitarian, efficient and universalist welfare state.

In the first part of this chapter, I will discuss several of Sweden's historic policy initiatives, demonstrating that these institutional innovations are best understood as technical solutions to planning problems. As Hugh Heclo pointed out many years ago, the major initiatives driving Swedish public policy were the product not of mass politics, where citizens rose to demand policies, but rather of elite decision-makers puzzling over policy dilemmas and promoting technical solutions to what they understood as technical problems: governing was seen as an engineering problem. I will then briefly discuss the politics of the mid-1970s and early 1980s, a period in which Swedish politics became more ideological and political. This was the era of the famous 'wage-earner funds' with which the Swedish left hoped finally to realize the ambition of socializing the Swedish economy. I will argue that this period broke the back of the Swedish model. As a result, the country's political economy went into decline.

Finally, I will examine the political economy of Sweden in recent years, which by virtually all accounts has witnessed a renewal. I will discuss some of the policy initiatives that have apparently helped rebuild Sweden's economic success. My central argument, however, is that at the core of the country's rediscovered success is a return to traditional technocratic policy-making. Today a centre-right government has taken on the role of the nation's engineers.

I argue that the unique features of the Swedish political economy are the product of a particularly successful brand of social democracy that was invented by a particularly technocratic and remarkably autonomous governing elite. In rather fundamental ways, Sweden's government has long been quite different from the more populist governments found in some other parts of Europe. I do not mean to suggest that there have been no politics in Sweden, nor do I believe that it does not have a democratic system. Huge political forces have been at work here, as elsewhere in Europe during the twentieth century. But Sweden's relatively homogeneous culture, small population, peculiar electoral institutions, rapid industrialization and wartime neutrality offered this country's elite an unusual degree of political autonomy which made it possible for them to construct an unusual egalitarian market economy (Steinmo 2010).

1 Corporatism not socialism

Many people believe that Sweden developed a successful 'socialist' economy within the capitalist world. This is simply wrong. Sweden has never been socialist but, rather, has been one of the most successful *market-based* economies in the world. The key to its economic success is that its political economy was adapted to the needs and demands of international capitalism. Rather than fight against capitalism and capitalists, the Swedish Social Democrats decided to work with the system.

Swedish neo- (or social) corporatism has been the subject of innumerable analyses over the years. In this system, representatives from the major union federation (LO), the major employer federation (SAF) and the government – which essentially meant elites from the Social Democratic Party (SAP) – met regularly and consistently to negotiate major decisions about future developments in the Swedish political economy.[2] It is sometimes less appreciated that this system was built within the context of an electoral system that was specifically designed to protect those in power at the time. In the early decades of the twentieth century, the ruling conservative elite constructed a complicated set of electoral rules, called the 'Conservative Guarantee'. These electoral rules divided the mandates for the Upper and Lower chambers of the Riksdag (Parliament) in such a way that several electoral cycles would pass before the control of both chambers would change hands following changes in the popular vote. The intention was to create an electoral system in which the vote of the people would be muted so that the Conservative government would be in a better position to protect its interests (Castles 1978: 115). Unsurprisingly, the Social Democrats fought against these electoral rules at the time, understanding that they would advantage the then ruling Conservative parties. What they failed to see, however, was that, once they gained power, these same rules would work to their advantage (see Steinmo 2010: 47–9).

This unusual electoral system shaped the political logic of all political actors and special interests. Whereas in a classical single-member district electoral system, relatively small changes in citizens' vote choices could result in significant changes in government, in the Swedish case governments were more insulated. Since all actors understood this basic fact, interest groups (known as 'social partners') on all sides had powerful incentives to compromise and deal with the government in power – and, from the mid-1930s to the mid-1970s, that government was the Social Democrats.

This system thus enabled quite a small group of leaders from the major economic interests in society to meet regularly under a fairly consistent set of expectations about the political future. This stability was clearly the foundation of what became known as the 'Politics of Compromise' (Rustow 1955). These elites would typically rely heavily on the professional advice of experts. Indeed, there are few countries in the world that have relied as heavily on expert commissions to address complicated or politically difficult policy issues. Even outside the famous *Statens Offentliga Utredningar* (SOU) process, it was commonplace to bring together the various 'social partners' with experts to seek out technical solutions to common problems. Once again, given the remarkable stability of the political system, there were few incentives for any of the partners to defect.

In effect, a *symbiotic relationship* developed between the organizations representing big business and big unions, and these also tolerated a powerful state. Specific policies favouring unions[3] were part of the system, as were policies that encouraged the concentration of capital and effectively discriminated against small business and entrepreneurs (Steinmo 2010).

The irony is that Sweden was largely able to achieve the highly egalitarian and progressive social and economic outcomes it did precisely because its political and economic elite (including the union elite) has been stable and remarkably isolated from the daily public pressures that confront political leaders in most other democratic nations. Ernst Wigforss, Sweden's famous and powerful minister of finance from 1932 to 1949, called this 'planmässig hushållning' (systemic management).[4]

Certainly, many factors contributed to Sweden's economic success in the 1950s and 1960s. But three particular policy choices stand out as significant. First, the Swedes embraced the famous Rehn–Meidner model of the labour market, in which unions and employers set national wage deals that explicitly and intentionally worked to squeeze out companies and sectors that could not afford to pay higher wages.[5] According to this model, Sweden would maintain an open economy, with low tariff barriers and low subsidies to domestic industry, so that inefficient and/or low-profit companies would be driven out of business and their resources reallocated by the market to more efficient firms. At the same time, trade unions would hold down wages in the most productive/profitable sectors (large firms, manufacturing, mining, etc.) and push up relative wages in the less productive/profitable sectors (textiles, farming, small firms). The idea was to encourage structural modernization and change in the economy by literally increasing profits in some sectors while driving other companies and sectors out of business. At the same time, the government was expected to invest in an active labour market policy to be used to help workers who were displaced to new jobs, industries and even locations.[6] In many ways this story is well known. What is less often appreciated, however, is the fact that this system, invented by two labour-union economists, strongly advantaged the biggest and most successful capitalists at the same time that it forced workers to bear the costs of economic adjustment. Whereas leftist political leaders in most other countries were demanding policies to protect workers from the market, Swedish elites passed policies that specifically exposed them to the market and demanded that they adjust to its demands, while allowing the richest capitalists in the nation to reap the short-term benefits.

Second, the Social Democrats effectively cut a deal with capital in which it was agreed that the government would build welfare-state programmes but would not tax capital or capitalists heavily. I discuss this at length elsewhere, so I will not elaborate here, other than to point out that, because of some very generous tax expenditures, Swedish capital enjoyed one of the lightest tax burdens in the advanced world, while Swedish workers bore the heaviest tax burden in the world (Steinmo 2002). For example, in the late 1950s the Social Democrats introduced consumption taxation even though there was no immediate fiscal pressure on the Treasury for these revenues. Unsurprisingly, the labour unions and the working class in general were opposed to the introduction of a new tax that explicitly would burden them the most. But the government persevered and was able to push through this regressive tax despite opposition from its own constituents (Steinmo 1993).

Finally, the government chose to initiate measures that encouraged women to enter the labour market instead of bringing in foreign workers to help meet the exploding demand for labour (Jordan 2006). It is important to see that labour-union members (as opposed to their elite representatives) did not demand these policies and for the most part opposed such ideas. Nor were these measures the product of the women's movement, which had yet to emerge. Instead, the government understood that there would be a shortage of labour as the economy expanded. Historic commitments to immigrant workers from Finland and Norway meant that, under Swedish law, a guest worker could relatively easily apply for and be granted permanent residence. Thus the idea of importing 'temporary' guest workers from Turkey, as the Germans had done, for example, was not a reasonable option. The government knew that Swedish law and tradition would have prevented them from kicking these workers out of the country if and when the economy retracted. Admitting women to the workforce, the Ministry of Finance concluded, would develop a more flexible labour force that would also prove to have fewer social problems for society.[7]

To be sure, these were unusual choices. One would not expect a Social Democratic government in the 1950s (or their labour-union allies) to agree to or to implement policies that explicitly increased taxes on working families and on consumption, especially when, at the same time, national wage deals were holding down wages in the most economically profitable sectors of the economy. It was no less surprising for a party to pass tax laws that effectively discriminated against traditional working-class families (where women traditionally did not work outside the home) in favour of middle-class families. But by the 1950s there was a very strong belief that the government could *and should* actively intervene in society to help make the economy more efficient, competitive and successful.

This system did not redistribute wealth from capital to workers in the normal sense of taking wealth or income from the rich or from enterprise to pay for programmes benefiting the workers or the poor. Instead, it was designed to facilitate economic growth and thereby produce wealth and income from which the working class could benefit through higher (albeit moderated) wage increases. Social investment was generous, and Sweden invested heavily in education, health care, housing and childcare. This was a moderate welfare state by international standards; however, these programmes were financed not by redistributive taxation but by the working and middle classes themselves.

These arrangements clearly worked to help build and modernize an internationally competitive and dynamic economy that produced high and stable profits and a growing standard of living. By 1970, Sweden had become one of the richest countries in the world and had achieved this while also building one of the most egalitarian societies in the West. It had nearly eliminated poverty and had educated one of the most dynamic and flexible workforces found in any capitalist economy, all while achieving high levels of economic growth. At the same time, Swedish capitalists became some of the most successful in the world. The arsenal of devices developed over the years worked to concentrate this small country's capital and labour resources in the hands of a remarkably small number of people. It was widely reported, for example, that the Wallenberg family holdings alone accounted for more that 30 per cent of private industrial employment in Sweden.

Rather than creating some kind of soft socialism, the Social Democrats in Sweden managed to build a highly competitive form of capitalism. This system was explicitly market-enhancing and eschewed most of the more radical policies of the left that were common in much of the rest of Europe. Instead of nationalizing industries to protect workers, Swedes implemented policies that pushed the weakest industries out of business and then financed programmes designed to make the workers more flexible and better trained for new jobs. The welfare state, in this sense, was intended not to compensate for the market but rather to help make it more efficient and more competitive. The famous active labour market policies in Sweden, then, did not decommodify labour; on the contrary, they in effect made Swedish labour a higher-value commodity.

One should also note that there is no evidence to suggest that there was corruption in these arrangements. Clearly, the Social Democrats, and the labour unions for that matter, had come to believe that cooperating with capitalists and employers would increase national wealth. But this did not imply that they had abandoned their beliefs in a more fair or equal society. Moreover, as Sweden became more economically successful, more and more Swedes moved into the middle class. There is considerable disagreement among academics as to *why* the Social Democrats increasingly came to argue for and develop policies that benefited the whole of society, rather than just the traditional working class (Castles 1978; Korpi 1983; Swenson 1989). For our purposes here, however, their motivations do not matter. Whereas the welfare state in many other European democracies is an explicit redistributive system that takes from one group (or sometimes takes from the whole) to give to another group (such as male breadwinners or pensioners) the welfare policies that Sweden built took from everyone *and* gave back to everyone. This model proved to be the most egalitarian in the world.

The many benefits of this system were plain enough to average Swedes. Their lives improved in significant and obvious ways, and this reinforced people's trust both in the system and in elites. Swedish society was becoming a middle-class society, and this middle class enjoyed what they were getting (even if they hadn't really demanded it). Perhaps unsurprisingly, then, the Social Democrats were rewarded with repeated electoral victories.

2 From planning to politics: the end of the Swedish model?

In retrospect, it seems that no sooner had Sweden become recognized as the premier example of the 'middle way' than its system began to crack. There is insufficient space in this essay to detail the evolution of the changes in the Swedish political economy from the 1970s through the 1980s, but a few general points can be noted so that we may better understand the new context in which policy began to change direction in the 1980s and 1990s.

The beginning of the end can be traced back to the early 1970s. Certainly the watershed event was a massive wildcat strike beginning in the iron mines in the north of Sweden (Kiruna) in 1969. This strike was exceptional because it was from the heart of the working class *against the union organization and their political allies in Stockholm.* Though the strike itself was eventually settled in favour of many of the miners' demands, the more basic accusations implied left serious doubts in the minds of the labour movement and the socialist leadership. What kind of union, and what kind of social democracy, would workers have to strike *against?*

These doubts led to significant self-examination and rethinking both within the party and inside the LO: unions became less quiescent and began to demand higher wages from employers in their national negotiations, more public spending from the Social Democratic government, and more explicitly redistributive (populist) tax measures. At the same time, the Social Democratic Party itself (at least significant portions of the left within the party) came to question its own legitimacy. Several substantial changes grew out of this self-examination: first, in 1974 the government introduced a constitutional change that was intended to make Swedish democracy more direct and more responsive to citizens.[8] Second, the LO began to demand structural changes in the economy, resulting in the implementation of a series of policies (including health and safety policies), but the most significant proposals were the demands for worker co-determination and the now famous 'wage-earner funds'. The wage-earner funds were certainly the most controversial of these proposals; their basic idea was that huge funds would be collected (to be financed through increases in both profits taxes and wage taxes) and would then be used to buy out the capital market. Though never fully implemented, the idea behind this policy was to realize the socialist ideal of workers owning the means of production.

Perhaps unsurprisingly, Swedish capital came to believe that the LO and the Social Democrats could no longer be trusted. At the same time, as Olof Ruin points out, 'at the parliamentary level the most important development in the 1970s, parallel to the new constitution, was the weakening of the executive.' Because of this weakening, he argues, the government was less able 'to take unpopular decisions' and to 'distance itself from special interests' (Ruin 1981).

The most obvious consequence of this new politics was a dramatic expansion in public spending, on the one hand, and decreased investment and private economic growth, on the other. Between 1960 and 1980, the scope of public spending expanded dramatically. Public expenditure on subsidies and transfers specifically grew from 9.3 per cent of GDP in 1960 to 16.2 per cent of GDP in 1970, and 30.4 per cent of GDP in 1980 (Tanzi and Schuknecht 2000: 31). Wage inflation shot up at the same time, with per hour labour costs growing at a rate of up to 17 per cent per annum in 1974 and 22.2 per cent per annum in 1975 (Lindbeck 1997). Economic growth stagnated and grew negative for several years in the late 1970s and early 1980s. In response to these macro-economic trends, the government was forced repeatedly to devalue the currency.[9] While these devaluations provided short-term relief for Swedish exporters, it was becoming increasingly clear that their gains were quickly being eaten away by higher wage demands. This cycle was both unproductive and unequal, for not all segments of society could recoup these losses on equal terms.

By the early 1980s, many members of the Swedish economic elite – both within the Ministry of Finance and in the economic profession more generally – viewed these developments as both an economic/fiscal crisis and a crisis of confidence. Whereas in the past these elites had believed they could manage their economy quite effectively, now they were more and more convinced that such management was no longer possible.[10] Entities that were once thought of as labour market partners were progressively regarded as simply 'interest groups'. The political system of the earlier era had insulated the fiscal elite and given them enormous policy autonomy, but now the political demands on both the tax side and the spending side were becoming increasingly difficult to shut out.[11]

The key player at the time was the minister of finance, Kjell Olof Feldt, who began publicly to question the long-term viability of the system that was evolving. He and his advisors believed that Sweden faced three huge policy problems: first, a steady stream of reports had demonstrated the economic inefficiencies and redistributive inequities of the extant system (Sverenius 1999).[12] Of course there was some variation in arguments and nuance, but during the 1980s it became virtually conventional wisdom among the economic elite, both inside and outside government, that the structure of the tax system was by now creating far too many problems for the economy. Second, the system was a major contributor to the wage and price inflation that was wreaking havoc on Swedish competiveness and thereby encouraging Swedish capital to abandon the country (Moses 2000). Third, the very high rates in the income tax system were now hitting even average workers. As a result, the system created incentives for people to cheat and engage in unproductive activities (such as buying a yacht) simply for tax reasons. These inequities also led others to question the fairness of Swedish society. The most important issue in Feldt's view was *trust* (Ahlquist and Engquist 1984; Feldt 1991; Sjöberg 1999).

By the early 1980s, the average industrial worker was suffering under a marginal income tax of over 50 per cent. Social democracy required a degree of social solidarity, and the obviously increasing abuse of the benefits system was making average Swedes doubt the efficacy of the system. Gunnar Myrdal (1982), one of Sweden's most prominent Social Democratic economists, sounded the alarm when he published an article on tax policy in which he worried that Sweden was becoming *et folk av fifflare* (a land of cheaters).

In sum, by the late 1970s and early 1980s, Sweden was in a process of undergoing substantial changes both in its political decision-making institutions and in the relationship between citizens and their state institutions. The Swedish model appeared to be crumbling.

It is worth pausing in our narrative a moment to consider the state of affairs at the end of the 1980s and in the early 1990s. We can perhaps now look back at this period of Swedish history as one of learning and restructuring. At the time, however, many thought that the 'Swedish experiment' was over (Lindbeck 1997). Those who argued in this direction had plenty of evidence on their side, of course. The Swedish economy was lagging behind its competitors, investment was down, the government was running high levels of debt, Sweden was confronting an ominous population crisis, and citizens appeared to be losing confidence in their government.

3 The return of the technocrats: re-establishing the Swedish model

There are several explanations for what happened in the following years to turn Sweden around. Subsequent governments made specific policy choices that clearly turned out to be very apposite: the tax system was radically restructured; the pension system was reformed; significant investments were made in families and children; and a long series of market-enhancing reforms were introduced in a wide array of public arenas, from the post office to primary school education. These reforms have been very important in helping the system become more competitive and dynamic in the context of a globalizing international economy, but to focus on the specific policies or budgetary priorities would still miss a significant part of the story. As important as these choices were, they were built upon a foundation of (a) a political system that offered policy-makers sufficient autonomy to make long-term decisions even when these might offend some of their most powerful constituents; (b) a relatively egalitarian social/economic structure; and (c) a remarkably efficient and non-corrupt political and administrative system (what is known as 'quality of government'). These three factors have worked together to reinforce citizens' trust both in their institutions and among themselves. In the next several pages I will offer a narrative of how this came together.

In the later years of the 1990s, conflict among Social Democratic elites and conflicts between the SAP and the labour unions became ever more open and public. The eventual result was that, even though the Social Democrats were still the largest party in the Riksdag after the 1991 election, they could not form a government. The Moderate Party was asked to step to the plate and form a minority government; the Social Democrats implied that they would not work to undermine the new government and would help support the Moderate Party in important legislation.

This was a particularly inauspicious time to come to government in Sweden. The financial and property markets were obviously overheated, the country's economic performance continued to decline, domestic productive investment was at a historic low, public and private debt was skyrocketing, and the currency was under extreme pressure from international speculators. Despite these challenges, it is fair to say that this government (with the explicit support of the Social Democratic elite) pursued a set of policies that helped the Swedish economy regain its footing and ultimately helped rebuild citizens' confidence in government. We cannot detail all the policies pursued in these years, but three major reforms stand out. The first of these is the comprehensive overhaul of the Swedish tax system.[13] The second is the successful management of the largest banking crisis in the nation's history, in which the government nationalized several banks and effectively took over the industry until it could be rebuilt and restabilized. The third is the adoption of what is widely considered to be the world's most comprehensive and forward-looking social security reform, which by virtually all accounts is both socially equitable and fiscally sustainable.

The social security reform and the banking crisis will be discussed briefly below, but what is important to note here is that these three cases shared one basic pattern:[14] a massive policy problem was approached as a technical issue, which was eventually (indeed remarkably quickly) solved through close and ongoing relationships between the key actors in the political system and/or the political economy. In each case, a very small group of actors engaged with the problem and produced technical solutions that were then passed on to the government, which then presented the legislation to the Riksdag. In each case, the conforming laws passed through Parliament with little significant controversy because the package had already been agreed to by the key elites representing the main parties. The meetings on social security reform were held behind closed doors, whereas tax reform (not discussed here) was a somewhat more open process. But, in each case, the key to the story was that a very small group of elite individuals were able to meet for a sustained period of time, negotiate over the technical features of a reform proposal, and finally put together a package that would not be subject to subsequent logrolling or legislative riders.

3.1 Social security reform: elite power behind closed doors

All advanced countries in the late twentieth century faced a looming demographic and fiscal problem. Sweden's problem was in fact worse than that of almost any other state. To put it bluntly, there were too many old people who felt they deserved very generous lifetime pension benefits and too few young people who earned too little money to fund their parents' and grandparents' benefit packages. The short-term answer to this dilemma in Sweden, as elsewhere, was borrowing. In the long term, however, the demographic picture would have been so out of balance that borrowing was not a sustainable option. By one UN estimate, pensioners would equal 54 per cent of the working-age population of Sweden by 2050 (Roberts 2003).

These demographic trends are *fiscal* issues because of the expectation on the part of most citizens that they have paid into a social security system from which they should be able to collect as they retire. In almost all countries, this is a fiscal illusion. We do not pay into a tangible fund that is just sitting there and waiting for us to collect from it in our old age; instead, social security is a system of intergenerational income transfer. Current workers pay social security taxes that go more or less directly into the benefit cheques of their retired parents and grandparents – even if the recipients are fundamentally richer than the payees (Chopel et al. 2005).

By the late 1980s, policy-makers around the world were keenly aware of the 'aging society' problem, but in most cases political leaders were deeply constrained by the fact that past commitments (both explicit and implicit) made to retirees prevented them from making cutbacks in benefits, at the same time as rising economic pressures cautioned against increasing social insurance taxes. This was a classic case of 'democracy in straightjackets'.

The Swedes, true to form, approached the problem by appointing a commission.[15] I will not detail the entire reform here, but two factors stand out.[16] First, the social pension system was divided into two parts: a basic guaranteed pension and an individual retirement account. In keeping with the basic principles of the universal welfare state, the new programme guarantees all citizens a basic and decent standard of living once they reach the age of retirement – whatever their work history.[17] In addition to and on top of the basic pension system, citizens born after 1954 will enrol in a defined-contribution scheme (a 'premium pension') that bears a remarkable resemblance to the privatized social security plan promoted by President Bush. In this system, 2.5 per cent of the social insurance tax goes to an individually owned pension account that is then invested by (or for) the income earner. Individuals, upon retirement, will collect from their funds in the form of an annuity, but, clearly, the longer a person pays into the system, the higher the benefits. The second important aspect of this radical reform was to build in what was called a fiscal balancing mechanism: the benefits in the basic pension would be tied directly to current contributions. Thus, as wages increase (or stagnate), so do benefits. In short, retirees benefit from the growth of the Swedish economy but do not have their benefits increased unless the society at large sees a growth in income.

This reform has drawn enormous interest and approval both within Sweden and around the world, because, by most accounts, it has solved the critical fiscal dilemma facing all advanced countries at the same time as it protects the elderly from falling into poverty as they age.[18] Because this new system offers strong incentives for workers to stay in the labour market longer and also directly ties old-age benefits to economic performance, it is expected to be fiscally viable in the long run. Few advanced societies can make this claim.

Bo Könberg, one of the key architects behind the reform, summed up his view of the process this way: 'In the Swedish literature the 1994 agreement has sometimes been described as the great pension compromise [*pension-skompromissen*] . . . no party achieved exactly what it wanted, rather everyone had to give and take' (Schøyen 2011). It is important to understand that what was agreed upon is fiscally sustainable because it takes benefits away from current and future retirees. In other words, Könberg and his small commission were able to impose costs on very powerful constituents. But, because of Sweden's long-term deference to power and authority, they were able to achieve a policy solution about which most countries' elites could only dream. Sweden was able to deal with this very difficult set of political issues by depoliticizing them and treating them as technical matters. By insulating the policy-makers from the demand pressures of public constituencies, the commission was thus able to propose practical solutions. The demographic/fiscal crisis bearing down on Sweden was averted largely because it was taken out of the political arena.

4 How to deal with a financial crisis

A second example of the Swedish policy-making system at work in the 1990s can be seen in the way in which the centre-right minority government dealt with the massive banking and financial crisis it confronted in 1992, almost immediately upon entering office. The new government's first response was to bring together experts from across the financial and political spectrum. It may well have been reasonable to expect these political leaders to try to run from the impending crisis or to blame the economy's problems on the past government. They chose instead to intervene decisively in the financial markets, inject liquidity, provide guarantees for doubtful loans, and ultimately steer the recovery process in a transparent way. They were able to achieve these remarkable policy ends with the political support of virtually all opposition parties. In the end, the recovery in the banking system and the larger economy was quick and the costs to the budget were relatively minimal.

How was this done? Bo Lundgren, the minister for economic affairs at the time and in charge of responding to the crisis, gathered his key advisors, as well as the leader of the Social Democratic Party at the time, and, in his words, 'put together a package'. The ministry quickly realized that extant Swedish law gave failing financial institutions six months to consolidate before the government could take them over. They understood that, during a crisis, such a long period before the government could act would give the errant managers and capitalists time to disperse their assets. Decisive government action was essential. The solution was to go to Johan Munck, the then president of the Swedish High Court, and ask him to draft a new law that would give the government the right to seize a bank's assets without the waiting period. With the support of the Social Democrats, Lundgren and his advisors then pushed the new law through Parliament in a shortened period which speeded up the legislative procedure, and *the bill became law in just three weeks*. From that point on, financial institutions understood that the government had both the tools and the intent to take whatever means were necessary to defend the economy, and not just the banks.[19]

The government injected equity capital directly into the banks which they felt had a chance of surviving, whereas banks that had no prospects of recovering and becoming profitable in the medium term were simply allowed to go bankrupt (Englund 1999: 91). When Lundgren was asked whether he felt much pressure from some of the special interests who would be negatively affected by the 'package' he had put together, he claimed quite bluntly that 'no one, nobody in government even approached me like that'. Recalling a personal entreaty made to him by SEB bank chairman Kurt G. Olssen, who asked for special dispensation for one of their subsidiary banks, Lundgren responded: 'So I called Olssen to come up, together with the CEO, and I said, "I'm not paying anything. Well, perhaps 1 krona." Then he started to say that his shareholders would take a great loss. So I told him, "That's not my problem."'[20]

Sweden's experience with its banking crisis has been studied by fiscal authorities around the world. Few, however, have been able to copy the efficient and straightforward way that this government addressed its crisis. To be sure, the eventual floating of the Swedish krona and the subsequent depreciation of currency constituted the main driving force behind the export-oriented recovery.[21] Moreover, Sweden yet again had the advantage of timing and was well placed to take advantage of the world economic expansion of the 1990s. The consequent fiscal expansion acted as an automatic stabilizer for the Swedish economy. The result was that, whereas the government had carried a massive budget deficit in 1992–4, by 1997 the budget had been balanced, and by the early 2000s Sweden had begun to pay down its debt (Jonung 2009: 12). Indeed, these years actually witnessed an *increase* in public spending, despite the fact that the centre-right government was at the helm.

5 The Social Democrats return

The Social Democrats who returned to office after the three years of Moderate Party rule were not the same Social Democrats who had held power for so long before. The damaging fights that had brought the party down in the late 1990s were not fully resolved, but the new leadership – especially under finance minister and then prime minister Göran Persson (1996–2006) – could be accurately described as technocratic.

Sweden's unofficial governing party quickly set about restabilizing the financial picture in the country. In many ways these 'socialists' now accepted the liberal logic that had swept across the globe. They did indeed cut back several social welfare policies, but careful analysis of these policies suggests that, rather than slashing programmes wholesale,[22] most of the reductions were in fact designed to remove some of the opportunities for abuse that the stunning generosity of these policies had created earlier on.[23] 'The upshot is that the policy implications from the case of Sweden are hard to classify on a simple right–left scale', economist Andreas Bergh notes. 'The welfare state survives because it coexists with high levels of economic freedom and well-functioning capitalist institutions . . .. Sweden also demonstrates that it is possible to increase economic freedom substantially without dismantling the welfare state' (Bergh 2010: 15).

This government clearly believed that markets could be more effective in delivering services than monopolies (even public monopolies), since they introduced a series of policy reforms designed to create greater competition in the delivery of public-sector services (see Olesen 2010). At the same time, however, several reforms were introduced that were explicitly designed to mitigate the growing inequality in Swedish society, including an increase in the top marginal rate of tax on very high-income earners and a 50 per cent reduction in the VAT rate on food. Public spending on childcare also increased.

By decade's end, Sweden's economic and fiscal situation had improved markedly: unemployment had been reduced, though not to the levels common during the heyday of the Swedish model. The budget was now in surplus. Investment had returned to levels not seen in many years. GDP growth was now at a healthy and sustainable rate. Instead of using the budget surpluses to cut taxes on mobile capital, as the right had demanded and many analysts had predicted would happen, the finance minister increased public spending on child support yet again and continued using the surplus to pay off Sweden's substantial public debt. Indeed, the first budget in the new century (2000) was widely heralded (and decried) as 'a classic Social Democratic budget' (Wettergren 2000).

Interestingly, the government also changed the electoral rules. Once again, a commission reported and the government obliged. In this case, the commission argued that the three-year election cycle in force since the constitutional reform of 1974 had made Swedish politics too vulnerable to electoral swings and the moods of the public. They recommended a four-year electoral term. *Remarkably, almost no one argued against the idea, and this major change in the electoral rules passed in the Riksdag with almost no opposition and very little public discourse.*

6 Choosing the best managers

The Social Democratic Party lost its mandate in 2006 and was replaced in government by a coalition led by the resurgent Moderaterna (Conservative) Party. This election (and the one that followed in 2010) should not be misunderstood as a rejection of Swedish social democracy, however. The Moderate Party, under the leadership of the young and progressive Fredrick Reinfeld, instead proved exceptionally successful in convincing the electorate that *they* would be the best defenders of the Swedish social democratic state. The sophisticated electoral campaigns clearly outshined the Social Democrats and offered voters a vision of a new party that would defend the traditional Swedish welfare state while at the same time modernizing it and making it even more efficient. Calling themselves 'the workers' party of today', the Moderates rejected traditional left/right categorization by declaring, for example, that they intended to lower taxes across the board, 'but most importantly for people who earn low incomes and who therefore need it most'.[24] A prominent Swedish journalist summarized the conservatives' electoral strategy in the following way: 'But the rebranding was, to a great degree, also a cloning. "Every promise the Social Democrats make on social welfare, we will agree to and improve," Reinfeldt said in one of his campaign speeches' (Engström 2006).

Only two years after the centre-right government was elected, the world economy went into a tailspin. At first this might have seemed like a repeat of past histories where a conservative government comes to office only to have to deal with another major economic disaster. But, unlike most of its European contemporaries, the Swedish government drew positive lessons from its 1991–2 experience and took a determinately pro-state approach to addressing the crisis. Instead of cutting back on public spending and declaring the need for austerity, it declared that it would expand the government and attempt to inflate the economy. Virtually as soon as it became aware that the crisis would be deep, the government initiated a stimulus plan that included significant increases in public spending on infrastructure, education, active labour market policies, specific supports for the automobile sector, and tax credits for home repairs and construction. Over the next year it introduced large increases in state subsidies to municipal governments, as well as income tax cuts across the board. Once again, the Social Democrats supported virtually all of these policies (with the exception of the income tax cuts) and offered policy prescriptions that actually differed little from those proposed by the Moderate government.

By 2011, these policies were being widely touted as some of the most effective responses to the global economic crisis found anywhere in the world. How was this done? Certainly, there are many possible interpretations and many parts to the puzzle. But the key factors appear to be that Sweden entered the crisis in a strong fiscal position, monitored the crisis very carefully, and learned its lessons from the banking crisis of 1991–2. Additionally, as the German group Bertelsmann observed in its comprehensive analysis of the politics and policies pursued by the Swedish government, there was a high degree of unity between political parties. Moreover, 'Sweden's democratic system lacks powerful (domestic) veto players' (Jochem 2010: 9):

Behind closed doors, cooperation between the government and the Riksbank functioned smoothly. Additionally, the government expanded the power of special authorities, which are tasked with coordinating economic policies between the central government and local/regional governments. In contrast to the early 1990s, the government struck no policy deals with the opposition. With its slim majority in parliament, the current coalition has not been forced to integrate opposition parties into the policy-making process. (Ibid.: 13)

In the meantime, the Social Democratic Party has been in disarray, apparently unable to find a clear message to convince voters that they would be any better at managing or improving social welfare than the conservatives. Clearly, many think that the government has gone too far with its market reforms. But the Moderates have been clever enough to argue that they have been following the same policy patterns established by the last Social Democratic government – but have been even more effective with their reforms.

Even as it espouses pro-welfare-state rhetoric, the conservative coalition government that has now been in power for five years has pursued a set of policies that have drawn significant scepticism from several analysts. For example, unemployment benefits and active labour market policies have been scaled back since 2006[25] in the name of 'making work pay' (Lindvall 2011). Perhaps more significantly, the Moderates have made a series of changes to the unemployment insurance system – a system which had long structurally advantaged organized unions (Rothstein 1992).[26] Although Sweden still has the highest union density of any country in the world, these reforms have clearly had some effect: in 2009, union membership in the workforce dropped to 71 per cent, from 77 per cent in 2006.

In the meantime, the Social Democrats have looked weak and confused. With the left tainted by several personal scandals and lacking a strong ideological position to confront the centre-right government,[27] one increasingly gets the impression that a new governing party has risen in Sweden.

7 The Svallfors Paradox[28]

Public support for key social welfare programmes in Sweden has *increased* rather than decreased in recent years. Given this fact, it is scarcely surprising that no major political party is demanding cutbacks in the welfare state. Even though median-income families pay substantial taxes, they also benefit from substantial direct social transfers from the state. A family at the median income level received nearly SEK40,000 in direct benefits (US$5,000 to $6,000, depending on exchange rates). These direct cash benefits do not include the value of public education for their children, national defence or other more indirect benefits advantaging citizens. In short, they pay a lot in, but they also can count on getting a lot out of the system.

One key to understanding the resilience of the Swedish welfare state is to appreciate that it is massively popular. As Stefan Kumlin (2002) demonstrates in his fascinating analysis, citizens' attitudes towards public services depend rather fundamentally on the character and delivery of those services. Stefan Svallfors, Sweden's leading expert on public attitudes towards the welfare state, summarizes his most recent findings as follows:

> There are two remarkable findings . . .. One is the sharply increased willingness between 2002 and 2010 to pay more taxes . . .. The second finding is that for all listed policies, the proportion that is willing to pay more taxes is actually *larger* than the proportion that wants to increase overall spending for that policy. (Svallfors 2011: 811)

Svallfors concludes the following from his data:

> Hence, no corrosive feedback effects from changing welfare policies may be detected in the Swedish public. It seems rather that the changes in institutional practices and political rhetoric that have taken place in the 1990s and 2000s have further strengthened middle-class support for the welfare state. In an ironic twist of fate, market-emulating reforms of the welfare

Table 4.1: Attitudes towards public spending in Sweden, 1997–2010 (%)

	1997	2002	2010
Individual willingness to pay taxes for welfare policies.			
Willingness to pay more taxes for ...			
Medical and health care	67	65	75
Support for the elderly	62	60	73
Support for families with children (child allowances, childcare)	42	39	51
Social assistance	29	25	40
Comprehensive and secondary schooling	62	61	71
Employment policy measures	40	31	54
Number of respondents	1,290	1,075	3,800

Source: Svalfors (2011: table 2).

state and the changed political rhetoric of the political right-of-center completed the full ideological integration of the middle class into the welfare state. The electoral base for any resistance against a high-tax, high-spending, collective welfare state now looks completely eroded. While the Social Democratic party suffers, the social democratic welfare state thrives. (Svallfors 2011: 815)

8 Conclusion

In a recent communication, one of the editors of this volume, Wolfgang Streeck, asked quite bluntly why there was 'so little discontent with democracy in Sweden'.[29] After all, he noted, in recent years Sweden has witnessed increased and sustained unemployment (at least in Swedish terms) and rising inequality (again, in Swedish terms), while at the same time there have been cutbacks in unemployment benefits and a rollback in union membership. Could it be, he implied, that the Swedish model is no longer the 'Swedish model', and that the majority of Swedes are happy with this?

My answer to this question depends on what one means by the 'Swedish model'. Many have assumed that Sweden has achieved its remarkable successes by being the most *democratic* country in the world. The fundamental assumption underlying much Swedish scholarship for the past several decades is that, because the outcomes have been progressive, the process must have been democratic. In my view, this assumption needs some qualifications. If what we mean by democracy is a system where the government is highly responsive to the expressed demands of its citizens, then Swedish democracy over the past decades must be brought into question. If, however, what we mean by this term is a political system in which elites may have considerable discretion and autonomy so that they can pursue what they believe to be the best interests of their citizens, and that the citizens can judge after the fact if these elites have actually delivered, then Sweden is indeed highly democratic.

There are many reasons to admire the Swedish system. It has provided remarkably high standards of living for its citizens, it is one of the most egalitarian political economies in the world, and it has proven to be resilient and able to adapt remarkably well to a dynamic and competitive world economy. But there is very little in this analysis that would lead us to conclude that Sweden has had a particularly responsive political democracy. Instead, we have seen a history of decisions that have been made by a talented and progressive elite in favour – and often in advance – of the country's citizens. Democracy, in Sweden, has effectively meant that citizens have the ability to judge the past performance of their governing elite. For most of the twentieth century, it was the Social Democrats who governed – and governed well. They were rewarded repeatedly for their judgements and in the process built a social welfare state that is massively popular. It appears today, however, that the Social Democrats have lost the ability to claim that they are the best managers of the system. Indeed, it is difficult to argue against the current government's performance in recent years. Despite the worldwide recession, the Swedish economy has posted positive growth and budget surpluses. Indeed, in 2010 the World Economic Forum declared Sweden the second most competitive economy in the world.[30]

9 A postscript: should we all be Swedes now?

Today we see straightjackets everywhere. The budget constraints, austerity programmes, and vast increases in economic distress witnessed across the industrialized world might lead one to conclude that what is needed in Europe are more autonomous governments of the Swedish kind. Tough decisions are necessary, and political autonomy is the key – or so the logic goes. In this view, the central problem in Europe today is that governments have been *too* responsive to their many constituencies and clienteles and that democracy needs straightjackets.

But, before we jump to the conclusion that Europe should now follow a Swedish model (as opposed to the neoliberal American model that was so popular only a few short years ago), it is important to remember that the Swedish system was built in a very particular way over a long span of time. More importantly, it was built within the context of a rather homogeneous polity that had one of the most concentrated economies in the world. Within Swedish society, social deference and trust was substantially easier to construct and maintain. Finally, the Swedish system has operated within, and has worked to reinforce, a remarkably fair and non-corrupt elite political culture. To try to build such a system in the larger, more diverse and more conflictual – to say nothing of corrupt – political economies found in some other parts of Europe strikes this author, at least, as both dangerous and foolhardy.

References

Agell, J. (1996) Why Sweden's welfare state needed reform, *The Economic Journal* 106: 1760–1771.
Ahlquist, B., and Engquist, L. (1984) *Samtal med feldt*. Stockholm: Tiden.

Bayram, I. E., DeWit, A., et al. (2012) The bumble bee and the chrysanthemum: comparing Sweden and Japan's response to fiscal crisis, unpublished manuscript. Florence, Italy.

Bergh, A. (2010) The rise, fall and revival of a capitalist welfare state: what are the policy lessons from Sweden?, unpublished manuscript. Stockholm.

Bundesregierung (German Federal Government) (2003) Pensions, 25 March; available at: http://eng.bundesregierung.de/frameset/index.jsp (accessed 23 June 2003).

Castles, F. (1978) The Social Democratic Image of Society. London: Routledge & Kegan Paul.

Chopel, A., Kuno, N., and Steinmo, S. (2005) Social security, taxation and redistribution in Japan, Public Budgeting and Finance 25(4): 20–43.

Dougherty, C. (2008) Stopping a financial crisis, the Swedish way, New York Times, 22 September; available at: www.nytimes.com/2008/09/23/business/worldbusiness/23krona.html (accessed 1 March 2012).

Englund, P. (1999) The Swedish banking crisis: roots and consequences, Oxford Review of Economic Policy 155: 80–97.

Engström, M. (2006) We still love the Swedish model, Open Democracy, 19 September; available at: www.opendemocracy.net/democracy-protest/swedish_model_3915.jsp (accessed 1 March 2012).

Feldt, K.-O. (1991) Alla dessa dagar [All those days]. Stockholm: Norstedts.

Hancock, M. D. (1972) The Politics of Post-Industrial Change. Ann Arbor, MI: Dryden Press.

Jochem, S. (2010) Sweden country report, in Managing the Crisis: A Comparative Analysis of Economic Governance in 14 Countries. Berlin: Bertelsmann Stiftung.

Jonung, L. (2009) The Swedish Model for Resolving the Banking Crisis of 1991–1993: Seven Reasons it Was Successful. Brussels: European Commission, Economics and Financial Affairs.

Jordan, J. (2006) Mothers, wives, and workers: explaining gendered dimensions of the welfare state, Comparative Political Studies 39(9): 1109–32.

Katzenstein, P. (1984) Small States in World Markets: Industrial Policy in Europe. Ithaca, NY: Cornell University Press.

Kjellberg, A. (2010) The decline of Swedish union density since 2011, Nordic Journal of Working Life Studies 1(1): 67–93.

Korpi, W. (1983) The Democratic Class Struggle. London: Routledge & Kegan Paul.

Kumlin, S. (2002) Institutions – experience – preferences: welfare state design affects political trust and ideology, in B. Rothstein and S. Steinmo (eds), Re-Structuring the Welfare State: Institutional Legacies and Policy Change. New York: Palgrave.

Lewin, L. (1970) Planhushallningsdebatten [The planning debate]. Stockholm: Almquist & Wicksell.

Lindbeck, A. (1997) The Swedish Experiment. Stockholm: Studieförbundet Näringsliv och Samhälle.

Lindvall, J. (2011) Politics and Policies in Two Economic Crises, working paper. Lund: Lund University.

Ministry of Finance (1995) *The Medium Term Survey of the Swedish Economy*. Stockholm: Ministry of Finance.

Moses, J. (2000) Floating fortunes: Scandinavian full employment in the tumultuous 1970s–1980s, in R. Geyer, C. Ingebritsen and J. Moses (eds), *Globalization, Europeanization and the End of Scandinavian Social Democracy?* London: Macmillan, pp. 62–84.

Muten, L. (1988) Tax reform – an international perspective, *Vårt economiska läge* [Our economic situation]. Stockholm: Sparfrämjandet.

Myrdal, G. (1982) Dags för ett bättre skattesystem [Time for a better tax system], in L. Jonung (ed.) *Skatter* [Taxes]. Malmö: Liberförlag.

OECD (Organization for Economic Cooperation and Development) (2002) *Taxing Wages Special Feature: Taxing Pensioners 2000–2001*. Paris: OECD.

Olesen, J. (2010) Privitizing health care in Sweden, Britain and Denmark: social and political science. PhD thesis, European University Institute, Florence.

Palme, J. (2003) The 'Great' Swedish Pension Reform, 24 March [online commentary] (accessed at www.sweden.se on 20 June 2003).

Roberts, A. (2003) Krybbe to grav [Cradle to grave]: is the much-loved welfare state still affordable?, *The Economist*, 12 June; available at: www.economist.com/node/1825083 (accessed 14 August 2012).

Rothstein, B. (1986) *Den Social-Demokratiska staten* [The Social Democratic state]. Lund: Lund Arkiv Avhandinesserie.

Rothstein, B. (1992) Labour market institutions and working class strength, in S. Steinmo, K. Thelen and F. Longstreth (eds), *Structuring Politics: Historical Institutionalism in Comparative Politics*. New York: Cambridge University Press, pp 33–56.

Ruin, O. (1981) Sweden in the 1970s: police-making [*sic*] becomes more difficult, in J. Richardson (ed.) *Policy Styles in Western Europe*. London: Allen & Unwin, pp. 141–67.

Rustow, D. (1955) *The Politics of Compromise*. Princeton, NJ: Princeton University Press.

Schøyen, M. A. (2011) The pension dilemma in Italy, Germany and Sweden: a common challenge, different outcomes, PhD dissertation, European University Institute, Florence.

Sjöberg, T. (1999) Intervjun: Kjell-Olof Feldt [Interview: Kjell-Olof Feldt]. *Playboy Skandinavia* 5: 37–44.

Steinmo, S. (1993) *Taxation and Democracy: Swedish, British and American Approaches to Financing the Modern State*. New Haven, CT: Yale University Press.

Steinmo, S. (2002) Globalization and taxation: challenges to the Swedish welfare state, *Comparative Political Studies* 35(7): 839–62.

Steinmo, S. (2010) *The Evolution of the Modern State: Sweden, Japan and the United States*. New York: Cambridge University Press.

Svallfors, S. (2011) A bedrock of support? Trends in welfare state attitudes in Sweden, 1981–2010, *Social Policy and Administration* 45(7): 806–25.

Sverenius, T. (1999) *Vad hände med Sveriges ekonomi efter 1970?* [What happened with the Swedish economy after 1970?], Demokrati Utredningen, vol. 31. Stockholm: Statens Offentliga Utredningar.

Swenson, P. (1989) *Fair Shares: Unions, Pay, and Politics in Sweden and West Germany.* Ithaca, NY: Cornell University Press.

Tanzi, V., and Schuknecht, L. (2000) *Public Spending in the 20th Century: A Global Perspective.* Cambridge: Cambridge University Press.

Thakur, S., Keen, M., Hovath, B., and Cerra, V. (2003) *Sweden's Welfare State: Can the Bumblebee Keep Flying?* New York: International Monetary Fund.

Von Sydow, B. (1989) *Vägen till enkammarriksdagen: demokratisk författningspolitik i Sverige 1944–1968* [The road to a one-chamber parliament: democratic constitutional politics in Sweden 1944–1968]. Stockholm: Tiden.

Wettergren, A. (2000) En traditionell socialdemokrat [A traditional social democrat]. *Götenburgs-Posten*, 30 May, p. 2.

5

Monetary Union, Fiscal Crisis and the Disabling of Democratic Accountability

Fritz W. Scharpf

1 Introduction

In capitalist democracies, governments depend on the confidence of their voters. But to maintain this confidence they also depend on the performance of their real economies and, increasingly, on the confidence of financial markets. To meet these requirements at the same time is difficult even under the best of circumstances. Compared with the situation up to the 1980s, however, international economic integration has added greatly to the difficulties of successful economic management at the national level. With the growing integration of capital markets, financial interpenetration made national economies vulnerable to crises originating elsewhere. At the same time, international and, more importantly, European rules on product and capital market liberalization imposed legal constraints that eliminated many policy options on which governments had previously relied to manage national economies. In the present chapter I focus on the European Monetary Union (EMU), which has removed crucial instruments of macro-economic management from the control of democratically accountable governments. Worse still, it has caused destabilizing macro-economic imbalances that member states find difficult or impossible to counteract with their remaining policy instruments. And, even though the international financial crisis had its origins beyond Europe, the Monetary Union greatly increased the vulnerability of member states to its repercussions. Its effects have undermined the economic and fiscal viability of some EMU member states and have frustrated political demands and expectations to an extent that may yet transform the economic crisis into a crisis of democratic legitimacy. Moreover, present efforts by EMU governments to 'rescue the euro' are more likely to deepen economic problems and political alienation than to correct the underlying imbalances.

The chapter begins with a brief reflection on the problematic relationship between democratic legitimacy and macro-economic management, followed by an equally brief restatement of the essential elements of Keynesian and monetarist policy models and their specific political implications. I then try to show how existing national regimes have been transformed by the creation of the European Monetary Union, and how the destabilizing dynamics of European monetary policy left some EMU member states dangerously vulnerable at the onset of the international financial crisis. In the concluding section, I examine the likely politico-economic and political consequences of programmes intended to rescue the euro and to reform the regime of the Monetary Union.

2 Democratic legitimacy and macro-economic management

After the Great Depression of the 1930s and the Second World War, governments in Western democracies had assumed political responsibility for preventing the return of similar economic catastrophes. This was to be achieved through macro-economic policies that would allow the state to increase or reduce aggregate economic demand in order to dampen the ups and downs of economic cycles, to prevent the rise of unemployment or inflation, and to ensure steady economic growth. The belief that macro-economic management could in fact realize these goals was largely confirmed in the Keynesian decades after the war, and it survived the monetarist counter-revolution of the 1980s as well, at least in the sense that economic crises continued to be seen as consequences of macro-economic mismanagement. But the very idea of effective macro-economic control has created an internal dilemma of democratic legitimacy – or, more precisely, a potential conflict between the input-oriented and the output-oriented dimensions of democratic legitimacy (Scharpf 1999: ch. 1).

Governments are supposed to carry out the 'will of the people' and they are also supposed to serve the 'common good'. In the *input* dimension, therefore, governors may be held accountable for policy *choices* that are in conflict with the politically salient preferences of their constituents, whereas, in the *output* dimension, they may be held accountable for *outcomes* attributed[1] to government policy that are seen to violate the politically salient concerns[2] of the governed. In both dimensions, what is initially at stake is political support for the government of the day. But, if it appears that elections and changes of government cannot make a difference, then the democratic legitimacy of the political regime itself may be undermined.

With regard to macro-economic management, the outcomes that potentially have very high political salience are rising mass unemployment and accelerating rates of inflation. Since these are not the direct object of policy choices, however, discussions of input legitimacy must focus on the policy instruments that may be employed to affect outcomes indirectly. In macro-economic theory, these include choices in monetary and exchange-rate policy, fiscal policy and wage policy – all of which are assumed to have a direct effect on aggregate economic demand and hence on economic growth, inflation and employment. They differ greatly, however, in their political salience, and hence in their potential relevance for input-oriented democratic legitimacy.

Under normal conditions, monetary policy has relatively low salience in the electoral arena. It is seen to involve highly technical decisions that are thought to be best left to specialists in central banks and finance ministries with an expertise in analysing and manipulating the aggregate supply of money in the economy. Ultimately, of course, monetary policy will also affect individuals and firms and may have massive distributional impacts. But these are not immediately visible and, when they occur, are not obviously related to specific policy choices. The same is true of policies affecting the exchange rate. Fiscal policy, by contrast, while also aiming at the public-sector deficit as an aggregate variable, must be implemented through disaggregated taxing and spending decisions that have a direct and visible impact on the incomes of individuals and firms. The same would be true if governments were to adopt policies (as they tried to do in some countries in the 1970s) that imposed direct wage controls.

Unlike monetary policy, therefore, choices of fiscal and wage policy are liable to become politicized. If they violate the politically salient *ex ante* preferences of constituencies, they may reduce the electoral support of governments and, in the extreme case, undermine input legitimacy, even though they may be necessary to achieve politically acceptable macro-economic outcomes. In other words, macro-economic management creates the possibility for a democratic dilemma: in attempting to maintain *output legitimacy* through functionally effective policies, governments may need to employ instruments that undermine their *input legitimacy* – and vice versa. In actual practice, however, the intensity of the dilemma depends not only on the type of economic challenges but also on the choice between the Keynesian and the monetarist models or paradigms of macro-economic management.

2.1 Keynesian politics of macro-economic management

In the Keynesian model, the government is supposed to employ all four instruments of macro-economic management in order to optimize the 'magic triangle' of full employment, price stability and external balance. And, since there is an assumed trade-off between the employment and inflation goals, left- and right-wing parties and governments will differ in their political priorities. In practice, the leading role is given to fiscal policy. In a recession, it should expand aggregate demand through tax cuts and deficit-financed expenditures; and, when the economy over-heats, demand should be reduced through tax increases and spending cuts. Monetary policy should be 'accommodating' – that is, to finance fiscal expansion at low interest rates and to avoid a collapse of domestic demand during fiscal retrenchment. And union wage policy should help to avoid wage-push inflation in the upswing and demand contraction in the downswing. In the US and the UK this model worked reasonably well during the early postwar decades. Even then, however, it was obvious that fiscal retrenchment in the upswing was politically more difficult to implement than fiscal expansion during a recession. And, when full employment was maintained, it proved difficult to prevent inflationary wage increases. Ultimately, however, the Keynesian model failed almost everywhere during the oil-price crises of the 1970s, when cost-push inflation and demand-deficient unemployment combined to create a 'stagflation' dilemma where fiscal expansion would have accelerated inflation, whereas fiscal retrenchment would have driven up mass unemployment (Scharpf 1991).

2.2 Monetarism and the Bundesbank's social compact

The monetarist paradigm owed its practical appeal to the failure of Keynesian policies in the 1970s but had its theoretical roots in pre-Keynesian neoclassical economics (Johnson 1971). Denying the existence of a trade-off between inflation and unemployment, it assigned norma-tive priority to price stability and functional priority to the monetary policy of a politically independent central bank. Everything else could and should be left to the operation of politically undisturbed and flexible markets. While generally associated with the Thatcher and Reagan governments, it was in fact the German Bundesbank which first established a monetarist regime in the early 1970s. After having dramatically dem-onstrated the destructive potential of monetary retrenchment in the crisis of 1973–4, the bank did in fact confront the government and the unions with the offer of an implicit social compact (Scharpf 1991: 128–39). It took pains to explain how monetary policy would not only ensure price stability but also produce politically justifiable macro-economic out-comes. Once inflation was under control, it would precisely monitor the state of the German economy and pre-announce annual monetary targets by reference to the current 'output gap'. Maximum non-inflationary growth would then be achieved if fiscal policy would just allow the 'automatic stabilizers' to rise and fall over the business cycle and if wages would rise with labour productivity. Thus fiscal policy would be relieved of its heroic Keynesian role, and unions would no longer be pressured to achieve counter-cyclical wage settlements. And, as governments and unions learned to play by the bank's new rules, the depoliticized monetarist regime did in fact work reasonably well, economically and politically, for Germany.

3 From monetarism in one country to Monetary Union

Monetarist as well as Keynesian models had originally been designed for national economies which were exposed to international competi-tion in product markets, but which retained control over their monetary regimes. But, following the 1970s, increasing capital mobility had created difficulties for both systems. Capital flight could frustrate Keynesian reflation, and monetarist strategies could not target the 'output gap' of a national economy when interest rates were being determined by inter-national capital markets. Moreover, capital mobility had increased the volatility of exchange rates, which was seen as a problem for exporters and importers in product markets. There were several reasons, there-fore, for European governments to be interested in creating a common exchange-rate regime.

The first such attempt, the European 'snake in the tunnel' of 1972, had quickly disintegrated in the oil-price crisis. Subsequently, the European Monetary System (EMS) of 1979 committed its member states to peg their currencies to a currency basket (the ECU). But, since Germany was the biggest economy and the most important trading partner for most other member states, the EMS in fact meant that these countries' curren-cies were pegged to the Deutschmark – which also implied that, in order to stay within the agreed-upon bandwidths, their central banks needed to mirror the stability-oriented monetary policy of the Bundesbank. For the other member states, this turned out to be difficult for several reasons.

First, the Bundesbank remained committed to the priority of price stability, and it continued to target its policies on conditions in the German economy – which sometimes differed significantly from those in other member economies.[3] Moreover, governments and unions outside

Germany did not necessarily appreciate the awesome power of monetary constraints. Nor did their central banks have a background of institutional autonomy, experience and credibility that would have allowed them to intervene with equal authority against public-sector deficits and wage settlements that diverged from the path defined for Germany. Even more important, however, were the institutional differences in national wage-setting systems. The monetarist regime worked in Germany because wage leadership was exercised by unified and economically sophisticated industrial unions that had learned to operate within given monetary constraints. In contrast, countries with powerful but fragmented and competitive unions, and decentralized wage-setting institutions, simply did not have the capacity to contain the inflationary pressures of wage competition (Calmfors 2001; Baccaro and Simoni 2010). As a consequence, inflation rates and the increase of unit labour costs continued to differ; and, to compensate for losses in international competitiveness, exchange rates and bandwidths were frequently readjusted. And because devaluation remained a possibility, the risk premiums of government bonds differed considerably among EMS member states. Moreover, any attempt to defend unrealistic exchange rates would invite currency speculation.

These problems persuaded European governments that moving from the EMS to a monetary union with irrevocably fixed exchange rates would be desirable. It would end their dependence on the Bundesbank, and it would eliminate the possibility of devaluation – and hence both the risk of currency speculation and the interest-rate differentials caused by the risk of devaluation. Germany, in turn, which was willing to accept the euro as the political price for German unification, was able to insist that the Bundesbank and its version of monetary stability should become the model for the European system, and that candidate countries would have to meet tough convergence criteria as a condition of admission (Delors 1989; McNamara 1998; Dyson and Featherstone 1999; Jones 2002; Vaubel 2010). In effect, therefore, the Maastricht Treaty protected the institutional independence of the European Central Bank (ECB) even more firmly than had been the case with the German Bundesbank. And, to ensure the ECB's monetarist orientation, the priority of price stability was specified in the treaty as well. Moreover, in order to gain access to the Monetary Union, EU member states had to remove all restrictions on capital mobility, to stabilize their exchange rates to the ECU, and to achieve convergence on low rates of inflation and low public-sector deficits. Perhaps unexpectedly, these 'Maastricht criteria' were in fact met by a considerable number of unlikely candidate countries – sometimes through creative accounting, but mainly through heroic efforts at budget consolidation and 'social pacts' with the unions, pacts whose short-term effectiveness was not necessarily sustainable over the longer term. In an attempt to forestall future lapses, Germany therefore also insisted on a 'Stability and Growth Pact' that defined permanent limits on national deficits and indebtedness together with seemingly tough sanctioning procedures (Heipertz and Verdun 2010).

4 From 1999 to 2007: monetarism in a non-optimal currency area

Initially, the Monetary Union did indeed fulfil the hopes of its support-ers. The widely resented dominance of the Bundesbank was replaced by a common European central bank that targeted its policy decisions on average inflation rates in the eurozone, rather than on the state of the German economy. National inflation rates that had steeply declined in the run-up to the euro continued to remain significantly lower than they had been in the 1990s and, most importantly, financial markets honoured the elimination of devaluation risks, so that interest rates on government bonds and commercial credit declined steeply, to the German level in all EMU member states (figure 5.1). The result was an initial boost to economic growth in those eurozone economies where interest rates had fallen – which, of course, was not the case in Germany. Despite the pre-1999 convergence, therefore, member states entered the EMU in significantly differing economic circumstances.

Such conditions had been discussed earlier under the rubric of whether the EMU could be considered an 'optimum currency area' (Mundell 1961; McKinnon 1963) – which would have presupposed relatively homogeneous member economies and a capacity to respond to 'asym-metric shocks' through a high degree of wage and price flexibility, considerable labour mobility, and a highly responsive system of inter-regional fiscal transfers. American authors found these conditions, when compared to interregional conditions in the United States, to be lacking in Europe (Eichengreen 1990; Eichengreen and Frieden 1994; Feldstein 1997) – and the same conclusion was reached by German authors referring to interregional economic relations in the Federal Republic (von Hagen and Neumann 1994; Funke 1997). But, given the political commitment to monetary unification, and the encouraging effects of national efforts to meet the Maastricht convergence criteria, optimism prevailed among economists in central banks and finance ministries, even in Germany.[4] Within their monetarist frame of reference, the overriding concern was whether the EMU would be able to maintain price stability, and the focus was on national public-sector deficits as a potential source

Figure 5.1: Interest rates of ten-year government bonds

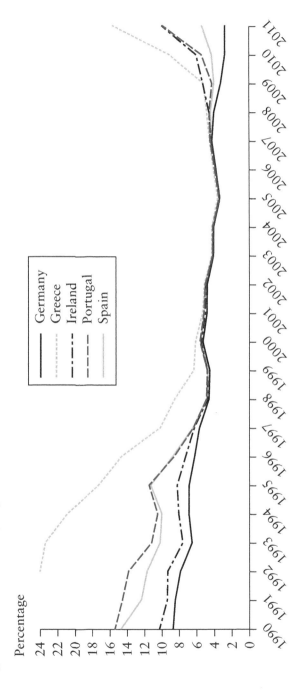

Percentage

Legend: Germany, Greece, Ireland, Portugal, Spain

Source: OECD.

of instability. But since the Stability Pact was designed to control these deficits, it was expected that the increasing integration of capital and goods markets would also ensure a continuing convergence of prices, wages and business cycles (Issing 2002). As it turned out, however, these expectations were misleading[5] for two related reasons.

On the one hand, the political crash programmes, through which unlikely candidate countries had achieved an impressive convergence on the Maastricht criteria, had generally not addressed the underlying structural and institutional differences that had originally caused economic divergence. Once access had been achieved, these differences would and did reassert themselves in the form of continuing (albeit reduced) differences in inflation rates (Lane 2006; Willett et al. 2010). On the other hand, ECB monetary impulses reflected average economic conditions in the eurozone and hence could not target the conditions of specific national economies. In effect, therefore, the crucial precondition of German-style monetarism – a precise fit between money supply and the growth potential of a specific economy – could not and did not exist in a heterogeneous monetary union. Thus, even if the European Central Bank could effectively control average consumer-price inflation in the eurozone, it was unable to ensure steady, inflation-free economic growth in the member economies of the EMU. Instead, its uniform monetary policy would amplify divergent dynamics in economies above and below the eurozone average (Enderlein 2004; Sinn et al. 2004; Lane 2006).

For countries with below-average rates of economic growth and inflation, the uniform ECB interest rates were too high, and the inflation-adjusted real interest rates faced by domestic consumers and investors were even higher – with the consequence that initially weak economic activity was depressed even further by restrictive monetary impulses. For countries with above-average rates of inflation, by contrast, ECB monetary policy was too loose, and real interest rates became extremely low or even negative (figure 5.2). Thus, the boost to economic activity that former soft-currency countries had received through the fall of nominal interest to German levels was subsequently intensified and accelerated by ECB monetary policy. Ironically, the first victim of European monetarism was Germany, the country whose government had imposed its model on the EMU.

4.1 Germany: the sick man of Europe rescued by union wage restraint

Before 1999, not only nominal interest rates but also real interest rates had been lowest in Germany. With entry into the Monetary Union, these comparative advantages were lost (Spethmann and Steiger 2005). Since nominal interest rates converged whereas German inflation rates contin-

Figure 5.2: Real long-term interest rates

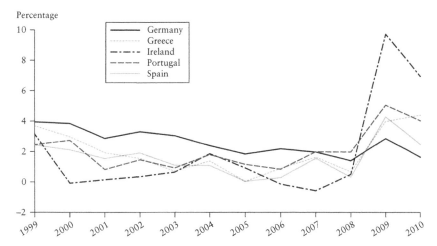

Percentage

Legend:
- Germany
- Greece
- Ireland
- Portugal
- Spain

Source: OECD.

ued to be lower, real interest rates in Germany became the highest in the eurozone. As a consequence, economic growth was lower in Germany than in almost all other EMU member economies; unemployment increased dramatically between 2000 and 2005 (figure 5.3), as did social expenditures, whereas tax revenues fell by 2.4 percentage points between 2000 and 2004.

In responding to this extended recession, Germany could not rely on the usual instruments of macro-economic management. Whereas the Bundesbank would have lowered interest rates in response to the rapidly increasing output gap, ECB interest rates continued to be too high for Germany. And where an autonomous government would have resorted to fiscal reflation, Germany came to violate the 3 per cent deficit limit of the Stability Pact merely by allowing the 'automatic stabilizers' to operate.[6] Moreover, any positive effects on domestic demand that unions might create through wage increases would have been overshadowed by job losses on account of their negative impact on export demand. In the absence of demand-side options, therefore, German policy-makers came to resort to supply-side strategies.

Thus Germany's industrial unions decided to protect existing jobs through wage restraint, which would increase the profitability of domestic production and the competitiveness of German exports. But, of course, stagnant or falling real wages, while stabilizing unit labour costs (figure 5.4), also reduced domestic demand even further – with negative effects on domestic growth and on imports. The Red–Green federal government

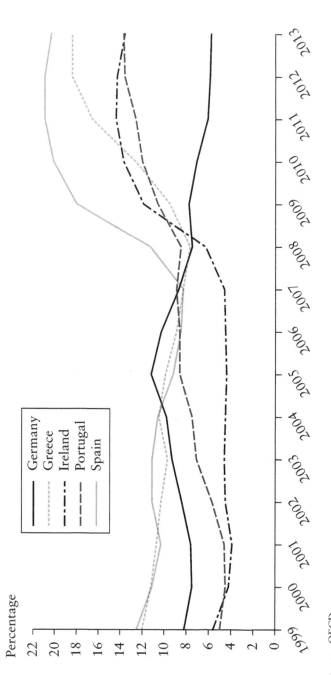

Figure 5.3: Unemployment rates (percentage of civilian labour force)

Percentage

Germany
Greece
Ireland
Portugal
Spain

Source: OECD.

Figure 5.4: Unit labour costs (total economy; Index 2000 = 100)

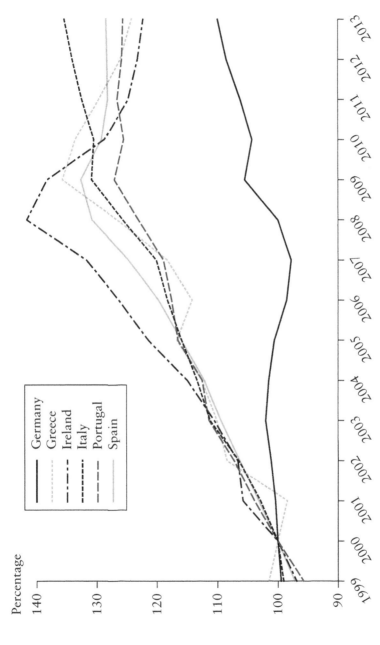

Source: Ameco database.

(a coalition of the Social Democrats and the Greens), for its part, reduced taxes on company profits and capital incomes, lowered the level of employment protection by deregulating temporary and part-time employment, and drastically cut benefits to the long-term unemployed in order to reduce the reservation wage of job-seekers (Trampusch 2009). There is no question that these supply-side policies lacked input legitimacy: they generated heated political debates, and, while they had the support of employers and the business press, they were extremely unpopular with the unions and the rank-and-file of the governing Social Democratic Party. In effect, mass demonstrations and the rise of a left-wing protest party brought about the defeat of Schröder's Red–Green government in the 2005 elections. And if the outcomes might arguably be justified in terms of output legitimacy, the political benefits were captured by Angela Merkel.

Economically, however, the combination of wage restraint practised by German unions and the government's supply-side policies achieved its hoped-for effect. Export demand increased, as, eventually, did employment in the export industries and in a growing low-wage sector, and registered unemployment began to decline after 2005 (figure 5.3). In effect, Germany, which had been the 'sick man of Europe' between 2000 and 2005, managed to pull itself out of the long recession to become again one of the strongest European economies at the onset of the international financial crisis in 2008. In an integrated economic environment, however, successful supply-side policies that reduce the cost and increase the profitability of domestic production in one country must inevitably have the effect of beggar-thy-neighbour strategies on its competitors (De Grauwe 2009: 112; Flassbeck 2010). In the process of coping with its own crisis, therefore, Germany also contributed to the economic vulnerability of other eurozone economies.

4.2 The rise and increasing vulnerability of GIPS economies

In the former soft-currency countries – I will look at Greece, Ireland, Portugal and Spain, labelling them GIPS economies – accession to the EMU had the initial effect of interest rates falling to the much lower German levels (figure 5.1). The sudden availability of cheap capital, whose domestic attractiveness was further increased by near-zero or even negative real interest rates, fuelled credit-financed domestic demand in Greece, Ireland and Spain (though less so in Portugal, for reasons that I have not been able to explore). In Spain and Ireland, in particular, cheap credit came to finance real-estate investments and rapidly rising housing prices, which eventually would turn into bubbles. As a consequence, economic growth was high, inflation remained above the European average, unemployment came down (figure 5.3) and real wages and unit labour costs (figure

5.4) increased steeply. As a consequence, imports would rise, export competitiveness would suffer, and deficits of current accounts (figure 5.5) – and hence the dependence on capital imports – would increase.

Even if they had considered the decline of their external balances a serious problem, however, the governments in GIPS economies found no effective way to counteract domestic booms that were driven by the cheap-money effect of uniform nominal and divergent real interest rates.[7] Spain and Ireland at least tried to achieve some restraint through the instruments of macro-economic policy that were still available nationally. But their attempts to contain wage inflation through a series of social pacts (Baccaro and Simoni 2010) and to practise fiscal constraint by running budget surpluses (figure 5.6) proved insufficient. What would have made a difference was monetary restraint, which would have impeded the credit-financed overheating of the Greek, Irish and Spanish economies. This, however, would have required differentiated, rather than uniform, monetary policies that would not be defined by eurozone averages but be targeted to the specific conditions and problems of the individual economies. Such approaches,[8] however, played no role in the construction of either the European Monetary Union or the Stability Pact (Heipertz and Verdun 2010), nor were they considered by mainstream monetary economics before the present crisis (De Grauwe 2009; but see De Grauwe 2011). Under the dominant view, the ECB was responsible only for average price stability in the eurozone as a whole, whereas all adjustment problems of individual economies were to be dealt with by individual EMU member states.

At the onset of the financial crisis, the GIPS economies therefore found themselves in extremely vulnerable positions, defined by severe current-account deficits and seriously overvalued real exchange rates (figure 5.7). For countries with independent currencies this process could not have continued for long. Under fixed exchange rates, it would have been stopped by a balance-of-payments crisis, and, under flexible rates, devaluation would have raised the price of imports and restored the competitiveness of exports. In the Monetary Union, however, external constraints were eliminated. Foreign investors and creditors were no longer concerned about currency risks, and banks in surplus countries such as Germany were happy to reinvest export incomes in bonds and asset-based securities issued by Greek, Spanish or Irish banks. Hence the rapidly increasing deficits of current accounts were not corrected but financed through equally increasing capital flows from surplus to deficit economies in the eurozone. By the same token, of course, divergent real effective exchange rates were stabilized as well, with Germany benefiting from an increasingly undervalued currency and GIPS economies suffering from overvaluation.

Figure 5.5: Current account as a percentage of GDP

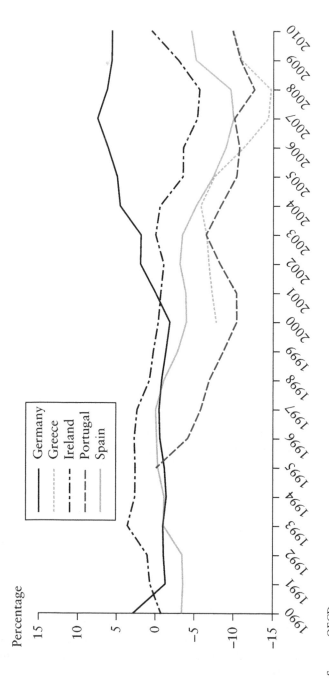

Figure 5.6: Total government budget deficit or surplus as a percentage of GDP

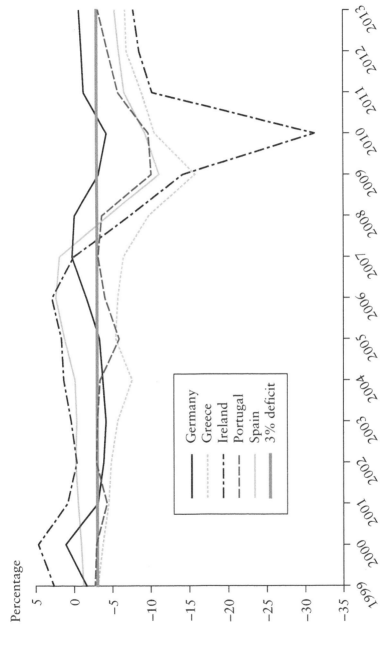

Source: Ameco database.

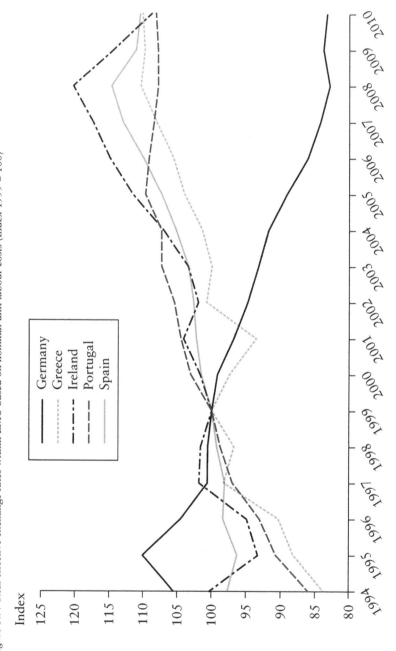

Figure 5.7: Real effective exchange rates within EMU based on nominal unit labour costs (Index 1999 = 100)

Source: eurostat.

What eventually mattered most was the increasing dependence on capital inflows and the rise of external – and mainly private[9] – indebtedness, which left GIPS economies extremely vulnerable to disturbances in international financial markets that might create credit squeezes. These vulnerabilities and the underlying imbalances of current accounts and real exchange rates were of no concern under the Stability Pact, which was supposed to deal only with excessive budget deficits. And while the pact should have been invoked against Greece, it was simply irrelevant for Spain and Ireland. Compared with Germany, their governments were models of fiscal probity, running budget surpluses in most years up to 2007 and reducing total public-sector debt far below the official target of 60 per cent of GDP (figure 5.8).

At the same time, the ECB also had seen no reason for alarm, as average eurozone inflation rates had remained within the limits to which ECB monetary policy was committed. And while all the GIPS economies had higher rates than Germany, they were not exorbitantly higher, and seemed not to accelerate. This may appear surprising, since the bursting of credit-financed real-estate bubbles in Ireland and Spain is now seen as a major cause of the present crises in these countries. But, technically, escalating real-estate and housing prices are defined as 'asset price infla-tion', which the ECB, like other central banks, will take into account only when the 'wealth effect' of such inflation is expected to increase consumer prices as well (Trichet 2005; De Grauwe 2009: 207–9).[10] And the rise of consumer prices in GIPS economies was effectively constrained not only by ECB policy but also by lower-priced imports.

5 From 2008 to 2011 and beyond: a sequence of three crises

How long the external imbalances in the eurozone could have contin-ued, and whether they could have been gradually corrected by market forces or would have ended in a crash, has become an academic issue. In the real world, the international financial crisis of 2008 triggered worldwide chain reactions which had the effect in the eurozone of trans-forming the vulnerability of deficit countries into a systemic crisis that is thought to challenge the viability of the Monetary Union itself. The much-researched story is far too complex to be retold here in any detail, but for present purposes a thumbnail sketch of three distinct but causally connected crises will suffice.

Initially, the direct impact of the American 'subprime mortgage crisis' and the Lehman bankruptcy was limited to European countries that had allowed their banks to invest heavily in 'toxic' American securities.

Figure 5.8: General government gross debt as a percentage of GDP

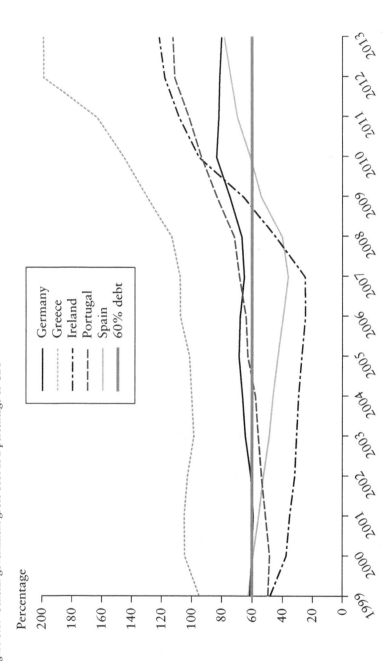

Source: Ameco database.

Apart from the UK, the main victims were Germany and Ireland, whereas banking regulations in Spain had effectively prevented Spanish banks from engaging in off-balance activities abroad. As a consequence, the budget deficits of countries that had to rescue 'system-relevant' private or public banks escalated above pre-crisis levels (figure 5.8).

The secondary impact of the international financial crisis was a dramatic credit squeeze in the real economy, as banks had to write off insecure assets on their balance sheets while mutual distrust brought interbank lending to a halt. As a consequence, economic activity declined, unemployment increased, and governments had to accept a steep decline in tax revenues and an equally steep rise in expenditures on unemployment and on the protection of existing jobs. Obviously, however, the impact of the credit squeeze was hardest in GIPS economies, which depended most on the availability of cheap credit and massive capital inflows. In Ireland and Spain, moreover, the real-estate bubble had burst under the impact of the recession, and mortgage defaults created a secondary banking crisis in which governments had to rescue even more financial institutions. The result was an even more dramatic rise in public-sector deficits and debt ratios even in countries such as Spain and Ireland, both of whose indebtedness had been far below the eurozone average. Ironically, therefore, they had to become deeply indebted to domestic and foreign banks in order to save their own banks.

In the process, a third crisis began as international rating agencies and investors ceased to be satisfied with the elimination of currency risks and finally began to worry about the sustainability of public-sector indebtedness – in particular for those countries whose current-account deficits suggested economic weaknesses that might also affect the government's capacity to meet financial commitments. As this happened, the price of outstanding bonds declined, refinancing as well as the placement of new issues became difficult, and the convergence of nominal interest rates to German levels came to an end. As a consequence, after 2008 the risk premiums on sovereign debt diverged again and rose to practically prohibitive levels in some of the GIPS countries (figure 5.9).

The spectre of 'sovereign default' arose first in Greece, which, unlike Spain and Ireland, had continually increased its public-sector debt even during the high-growth years following its accession to the eurozone in 2001. At the same time, moreover, by 2008 the Greek current account had reached a record deficit of –15 per cent of GDP. Outside of the Monetary Union, such deficits would have provoked a currency crisis because financial markets would challenge the state's capacity to maintain an unrealistic exchange rate. Inside the EMU, however, the same current-account deficits did provoke challenges to the state's capacity to serve its accumulated debt.

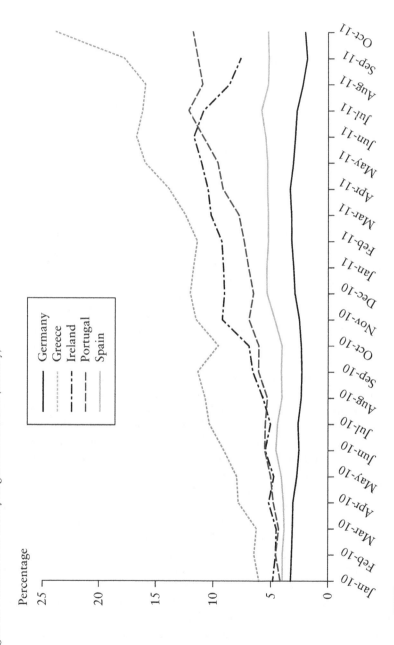

Figure 5.9: Interest rates of ten-year government bonds (monthly)

Percentage

Germany
Greece
Ireland
Portugal
Spain

Source: OECD.

Initially, the German and other EMU governments would have liked to invoke the treaty's no-bailout clause (Article 125 TFEU), leaving the Greeks to cope with their problems on their own. But Germany and the others came to realize that the integration of European capital markets had turned the clause into a trap: if the governments allowed Greek insolvency, the outcome could be another banking crisis in France, Germany and other countries whose banks were heavily invested in Greek government bonds. Hence even Germany agreed reluctantly to create a common 'Stability Mechanism' that would allow the Greek government to obtain credit at reduced rates. This mechanism was followed by increasingly extensive financial commitments by EMU member states to the present European Financial Stability Fund (EFSF), whose protection was soon extended to Ireland and Portugal and is now considered for Spain and Italy.

Unfortunately, however, these commitments were and still are shaped by the perception that the euro crisis was caused by irresponsible GIPS governments recklessly raising public-sector debt (debt which, incidentally, is still lower in Spain than in Germany) – rather than by current-account deficits and the underlying structural deficiencies of the Monetary Union. Hence the 'rescue' guarantees and credits come with stringent 'conditionalities' requiring massive expenditure cutbacks and tax increases in order to reduce budget deficits. But, as expected, massive fiscal retrenchment in a recession depresses economic activity further, increases unemployment (figure 5.3) and reduces public revenues even more. The consequence so far has been a continual escalation of financial-market challenges to the solvency of EMU states, followed by further retrenchment and further increasing demands on the rescue funds that were meant to stave off insolvency threats confronting ever more EMU states.

6 Beyond the rescue operations: options for a viable EMU?

When the financial markets crisis turned into a sovereign debt crisis, Greece and other deficit states might have left the Monetary Union to re-establish the international viability of their economies through devaluation. GIPS governments rejected the option because the transition would have been painful and fraught with technical difficulties. The Commission, the ECB and the governments of surplus countries came to the same conclusion for reasons of their own, which, not necessarily in the order of their importance, could be listed as follows: (1) if Greece left the EMU, it would be seen as a major setback for European integration; (2) a departure by Greece would encourage speculative attacks on other EMU member states; (3) bankruptcies of GIPS states would entail heavy losses for banks in surplus countries and for the ECB; and (4) the expected revaluation of the euro would hurt export industries in Germany and other surplus economies that had been benefiting from an undervalued real exchange rate. In early 2010, the lesser evil clearly seemed to be to ignore the no-bailout clause of the treaty and initiate a rescue-cum-retrenchment programme for Greece.

6.1 Two crucial challenges to economic recovery within the EMU

Thus all present debates are about how to solve the GIPS crises in the context of a continuing Monetary Union. But, in order to evaluate their chances of success, one needs to be clear about the challenges. As I have tried to show, the euro crisis was caused by structural deficiencies of the Monetary Union, and it can only be resolved if two crucial problems of GIPS economies are overcome. By the same token, structural reforms of the Monetary Union will only be effective if they are able to prevent the recurrence of these problems, whose nature can be summarized in three diagrams describing the basic obstacles to the recovery of GIPS economies. The first illustrates the continuing discrepancy of current accounts (figure 5.5), the second represents the imbalance of real effective exchange rates (figure 5.7) and the third documents the recent divergence of real interest rates (figure 5.10). When considered together, they point to two crucial challenges.

6.1.1 The challenge of lost competitiveness

The persistence of current-account deficits implies the continuing dependence of GIPS economies on capital imports. In order to overcome the vulnerability of these economies to the vagaries of international capital markets, imports must be reduced and exports increased. The gaps have narrowed in recent years because the recession, which was deepened by massive fiscal retrenchment, has greatly reduced consumer demand, including the demand for imports. But, unless export competitiveness is increased as well, reducing import demand will only reflect the deepening economic crisis. The lack of competitiveness is reflected by the imbalance of real effective exchange rates (figure 5.7). It implies that German exports are subsidized by an undervaluation of about 10 per cent, whereas GIPS exports are penalized by a similar overvaluation.

Since the decision to maintain the Monetary Union rules out any adjustment of nominal exchange rates, these imbalances can only be overcome through real revaluations – meaning that wages and prices should rise in Germany and fall in GIPS economies. In fact, the current crisis has

Figure 5.10: Real long-term interest rates (monthly)

Percentage

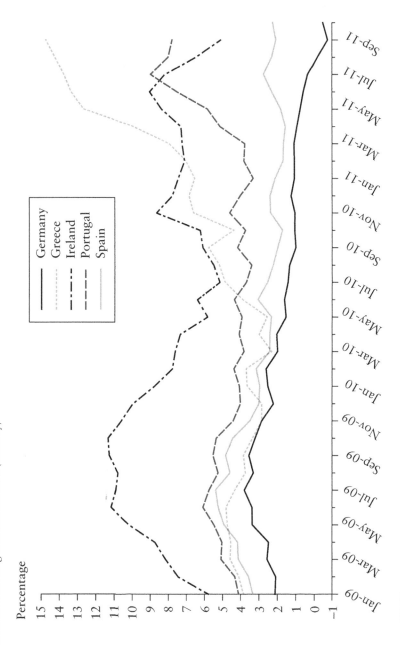

Source: OECD.

already narrowed the huge gap in unit labour costs that existed in 2009 (figure 5.4). But much more progress will be needed, and in GIPS countries this will require not only the further reduction of nominal wages in the export-oriented sectors but also productivity-increasing private and public investment. But directly to reduce nominal wages in the private sector is beyond the powers of governments in most constitutional democracies. And private-sector investment is unlikely to increase as long as the economy remains depressed and non-competitive. At the same time, public investments in R&D, education and training, and production-related infrastructure are severely constrained by the requirements of fiscal retrenchment. But this is not the only obstacle to economic recovery.

6.1.2 The challenge of counterproductive real interest rates
In the early years of the Monetary Union, the German economy was depressed by high real interest rates, and domestic growth in the GIPS economies was fuelled by very low or even negative rates (figure 5.2). After the international financial crisis, however, the impact of monetary impulses was reversed – but it is again economically counterproductive (figure 5.9). The strong German economy is now benefiting not only from an undervalued real exchange rate but also from very low or even negative real interest rates, whereas GIPS economies are struggling with extremely high real interest rates that must deter private investment and depress private consumption. And even if euro bonds or an ECB bazooka were to stop the debt crisis, they would reduce interest rates only for the state, not for private investors. Interest-rate subsidies for private investments could help – if they could be financed under conditions of fiscal retrenchment and were allowable under EU competition rules. What would really make a difference would be monetary expansion targeted to GIPS economies – but the ECB remains firmly oriented towards average conditions in the eurozone and does not even consider the possibility of differentiated monetary policy to accommodate the needs of different member economies (Stark 2011).

These are extremely difficult challenges to deal with at the national level, and it is obvious that GIPS governments, acting under the pressure of financial markets as well as under the economic constraints of the Monetary Union and the political constraints of national democratic accountability, have not been able to cope successfully. As a consequence of their loss of output legitimacy (and in the absence of convincing 'communicative discourses' (Schmidt 2006, 2012) that might have generated input legitimacy), governments of the day have lost their political support in Ireland, Portugal, Greece, Italy and Spain, and have been replaced not by the opposition but by non-political 'expert' governments that do not claim input-oriented democratic legitimacy in Greece or Italy. The question is whether European interventions did, or could have done, any better.

6.2 European responses to the GIPS crises

European responses were aimed initially at preventing the sovereign default of Greece, Ireland and Portugal through loan guarantees, credits and ECB interventions that would reduce the interest rates at which GIPS governments could obtain new credit. But even though these 'rescue' operations achieved their immediate goal, they have not yet succeeded in restoring the 'confidence' of capital markets. Risk premiums on government bonds remain extremely high (figure 5.9), and vulnerability is spreading as rating agencies and speculative attacks have begun to question the solvency of other EMU member states and the adequacy of presently available rescue funds. Beyond satisfying the immediate credit needs of GIPS governments, therefore, the rescue programmes should also create a guarantee mechanism that would deter future speculative attacks testing the solvency of all EMU member states. How this is to be achieved is still controversial at the time of writing (December 2011). But at least outside of Germany, it is widely believed that success would be possible if Berlin gave up its veto against euro bonds or allowed the ECB to act as 'lender of last resort' for EMU member states as well as for European banks.

In contrast to conflicts over the nature and size of rescue mechanisms, the conditions under which GIPS governments could ask for credit support seem to have raised hardly any controversies at the summit level. The summit's primary instruments are quarterly 'Memorandums of Understanding', which, under the authority of the Euro group of the ECOFIN Council, are defined by the Commission and supervised by a 'Troika' of agents of the IMF, the ECB and the Commission. Ostensibly intended to reduce the credit needs of GIPS governments, their primary focus has been on rigorous fiscal retrenchment through cuts in welfare spending, public-sector employment, wages and pensions, as well as through VAT increases and the privatization of public assets. In the meantime, however, it is obvious that, at least in the short term, these measures have done nothing to reduce the dependence of debtor states on foreign credit: fiscal retrenchment and the loss of mass incomes deepened the recession of GIPS economies, which then reduced public-sector revenues and increased public-sector debt (figure 5.8).

As this effect must have been foreseen by economists at the Commission, one must presume that the conditions were guided by a longer-term perspective on economic recovery. And, indeed, the memorandums did go far beyond obviously deficit-related requirements to include a wide range of institutional changes in public administration, taxation, banking regulation, social policy, health-care systems, industrial relations and the regulated professions. They generally seek to increase the market flexibility of wages and prices, to reduce reservation wages, and to reduce the bureaucratic burdens on the private sector. In effect, since nominal devaluation is ruled out by the commitment to maintain the Monetary Union, the conditions imposed seem to deal with overvalued real exchange rates by promoting a real devaluation of GIPS economies solely through the combination of supply-side reforms and real wage decline that allowed Germany to escape its recession after 2005.

But, of course, the differences between GIPS economies in 2010–11 and Germany in 2004–5 are enormous. Unemployment is very much higher (figure 5.3), and domestic consumer and investment demand is depressed by real interest rates that are in some cases three or five times higher than they were in Germany during its recession (figure 5.10). Also, current accounts are in deficit whereas Germany had already been achieving surpluses (figure 5.5). And real effective exchange rates are so highly overvalued (figure 5.7) that drastic cuts of nominal wages, rather than mere union wage restraint, would be needed to achieve international competitiveness. Moreover, Germany had a strong industrial base that was well inserted in world markets and thus could benefit immediately from any reduction in production costs. With the possible exceptions of Ireland, Northern Italy, Catalonia and the Basque region, this is not true of the economies that are presently in trouble.

In short, it seems quite unlikely that the supply-side strategies that succeeded in Germany[11] over a period of three or four years will generally be able to restore the viability of GIPS economies within the foreseeable future. If this is borne out, the prospect will be one of long periods of economic stagnation, persistent mass unemployment, and rising inequality and poverty in the southern member states of the Union.

7 Longer-term institutional reforms

Looking beyond rescue operations, European policy-makers have recently also focused on institutional reforms establishing a form of *gouvernement économique* that is supposed to prevent future crises of the euro. So far, these efforts have produced a 'six-pack' of regulations and directives, establishing a revised 'Excessive Deficit Procedure' under Article 126 and a new 'Excessive Imbalance Procedure' under Article 121 of the TFEU.[12] While these were adopted by the ECOFIN Council and the European Parliament in October 2011 and came into force in

December, the euro area heads of state or government found it useful to add a new Fiscal Compact at the European Summit of 9 December 2011.

The 'Excessive Deficit Procedure' (EDP) represents a tougher version of the Stability Pact, with greater emphasis on the rapid and continuous reduction of total public-sector debt. It emphasizes the preventive and corrective supervision of national budgeting processes by the Commission and is characterized by earlier scrutiny, economic analyses, recommendations, and sanctions for non-compliance, and ultimately by more severe fines that will become effective as proposed by the Commission – unless the proposal is rejected by a qualified majority in the Council. Though these rules are meant to be tough, they apparently were still too soft in the eyes of governments in Berlin and Paris, who pushed for a treaty revision.[13] Since the UK government would not agree, however, the German and French governments were able to obtain only the commitment to a Fiscal Compact in the form of an international agreement that would run parallel to the EU Treaty. The main innovations of the compact will be the application of the reverse qualified majority vote (QMV) rule to all decisions once the Commission has determined a breach of the 3 per cent deficit ceiling, and the commitment of EMU governments to introduce balanced-budget requirements in their national constitutions.

Like the old Stability Pact, both the EDP and the Fiscal Compact are based on the belief that the present euro crisis was caused by excessive budget deficits and rising public-sector debt, that it could have been prevented if existing rules had been enforced, and that future crises may be averted by more stringent constraints on fiscal policy and more effective sanctions. On the basis of my analysis presented above, this view misreads the past and underestimates the difficulty of present problems – and the Excessive Imbalance Procedure (EIP) demonstrates that at least the Commission has come to have similar doubts.

The EIP recognizes that imbalances of current accounts and other macro-economic aggregates were proximate causes of the crisis, and that these must be corrected and prevented in order to ensure the 'proper and smooth functioning of the economic and monetary union'.[14] The main instrument of the procedure will be a 'scoreboard' of internal and external macro-economic imbalances, complete with 'indicators' and upper and lower 'alert thresholds'.[15] Based on statistical data and its own economic judgement, the Commission will identify member states 'deemed at risk of imbalance', followed by 'country-specific in-depth reviews', 'preventive recommendations' and, in the event of 'excessive imbalances', Council recommendations of corrective action, with deadlines attached and with compliance to be monitored by the Commission. If governments fail to comply, the Commission may again propose fines that the Council can oppose only through qualified majority vote.

Quite apart from the reverse QMV rule, the legal implications of the EIP appear remarkable for a number of reasons. First, in contrast to the rule-based approach of the Maastricht Treaty and the Stability Pact, the EIP will establish a broadly discretionary regime of supranational economic supervision and management that must depend on disputable hypotheses regarding the causal relevance of specific indicators for economic performance and the critical significance of upper and lower thresholds.[16] Practically all the indicators suggested refer to economic conditions that, unlike public-sector budgets, are not under the direct control of national governments. Moreover, the use of policy instruments that might be used to achieve an indirect influence over wages, labour productivity, private savings or consumer credit is tightly constrained by European guarantees of economic liberties and competition law.

In any case, however, the policies that might have a *de facto* influence on imbalances are by no means limited to those that are included *de jure* in the EU's portfolio of delegated powers. But, just as was true of the Troika's memorandums of understanding, the exercise of these powers is nevertheless to be controlled by the Commission's sanction-clad 'recommendations'. Thus Regulation (EU) no. 1176/2011 provides explicitly (at §120) that these '*recommendations . . . should be addressed to the Member State concerned to provide guidance on appropriate policy responses. The policy response of the Member state . . . should use all available policy instruments under the control of public authorities.*' And, if compliance should be deficient, the Commission may define sanctions that could then be stopped only by reverse QMV in the Council. In other words, the fine-tuned allocation of European and national competence achieved after long negotiations in the Lisbon Treaty will no longer play a role once the Excessive Imbalance Procedure has been initiated. In effect, this amounts to a constitutional revolution. And it seems even more remarkable that this policy change was adopted in the form of Council regulations (which need not be transposed by national parliaments) without significant public debate by a unanimous ECOFIN Council and with the full support of the European Parliament (which tried hard to automate sanctions even further).

8 EMU economic governance reforms: effective and legitimate?

Let us assume that the euro will survive because rescue guarantees will somehow succeed in deterring further speculative attacks on the bonds of eurozone states. As a consequence, the high risk premiums on GIPS government bonds may come down and the conditionalities attached to rescue credits could be phased out. Nevertheless, the eurozone would still be a non-optimal currency area. Germany and a few other countries would still benefit from undervalued real exchange rates, whereas GIPS economies would still be struggling with an economic decline that would be reinforced by high real interest rates and overvalued real exchange rates. Under these conditions, how would the structural reforms presently adopted affect the future economic fates of EMU member states and the legitimacy of economic governance in the eurozone?

8.1 Effectiveness

At the outset, it needs to be understood that present reforms do not envisage the creation of central-level European remedies for the plight of EMU member states. First, these reforms do not address the causal effect of unitary monetary policy on macro-economic imbalances in a non-optimal currency area, and they do not even discuss the possibility of targeting some of the ECB's policy instruments to the specific problems of individual economies. Second, they also ignore the crucial role of central-government fiscal policy in dealing with economic heterogeneity in a non-optimal currency area. In large economies, such as the United States, the large national budget and the territorial impact of tax revenues and expenditures will automatically generate large fiscal transfers between prosperous and stagnant regions (Feldstein 1997). Within Germany, of course, explicit programmes of fiscal equalization are even more effective. In the eurozone, however, the minute size of the EU budget rules out the possibility of automatic fiscal compensation, and the new Fiscal Compact launched at the Summit of 9 December 2011 carefully excludes all references to the possibility of horizontal fiscal transfers among EMU member states.

In other words, there will be neither monetary nor fiscal relief from the European level for the distortions generated by the European Monetary Union. Any problems arising in national economies must be coped with by national governments with the policy instruments and the resources that happen to remain available at the national level. The only contribution that European authorities will make under the EDP, EIP and Fiscal Compact reforms is to dictate how national governments should employ these instruments – and to impose sanctions for non-compliance.

Instead of providing *centralized* European solutions, present reforms envisage a radical extension of *hierarchical* European controls over national policy choices. There is also no suggestion that the legal prohibitions constraining national solutions might be relaxed. Thus European internal-market and competition rules will continue to eliminate all options that would restrain imports, subsidize exports or restrain unfettered capital mobility. In theory, therefore, European intervention will not enlarge the space for solutions available at the national level.

Moreover, given the variety and contingency of economic, social and institutional conditions in seventeen EMU member states, it would be difficult to argue that European interventions could benefit from comparative cognitive advantages. Commission experts could not draw on more valid information or better expertise than national governments when it comes to designing and evaluating policy options that might have a chance of succeeding under specific national conditions. Thus the only advantage that the policies defined by the Commission and the quasi-automatic sanctions imposed under Council authority will have over autonomous national policy choices is their capacity to disable national democratic processes[17] that might undermine the political feasibility of real-devaluation and supply-side policies in view of their disastrous impact on unemployment, poverty and social inequality.

8.2 Legitimacy

If such capacity is realized, the policies imposed under the regime of the EDP, the EIP and the new Fiscal Compact will lack input-oriented democratic legitimacy at the national level.[18] And, even though claims to output-oriented legitimacy – implying problem-solving effectiveness and justice of outcomes – cannot yet be empirically evaluated, it would take very brave governments to bet on their vindication for subsequent elections.

At the European level, however, the EDP and the EIP regulations were adopted with the agreement of the ECOFIN Council and the European Parliament; the Fiscal Pact needs to be ratified by parliaments or through referendums in all participating states, and the sanctions imposed will be formally attributed to Council decisions. So the regimes themselves are supported by intergovernmental agreements and by majority votes in the European Parliament. But would that suffice to ensure the legitimacy of the policies adopted? In discussions about the legitimacy of European policy choices, the indirect link to the unanimous agreement of politically accountable governments has long been considered sufficient. This argument was obviously weakened with the move from intergovernmental unanimity to qualified majority voting in the Council, and with the increasing role of supranational agents lacking political accountability. Nevertheless, broad consensus in the Council is still seen as an important legitimating argument in support of European legislation adopted by the 'Community method'. By its own logic, however, this argument cannot be invoked to claim indirect democratic legitimacy for decisions adopted in the Excessive Deficit and the Excessive Imbalance procedures. An obvious reason is the decision rule of reverse QMV, which empowers the Commission or a small blocking minority of governments to impose sanctions – a process that is obviously meant to eliminate consensual intergovernmental control over policies designed by the Commission. But the problem is more fundamental.

Democracy is about collective self-government – common rules by which we, acting as a collectivity, agree to be jointly bound. By the same logic, intergovernmental agreements may legitimate common rules serving national interests that cannot be realized nationally. But establishing a common rule is not the same as establishing a discretionary authority with sanctioning powers whose application cannot be controlled by the governments that have created it. Even if the rule-based original Stability Pact might have been acceptable, the EIP goes beyond the pale: its economic logic dictates that it must operate without any predefined rules and that the Commission's ad hoc decisions must apply to individual member states in unique circumstances rather than to EMU states in general. Regardless of the comparative quality of its economic expertise, the Commission lacks legitimate authority to impose highly intrusive policy choices on member states – choices that are fundamentally controversial and have massively unequal distributive impacts (Majone 1996, 2009).

But even if such decisions were adopted in the Council (without the participation of the states affected) they would not achieve democratic legitimacy. The chain of delegation merely authorizes governments to speak for their own constituencies. These may accept sacrifices of their own in the name of European solidarity or of a normative commitment to the 'inclusion of the other'. But individual governments have no democratic mandate for ad hoc decisions that would impose sacrifices and punitive sanctions on the governments and citizens of other member states – under conditions, *nota bene*, where the citizens of the affected state have no possibility of holding these other governments accountable for the policies they are made to suffer. In other words, intergovernmental input legitimacy would not support the policy choices imposed by EDP and EIP processes under Council authority. And this conclusion would not change if the European Parliament (EP) had its way and were also involved in the process.

The EP has continually increased its powers in the legislative process, and its deliberations and effective bargaining strategies have generally helped to improve the substantive quality of European legislation. But EP elections do not provide a political link between citizens and European policy choices. And, unlike national governments, policy-makers at the

European level have no reason to anticipate the possibility of electoral sanctions should their policies violate highly salient popular interests. And, worse still, if European policy choices were in fact politicized in EP elections, the highly salient national interests of deficit and surplus countries would be mobilized against each other, effectively destroying the legitimacy of majority votes in the EP.

In other words, the present set of European policy responses to the euro crisis lacks democratic input legitimacy. It must be seen as a gamble on achieving output legitimacy over the medium term. On the basis of the analyses presented here, that appears to be a long shot. If it should fail, the legitimacy of the European Union is likely to suffer, and the sense of a common European interest that has developed over many decades may be severely damaged.

References

Baccaro, L., and Simoni, M. (2010) Organizational determinants of wage moderation, *World Politics* 62(4): 594–635.

Calmfors, L. (2001) *Wages and Wage Bargaining Institutions in the EMU: A Survey of the Issues*, CESifo Working Paper no. 520. Munich: CESifo.

De Grauwe, P. (2009) *Economics of Monetary Union*. 8th edn, Oxford: Oxford University Press.

De Grauwe, P. (2011) *The Governance of a Fragile Eurozone*. Leuven: University of Leuven; available at: www.econ.kuleuven.be/ew/academic/intecon/Degrauwe/PDG-papers/Discussion_papers/Governance-fragile-eurozone_s.pdf (accessed 1 March 2012).

Delors, J. (1989) *Report on Economic and Monetary Union in the European Community*. Brussels: Committee for the Study of Economic and Monetary Union.

Dyson, K., and Featherstone, K. (1999) *The Road to Maastricht: Negotiating Economic and Monetary Union*. Oxford: Oxford University Press.

Eichengreen, B. (1990) *Is Europe an Optimum Currency Area?*, CEPR Discussion Paper 478. London: Centre for Economic Policy Research.

Eichengreen, B., and Frieden, J. (eds) (1994) *The Political Economy of European Monetary Unification*. Boulder, CO: Westview Press.

Enderlein, H. (2004) *Nationale Wirtschaftspolitik in der europäischen Währungsunion*. Frankfurt am Main: Campus.

Feldstein, M. (1997) *The Political Economy of the European Economic and Monetary Union: Political Sources of an Economic Liability*, Working Paper 6150. Cambridge, MA: National Bureau of Economic Research.

Fischer-Lescano, A., and Kommer, S. (2011) *Verstärkte Zusammenarbeit in der EU: Ein Modell für Kooperationsfortschritte in der Wirtschafts- und Sozialpolitik?* Berlin: Friedrich-Ebert-Stiftung.

Fitz Gerald, J. (2006) *The Experience of Monetary Union – Ireland and Spain*, ESRI Working Paper. Dublin: Economic and Social Research Institute.

Flassbeck, H. (2010) *Die Marktwirtschaft des 21. Jahrhunderts*. Frankfurt am Main: Westend.

Funke, M. (1997) The nature of shocks in Europe and in Germany, *Economica* 64: 461–9.

Giegold, S. (2011) *Umsetzung des Economic Governance-Pakets: Präsident des EU-Parlaments weist Kommission und Bundesregierung in die Schranken*, 16 November 16; available at: www.sven-giegold.de/2011/prasident-des-europarlaments-weist-kommission-und-bundesregierung-bei-umsetzung-der-economic-governance-in-die-schranken (accessed 29 February 2012).

Häde, U. (2011) Art. 136 AEUV – eine neue Generalklausel für die Wirtschafts- und Währungsunion?, *Juristenzeitung* 66(7): 333–40.

Heipertz, M., and Verdun, A. (2010) *Ruling Europe: The Politics of the Stability and Growth Pact*. Cambridge: Cambridge University Press.

Issing, O. (2002) On macroeconomic policy co-ordination in EMU, *Journal of Common Market Studies* 40(2): 345–58.

Johnson, H. G. (1971) The Keynesian revolution and the monetarist counter revolution, *American Economic Review* 61(2): 91–106.

Jones, E. (2002) *The Politics of Economic and Monetary Union: Integration and Idiosyncracy*. Lanham, MD: Rowman & Littlefield.

Lane, P. R. (2006) The real effects of Monetary Union, *Journal of Economic Perspectives* 20(4): 47–66.

McKinnon, R. I. (1963) Optimum currency areas, *American Economic Review* 53(4): 717–25.

McNamara, K. R. (1998) *The Currency of Ideas: Monetary Politics in the European Union*. Ithaca, NY: Cornell University Press.

Majone, G. (1996) *Regulating Europe*. London: Routledge.

Majone, G. (2009) *Europe as a Would-Be World Power*. Cambridge: Cambridge University Press.

Marsh, D. (2011) *The Euro: The Battle for the New Global Currency*. New edn, New Haven, CT: Yale University Press.

Mundell, R. A. (1961) A theory of optimal currency areas, *American Economic Review* 51(4): 657–65.

OECD (Organization for Economic Cooperation and Development) (2008) Country note Germany (in German): Deutschland. *Growing Unequal? Income Distribution and Poverty in OECD countries*. Paris: OECD; available at: www.oecd.org/dataoecd/45/27/41525386.pdf (accessed 29 February 2012).

Ohler, C. (2010) Die zweite Reform des Stabilitäts- und Wachstumspaktes, *Zeitschrift für Gesetzgebung* 25(4): 330–45.

Scharpf, F. W. (1991) *Crisis and Choice in European Social Democracy*. Ithaca, NY: Cornell University Press.

Scharpf, F. W. (1999) *Governing in Europe: Effective and Democratic?* Oxford: Oxford University Press.

Schmidt, V. A. (2006) *Democracy in Europe: The EU and National Politics*. Oxford: Oxford University Press.

Schmidt, V. A. (2012) Democracy and legitimacy in the European Union revisited: input, output *and* throughput, *Political Studies*; available at: http://dx.doi.org/10.1111/j.1467-9248.2012.00962.x.

Sinn, H.-W., Widgrén, M., and Köthenbürger, M. (eds) (2004) *European Monetary Integration*. Cambridge, MA: MIT Press.

Spethmann, D., and Steiger, O. (2005) Deutschlands Wirtschaft, seine Schulden und die Unzulänglichkeiten der einheitlichen Geldpolitik im Eurosystem, in D. Ehrig and U. Staroske (eds), *Dimensionen angewandter Wirtschaftsforschung: Methoden, Regionen, Sektoren: Festschrift für Heinz Schäfer zum 65. Geburtstag*. Hamburg: Verlag Dr. Kovac, pp. 255–85.

Stark, J. (2011) Staatsschuld und Geldpolitik: Lehren aus der globalen Finanzkrise, lecture, Munich, 20 June; available at: www.ecb.int/press/key/date/2011/html/sp110620.de.html (accessed 1 March 2012).

Trampusch, C. (2009) *Der erschöpfte Sozialstaat: Transformation eines Politikfeldes*. Frankfurt am Main: Campus.

Trichet, J.-C. (2005) Asset price bubbles and monetary policy, lecture by the president of the European Central Bank at the Monetary Authority of Singapore, 8 June; available at: www.bis.org/review/r050614d.pdf (accessed 1 March 2012).

Vaubel, R. (2010) The euro and the German veto, *Econ Journal Watch* 7(1): 82–90.

Von Hagen, J., and Neumann, M. J. M. (1994) Real exchange rates within and between currency areas: how far away is EMU?, *Review of Economics and Statistics* 76(2): 236–44.

Willett, T. D., Permpoon, O., and Wihlborg, C. (2010) Endogenous OCA analysis and the early euro experience, *World Economy* 33(7): 851–72.

6

Smaghi versus the Parties: Representative Government and Institutional Constraints[1]

Peter Mair

1 Introduction

My focus in this chapter is on the problems facing the good functioning of representative government in contemporary parliamentary democracies. In brief, I argue that these systems are characterized by a sharply growing tension between the demands of representation, on the one hand, and the demands of government, on the other – or, as I put it in an earlier version of this essay, between the demands of responsiveness and the demands of responsibility.[2] Although tensions such as these have always existed in one form or another in most democracies, I argue that they have become substantially more acute in the past two decades. There are a variety of reasons for this, and these are summarized later in the chapter. In addition, and for a variety of other reasons, I argue that contemporary governments are finding it more and more difficult to manage this tension: not only is there a growing gap between representation and government, but the capacity of political actors to bridge that gap is itself diminishing.

I focus on parliamentary democracies for two reasons. First, I assume that the problems discussed here are more acute in systems where party government tends to prevail and where executive and legislative powers are fused. In systems where these powers are separated, there is less pressure on the executive to manage government in a manner that is both representative and responsible. It is not that the executive in these systems can afford to ignore representative demands – that is clearly impossible – it is simply that elsewhere in the institutions there are other actors, those working within the legislative arena, that are independent of the executive and that can afford to give priority to representative claims. This inevitably reduces the representative pressure on the executive. In other words, the executive is more likely to be willing to act responsibly in the knowledge that political representation is also being looked after elsewhere in the system. This is obviously more easily managed in systems with a non-elected executive, as in the European Union political system, than with an elected executive, as in the US. Nonetheless, in both systems the executive is clearly less constrained by the tension between representation and responsibility than in a parliamentary system, where the executive, usually in the form of a party government, must also represent the people, and where no other institution is sufficiently independent to take up that latter role (indeed, in most parliamentary systems, the executive also more or less dominates the legislature, thereby further undermining its functional autonomy).

The second reason for the focus on parliamentary regimes is because, as Müller and his colleagues (2003: 20) emphasize, these are regimes which, within the terms of principal–agent theory, epitomize a clear and singular 'chain of delegation':

> The ideal-typical parliamentary democracy thus features an indirect chain of command, in which at each stage a single principal delegates to only one agent (or several non-competing ones), and where each agent is accountable to one and only one principal. Thus, indirectness and singularity set parliamentarism apart from other constitutional designs, such as presidentialism.

The distinctiveness of parliamentary systems in this regard is also emphasized by Neto and Strøm (2006: 632):

> Different constitutions imply different regimes of delegation and accountability – different ways in which political principals select agents, transfer authority to them and subsequently hold them to account. In the parliamentary chain of delegation, voters delegate to individual members of parliament, members of parliament to parliamentary majorities, parliamentary majorities to a prime minister, a prime minister to policy makers in the cabinet and cabinet ministers to civil servants. Parliamentary democracy thus means a long and indirect chain of delegation, in which few political agents are selected directly by the citizens.

In this chapter, I contend that the parliamentary chain of delegation faces increasing difficulty in functioning in the ideal-typical way that Müller, Strøm and their colleagues have sketched. There are two problems here. In the first place, the earliest and most important link in the chain – that connecting voters to their elected representatives – is becoming more and more problematic, in that elected representatives – or at least their organizations – appear to be less willing or able to respond to the voice of the ordinary voter, and in that this voice itself has become increasingly inchoate and inaudible. Or, while audible, it is less easily tuned in and – as parties might put it – less easily aggregated. I come back to this issue later on. Since every chain is only as strong as its weakest link, the problem for the parliamentary chain of delegation is made even more acute by virtue of the weakest link also being the earliest.

The second problem, as the Irish case below shows all too clearly, is that the chain is no longer very singular. That is, while each prior principal in the chain – the voters, the members of Parliament, the majority, the prime minister, etc. – clearly seeks to delegate to the subsequent agent, and while each agent is also theoretically accountable to the prior principal, these are not the only actors involved. Rather, agents at all stages in the chain, but particularly at the executive level – both the political and the administrative executive – are also subject to increasing pressure and demands from outside the formal chain itself. These may come from lobbyists and special interests, to whom some agents also feel obliged to listen, and who are often deemed by these agents to have legitimate authority; or, more importantly, they may come from other institutions or supranational or international bodies that have a right to be heard and, indeed, the authority to insist. Even beyond those directly engaged in the chain of delegation itself, there are therefore many other competing principals that intervene along the way and that might seek to divert the agents in a different direction than that intended by their immediately prior principals in the chain. Indeed, the agents may sometimes even be persuaded that they owe a greater duty of accountability to these 'external' principals than to their own domestic principals (e.g., Börzel and Risse 2000; Papadopoulos 2010: 1034–6). If instead of the metaphor of the chain of delegation, we think of the process as similar to Newton's cradle – the executive toy made up of swinging balls that hit back and forth – then the external principals are like other balls that come in and hit from an obtuse angle, thereby disrupting and blocking the sequences of action (representation) and reaction (accountability).

This problem is typified very clearly by the Irish example, which I deal with extensively in section 2. Not only is the external pressure – the weight of the external principals – very evident in the Irish case, which is a small open economy in crisis, but there is also a strong tradition of localism in electoral politics, which keeps the elected representatives very close to their local constituencies and thereby 'frees up' the national policy-makers to pay more attention to their own preferences or those of others outside the chain.[3] Following the analysis of the Irish case, I then go on to outline the growing tension between representative and responsible government (section 3), and conclude with a discussion of the potential implications of the argument (section 4).

2 A story of Irish banking

'"Everything depends on everything else", a close political adviser to Dr. Merkel told The Irish Times' (Ó Caollaí 2011).

In the early morning of 30 September 2008, two weeks after the collapse of Lehman Brothers in New York and following a rapid haemorrhaging of funds from some of the major Irish banks, a group of leading Irish bankers met to discuss the crisis with a small number of senior politicians and civil servants, including the taoiseach (prime minister), the minister for finance, the attorney general, the governor of the Central Bank of Ireland and various officials. The immediate cause for concern was a run on a relatively new bank, the Anglo Irish Bank, which had engaged in reckless lending to property developers during the boom years of the Celtic Tiger, and which was now risking meltdown. Since the collapse of Lehman Brothers, the bank had been losing about €1 billion a day, and by late September it was facing a cash shortfall of €12 billion. According to Merrill Lynch, advisors to the government, the bank had exhausted its liquidity and faced an immediate funding deficit of €100 million. It no longer had the funds to meet its obligations and, despite frantic last-minute efforts by its senior officials, was unable to raise emergency funds from the other major banks in the system. In fact, these other banks were also in trouble, including the long-established Bank of Ireland and Allied Irish Banks (AIB). Both were losing major deposits on a daily basis and were facing a collapse in their share price. Two weeks after Lehman, it seemed that the entire Irish banking system was about to go under.

The response of the Irish government early that morning was to issue a guarantee, on behalf of the state, of the liabilities of all of the troubled banks, including those not directly represented at the actual meeting. The decision was taken at around 3 a.m. by the three politicians, all of whom belonged to the same leading party in the then coalition, and by their senior advisors. Other ministers were contacted by telephone and gave their approval. At 6 a.m. the decision was also communicated to the French finance minister, then chair of the EU finance ministers, and to the Luxembourg prime minister, then head of the eurozone member states. It was announced publicly at 6:45 a.m.[4] The total amount of the deposits and liabilities covered by the guarantee on the night it was issued was estimated at €334 billion, of which over €50 billion was required immediately or in immediate pledges. Ireland's GDP is roughly €160 billion. This was, as O'Toole (2010: 16) later put it, 'the most momentous political decision in the history of the state'.

There are a number of observations that can be drawn from this story, some of which are not necessarily relevant to this essay. In the first place, we can see that a political decision with fundamental and possibly very long-term consequences for the citizens of the polity can nevertheless be taken very quickly and perhaps even carelessly. The issue had been rumbling on for some time, and had become acute during the two weeks following Lehman. It reached crisis point on the night of 29–30 September, and the decision was effectively taken around 3 a.m., when those involved were clearly tired and stressed. In other words, within the space of a few hours, a decision was made that will clearly have serious repercussions on the finances of the state for decades to come. Moreover, as later became apparent, it was not a very well-informed decision. The banks had not been completely up front about their liabilities, and the guarantee was eventually to encompass a much larger sum than originally envisaged. It also involved the effective nationalization by the state of the main banks involved.

Second, in a majoritarian polity such as Ireland, we can see that a decision-making circle can actually be very small: in this case, just three senior politicians, including the prime minister and the finance minister, various senior government officials and a handful of top bankers. Third, although it shows that parties matter and make a difference – it was a group of party leaders who were responsible for this 'momentous political decision' – it does *not* show that party *differences* make a difference, which has always been the more interesting question for students of parties and public policy. In fact, at a special emergency debate in the Dáil held later on 30 September to ratify the guarantee, the government decision was supported not only by the main opposition party, Fine Gael, but also by one of the more important fringe populist parties, Sinn Féin. The only party opposing the decision was the small Labour Party, which was reluctant to commit to an open-ended guarantee. In the event, the government's proposal was accepted by a margin of 124 to 18, an encompassing consensus.

During the late 1990s and early 2000s, record Irish growth levels had followed from the huge expansion of inward investment, principally in the high-tech and pharmaceutical sectors, leading to what observers famously dubbed the 'Celtic Tiger'. Thereafter, as this particular engine of growth slowed, the boom was fuelled instead by an extraordinary property bubble, which in turn was built on massive private debt, including both the huge loans made by the Irish banks to various property companies and the host of smaller but still substantial loans to private home buyers. One consequence of the boom, in both its guises, was great buoyancy in government revenues and hence also a substantial reduction in sovereign debt. This, together with the exceptional growth levels, had left Ireland appearing to be one of the model citizens of the eurozone: by early 2008, national debt (sovereign debt) had been reduced to just €46 billion, representing one of the lowest ratios to GDP in the eurozone, while budget deficits were almost non-existent. The labour force had expanded dramatically, not least as a result of substantial inward migration from the new accession states, and there was virtually no unemployment. And while in other circumstances the combination of these positive indicators would have likely led to major domestic inflation, and did so in practice in Ireland, the monetary effects of this inflation were smothered by the euro.

All of this changed completely in September 2008. In taking over the liabilities of the banks, the government transformed what had been an enormous private debt into a sovereign debt, thereby doubling and potentially tripling the liabilities incurred by the state. A sovereign debt of some 40 per cent of GDP was doubled overnight – literally overnight – to close to 80 per cent, with a potential further stretch to up to 110 per cent or 120 per cent still to come. In addition, the need to pump so much money into so many banks in such a short space of time pushed what had been a small and sometimes non-existent budget deficit to an astonishing 32 per cent in 2010. Government revenues were also suffering in a more general sense. before the crash, the centre-right Fianna Fáil–Green coalition, encouraged by the opposition parties, had sought to burn the policy candle at both ends by increasing public spending at the same time as lowering taxes, making up the shortfall through commercial property taxes, stamp duty and other exceptional revenue sources that were mainly connected directly or indirectly to the property bubble. By late 2008, this circle could no longer be squared. By then, indeed, the former poster-boy of the eurozone had become effectively insolvent.[5]

The consequence is now well known: an emergency loan from the EU and the IMF, plus some indigenous Irish funds, totalling some €85 billion. Some of this was intended for the banks. Some was for the normal running costs incurred in governing the state, in that recourse to the normal bond market had become prohibitively expensive as a result of the doubling of the sovereign debt. Not all of the €85 billion needed to be drawn down immediately, but every tranche that is taken comes with an interest rate of 5.8 per cent, a figure which is generally seen as potentially crippling the Irish economy. Moreover, the government has also pledged to reduce its budget deficit down to 3 per cent by 2015 or

2016 – there may be some flexibility as far as this target date is concerned – which is seen to require the adoption of a very severe austerity programme. These, at least, are the very demanding terms that were agreed with the EU, the ECB and the IMF by the outgoing Fianna Fáil–Green government, and that were also approved in broad outline in a rushed procedure in the Dáil at the beginning of February 2011, with support from both Fine Gael and Labour (but with opposition from Sinn Féin).

2.1 Smaghi (and Chopra) versus the parties

But there are still some doubts about how demanding it will turn out to be in practice, and this brings me to the core of the chapter. Although the broad outline of the EU/IMF loan package has been agreed by all mainstream parties, including Fine Gael and Labour, who are expected to form a new coalition following the election called for 25 February, the precise terms are still considered up for negotiation.[6] The target date for reducing the deficit to 3 per cent is still somewhat open, for example, and all parties accept this. Flexibility regarding the interest rate is disputed, however. The outgoing Fianna Fáil–Green government claims the terms were the best available in the circumstances and cannot be changed. The opposition Fine Gael and Labour parties, on the other hand, claim that a more favourable rate was offered to Greece, and, although the parties have avoided concrete commitments, they both pledged on the eve of the election campaign that they would seek to renegotiate the 5.8 per cent figure.[7] In a special RTE *Prime Time* programme on the issue, broadcast on 27 January 2011, spokespersons from both parties suggested that they might try to lower the figure to closer to 3 per cent or 3.5 per cent.[8]

Although this was clearly an attractive election pledge, since it promised the possibility of being able to pull back from the most severe elements of the austerity programme, it also seemed unrealistic. Interviewed for the same RTE programme, Lorenzo Bini Smaghi, a member of the ECB executive board and the official in charge of European and international relations, flatly denied the possibility that the loan might be renegotiated:

> A government engages a country when it signs the agreement. It went through parliament [and] so the democratic process. So it doesn't happen that when you have a change in government the next government reneges on commitments. It enters of course into discussion of the implementation of the programme, but the programme is there, has been signed, and has to be implemented.

This view was echoed by Ajai Chopra, who had headed the IMF mission to Ireland, and who also viewed the agreement as committing the nation rather than the particular government and thereby viewed it as given. The following is extracted from the transcript of an interview from the IMF website:[9]

> QUESTIONER: The people who you've negotiated this agreement with, the current government, is very, very unlikely to be in power much beyond March of next year and the opposition parties have made it clear that they are not happy with the terms of this overall package . . .. How big a risk do you think it is that after the election, whenever that happens, the commitment to following through on these measures will wane and you'll be left going back in there to renegotiate?
>
> MR. CHOPRA: I think the key point to make over here is that this is a programme for Ireland and that this is a national response. The IMF has had experience of dealing with such situations where there is a change in government. What we need to do is look at the public record of what the parties have said, and here there is a copious public record. We've looked at the statements made by party leaders on their websites . . .. There is nothing that we've seen in terms of the public pronouncements by the opposition parties in terms of the approach to achieving the goals of fiscal and financial stability that would cause undue problems to achieving the overall goals of the programme.
>
> QUESTIONER: One additional question. Therefore do the opposition parties have any chance of renegotiating the overall rate?
>
> MR. CHOPRA: For the IMF, no. This is the rate that is applied to all member countries.

Since these discussions and negotiations are very current at the time of writing, it is obviously impossible to predict what will happen under any new government that is likely to take office in March. Moreover, although general grandstanding on the issue on the part of the opposition parties is easily documented, both Fine Gael and Labour are being very careful not to make specific and hence potentially accountable pledges. Nonetheless, by entering an election and competing against the outgoing governing parties, they were both clearly keen to give the impression that they could renegotiate the agreement, and they both clearly expected that this stance would deliver electoral support.[10] Against this, the ECB and the IMF, in the persons of Smaghi and Chopra, insisted that the agreement had been negotiated on behalf of the Irish state rather than on behalf of any short-term government, and hence that it was more or less set in stone – particularly as far as the rate of interest was concerned. All of this has the potential to lead to a conflict between a set of parties that enter government with a representative mandate to renegotiate a loan and a set of lenders that insist on sticking to the terms of an agreement that has already been signed by 'the state'.[11]

2.2 Cui bono?

Conflicts between what a government or its voters might like to happen, on the one hand, and what various institutional and other constraining forces 'allow' to happen, on the other, are of course congenital in any modern democracy. To paraphrase an earlier analysis (Katz 1986), the party-ness of modern party government is often in conflict with its government-ness. At the same time, however, I should emphasize that this is not a conflict between input and output legitimacy (Scharpf 1999) or between government by the people and government for the people. In the Irish case, to push for a renegotiation of the EU/IMF agreement after the election might well be considered expressive of government *by* the people, and hence we see this side of the equation in action. The parties favouring renegotiation – even if without precise detailed plans – are those currently preferred by the electorate and are likely to win a commanding majority. Indeed, the agreement has become extremely unpopular with voters, as has the austerity which it promises, and according to a pre-election poll (Millward Brown Lansdowne 2011), more than 80 per cent of the electorate favoured renegotiation. Should the people decide, it would be likely in favour of new terms. This would be a decision *by* the people.

On the other side of the equation, however, it is difficult to view acceptance of the status quo, and hence acceptance of the Smaghi–Chopra arguments, as being expressive of government *for* the people. According to many interpretations, including those of the renowned economists Ken Rogoff and Paul Krugman, as well as the financier George Soros, this agreement is actually damaging to the interests of the Irish people and to the long-term prosperity of the Irish state. 'How long can Ireland take the pain that's necessary?', asked Rogoff recently. 'A year, two years? Maybe. But three or four? Countries outside of Romania maybe, under Ceausescu, really haven't done this and so it's possible but it's very demanding' (Beesley 2011b). According to Krugman (2010), 'you have to wonder what it will take for serious people to realize that punishing the populace for the bankers' sins is worse than a crime; it's a mistake.' For Soros (2010), finally, it is a case of 'the bondholders of insolvent banks . . . being protected at the expense of taxpayers. This is politically unacceptable. A new Irish government to be elected next spring is bound to repudiate the current arrangements.' Staying with the present commitments does not therefore seem to be expressive of government *for* the people. Indeed, for some commentators, as we've seen, it is government *against* the people.

So, in whose interests was it? And for whom was the decision made? In the first place, and most obviously, it was in the interests of the banks that were bailed out, and in the interests of the senior management of these banks who were busy lobbying the party leadership on the night of 30 September. Subsequent to the declaration of the bank guarantee, there has been a lot of speculative comment in the Irish media regarding the personal relationships between the bankers themselves and senior government ministers, and it has often been suggested that the decision was owed to cronyism and political favouritism (e.g., O'Toole 2010). This also means that it was in the interests of the bondholders of the failing banks, who are mainly European banks, and who are together owed an estimated €360 billion, including €100 billion to German banks and €110 billion to UK banks. Since any default would have major knock-on effects on their balance sheets, it is also clearly in the interests of these other European banks and their national governments that the debts are covered. Finally, the decision was also taken in the interests of the ECB and the leadership of the eurozone more generally, as well as in the interests of the EU authorities, since an Irish default would seriously undermine the euro and hence risk irreparable damage to the EU itself. Indeed, it was argued by some Irish commentators and politicians that the ECB and the EU had forced the rescue package on Ireland in an effort to protect the European banks and the currency. Perhaps, then, the decision is expressive of government for the *European* people(s).

Issues of interest and culpability were also the subject of a heated exchange in the European Parliament, connecting the problem to moral hazard not just on the part of the Irish banks but also on the part of their counterparts in Europe, and thereby connecting also to a wider discussion as to whether the blame for the crisis lay with the Irish banks, who loaned recklessly in the property market, or with those European banks that provided the funds to allow Irish banks to make the loans in the first place. An Irish Socialist MEP, Joe Higgins, placed the blame on both the Irish and the European banks, and condemned the transferring of the costs of the bailout to the Irish taxpayers, whom he claimed were not responsible. The bailout mechanism, he argued, 'is in practice nothing more than another tool to cushion major European banks from the consequences of their reckless speculation on the financial markets'. To which the president of the European Commission, José Manuel Barroso, responded angrily: 'The problems of Ireland were created by the irresponsible financial behaviour of some Irish institutions and by the lack of supervision in the Irish market . . .. Europe is now part of the solution; it is trying to support Ireland. But it was not Europe that created this fiscally irresponsible situation and this financially irresponsible behaviour. Europe is trying to support Ireland. It is important to know where the responsibility lies' (EP Debates 2011).

Lorenzo Bini Smaghi was also explicit on this issue, emphasizing that the whole problem was the responsibility of the Irish, and that it was 'totally wrong' to suggest that the ECB had pressured the government: 'Democracies have to be accountable and consistent with their own choices. I don't think anybody outside Ireland should tell Ireland what to do, but you should not complain if now you have to increase taxes as a result of the choice of economic model the Irish people made . . .. The driving force was the collapse of investor confidence and the decision was entirely the Government's own' (Beesley 2011a). Brian Cowen, the soon-to-be outgoing taoiseach, pushed the same line, emphasizing that the request for European help had not been forced on his government: 'It was an Irish decision made by Irish people', he insisted.[12]

3 Representative and responsible government

For a variety of reasons – social, structural, organizational and geopolitical, as well as simply the sheer force of attrition – the character of parties and party competition in many of the European polities is changing in ways that are making it more and more difficult for parties to respond to their voters, and hence to represent and act on their opinions. In other words, it is changing in ways which challenge the integrity of the chain of delegations. These problems emerge at two levels. First, parties find it more difficult to listen to voters and to understand, aggregate or process their demands. Second, parties have less freedom in which to treat their voters as principals and to act as their agents.

3.1 Representative parties

In traditional understandings of the development of representative government in modern Europe, parties were seen to have played two crucial roles. In the first place, they played a crucial representative role – articulating interests, aggregating demands, translating collective preferences into distinct policy options, and so on. They linked civil society to the polity and did so from a very strong and well-grounded foundation in society. Parties gave voice to the citizenry. In the second place, they governed. They organized and gave coherence to the institutions of government, and from their positions in government, and in opposition, they sought to build the policy programmes that would serve the interests of their supporters and of the wider polity. The combination of both these crucial roles into one was the unique contribution parties offered to the development and legitimation of modern democracy. That is, within one party agency, and within one party organization, were developed the key representative and governing functions of the polity. This was the key to the legitimation of representative government in democratic political systems. In such a process, there were few, if any, principal–agent problems: there was usually only one principal, and this principal was also the agent (see Katz and Mair forthcoming: ch. 2).

In contemporary democracies, by contrast, these two functions have begun to grow apart, with many of today's mainstream parties downplaying, or being forced to downplay, their representative role, and enhancing, or being forced to enhance, their governing role (Mair 2006; Katz and Mair 1995). In other words, as part of the process by which parties have moved their centres of gravity from civil society to the state, they have also began to shift from *combining* representative and governmental roles (or combining representative and procedural or institutional roles) to building on their governmental role alone.

Another way of looking at this is to suggest that these parties have moved from making representations on behalf of citizens to the state to making representations on behalf of the state to the citizens. The representation of the citizens, meanwhile, to the extent that it still occurs at all, is increasingly given over to other, non-governing organizations and practices – to interest groups, social movements, advocacy coalitions, lobbies, the media, self-representation, etc. – that are disconnected from the parties and the party system and that can talk directly to government and the bureaucracy. In this way, the representation of interests – government by the people – becomes less and less a function of the activities of partisan political organizations. This also implies the possible emergence of a new division of labour within the democracy polity, whereby the mainstream parties would govern, or primarily govern, while other agencies would look after the citizens' representative needs. There is one important exception here, of course, in that one channel of representation that does remain within the electoral channel is that which is trumpeted by the new 'niche' or 'challenger' parties (Meguid 2005), often populist in tone, who may also downplay their governing ambition or lack a governing capacity. Needless to say, these developments severely challenge the strength and coherence of the first link in the parliamentary chain of delegation. This is not only because, as Müller and his colleagues (2003: note 12, citing Riker [1982]) acknowledge, it may simply be impossible for the parties to know what citizens want, but also because the parties that govern seem now less willing or able to listen, while the citizens themselves prefer to address other agencies.

There are at least four good reasons to believe that parties are now less inclined and less able to listen to voters and less capable of processing their demands. In the first place, parties find it increasingly difficult to know what voters want. Since the development of the catch-all party in the 1960s, resources and power inside the parties have increasingly shifted upwards, privileging those whom Kirchheimer (1966) spoke of as 'the top leadership groups'. Although this has allowed the parties greater flexibility in competing for office and has freed the leaderships from the constraints of more purposeful mass organizations and memberships, it has also had its costs. Party organizations became more top-heavy and capital intensive, membership levels began to fall, and the general rootedness of parties within the wider society began to erode. Levels of popular identification with parties waned, loyalties declined, voters grew more distant and less engaged, and electoral preferences became more volatile and contingent. It was not only the case that voters no longer belonged to the parties – as Parisi and Pasquino (1979) had once argued, instancing the general shift from 'a vote of belonging' to a 'vote of opinion' – but also that the parties no longer belonged to the voters. When party organizations were embedded within a wider network of organized cleavages, and when both leaders and voters were more less part of the same milieu, it was easy for party leaders to listen to voters and to understand what they were saying. In contemporary party organizations, by contrast, leaders (or their professional consultants) who wish to listen to their voters are obliged to rely on opinion polls, focus groups and the independent media, none of which seems able to offer a clear and unambiguous message, with much of what is expressed being a sense of disappointment at the inability of parties and governments to do what might be desired (e.g., Russell 2005; Hay 2007).

Parties also have problems listening to voters simply because electoral representation itself has become more difficult. The decline of the traditional large collective constituencies, the fragmentation of electorates, the particularization of voter preferences, and the volatility of issue preferences and alignments – that whole process which the Dutch refer to as *ontzuiling* and individualization – made it more and more difficult for parties to translate popular interests into distinct policy alternatives (see also Schmitter 2008). This was especially so since many of the traditional representative guidelines no longer functioned, but instead were part of a context in which, as Rudy Andeweg (2003: 151) has noted, 'religion is increasingly expressed outside churches, interest promotion is taken care of outside interest associations . . . physical exercise outside sports clubs . . . work outside permanent employment, love outside marriage, and even gender differences are becoming divorced from sex differences.' In other words, even if parties wanted to listen to voters, and even if they managed to do so, the result was often a cacophony of different voices. This made it harder for them to synthesize the various demands, let alone aggregate them into coherent electoral and governing programmes – itself the classic representative function performed by parties within democracies.

[handwritten margin notes: too complex for politicians ↓ I'm not convinced EU level, then not undemocratic]

Third, it is likely that parties will have become less inclined to listen to voters to the extent that they cannot effectively process the demands that voters express. For a variety of reasons, parties in national governments in recent years have ceded much of their capacity and authority to make binding decisions in a host of different policy areas. In part this is because of the sheer complexity of the issues involved (Papadopoulos 2003) and results from the tendency to delegate decision-making authority to expert institutions and agencies lying outside the formal electoral arena. However, it is also the result of a gradual shift in competences, with the European level in particular assuming an increasing responsibility in many policy areas and thereby reducing the capacity of parties to offer meaningful policy alternatives to their voters (Dorussen and Nanou 2006; Nanou and Dorussen 2010). Given that national governments now often lack the resources to determine policies autonomously, the parties occupying these governments are unlikely to encourage voters to give voice in these areas in electoral contexts.

Finally, the steady opening-up of the governing process to an ever wider range of parties in the 1970s and 1980s turned the ambition to govern into a much more realistic and manageable goal for more and more party leaders. Indeed, holding office in government became part of the conventional career cycle and ambition for both parties and their leaders – a process which, as Borchert (e.g., 2008) shows, went hand in hand with the growth of political professionalization. This also became part of the more general change in party strategy, whereby the shift of resources inside parties from the party on the ground and from the party in the central office to the party in public office allowed the ambitions of the party in public office to be transformed into the ambitions of the party as a whole (Katz and Mair, forthcoming). For many party leaders, parties were governors or they were nothing, a perspective which clearly leaves little room for listening to voters.

3.2 Responsible government

The second source of difficulty in the parliamentary chain of delegation connects directly to the notion of responsibility. It is a commonplace to note that all democratic governments, always, have had to maintain a balance between demands for responsiveness, on the one hand, and demands for responsibility, on the other, or, echoing Scharpf (1999), all governments have had to maintain a balance between democracy and efficiency. Today, however, in the new circumstances of party politics, these two demands have come increasingly in tension, and it is becoming more and more difficult to reconcile them. Moreover – and this is where I come to the core of my argument – not only are the demand for responsiveness and the demands for responsibility increasingly at odds with one another, but there has also been an undermining of the parties' capacity to reconcile and resolve this growing tension. In other words, the tension itself is becoming steadily more acute, and the means of handling that tension are steadily waning.

Responsibility is, of course, a difficult and contested term. For Sartori (1976: 18–24), for example, as well as for many of the US advocates of the 'responsible party model' in the 1950s and 1960s (e.g., APSA 1950), responsibility essentially boils down to accountability. Political actors and their parties and their governments give account to parliament and/or to the people, and are in this sense accountable and, thereby, responsible. For Downs (1957: 105), by contrast, responsibility implies predictability and consistency: a party is responsible 'if its policies in one period are consistent with its actions (or statements) in the preceding period', and hence 'the absence of responsibility means party behaviour cannot be predicted by consistently projecting what parties have done previously.' For Rieselbach (1977: 8–10), who proposes responsibility, responsiveness and accountability as three standards against which the US Congress – or any legislature – might be evaluated, responsibility implies efficiency and effectiveness: 'a responsible institution provides reasonably successful policies to resolve the major problems it is faced with. The emphasis of the responsibility criterion is on speed, efficiency, and, of course, success.' Finally, for Birch (1964), in his classic study of the British constitution, responsibility implies not only responsiveness and accountability – the two notions highlighted by the US advocates of the 'responsible party model', for example – but also 'prudence and consistency on the part of those taking decisions'. As Birch goes on to emphasize, this latter meaning evokes notions of duty and of moral responsibility, and here too it is contrasted with reckless or inconsistent decision-making.

We are therefore confronted with three distinct concepts, each of which is in some way associated with the broader notion of responsibility. The first is responsiveness, whereby political leaders or governments listen to and then respond to the demands of citizens and groups. This may also be associated with the traditional understanding of party government and party democracy, in which parties and their leaders acquire a mandate through elections and go on to implement the chosen policies while in government. The second concept is accountability, whereby political leaders or governments are held to account by parliaments or by voters. The judgement of these citizens or parliaments may be based on evaluations of how responsive the leaders have been and how well they have acted as delegates or agents of the bodies or principals carrying out the evaluation; or it may reflect a 'trustee' type of relationship, in which the leaders make their own judgements and are subsequently evaluated on their performance. Either way, both judgements involve *ex post* evaluation, and, following Andeweg (2003), this seems to have become more important as traditional *ex ante* representation – responsiveness – becomes more difficult to realize. In other words, there is a potential trade-off between responsiveness and accountability, with a weakening of the former being compensated by a greater emphasis on the latter; or, in Scharpf's (1999) terms, with the failings of input-oriented legitimacy being compensated by a greater reliance on output-oriented legitimacy.

The third concept, following Birch, is responsibility in the narrower and more formalized sense of the term, whereby leaders and governments are expected to act prudently and consistently and to follow accepted procedural norms and practices. This also means living up to the commitments that have been entered into by their predecessors in office and abiding by agreements that these predecessors have made with other governments and institutions. In other words, responsibility involves an acceptance that, in certain areas and in certain procedures, the leaders' hands will be tied. Of course, the ties may also eventually be loosened, and the leader may break with established traditions and practices – but, even in these cases, to act responsibly means to effect changes according to accepted procedures and to avoid random, reckless or illegal decision-making. In terms of procedures, responsible government is therefore 'good' government.

So how do these three notions fit together? The first two obviously fit together in the sense that the declining representative capacity of parties leads to retrospective accountability acquiring a greater emphasis than prospective mandates. Indeed, regardless of whether the parties in government are standing in relation to parliament and the voters as accountable trustees or as responsive delegates, there is a clear and relatively unambiguous principal–agent relationship involved. The parties in government are the agent, and voters – whether mandating *ex ante* or accountable *ex post* – are the principal. The chain of delegation is clear.

The relationship of both concepts with responsibility in the Birch sense is much more problematic, however. Here there is not one more or less straightforward principal that the parties in government meet when dealing with the voters or parliament, but rather a host of different and sometimes contradictory principals constituted by the many veto and semi-veto players who now surround government in its dispersed multi-level institutional setting: the central banks, the courts, the European Commission, the Council of Europe, the WTO, the United Nations and its various offshoots, and so on, and who, as we have seen, are proving so powerful in the Irish case. It is to these sometime principals that parties in government are also accountable, and it is when these governing parties continue to respect the rulings and procedures laid down by these institutions that we can speak of them being consistent, prudent and responsible.

With responsiveness and accountability, the integrity of the parliamentary chain of delegation remains intact, in that there is one key principal and one key agent at each of the points, and there is also singularity. Once we introduce the notion of responsibility, on the other hand, the integrity is undermined, since other principals external to the chain of delegation begin to assert themselves. The key difference is therefore not between prospective responsiveness and retrospective accountability, which governments can try to square in any case, but between both of these forms of control, on the one hand, each with the same basic principal, and the problem of responsibility, on the other, with its host of different and sometimes competing – and often legitimate – principals. As is more than evident in the Irish case, for example, it is here that the key incompatibilities lie, with the demands of responsiveness both to voters and to parliament, and hence also the demands of representation, proving particularly difficult to reconcile with the demands of responsibility. This is therefore also where the parliamentary chain of delegation runs into problems.

But this is also an old problem, and one that connects closely to Dahl's (1956) traditional distinction between populistic and Madisonian democracy, as well as to the more common contemporary distinction between efficient and democratic government (e.g., Scharpf 1999). Moreover, the problems that institutional diversity poses for the chain of delegation are also recognized by Müller et al. (2003), as well as by some of the more general work on principal–agent theory. A recent evaluation of the literature on bureaucratic control concluded, for example, 'that bureaucratic actions are influenced by multiple potential principals and that these potential principals are often in competition with one another' (Worsham and Gatrell 2005: 364; see also Wood and Waterman 1993), while Kaare Strøm (2003: 60) also points out that external political constraints can get in the way of representative politics by prohibiting certain forms of agency or by 'forcing agents into behaviour that neither they nor their [own, domestic] principals would have freely chosen'. So why should this familiar tension between responsiveness and responsibility now be a matter of particular concern? What is different in contemporary democracy?

3.3 A growing tension

There are four factors in particular that are important here, all of which point to a difference in scale rather than a difference in kind, but which together cumulate in a manner that constitutes a fundamental challenge to the good functioning of representative government. In the first place, and as already discussed above, governments are finding it ever more difficult to respond to voters and to electoral opinion, and ever more difficult to read and aggregate preferences and to persuade voters to align behind their policies. As we have seen, this is partly because they have withdrawn from civil society and, hence, are out of touch with electoral demands, and partly because they now maintain smaller and increasingly unrepresentative party memberships and lack mechanisms for steering communication upwards through the party organization. Moreover, the parties have tended to loosen their ties with the major mass organizations in civil society – organizations which in any case are themselves less able to communicate with the wider citizenry and hence lack access to that particular channel of communication. As noted, it is also increasingly difficult for parties to respond to voters in policy terms, since, at least in Europe, much of the policy discretion and room for manoeuvre open to governments has been severely curtailed by the transfer of decision-making authority to the supranational level. All of these factors have acquired greater weight in recent years, and for this reason the problems that they cause assume greater weight as well.

It is not just top-down change that is relevant here, however. Mass electoral opinion has become more fragmented and volatile, with the result that there are fewer and fewer stable landmarks around which the parties can orient themselves. As Russell Hardin (2000) has argued, the general decline in the importance of left–right economic competition and the general growth in a host of often complex issues that are unrelated to one another together undermine the capacity to organize politics along a single simple dimension. The result is that, even if parties in government were in a position to respond to popular demands, they would find it difficult to do so because of the challenge of knowing what those demands actually were. This also makes parties and governments more susceptible to the influence of lobbyists and special interests. The tension therefore becomes more acute simply because it has become more difficult for parties to be responsive to the citizenry as a whole.

Second, in seeking to act responsibly – that is, in trying to do what they are expected to do as governments, and in trying to meet the everyday responsibilities of office – governments now find themselves more and more constrained by other agencies and institutions. As we have seen very clearly in the Irish case, the range of principals who oblige governments to behave in a particular way, and who define the terms of reference of responsibility, has expanded enormously. This is a growing problem, in that the Europeanization and internationalization of policy parameters, reflected in what Ruggie (1997) and Scharpf (2000) treat as 'the decline of embedded liberalism', oblige governments to be accountable to an increasing number of principals, many of whom are not located within the domestic realm, and most of whom are difficult to control. In other words, by disembedding liberalism, globalization in general and Europeanization in particular create many new principals to whom governments owe account. This also makes it even more difficult for voters to see or understand the rationale behind certain decisions, and hence this also provokes tensions. Even though governments might be willing to heed their voters' demands – if they could read them properly – they may well be limited in doing so by having 'other constitutionally prescribed roles to play' (Strøm 2003: 60). This is not a new problem, to be sure, but it has become weightier and more serious in recent years. We are dealing not only with a problem of voter demands that are not so easily understood by parties in government, but also with governments that are not always in a position to respond to those that they do understand.

There is also a third, cumulating factor at work here, which was originally highlighted by Richard Rose (e.g., 1990) some time ago, and which concerns the constraints imposed by the legacies inherited by governments. As Rose argued, most of what governments do is a function of what they have inherited rather than what they have chosen. In the mid-1980s, for example, the then radical Thatcher government was still maintaining and funding 207 of the 227 programmes which it had inherited from the previous Labour regime (many of which had also been inherited by Labour) and, after six years in office, it had initiated just twenty-eight new programmes. In terms of the total programme cost to the government in 1985, less than 6 per cent of expenditure was occupied by newly created programmes (Rose 1990: 279–80). In acting 'responsibly', governments are therefore limited not only by their traditional constitutional constraints and by the growing weight of international constitutional constraints – deriving from the EU or the Council of Europe in the European case, and from the UN and the international legal system more globally – but also by the weight of prior policy commitments. Indeed, with time, the inherited weight of these prior commitments has grown enormously, and hence the room for discretionary manoeuvre available to any one government at any one time has become correspondingly curtailed.[13]

In his discussion of responsible government in the British case, Birch (1964: 170) emphasizes the familiar point that, although responsiveness and responsibility are both generally seen as desirable, they are not always compatible. This is also my main point here. Not only are these features of party government sometimes incompatible, they are also *increasingly* incompatible, in that prudence and consistency, as well as accountability, require conforming to external constraints and legacies and not just to public opinion, and these external constraints and legacies have grown in weight in recent years, while public opinion, in its turn, has become harder and harder to read. This is the growing imbalance.

The fourth factor that I wish to emphasize here is that, while the traditional (and lesser) incompatibility between responsiveness and responsibility that was experienced in the past could often be bridged or 'managed' by parties who were able to persuade voters on their side through partisan campaigns and appeals to partisan loyalty, this is less conceivable today. The incompatibility has always troubled parties, of course, and many party governments in the past have been quick to cite difficult circumstances, inauspicious developments or simple misjudgements in order to justify the evasion of election commitments or the reneging on promises. In addition, parties could also sometimes pull their voters with them through the change of direction by appealing to popular loyalty and trust. In contemporary circumstances, however, this option is no longer effectively available. Parties have almost no members to help mobilize public opinion, and they have an ever shrinking number of strong partisan identifiers within the electorate who might take them at their word. They rarely control the means of political communication and hence have to rely on others for their persuasive capacities. Moreover, as is now well attested, political parties are by far the least trusted institution within modern democracies. For all of these reasons, their mobilization capacities, and hence also their persuasive capacities, are now severely reduced. Parties, in short, now appear to exacerbate rather than alleviate the problem.

4 Implications

'Democracy means not only that people can vote in free and fair elections, but that they can influence public policy as well. What people think matters at least as much as what governments do' (Krastev 2002: 45).

A number of implications follow from these arguments. As far as the particular case of Ireland is concerned, the politics of the future will almost certainly, and enduringly, be a politics of austerity. It is not simply the size of the newly enlarged sovereign debt that matters here – given that there is likely to be at least some level of default on the debts owed by the banks, there should be an eventual reduction in the overall debt owed by the state – but also the rate of interest which is being paid on the sums borrowed from the EU and the IMF. Should this rate remain at 5.8

per cent – and this decision is obviously not in Irish hands – it will almost certainly squeeze the Irish economy severely, thereby ensuring that Irish democracy remains in a straightjacket for years to come. In such a context of 'democracy without choices' (Krastev 2002), it makes little sense to speak of the parliamentary chain of delegation: it is the external principals who will be making the demands and constraining the decisions, while the voice of Irish voters will count for little. It will be difficult for the parties to beat Smaghi (or to beat the Germans or the Dutch).

Beyond the Irish case, however, there are also wider implications. First, and most obviously, it is clear that the task of governing has become extremely complex, time-consuming and demanding, and is something that does not afford much room for partisan mobilization either as a core activity or even on the side. It therefore follows that parties that are busy governing are busier as governments than they are as parties. If they are busy as parties, then either someone else is governing – through the displacement of the real decision-making power – or the parties are governing badly. This is a problem for the parties as well as for democracy. Moreover, because parties are busy governing, because governing demands so much of them, and because there is so little room for partisanship in this governing process, much of what they do is inevitably depoliticized. But this in itself leads to a paradox, which eats away at their standing: the more the parties depoliticize policy-making, the more they are obliged to justify their choices – because these choices, being depoliticized, are no longer self-evident choices for their supporters and voters; yet the more parties depoliticize, particularly within contemporary circumstances, the more difficult it becomes – as parties – to justify these choices.

Second, there are signs that the growing gap between responsiveness and responsibility, and the declining capacity of parties to bridge or manage that gap, is leading to the bifurcation of a number of party systems and to a new form of opposition (Katz and Mair 2008). In these systems, governing capacity and vocation become the property of one more or less closely bounded group of political parties. These are parties which are clearly within the mainstream, or 'core' (Smith 1989), of the party system, and it is these which may be able to offer voters a choice of government. Representation or expression, on the other hand, or the provision of voice to the people, when it doesn't move wholly outside the arena of electoral politics, becomes the property of a second group of parties, and it is these parties that constitute the new opposition. These latter parties are often characterized by a strong populist rhetoric. They rarely govern and also downplay any office-seeking motives. On the rare occasions when they do govern, they sometimes have severe problems in squaring their original emphasis on representation and their original role as the voice of the people with the constraints imposed by governing and by having to compromise with coalition partners. Moreover, though not the same as the anti-system parties identified by Sartori (1976: 138–40), they share with those parties a form of 'semi-responsible' or 'irresponsible' opposition, as well as a 'politics of outbidding'. In other words, it is possible to speak of a growing divide in European party systems between parties which claim to represent, but don't deliver, and those which deliver, but are no longer seen to represent.

Finally, the growing gap between responsiveness and responsibility – or between what citizens might like governments to do and what governments are obliged to do – and the declining capacity of parties to bridge or manage that gap, lies at the heart of the disaffection and malaise that now suffuses democracy. This also echoes Jean Leca's (1996) conclusion that there is a growing separation between the world of public opinion, on the one hand, and the world of problem-solving, on the other (see also Papadopoulos 2010). Governments try to solve problems, and hence parties in government try to solve problems, but they do so at an increasing remove from public opinion.

Seen in this way, and framed as the growing and potentially unbridgeable gap between responsive government and responsible government, it becomes very difficult to conceive of how the malaise might be treated or overcome. This is particularly so since we are dealing with a problem that can only grow worse in a period of fiscal austerity, when external constrains and financial limits become much more powerful, and when the governing parties are even less able to meet the demands of voters.

Some years ago, in an evaluation of the development of democracy in the Balkan states, Ivan Krastev (2002: 51) emphasized how the stability of public policy had been 'ensured largely by outside pressure and constraints in the form of EU or IMF conditionalities, currency pegs and the like'. The current situation in Ireland, which is one of the longest enduring of the European democracies, is of course little different. But, even if to a lesser degree, this situation is comparable to that of many more of Europe's long-standing democracies, which are also constrained by debt and the legacy of past policies, and which are now also pressured by external lenders, bondholders and supranational authorities. In such circumstances, as Krastev goes on to argue, relations between politicians and the public worsen, since in such circumstances we see regimes 'in which the voters can change governments far more easily than they can change policies'. In the Balkans, he argues, this signals the failure of representation and the onset of a democracy without choices. Elsewhere in Europe, where democracies are more established, such failures are also increasingly evident.

References

Andeweg, R. B. (2003) Beyond representativeness? Trends in political representation, *European Review* 11(2): 147–61.

APSA (American Political Science Association) (1950) Towards a more responsible two-party system: a report on the Committee on Political Parties, *American Political Science Review* 44(3): supplement.

Beesley, A. (2011a) Ireland's meltdown is the outcome of the policies of its elected politicians, *Irish Times*, 15 January.

Beesley, A. (2011b) Burden of bank debt 'must be shared', *Irish Times*, 27 January.

Beesley, A., Scally, D., and De Bréadún, D. (2011) Rehn says terms of bailout may be changed in future, *Irish Times*, 15 February.

Birch, A. H. (1964) *Representative and Responsible Government*. London: Allen & Unwin.

Borchert, J. (2008) Political professionalism and representative democracy: common history, irresolvable linkage and inherent tensions, in K. Palonen, T. Pulkkinen and J. M. Rosales (eds), *The Ashgate Research Companion to the Politics of Democratization in Europe*. Aldershot: Ashgate, pp. 267–83.

Börzel, T. A., and Risse, T. (2000) *When Europe Hits Home: Europeanization and Domestic Change*, European Integration online papers 4; available at: http://eiop.or.at/eiop/texte/2000-015.htm (accessed 16 August 2012).

Cahill, A. (2011) FG pledge to revise EU–IMF loan conditions, *Irish Examiner*, 29 January; available at: http://www.irishexaminer.com/ireland/fg-pledge-to-revise-eu-imf-loan-conditions-143614.html (accessed 29 February 2012).

Carswell, S. (2010) The big gamble: the inside story of the bank guarantee, *Irish Times*, 25 September.

Cowen, B. (2010) Interview with Miriam O'Callaghan, *Prime Time*, 8 December. Dublin: Raidió Teilifís Éireann (RTÉ) [television programme].

Dahl, R. A. (1956) *A Preface to Democratic Theory*. Chicago: University of Chicago Press.

Dellepiane, S., and Hardiman, N. (2010) The European context of Ireland's economic crisis, *Economic and Social Review* 41(4): 471–98.

Dorussen, H., and Nanou, K. (2006) European integration, intergovernmental bargaining, and convergence of party programmes, *European Union Politics* 7(2): 235–56.

Downs, A. (1957) *An Economic Theory of Democracy*. New York: Harper & Row.

Farrell, D., Wall, M., and Ó Muineacháin, S. (2011) Courting, but not always serving: perverted Burkeanism and the puzzle of the Irish TD under PR-STV, draft paper prepared for the Workshop on Intraparty Democracy, Carleton University, Ottawa, August.

Hardin, R. (2000) The public trust, in S. J. Pharr and R. D. Putnam (eds), *Disaffected Democracies: What's Troubling the Trilateral Countries?* Cambridge: Cambridge University Press, pp. 31–51.

Hay, C. (2007) *Why We Hate Politics*. Cambridge: Polity.

Katz, R. S. (1986) Party government: a rationalistic conception, in F. G. Castles and R. Wildenmann (eds), *Visions and Realities of Party Government*. Berlin: de Gruyter, pp. 31–71.

Katz, R. S., and Mair, P. (1995) Changing models of party organization and party democracy: the emergence of the cartel party, *Party Politics* 1(1): 5–28.

Katz, R. S., and Mair, P. (2008) *MPs and Parliamentary Parties in the Age of the Cartel Party*. Rennes: ECPR Joint Sessions.

Katz, R. S., and Mair, P. (forthcoming) *Democracy and the Cartelisation of Political Parties*.

Kirchheimer, O. (1966) The transformation of the Western European party systems, in J. LaPalombara and M. Weiner (eds), *Political Parties and Political Development*. Princeton, NJ: Princeton University Press, pp. 177–200.

Krastev, I. (2002) The Balkans: democracy without choices, *Journal of Democracy* 13(3): 39–53.

Krugman, P. (2010) Eating the Irish, *New York Times*, 25 November; available at: http://www.nytimes.com/2010/11/26/opinion/26krugman.html (accessed 29 February 2012).

Leca, J. (1996) Ce que l'analyse des politiques publiques pourrair apprendre sur le gouvernement démocratique? *Revue Française de Science Politique* 46(1): 122–33.

McDermott, V. (2010) Renegotiating the EU/IMF loans package – just how realistic is that?, 30 December; available at: www.irishelection.com/2010/12/renegotiating-the-euimf-loans-package-just-how-realistic-is-that/ (accessed 29 February 2012).

McGee, H. (2011) Gilmore vows to renegotiate 'bad deal' on EU–IMF bailout package, *Irish Times*, 4 February.

Mair, P. (2006) Ruling the void: the hollowing of Western democracy, *New Left Review* 42(Nov–Dec): 25–51.

Mair, P. (2009) *Representative versus Responsible Government*, MPIfG Working Paper 09/8. Cologne: Max Planck Institute for the Study of Societies.

Meguid, B. (2005) Competition between unequals: the role of mainstream party strategy in niche party success, *American Political Science Review* 99(3): 347–59.

Millward Brown Lansdowne and the Sunday Independent (2011) *National Opinion Poll*, 28 January; available at: http://politicalreform.ie/2011/01/29/sunday-independentmbl-poll-30th-january-2011-plus-ca-change/ (accessed 17 August 2012).

Müller, W. C., Bergman, T., and Strøm, K. (2003) Parliamentary democracy: promise and problems, in K. Strøm, W. C. Müller and T. Bergman (eds), *Delegation and Accountability in Parliamentary Democracies*. Oxford: Oxford University Press, pp. 3–33.

Nanou, K., and Dorussen, H. (2010) European integration and electoral democracy: how the EU constrains party competition in the member states, unpublished paper.

Neto, O. A., and Strøm, K. (2006) Breaking the parliamentary chain of delegation, *British Journal of Political Science* 36(4): 619–43.

O'Brien, D. (2011) The opposition parties want to renegotiate the bailout: is it possible? *Irish Times*, 1 February.

Ó Caollaí, É. (2011) Kenny accused of 'misleading' public, *Irish Times*, 15 February.

O'Regan, M. (2011) Sinn Féin will tell the IMF 'to go home', Adams insists, *Irish Times*, 31 January.

O'Toole, F. (2010) *Enough is Enough: How to Build a New Republic*. London: Faber.

Papadopoulos, Y. (2003) Cooperative forms of governance: problems of democratic accountability in complex environments, *European Journal of Political Research* 42(4): 473–501.

Papadopoulos, Y. (2010) Accountability and multi-level governance: more accountability, less democracy? *West European Politics* 33(5): 1030–49.

Parisi, A., and Pasquino, G. (1979) Changes in Italian electoral behaviour: the relationships between parties and voters, *West European Politics* 2(1): 6–30.

Rieselbach, L. N. (1977) *Congressional Reform in the Seventies*. Morristown, NJ: General Learning Press.

Riker, W. H. (1982) *Liberalism against Populism: A Confrontation between the Theory of Democracy and the Theory of Social Choice*. San Francisco: W. H. Freeman.

Rose, R. (1990) Inheritance before choice in public policy, *Journal of Theoretical Politics* 2(3): 263–91.

Ruggie, J. G. (1997) *Globalization and the Embedded Liberalism Compromise: The End of an Era?*, MPIfG Working Paper 97/1. Cologne: Max Planck Institute for the Study of Societies.

Russell, M. (2005) *Must Politics Disappoint?* London: Fabian Society.

Sartori, G. (1976) *Parties and Party Systems: A Framework for Analysis*. Cambridge: Cambridge University Press.

Scharpf, F. W. (1999) *Governing in Europe: Effective and Democratic?* Oxford: Oxford University Press.

Scharpf, F. W. (2000) Economic changes, vulnerabilities, and institutional capabilities, in F. W. Scharpf and V. A. Schmidt (eds), *Welfare and Work in the Open Economy*, Vol. 1: *From Vulnerability to Competitiveness*. Oxford: Oxford University Press, pp. 21–124.

Schmitter, P. C. (2008) The changing politics of organised interests, *West European Politics* 31(1–2): 195–210.

Smith, G. (1989) Core persistence: change and the 'people's party', *West European Politics* 12(4): 157–68.

Soros, G. (2010) Europe should rescue banks before states, *Financial Times*, 14 December; available at: http://www.ft.com/cms/s/0/76f69cd8-077a-11e0-8d80-00144feabdc0.html#axzz23oeUXInL (accessed 29 February 2012).

Streeck, W. (2006) A state of exhaustion? A comment on the German election of 18 September, *Political Quarterly* 77(1): 79–87.

Streeck, W. (2007) *Endgame? The Fiscal Crisis of the German State*, MPIfG Discussion Paper 07/7. Cologne: Max Planck Institute for the Study of Societies.

Strøm, K. (2003) Parliamentary democracy and delegation, in K. Strøm, W. C. Müller and T. Bergman (eds), *Delegation and Accountability in Parliamentary Democracies*. Oxford: Oxford University Press, pp. 55–106.

Willis, A. (2011) FG leader meets Barroso over bailout, *Irish Times*, 29 January.

Wood, B. D., and Waterman, R. (1993) The dynamics of political-bureaucratic adaptation, *American Journal of Political Science* 37(2): 497–528.

Worsham, J., and Gatrell, J. (2005) Multiple principals, multiple signals: a signaling approach to principal–agent relations, *Policy Studies Journal* 33(3): 363–76.

7

Liberalization, Inequality and Democracy's Discontent[1]

Armin Schäfer

1 Introduction

In the 1970s, the postwar era came to an end after thirty years of vigorous growth. The collapse of Bretton Woods, rising unemployment, high rates of inflation and industrial strife, and diminished growth rates were unmistakable signs that the *trente glorieuses* were over. While most observers shared a sense of crisis, they had different interpretations of its causes: while the left claimed that contradictions inherent to capitalism had finally resurfaced and eventually had brought about a 'legitimation crisis' (Habermas 1973; Wolfe 1977), conservatives argued that growing political demands for redistribution, wage increases and job security had put an unbearable burden on the capitalist economy; they asserted that 'government overload' was at the heart of the crisis. In a democracy, so the latter group reasoned, politicians had to meet voters' demands in order to stay in office, and rising public expenditures therefore seemed inescapable. The conservative interpretation found much resonance politically, as evidenced by the fact that so many market-oriented parties won political office after 1979. Responding to the economic turbulences of the 1970s, these governments began to remake national economies in the hope of reinvigorating growth. From the 1980s onwards, many countries privatized public enterprises, liberalized markets and started to cut back on the welfare state.

Whatever the economic merits of these cures have been, they did not serve democracy well. Almost everywhere today, fewer people turn out to vote than was the case in the 1970s or 1980s – and turnout is lowest in countries with high inequality. With income inequality growing, citizens seem to have lost their faith in electoral politics as well. Contrary to the 'government overload' thesis, democracy's discontent is actually least pronounced in egalitarian countries with strong trade unions and high levels of public expenditure. In the next section, we will revisit the conservative diagnosis of government overload that occurred in the late 1970s. Section 3 will use broad empirical trends in OECD countries to demonstrate how governments have pursued distributive and regulatory liberalization. Western governments have fended off popular demands for redistribution by asserting the position of the market and reducing their own involvement in economic affairs. Income inequality has consequently increased over the last twenty-five years, as section 4 documents. Section 5 then asks what effect setting markets free has had on the quality of democracy. More specifically, it looks at the impact of inequality on turnout as well as trust in parliament and government. The final section asks what this analysis tells us about the future prospects of democracy in the face of vastly increased debt during the financial crisis. Since governments – independently of their ideological leanings – are forced to cut spending in an attempt to limit deficits, their citizens may grow even more alienated from democratic politics than they are at present.

2 Government overload

The literature on government overload that flourished in the 1970s is riddled with dramatic statements and doomsday scenarios. For example, Brittan (1975: 129) assumed that adults at the time would live to see democracy crumble. Crozier and his colleagues (1975: 2) quoted Willy Brandt, who is supposed to have predicted in the 1970s that democracy would collapse within the next twenty to thirty years. These authors saw flaws in the way democratic politics worked:

> There is deeper reason for pessimism if the threats to democracy arise ineluctably from the inherent workings of the democratic process itself. Yet, in recent years, the operations of the democratic process do indeed appear to have generated a breakdown of traditional means of social control, a delegitimation of political and other forms of authority, and an overload of demands on government, exceeding its capacity to respond. ... The demands on democratic government grow, while the capacity of democratic government stagnates. This, it would appear, is the central dilemma of the governability of democracy which has manifested itself in Europe, North America, and Japan in the 1970s. (Crozier et al. 1975: 8–9)

Two reasons in particular were purported to be responsible for government overload: the strength of trade unions and the need for political parties to outcompete their rivals in responding to popular demands for redistribution (Brittan 1975: 129).

First, government overload theorists held trade unions responsible for economic ungovernability. Governments depended on union cooperation in order to be able to control inflation and unemployment simultaneously, yet, as their organizational power grew, unions prevailed in increasing wages, which created inflationary pressure. Fighting inflation was politically dangerous for governments, because of the assumption that price stability and employment were negatively correlated. All attempts to stop inflation led by necessity to an increase in unemployment. To accept this would have torpedoed any office-holder's chances at re-election, since the Keynesian postwar consensus attributed the responsibility for full employment to government.[2] This made government overload theorists all the more pessimistic about the future of democracy, because governments, should they fail to disempower unions, would have the choice only between inflation and unemployment – and both were considered incompatible with democracy (Brittan 1975: 143). 'In this sense, inflation is the economic disease of democracy' (Crozier et al. 1975: 164).

A few years later, Olson (1982) provided the most thorough analysis of the connection between union power and government overload.[3] In *The Rise and Decline of Nations*, he argued that distributional coalitions were gaining more and more influence in democratic countries. These coalitions were themselves not productive but fought primarily for economic rents. Olson attributed the stagflation of the 1970s – the simultaneous emergence of low economic growth and high rates of inflation – to the influence of these 'growth-retarding organizations' (1982: 98). Although the argument applied to special interest groups in general, Olson was referring above all to trade unions (ibid.: 48–9, 111, 201–2), holding that they created cartels, controlled access to the labour market and negotiated non-market prices that led to unemployment. Encompassing organizations, however, would have to take (macro-) economic consequences of their actions into account.

Olson's argument gained plausibility in light of the different developments experienced by European countries in the 1970s. Corporatist countries with centralized and unitary organizations were more successful at handling the negative impact of the oil crisis than were those with strong but fragmented unions competing against one another (Scharpf 1987). Against this backdrop, it is not surprising that Great Britain in particular was thought to be ungovernable (Crozier et al. 1975: 11). Throughout the 1970s, various British governments negotiated with the trade unions to get a grip on accelerating inflation rates. Wage policy guidelines were determined time and again, yet they seldom lasted longer than a year. Many trade union critics perceived the 'British disease' as the precursor to future developments in other countries (Guggenberger 1975: 33). Since Olson expected the number of special interest groups to increase over time, he predicted a further slowdown in economic growth for stable democracies. Again, the very logic of democracy – the freedom of association – was seen to have detrimental economic effects.

Second, in line with the public choice literature, overload theorists identified another threat to prudent government behaviour: they saw a growing demand for redistribution from the public and expected parties to overbid themselves to meet these demands in their quest for office (Crozier et al. 1975: 9). Taken together, the demand and supply culminated in the 'principle of self-propelling motion' that Luhmann (1981: 37) compared to a swarm of migrating locusts with no internal rules to stop the dynamics of its own action. Instead of rejecting spiralling demands, the advanced welfare state took on more and more tasks, for which additional revenue was needed. In doing so, government absorbed an ever larger percentage of GDP after taxes and social security contributions.

Whereas public choice scholars attributed the expansion of public expenditure to the very logic of party competition, others saw long-term trends at work: 'Once upon a time, then, man looked to God to order the world. Then he looked to the market. Now he looks to government' (King 1975: 288). The crisis of democracy was inevitably the consequence of 'a revolution of growing demands' (Bell 1991: 32; author's translation) that politics had evoked but could not fulfil. What remained controversial was the question of whether the necessary departure from the 'too much government' (*Vielregiererei*) was possible in an 'unbridled democracy' or whether the 'dethronement of politics' could succeed (Hayek 1978: 17; author's translation). The majority of observers interpreted growing public expenditures as an unavoidable trend, whereas Huntington (1975: 84, 113) saw government overload as resulting from a temporary 'excess of democracy'. To save democracy from these excesses, politics and markets would have to be depoliticized.

In sum, overload theorists – many of them economic liberals – found democratic governments ill-equipped to deal with the economic challenges of the time. The cure they proposed consisted of welfare-state retrenchment and the depoliticization both of the market and of democracy. Politically, the conservative crisis diagnosis has proven highly influential. Since the early 1980s, OECD countries have pursued reforms that correspond to its recommendations: almost everywhere, governments have – albeit in a piecemeal, stop-and-go fashion – taken on the task of liberalizing markets. This strategy did not start everywhere at the same time, and not all governments have pursued it with the same rigour, but nowhere has it been thoroughly ignored, as the next sections show.

3 Setting the market free

Following Höpner et al. (2011: 3; author's translation), we can define political liberalization as the 'politically legitimized transfer of allocation and distribution decisions to markets'. Hence liberalization directly affects the causes of government overload, since political actors can point towards markets to ward off popular demands. Höpner and his co-authors track liberalization trends for twenty-one OECD countries since 1980 and distinguish two dimensions of liberalization: regulatory and distributive. They find that regulatory liberalization has proceeded more quickly than distributive liberalization. More importantly, however, the overall conclusion of their study is that not only have all countries pursued liberalization policies, but the least market-oriented ones have liberalized most, prompting convergence (ibid.: 22).

Much of the welfare state retrenchment literature has focused on distributive liberalization and has somewhat neglected regulatory liberalization. Nonetheless, disagreements persist about the degree to which welfare cuts have taken place (see Starke 2006 for a literature review). Looking at aggregate expenditure data between 1960 and 2001, Castles (2006) stresses welfare-state resilience. While there have been substantial cuts in areas such as military spending, social expenditure has hardly decreased. In line with the 'new politics of the welfare state' thesis (Pierson 1996), the argument is that sluggish growth and high debt have made some retrenchment necessary, but that governments have shied away from cutting popular programmes and instead have focused on less visible ones to avoid electoral punishment.

Figure 7.1, depicting average spending and taxation levels for twenty-three countries in the period from 1970 to 2007, at first sight corroborates this impression.[4] While overall expenditure (total disbursement as a percentage of GDP) has declined during the last two decades and now hovers at the level of 1979, there is little evidence for a decline in aggregate taxation or social spending. In fact, both tax revenue and social expenditure have stagnated during the last fifteen years. Yet table 7.1 offers a more nuanced picture. If we compare the figures of the latest available year to the minimum, all countries show higher spending. Compared to the maximum, however, current social spending is lower in seventeen countries and the level of taxation is below the maximum value in twenty-one countries. Cuts in spending and taxation have

Figure 7.1: Average expenditure and taxation levels as a percentage of GDP in twenty-three countries

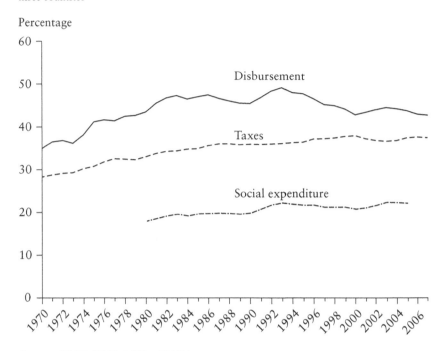

Percentage

Source: OECD (2007, 2010a, 2010b).

generally been smallest in Southern Europe and highest in Anglo-Saxon and Scandinavian countries.

The welfare resilience hypothesis has been criticized because developments at the macro-level do not necessarily correspond with those on the micro-level (Scruggs 2008: 63–5). Even if individual entitlements are cut, the sum of benefits can increase because of a larger number of beneficiaries. This is why Korpi and Palme (2003) as well as Allan and Scruggs (2004) study individual entitlements rather than aggregate social spending. Figure 7.2 shows the replacement rates for an average production worker in four social policy areas for eighteen countries (1960 to 2000). In all cases, benefit entitlements are lower in the year 2000 than they were in the early 1980s – although replacement rates still exceed the level of 1960. Clearly, welfare states are less generous today than they used to be. This holds for all country groups, even though cuts have been more modest in Japan and continental Europe than in Scandinavia or the Anglo-Saxon countries.

Turning to regulatory liberalization reveals even less ambiguous trends. The existing evidence suggests that all OECD countries have

Table 7.1: Trends in social expenditure and taxation, 1970–2005

	Social expenditure (% of GDP)					Total tax revenue (% of GDP)				
	2005	Minimum	Maximum	2005-min	2005-max	2008	Minimum	Maximum	2008-min	2008-max
Australia	17.1	10.8	17.9	6.3	-0.8	27.1	20.9	30.3	6.2	-3.2
Canada	16.5	14.1	21.3	2.4	-4.8	32.3	30.1	36.7	2.2	-4.4
Ireland	16.7	13.4	22.0	3.3	-5.3	28.8	27.9	36.8	0.9	-8.0
New Zealand	18.5	17.1	22.2	1.4	-3.7	33.7	25.0	37.6	8.7	-3.9
United Kingdom	21.3	16.6	21.3	4.7	0.0	35.7	31.2	38.5	4.5	-2.8
United States	15.9	12.9	16.2	3.0	-0.3	26.1	24.9	29.5	1.2	-3.4
	17.7	**14.2**	**20.1**	**3.5**	**-2.5**	**30.6**	**26.7**	**34.9**	**4.0**	**-4.3**
Austria	27.2	22.6	27.5	4.6	-0.3	42.7	33.8	45.3	8.9	-2.6
Belgium	26.4	23.5	27.0	2.9	-0.6	44.2	33.9	45.1	10.3	-0.9
France	29.2	20.8	29.2	8.4	0.0	43.2	33.5	45.1	9.7	-1.9
Germany	26.7	22.5	27.4	4.2	-0.7	37.0	31.5	37.2	5.5	-0.2
Luxembourg	23.2	19.8	25.3	3.4	-2.1	35.5	23.5	39.8	12.0	-4.3
Netherlands	20.9	19.3	26.6	1.6	-5.7	39.1	35.6	45.5	3.5	-6.4
Switzerland	20.3	13.5	20.3	6.8	0.0	29.1	19.0	30.0	10.1	-0.9
	24.8	**20.3**	**26.2**	**4.6**	**-1.3**	**38.7**	**30.1**	**41.1**	**8.6**	**-2.5**
Greece	20.5	11.5	22.3	9.0	-1.8	32.6	18.1	35.9	14.5	-3.3
Italy	25.0	18.0	25.0	7.0	0.0	43.3	23.9	43.4	19.4	-0.1
Portugal	23.1	10.8	23.1	12.3	0.0	35.2	17.0	35.2	18.2	0.0
Spain	21.2	15.5	23.2	5.7	-2.0	33.3	15.9	37.3	17.4	-4.0
	22.5	**14.0**	**23.4**	**8.5**	**-0.9**	**36.1**	**18.7**	**38.0**	**17.4**	**-1.9**

Table 7.1 (continued)

	Social expenditure (% of GDP)					Total tax revenue (% of GDP)				
	2005	Minimum	Maximum	2005-min	2005-max	2008	Minimum	Maximum	2008-min	2008-max
Denmark	27.1	23.4	29.4	3.7	-2.3	48.2	38.4	50.8	9.8	-2.6
Finland	26.1	18.4	33.6	7.7	-7.5	43.1	31.6	47.2	11.5	-4.1
Iceland	16.9	14.0	18.2	2.9	-1.3	36.8	27.4	41.5	9.4	-4.7
Norway	21.6	16.9	24.6	4.7	-3.0	42.6	34.5	44.5	8.1	-1.9
Sweden	29.4	28.6	36.2	0.8	-6.8	46.3	37.9	52.2	8.4	-5.9
****	**24.2**	**20.3**	**28.4**	**4.0**	**-4.2**	**43.4**	**34.0**	**47.2**	**9.4**	**-3.8**
Japan	18.6	10.3	18.6	8.3	0.0	28.1	19.6	29.7	8.5	-1.6

Source: See figure 7.1.

Figure 7.2: Average replacement rates of an average production worker in eighteen countries

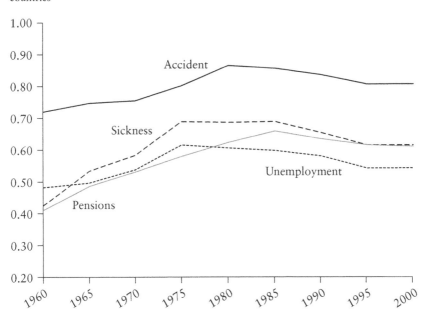

Source: Korpi and Palme (2007).

adopted measures to liberalize markets: they have privatized state-owned enterprises, introduced competition where in the past state monopolies provided services of general interest – postal services, electricity, public transport, etc. – and eased employment protection, especially for non-standard employment. Regulatory liberalization has meant that an increasing number of people have jobs that are no longer protected from competition, and remuneration has started to reflect market prices.

Unfortunately, there are few long-term indicators for the overall degree of regulatory liberalization. The Fraser Institute calculates an 'Economic Freedom of the World Index' ranging from 1 to 10, however, with higher values indicating 'freer' markets.[5] The overall index includes levels of taxation and government size as well as features of the legal system, trade openness and market regulation. Figure 7.3 shows the development of the overall Economic Freedom Index as well as the sub-index on (market) regulation and its sub-index of labour-market regulation. All three indicators show that advanced democracies have become less interventionist and have removed barriers to economic transactions, in particular between 1985 and 2005. Despite slightly decreasing values after 2005, markets at the end of the period are less politically regulated than they

Figure 7.3: Economic freedom index and regulation in twenty-three countries

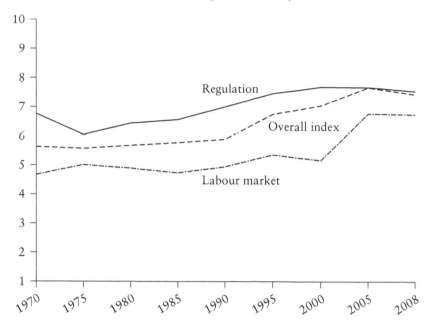

Source: Gwartney et al. (2010).

were in 1970. Declining coefficients of variation over time (not reported in the figure) indicate that countries have been converging towards the pole of 'economic freedom'.

A similar story holds for state subsidies. Until the early 1980s, subsidies mounted as governments sought to offset rising unemployment and structural change through higher subsidies. Thereafter, however, subsidies have been cut almost everywhere. Since 1999, state subsidies have been below the level of the 1970s (figure 7.4). Another way in which governments have sought to unburden themselves has been the privatization and liberalization of services of general interests such as telecommunications, postal services, energy and public transport (Henisz et al. 2005). Without exception, OECD countries have introduced market mechanisms to govern these sectors. The OECD provides an indicator that measures regulatory provisions on a scale from 0 to 6 (lower values stand for less regulation) for seven sectors: telecommunications, electricity, gas, post, rail, air transport and road freight. As figure 7.5 shows, these services of general interest have experienced fierce liberalization since the 1980s. Combined with similar figures on privatization, these changes suggest that the state has cut down its entrepreneurial

Figure 7.4: Subsidies as a percentage of GDP for twenty-three countries

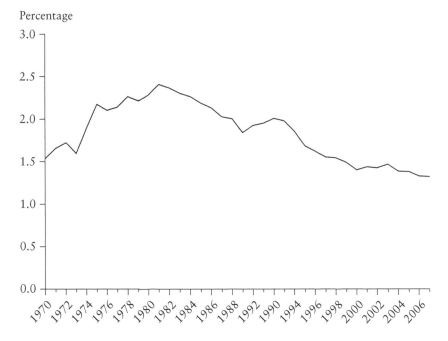

Source: OECD (2010a).

activities substantially, not least because privatization revenues have helped to limit deficits (Obinger and Zohlnhöfer 2007).

Finally, the spectre of the trade union state has lost whatever credibility it once had. Trade unions have been losing members in the vast majority of countries (Scruggs 2002). In the nineteen non-Scandinavian countries, trade union density between 1970 and 2007 declined from just under 40 per cent to 23 per cent. The catchphrase watchword of the trade union state appeared plausible to observers in the 1970s because militancy in the labour movement had been on the increase since 1968. Until the first wave of strikes in the early 1960s, industrial conflicts were rare occurrences in the postwar period. Between 1968 and 1975, however, nearly all Western countries experienced sustained strikes. Work stoppages remained quite common in several countries well into the 1980s, but since the beginning of the 1990s the number of workdays lost to strikes has dropped again to the level of the early 1970s (Glyn 2006: 6). Trade unions today are much weaker than they used to be and use strike action much less frequently than in the past.

Figure 7.5: Summary index of regulation in services of general interest

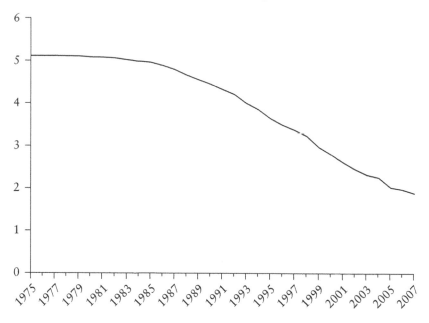

Source: OECD (2012). The ETCR-Indicator summarizes regulatory provisions in seven sectors: telecomunications, electricity, gas, post, rail, air passenger transport and road freight.

In sum, the evidence suggests that advanced democracies – at least from the mid-1980s onwards – acted upon the cure that overload theorists had prescribed in the 1970s. Albeit slowly and to different degrees, these countries have managed to stop or even to reverse the growth of public expenditure, have cut back welfare entitlements for individuals, and have liberalized markets. Although the twenty-three countries under review have not converged on a single welfare and production regime, they all have grown more market-oriented in the last twenty-five years.

4 Liberalization and rising inequality

For the first three-quarters of the twentieth century, income inequality fell. Over this period, the richest 10 per cent of the population's share of overall income declined. Such was the case in Australia, France, Germany, Britain, Ireland, Canada, the Netherlands, Switzerland and the United

Figure 7.6: Gini index of disposable income for twenty-three countries

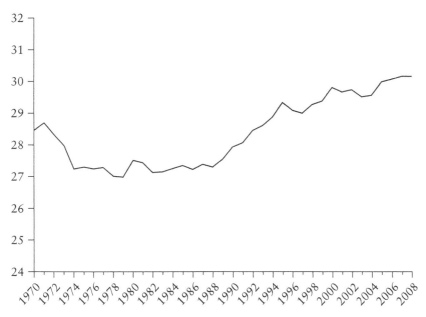

Source: Solt (2008–9).

States (Atkinson and Piketty 2007: 540). However, the subsequent move towards freer markets has left its imprint on the distribution of incomes. Income inequality began to rise, first in Anglo-Saxon countries and later in almost all other countries (Brandolini and Smeeding 2008; Goesling 2001). Referring to this development, Alderson and Nielsen (2002) speak of a 'great U-turn' in income inequality.

Figure 7.6 shows the development of the Gini coefficient (of disposable incomes) between 1970 and 2008. During the first half of the 1970s, income inequality was still declining. Between the mid-1970s and the late 1980s, different country groups followed different trajectories. While inequality started to rise in the Anglo-Saxon world, it remained fairly stable in continental Europe and even declined in the Scandinavian countries. Over the last ten to fifteen years, however, inequality has been growing in all country groups (OECD 2011: 24).

In line with the discussion in the previous section, which presented clear evidence of regulatory liberalization but more mixed evidence of distributive liberalization, table 7.2 demonstrates that market incomes have become unequal more rapidly than disposable incomes. This might, in fact, help to explain why (aggregate) social expenditure has

Table 7.2: Trends in income inequality, mid-1980s to mid-2000

	Market income			Disposable income		
	Mid-1980s	Mid-2000s	% change	Mid-80s	Mid-2000s	% change
Australia	–	0.46	–	–	0.30	–
Austria	–	0.43	–	0.24	0.27	11.1
Belgium	0.45	0.49	8.2	0.27	0.27	0.0
Canada	0.40	0.44	9.1	0.29	0.32	9.4
Denmark	0.37	0.42	11.9	0.22	0.23	4.3
Finland	0.33	0.39	15.4	0.21	0.27	22.2
France	0.52	0.48	-8.3	0.31	0.28	-10.7
Germany	0.44	0.51	13.7	0.26	0.30	13.3
Greece	–	–	–	0.34	0.32	-6.3
Iceland	–	0.37	–	–	0.28	–
Ireland	–	0.42	–	0.33	0.33	0.0
Italy	0.42	0.56	25.0	0.31	0.35	11.4
Japan	0.35	0.44	20.5	0.30	0.32	6.3
Luxembourg		0.45	–	0.25	0.26	3.8
Netherlands	0.47	0.42	-11.9	0.26	0.27	3.7
New Zealand	0.41	0.47	12.8	0.27	0.34	20.6
Norway	0.35	0.43	18.6	0.23	0.28	17.9
Portugal	–	0.54	–	–	0.38	–
Spain	–	–	–	0.37	0.32	-15.6
Sweden	0.40	0.43	7.0	0.20	0.23	13.0
Switzerland	–	0.35	–	–	0.28	–
United Kingdom	0.44	0.46	4.3	0.33	0.34	2.9
United States	0.40	0.46	13.0	0.34	0.38	10.5
Average	**0.41**	**0.45**	**9.94**	**0.28**	**0.30**	**5.94**

Source: OECD (2008).

not declined: as market incomes grow apart, incomes at the lower end of the distribution can fall below the subsistence level and qualify for transfer payments. Free markets can prove expensive under these circumstances.

Which factors discussed in section section 3 trigger inequality? Table 7.3 displays the result of a pooled time-series cross-sectional regression analysis for all twenty-three countries and the period from 1980 to 2007. Unfortunately not all indicators are consistently available for a reasonable number of years or for all countries, so the analysis is limited to those that are. The first two factors (social expenditure and taxation) reflect the degree of distributive liberalization; union density, regulation and employment protection reflect regulative liberalization, while the other variables serve as controls. Higher values for the first five variables indicate less liberalization. Model 1 includes all of these variables as well

Table 7.3: Determinants of income inequality (OLS regression with PCSE)

	Model 1	Model 2	Model 3
Social expenditure	−0.116[a]	−0.322[c]	−0.309[c]
	(0.047)	(0.074)	(0.074)
Taxation	−0.149[b]	−0.143[b]	−0.136[a]
	(0.033)	(0.033)	(0.033)
Union density	−0.449[c]	−0.432[c]	−0.341[c]
	(0.011)	(0.011)	(0.016)
Regulation of services of	−0.162[c]	−0.173[c]	−0.177[c]
general interest	(0.164)	(0.165)	(0.165)
Employment protection	−0.111[a]	−0.525[c]	−0.487[c]
	(0.202)	(0.611)	(0.615)
Unemployment rate	−0.020	−0.011	−0.011
	(0.047)	(0.045)	(0.045)
Debt (log)	0.125[c]	0.125[c]	0.108[b]
	(0.347)	(0.332)	(0.342)
GDP (log)	−0.263[c]	−0.297[c]	−0.276[c]
	(1.098)	(1.093)	(1.129)
1990s	0.069[b]	0.074[b]	0.071[b]
(reference: 1970s)	(0.204)	(0.218)	(0.216)
2000s	0.137[c]	0.151[c]	0.147[c]
(reference: 1970s)	(0.294)	(0.316)	(0.314)
Employment protection*		0.508[b]	0.480[b]
social expenditure		(0.027)	(0.027)
Scandinavia			−0.120
(1 = yes; 0 = no)			(0.787)
R[2]	0.898	0.901	0.902
N	444	444	444

Notes:
[a] p<.05.
[b] p<.01.
[c] p<.001.
* Indicates an interaction effect, where two variables have been multiplied.
Models correct for first-order autocorrelation and report standardized coefficients with panel-corrected standard errors in parentheses.

as two time-period dummy variables. The second model introduces an interaction term for employment protection and social expenditure, since these two could be functionally equivalent in reducing inequality. Model 3 includes a dummy variable for the Scandinavian countries to check whether the results are driven by this group of countries. No matter how the model is specified, the results are clear: higher values on the first five variables – indicating politically constrained markets – reduce inequality. A recent OECD report shows that the very same factors that generate employment – for example, declining trade union membership, less employment protection, product market deregulation and lower unemployment replacement rates – lead at the same time to a higher degree of wage dispersion. As welfare states have become less able to offset the increasing spread of market incomes in recent years, the inequality of disposable incomes has been mounting too (OECD 2011: 32): free markets inevitably lead to higher income inequality.[6]

As expected, social expenditure conditions the effect of employment protection. If the former is below 22 per cent of GDP, the latter has a significant impact on income inequality. Once social spending exceeds this level (which is true for 40 per cent of the country years), strict employment protection does not additionally lower inequality.[7] Higher debt rates also lead to income inequality. During the financial crisis debt has been rising for all countries and skyrocketing in some, so a further rise in inequality can be expected. Finally, the results reported in the first two models are not driven simply by the Scandinavian countries. They remain significant even if we introduce a 'Scandinavia dummy' or drop these countries altogether (not shown in the table).

5 Inequality and democracy's discontents

Overload theorists have championed less government and freer markets for the sake of democracy. Given the trends discussed in section 3, democracy should be in better shape today than it was twenty-five years ago: the power of labour unions has been curbed, inflation and strikes have levelled off, the involvement of government in economic affairs has been reduced, and public expenditures are not increasing uncontrollably but rather are stagnating or even declining. Yet there still are signs of democratic distemper. Confidence in parliaments and politicians is declining, electoral participation is sinking, and dissatisfaction with the way democracy works is widespread (Putnam et al. 2000: 15–16, table 1.1; Dalton 2004: 29–30, table 2.2). Free markets do not comfortably coexist with democracy when rising inequality breeds apathy and discontent.

To address this issue, we will now look at the impact of inequality on voter turnout and confidence in parliaments and governments. In a first step, we ran a pooled time-series cross-section regression for twenty-three OECD countries and the years 1970 to 2008 to determine whether income inequality has an impact on turnout (table 7.4). The first model simply includes a number of variables that have frequently been found to affect turnout (see Blais 2006). Except for 'closeness' – the difference between the strongest and the second-strongest party – the effects are in

Table 7.4: Determinants of turnout in twenty-three countries, 1970–2008 (OLS regression with PCSE)

	Model 1	Model 2	Model 3
Gini coefficient	−1.227[c]	−0.942[c]	−0.215[b]
(0–100)	(0.121)	(0.105)	(0.076)
Compulsory voting	11.693[c]	10.055[c]	2.536[b]
(0 = no; 1 = yes)	(1.249)	(1.065)	(0.838)
Proportional representation	7.952[c]	2.038	0.446
(0 = no; 1 = yes)	(1.639)	(1.586)	(0.974)
Presidentialism	−20.417[c]	−7.477[c]	−2.326
(0 = no; 1 = yes)	(1.662)	(2.252)	(1.359)
Bicameralism	−4.065[a]	3.778[a]	1.242
(0 = no; 1 = yes)	(1.596)	(1.598)	(0.933)
Effective number of parties	−0.087	−0.639[b]	−0.274[a]
	(0.315)	(0.231)	(0.134)
Closeness	−0.216[b]	−0.131[a]	−0.050
	(0.071)	(0.061)	(0.038)
Population (log)	0.490	−1.461[b]	−0.379
	(0.570)	(0.556)	(0.325)
Switzerland		−26.605[c]	−4.087
(0 = no; 1 = yes)		(3.405)	(2.332)
USA		−26.044[c]	−14.863[c]
(0 = no; 1 = yes)		(3.352)	(1.965)
Turnout (lag)			0.801[c]
			(0.045)
Constant	105.876[c]	119.924[c]	25.452[c]
	(6.792)	(5.624)	(5.613)
R^2	0.738	0.807	0.934
N	221	221	215

Notes:
[a] $p<.05$.
[b] $p<.01$.
[c] $p<.001$
All models are pooled time-series cross-section OLS-regression and report panel-corrected standard errors in parentheses. The results stay substantially the same with a feasible least-squares regression, which controls for autocorrelation or heteroskedasticity.

Sources: Armingeon et al. (2010), except compulsory voting: www.idea.int/vt/compulsory_voting.cfm (accessed February 2010).

line with the results from earlier studies. Taken together, these variables explain a considerable share of the variance, and the effect of inequality on turnout is robust for different model specifications. All else being equal, moving from the most equal to the most unequal country lowers turnout by roughly 18 points (this refers to the second model). Model 3 includes the lagged dependent variable which reduces the explanatory power of other variables (Achen 2001), yet income inequality remains

Table 7.5: Probability of voting (multi-level regression analysis)

	Model 1	Model 2	Model 3	Model 4
Household income	0.072[d]	0.072[d]	0.107[d]	0.105[d]
	(0.016)	(0.016)	(0.013)	(0.013)
Education	0.255[d]	0.254[d]	0.276[d]	0.275[d]
(1 = low to 5 = high)	(0.011)	(0.011)	(0.008)	(0.008)
Gini coefficient	−0.083[c]	−0.083[c]	−0.068[c]	−0.067[c]
	(0.031)	(0.031)	(0.025)	(0.025)
Income[b] Gini		0.001	−0.001	
		(0.004)	(0.003)	
Education[b] Gini				0.002
				(0.002)
Age	0.123[d]	0.123[d]	0.141[d]	0.141[d]
	(0.004)	(0.004)	(0.003)	(0.003)
Age^2/100	−0.090[d]	−0.090[d]	−0.108[d]	−0.108[d]
	(0.004)	(0.004)	(0.003)	(0.003)
Female	−0.046[a]	−0.046[a]	−0.078[d]	−0.078[d]
(0 = no; 1 = yes)	(0.024)	(0.024)	(0.018)	(0.018)
Unemployed	−0.398[d]	−0.397[d]		
(0 = no; 1 = yes)	(0.052)	(0.052)		
Trade union member	0.351[d]	0.351[d]		
(0 = no; 1 = yes)	(0.035)	(0.035)		
Leftist	0.208[d]	0.208[d]		
(0 = no; 1 = yes)	(0.026)	(0.026)		
Population (log)	0.041	0.041	−0.047	−0.047
	(0.105)	(0.105)	(0.091)	(0.091)
Closeness (difference between	−0.000	−0.000	−0.003	−0.003
the two strongest parties)	(0.017)	(0.017)	(0.015)	(0.015)
Effective number of parties	−0.043	−0.043	−0.040	−0.040
	(0.077)	(0.077)	(0.062)	(0.062)
Compulsory voting	1.315[d]	1.315[d]	1.527[d]	1.527[d]
(0 = no; 1 = yes)	(0.328)	(0.328)	(0.258)	(0.258)
Proportional representation	0.283	0.283	0.126	0.126
(0 = no; 1 = yes)	(0.359)	(0.359)	(0.316)	(0.316)
Presidentialism	−1.008[c]	−1.008[c]	−0.769[c]	−0.768[c]
(0 = no; 1 = yes)	(0.306)	(0.306)	(0.259)	(0.259)
Bicameralism	−0.138	−0.138	0.108	0.108
(0 = no; 1 = yes)	(0.271)	(0.271)	(0.233)	(0.233)
Constant	2.102[d]	2.102[d]	1.906[d]	1.906[d]
	(0.326)	(0.326)	(0.288)	(0.288)
Deviance	47522.794	47522.738	78269.177	78267.541
N	74658	74658	108204	108204
N_g	67	67	79	79

Notes:
[a] p<.1.
[b] p<.05.
[c] p<.01.
[d] p<.001.

Table 7.5: (continued)

Standard errors in parentheses. Continuous individual level variables are centred at the country mean; continuous level II-variables are grand mean-centred.
Missing values for income have been replaced with the country mean. Running the analysis without imputation does not change the results.
This analysis does not weight voters and non-voters according to real turnout. Doing so does not, however, affect the results.
For a list of elections and surveys used for this analysis, see table 7.7.

Figure 7.7: Marginal effect of income and education on turnout as inequality changes

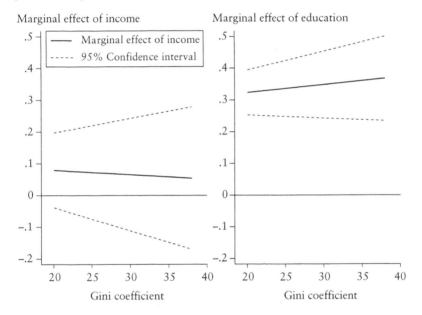

Source: See table 7.7.

statistically significant. Substantially, this means that income inequality reduces turnout independently of other trends by 4 points.

We then complement the table 7.4 regression analysis with a multi-level logistic regression for twenty-three countries and seventy-nine elections that involves controls for each of the three levels (individual, election, country).[8] Table 7.5 shows the results. Individual resources such as income and education increase the probability of voting, whereas income inequality reduces this probability. There is a curvilinear relationship between age and voting (young and old citizens are less likely to vote than those in the middle). Unemployment also decreases the likelihood of voting, while membership in a trade union and left-leaning political views increase it. Compulsory voting increases turnout, while presidentialism lowers it. By and large, these results confirm what we already know. At first sight, however, model 3 fails to support the claim that the voting gap between rich and poor is higher in more unequal countries. The interaction term is not significant (see also figure 7.7). These results suggest, in contrast to Solt (2008) but in line with Anderson and Beramendi (2008), that greater income inequality does not widen the participatory gap between those at the bottom and those at the top of society. Yet many interviewees refused to reveal their family income, and responses may generally be unreliable. This is why model 4 tests instead whether the effect of education as a measure of social stratification changes with rising inequality. As figure 7.7 shows, it does indeed. Substantively this means that the turnout gap between the poorly educated and the well-educated widens from 10 to almost 19 percentage points if we move from the most egalitarian to the most unequal country. This finding suggests that inequality not only lowers turnout, it also renders it more socially unequal.

The final analysis checks whether income equality has any effect on the confidence citizens have in their national parliament or government. All models in table 7.6 are based on data from the World Value Surveys and European Value Surveys for the years 2005–8, which allow the inclusion of a larger range of individual-level variables. The Gini index, compulsory voting, presidentialism, single-member district and bicameralism are used at the country level. The individual-level variables are in line with what is to be expected and will not be discussed in any detail. As in previous analyses, both household income and education positively influence the probability of confidence in national parliaments and governments, whereas income inequality reduces the probability of confidence: inequality thus undermines citizens' trust in democratic institutions.

Model 2 and model 4 also include an interaction between individual income and income distribution to test whether differences between income groups are larger in more unequal societies. Figure 7.8 shows that differences in confidence between income groups decline with growing inequality.[9] In unequal countries, distrust seems to depend less on individual traits than on the context of inequality, which means that everyone has less confidence. In egalitarian societies, in turn, confidence in parliament and government is generally higher but also more differentiated between income groups.

In sum, using different methods and looking at different indicators confirms that inequality reduces citizens' propensity to vote as well as their confidence in parliament and government. The attempt to reinvigorate growth through liberalization has left its imprint on democracy. As countries have grown more unequal, citizens have lost their faith in

Table 7.6: Confidence in parliaments and governments (random intercept model)

	Confidence in parliament		Confidence in government	
	Model 1	Model 2	Model 3	Model 4
Household income	0.037[d]	0.036[d]	0.041[d]	0.040[d]
	(0.006)	(0.006)	(0.006)	(0.006)
Education	0.075[d]	0.075[d]	0.033[c]	0.033[c]
	(0.012)	(0.012)	(0.012)	(0.012)
Gini index	−0.063[b]	−0.062[b]	−0.048[a]	−0.047[a]
(0–100)	(0.027)	(0.027)	(0.029)	(0.029)
Gini* income		−0.002		−0.001
		(0.001)		(0.001)
Individual controls				
Age	−0.028[d]	−0.028[d]	−0.030[d]	−0.030[d]
	(0.005)	(0.005)	(0.005)	(0.005)
$Age^2/100$	0.033[d]	0.034[d]	0.033[d]	0.033[d]
	(0.005)	(0.005)	(0.005)	(0.005)
Female	0.016	0.016	−0.083[c]	−0.083[c]
	(0.031)	(0.031)	(0.031)	(0.031)
Extremism (distance to	−0.010	−0.010	0.023[a]	0.023[a]
ideological mean)	(0.013)	(0.013)	(0.013)	(0.013)
Party member	0.171[c]	0.171[c]	0.032	0.032
(0 = no; 1 = yes)	(0.057)	(0.057)	(0.055)	(0.055)
Trade union member	−0.057	−0.058	−0.142[d]	−0.144[d]
(0 = no; 1 = yes)	(0.042)	(0.042)	(0.042)	(0.042)
Political interest	0.428[d]	0.428[d]	0.349[d]	0.349[d]
(0 = no; 1 = yes)	(0.033)	(0.033)	(0.034)	(0.034)
Church attendance	0.341[d]	0.340[d]	0.452[d]	0.451[d]
(0 = no; 1 = yes)	(0.039)	(0.039)	(0.039)	(0.039)
Life satisfaction	0.046[d]	0.045[d]	0.058[d]	0.057[d]
(1 = low; 10 = high)	(0.009)	(0.009)	(0.009)	(0.009)
Trust in other people	0.375[d]	0.374[d]	0.314[d]	0.314[d]
(0 = low; 1 = high)	(0.033)	(0.033)	(0.033)	(0.033)
Country controls				
Compulsory voting	−0.199	−0.199	−0.249	−0.249
	(0.297)	(0.297)	(0.318)	(0.318)
Presidentialism	0.383	0.382	0.404	0.403
	(0.303)	(0.303)	(0.324)	(0.324)
Single-member district	−0.753[b]	−0.753[b]	−0.265	−0.265
	(0.331)	(0.331)	(0.354)	(0.354)
Bicameralism	−0.239	−0.240	0.051	0.050
	(0.221)	(0.221)	(0.236)	(0.236)
Constant	−0.573[d]	−0.572[d]	−0.889[d]	−0.888[d]
	(0.150)	(0.150)	(0.160)	(0.160)
N (individuals)	20168	20168	20235	20235
N (countries)	23	23	23	23

Table 7.6 (continued)

Notes:
[a] p<.1.
[b] p<.05.
[c] p<.01.
[d] p<.001.
* Indicates an interaction effect, where two variables have been multiplied.
Standard errors in parentheses.

Source: World Value and European Value Surveys, 2005/2008.

Figure 7.8: Marginal effect of income on confidence in parliament and government as inequality changes

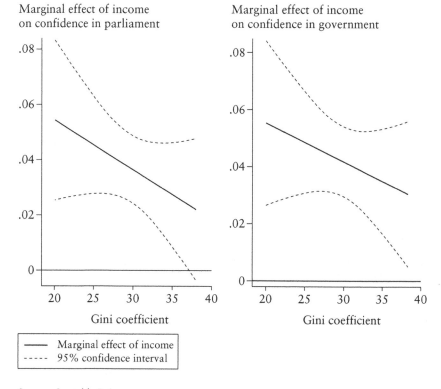

Marginal effect of income on confidence in parliament

Marginal effect of income on confidence in government

——— Marginal effect of income
- - - - 95% confidence interval

Source: See table 7.6.

elections, parliaments and governments. Government overload theorists in the 1970s demanded less politicized markets and depoliticized democracy, and that is just what has happened in the countries where their economic recommendations have been realized to the fullest. Contrary to

Table 7.7: Elections and surveys

Country	1980s	1990s	2000s
Australia	1984[a]	1990[c], 1993[e]	2004[g]
Austria		1991[d], 1994	2002[h]
Belgium	1987[b]	1991[d], 1999[f]	2003[h], 2007[j]
Canada		1993[e]	2004[g], 2006[i]
Denmark	1987[b]	1994[d], 1998[f]	2005[g]
Finland		1995[d]	2003[g], 2007[j]
France	1986[b]	1993[e]	2002[g], 2007[j]
Germany	1983[a], 1987[b]	1994[e]	2005[g]
Greece	1985[b]	1993[d]	2004[h], 2007[j]
Iceland		1999[f]	2003[h]
Ireland	1987[b]	1992[e]	2002[g], 2007[j]
Italy	1987[b]	1994[e]	2001[h], 2006[i]
Japan		1993[e]	2005[g]
Luxembourg		1994[d]	2004[h]
Netherlands	1986[b]	1994[d], 1998[f]	2006[h]
New Zealand		1996[e]	2002[g], 2005[i]
Norway		1993[e]	2001[g], 2006[i]
Portugal	1987[b]	1991[d], 1999[f]	2002[g], 2005[i]
Spain	1986[b]	1993[e]	2004[g], 2008[j]
Sweden		1994[e]	2002[g], 2006[i]
Switzerland		1999[f]	2003[h], 2007[j]
United Kingdom	1987[b]	1992[e]	2005[h]
United States	1984[a], 1988[c]	1992[e]	2004[g]

Surveys: [a]International Social Survey Programme (ISSP) I; [b]Eurobarometer 30.0; [c]ISSP II; [d]Eurobarometer 44.1; [e]ISSP III; [f]Comparative Study of Electoral Systems (CSES) I; [g]ISSP IV; [h]European Social Survey (ESS) II and ESS III; [i]CSES II; [j]ESS IV.

their predictions, there are fewer signs of democratic disaffection in the most egalitarian countries, which still have comparatively high levels of taxation and public spending.

6 Conclusions

Many observers during the 1970s were pessimistic about the future prospects of Western democracy because they thought governments would inevitably prioritize demands from special interest groups or voters above economic prudence. Parties would outdo each other to promise higher spending, and governments would be too weak to confront well-organized trade unions. Despite these predictions, governments were still able to cut welfare benefits and reduce involvement in economic affairs. Radical welfare reforms may have been rare, but piecemeal changes, accumulating over time, have taken place everywhere. Between the mid-1980s and the late 2000s, rich OECD countries have liberalized their economies and delegated decisions to markets even at the cost of citizen disaffection.

The achievements of the long struggle to cut public spending and lower public debt were reversed by the financial crisis in the years after 2007, however. Within a few years, deficits and debt have risen to record levels as governments have sought to stabilize the banking sector and to avert economic collapse. The most spectacular increases in public debt resulted from the need to save liberalized markets from themselves (see Streeck, chapter 11 in this volume). As the financial crisis puts strains on national budgets, the dissatisfaction with the way democracy works is likely to be exacerbated. High deficits and huge public debt will force governments to curb spending, shrink the public sector, and look for further revenues from privatization for years to come. Many governments have already announced deep cuts to take effect over the next several years to restore sound public finances. If governments are forced to follow this path independently of their ideological leanings or their constituencies, it could become even more difficult for voters to detect differences between parties, and the incentives to vote might decline further. Even worse is that income inequality will increase as austerity measures begin to work – and citizens' faith in democratic politics is likely to erode further as a result.

References

Achen, Christopher (2001) Why lagged dependent variables can suppress the explanatory power of other independent variables, paper presented at the annual meeting of the Political Methodology Section of the American Political Science Association, UCLA, 20–22 July.

Alderson, A. S., and Nielsen, F. (2002) Globalization and the great U-turn: income inequality trends in 16 OECD countries, *American Journal of Sociology* 107: 1244–99.

Allan, J. P., and Scruggs, L. (2004) Political partisanship and welfare state reform in advanced industrial societies, *American Journal of Political Science* 48: 496–512.

Armingeon, K., et al. (2010) *Comparative Political Data Set 1960–2008*. Berne: University of Berne, Institute of Political Science.

Anderson, C. J., and Beramendi, P. (2008) Income, inequality, and electoral participation, in P. Beramendi and C. J. Anderson (eds), *Democracy, Inequality, and Representation: A Comparative Perspective*. New York: Russell Sage Foundation.

Atkinson, A. B., and Piketty, T. (2007) Towards a unified data set on top incomes, in A. B. Atkinson and T. Piketty (eds), *Top Incomes over the*

Twentieth Century: A Contrast between Continental European and English-Speaking Countries. Oxford: Oxford University Press.

Bell, D. (1991) *Die kulturellen Widersprüche des Kapitalismus.* Frankfurt am Main: Campus.

Blais, A. (2006) What affects voter turnout, *American Review of Political Science* 9: 111–25.

Brandolini, A., and Smeeding, T. M. (2008) Inequality patterns in Western democracies: cross-country differences and changes over time, in P. Beramendi and C. J. Anderson (eds), *Democracy, Inequality, and Representation.* New York: Russell Sage Foundation, pp. 25–61.

Brittan, S. (1975) The economic contradictions of democracy, *British Journal of Political Science* 5: 129–59.

Castles, F. G. (2006) *The Growth of the Post-War Public Expenditure State: Long-Term Trajectories and Recent Trends,* TranState Working Papers 35. Bremen: Sonderforschungsbereich 597 'Staatlichkeit im Wandel'.

Crozier, M. J., Huntington, S. P., and Watanuki, J. (1975) *The Crisis of Democracy: Report of the Governability of Democracies of the Trilateral Commission.* New York: New York University Press.

Dalton, R. J. (2004) *Democratic Challenges, Democratic Choices: The Erosion of Political Support in Advanced Industrial Democracies.* Oxford: Oxford University Press.

Glyn, A. (2006) *Capitalism Unleashed: Finance Globalization and Welfare.* Oxford: Oxford University Press.

Goesling, B. (2001) Changing income inequality within and between nations: new evidence, *American Sociological Review* 66: 745–61.

Guggenberger, B. (1975) Herrschaftslegitimierung und Staatskrise: Zu einigen Problemen der Regierbarkeit des modernen Staates, in M. T. Greven, B. Guggenberger and J. Strasser (eds), *Krise des Staates? Zur Funktionsbestimmung des Staates im Spätkapitalismus.* Neuwied: Luchterhand, pp. 9–59.

Gwartney, J. D., Hall, J. C., and Lawson, R. (2010) *Economic Freedom of the World: 2010 Annual Report.* Vancouver: Fraser Institute; available at www.freetheworld.com.

Habermas, J. (1973) *Legitimationsprobleme im Spätkapitalismus.* Frankfurt am Main: Suhrkamp.

Hayek, F. A. von (1978) Die Entthronung der Politik, in D. Frei (ed.), *Überforderte Demokratie?* Zürich: Schulthess Polygraphischer Verlag, pp. 17–30.

Hayek, F. A. von (1980) *Studies in Philosophy, Politics, and Economics.* 2nd edn, Chicago: University of Chicago Press.

Henisz, W. J., Zelner, B. A., and Guillén, M. F. (2005) The worldwide diffusion of market-oriented infrastructure reform, 1977–1999, *American Sociological Review* 70: 871–97.

Höpner, M., et al. (2011) Liberalisierungspolitik: Eine Bestandsaufnahme des Rückbaus wirtschafts- und sozialpolitischer Interventionen in entwickelten Industrieländern, *Kölner Zeitschrift für Soziologie und Sozialpsychologie* 63: 1–32.

Huntington, S. P. (1975) The United States, in M. J. Crozier, S. P. Huntington and J. Watanuki (eds), *The Crisis of Democracy: Report on the Governability of Democracies to the Trilateral Commission.* New York: New York University Press, pp. 59–118.

King, A. (1975) Overload: problems of governing in the 1970s, *Political Studies* 23: 284–96.

Korpi, W., and Palme, J. (2003) New politics and class politics in the context of austerity and globalization: welfare state regress in 18 countries, 1975–95, *American Political Science Review* 97: 425–46.

Korpi, W., and Palme, J. (2007) *The Social Citizenship Indicator Programme (SCIP).* Stockholm University: Swedish Institute for Social Research; available at: https://dspace.it.su.se/dspace/handle/10102/7.

Luhmann, N. (1981) *Politische Theorie im Wohlfahrtsstaat.* Munich: Olzog.

Obinger, H., and Zohlnhöfer, R. (2007) The real race to the bottom: what happened to economic affairs expenditure after 1980?, in F. G. Castles (ed.), *The Disappearing State? Retrenchment Realities in an Age of Globalization.* Cheltenham: Edward Elgar, pp. 184–214.

OECD (Organization for Economic Cooperation and Development) (2007) *OECD Factbook 2007: Economic, Environmental and Social Statistics.* Paris: OECD.

OECD (Organization for Economic Cooperation and Development) (2008) *Growing Unequal? Income Distribution and Poverty in OECD Countries.* Paris: OECD.

OECD (Organization for Economic Cooperation and Development) (2010a) *OECD Economic Outlook No. 88,* available at: www.oecd-ilibrary.org/economics/data/oecd-economic-outlook-statistics-and-projections/oecd-econo mic-outlook-no-88_data-00533-en.

OECD (Organization for Economic Cooperation and Development) (2010b) *Revenue Statistics: Comparative tables*; available at: www.oecd-ilibrary.org/taxation/data/revenue-statistics/comparative-tables_data-00262-en.

OECD (Organization for Economic Cooperation and Development) (2011) *Divided We Stand: Why Inequality Keeps Rising.* Paris: OECD; available at: www.bmask.gv.at/cms/site/attachments/8/3/3/CH2267/CMS1313474232347/oecd_divided_we_stand_2011.pdf.

OECD (Organization for Economic Cooperation and Development) (2012) *OECD.Stat: Regulation in Energy, Transport and Communications*; doi: 10.1787/data-00285-en.

Olson, M. (1982) *The Rise and Decline of Nations: Economic Growth, Stagflation, and Social Rigidities.* New Haven, CT: Yale University Press.

Pierson, P. (1996) The new politics of the welfare state, *World Politics* 48: 143–79.

Putnam, R. D., Pharr, S. J., and Dalton, R. J. (2000) Introduction: what's troubling the trilateral democracies?, in S. J. Pharr and R. D. Putnam (eds), *Disaffected Democracies: What's Troubling the Trilateral Countries?* Princeton, NJ: Princeton University Press, pp. 3–27.

Scharpf, F. W. (1987) *Sozialdemokratische Krisenpolitik in Europa: Das 'Modell Deutschland' im Vergleich*. Frankfurt am Main: Campus.

Scruggs, L. (2002) The Ghent system and union membership in Europe, 1970–1996, *Political Research Quarterly* 55: 275–97.

Scruggs, L. (2008) Social rights, welfare generosity, and inequality, in P. Beramendi and C. J. Anderson (eds), *Democracy, Inequality, and Representation: A Comparative Perspective*. New York: Russell Sage Foundation, pp. 62–90.

Solt, F. (2008) Economic inequality and democratic political engagement, *American Journal of Political Science* 52: 48–60.

Solt, F. (2008-9) *The Standardized World Income Inequality Database*, available at: http://dvn.iq.harvard.edu/dvn/dv/fsolt/faces/study/StudyPage.xhtml?studyId=36908.

Starke, P. (2006) The politics of welfare state retrenchment: a literature review, *Social Policy and Administration* 40: 104–20.

Wolfe, A. (1977) *The Limits of Legitimacy: Political Contradictions of Contemporary Capitalism*. New York: Free Press.

8

Participatory Inequality in the Austerity State: A Supply-Side Approach

Claus Offe

1 Introduction

In this chapter, I explore some of the links that exist between three bundles of variables. Two of these are macro-variables that are tied together in the concept of (contemporary) *democratic capitalism* (Streeck 2010, 2011a): *declining* and *unequal* voter turnout. The third is the micro-variable of individual citizens' political participation. Participation is a multifaceted phenomenon (voting, joining, discussing politics, etc.) that requires references to various meso-phenomena (political parties, associations) in order to be understood. The question that guides the discussion of these extremely complex relations is how empirical trends in political participation – citizens' overall disengagement with political life (Mair 2006) and the increasingly *unequal* pattern of that disengagement – can be accounted for in terms of developments taking place at the level of the democratic state and its policies, on the one hand, and the capitalist economy, on the other.

2 Two trends: declining and unequal turnout

The topic of why people don't vote – or why they don't participate in political life in other ways – has a long history in political science. It has attracted fresh scholarly interest since the mid-1990s. Two questions are being asked and need to be answered. First, why are we seeing an *overall decline* in voting – as well as in other forms of political participation – in most liberal democracies, old ones as well as new? Second, why is non-participation a phenomenon that is far from randomly distributed across the population of eligible citizens, and instead *disproportionally affects the less privileged strata* of constituent populations? To the extent that either or both of these phenomena – the average *level* of participation of the entire (eligible) population and the distributional *patterns* of partici-patory practices across the social structure – are considered problematic from points of view spelled out by normative democratic theory, there are conceivable solutions to each respective problem. The following logic will apply in cases where such solutions are available and attempted: any workable solution to problem (1) – e.g., making voting mandatory or incentivizing it through positive or negative sanctions – would also take care of problem (2), but the inverse is not necessarily true; participatory practices can remain low on average even if they are evenly distributed across structural hierarchies.

Whenever we conceptualize a social phenomenon as a 'problem', we need to specify which groups are affected or, more generally, which evaluative perspective would consider the given phenomenon a 'problem' – meaning a condition that calls, or inspires the search for a 'solution'. Thus we need to understand for whom and according to what kind of evaluative standard our first problem – the low overall turnout in elections (or, for that matter, low rates of other kinds of political participation) – should constitute a problem.

There are two kinds of answers to this question. One starts with the intuition that citizens, by participating, confer *political resources*, and that political elites depend on the supply of these resources for the sake of their legitimacy, as well as for the proper functioning of the political system as a whole.[1] The more members political parties and functional associations have – i.e., the more people who decide to join – the greater the pool of material resources for these groups (in the form of member-ship dues) and the more credible their legitimacy-conferring claim to representativeness.[2] Conversely, the entire political system would suffer considerable embarrassment and loss of credibility if the turnout on election day were to drop below the level of, say, 30 per cent of those eligible. Such an outcome would be perceived as signalling worries in large parts of the electorate about either the *relevance* of the alternatives (candidates, platforms) between which voters are called upon to decide or the perceived *fairness* of the procedures according to which the system operates, or both. It would also leave the resulting governing coalitions vulnerable to criticism that, in the limiting case, they represented just a tiny minority (in this case 15.01 per cent) of the overall polity, thus con-siderably weakening a government's claim to democratically constituted political authority. Political elites must be interested in absorbing the hopes, fears, loyalties and interests of citizens into the institutional channels of 'normal politics', thereby *integrating* the political community at the level of 'diffuse support' for the democratic form of government and strengthening a second-order consensus concerning the rules by which first-order conflict and dissent is to be processed. Absent such support and consent, it is likely that such motivations will seek, and eventually find, their expression in non-institutional, potentially disruptive forms of participation. High degrees of electoral disengagement and abstention will also undercut political input legitimacy ('Low levels of input legitimacy [can] have a negative impact on the government's ability to ensure compliance with government regulations' [Quintelier et al. 2011: 399]) and hence the effectiveness of governance.

The other way that low electoral turnout can constitute a problem derives from a well-founded empirical generalization. This claims that, the further the level of participatory practices *deviates* from the 100 per cent maximum, the more *unequal* the pattern of participation is bound to be. The lower the overall rate of participation, the more socially *distorted* it will be according to stratification dimensions such as income, education, class, status security and life satisfaction (Kohler 2006; Gallego 2007; Solt 2010). Distorted patterns of participation, once they are known to exist and are anticipated by competing political parties, have a direct impact on both the content of parties' programmatic platforms and the policy output of governing parties. In particular, parties and governing coalitions will tend to form rational strategies that are biased in favour of those social categories known to participate and that ignore or downgrade those less likely to do so; these political entities will tend to 'optimize the allocation of pains to [known] non-voters' (Streeck 2007: 28). 'Who votes and who doesn't has important consequences . . . for the content of policies' (Lijphart 1997: 4). In the second step of this developing circular dynamic, those who perceive themselves to be 'left out' (due to such strategies by parties and rulers) will probably have ever fewer motives to participate, which in turn will further diminish parties' willingness to take their interests on board – and so on.[3] The net result is a nominally democratic political system that is systematically biased to favour the middle class and everyone above it, while depriving all those below it of the effective use of their political resources – i.e., the political rights of citizenship. Such a system amounts to a gross *de facto* violation of the normative standard of *civic equality* that we associate with the idea of democracy (Schäfer 2010, 2011a). Note that this line of reasoning leads us right to the fusion of the two problems that we have distinguished at the outset. We might now paraphrase the problem by saying that the first phenomenon – overall *decline* of participation – is both a problem in itself (because of the issues of legitimacy and political integration, as perceived by political elites) and a *cause* of the problem of *distorted* participation (our second phenomenon) that it invariably involves.

3 Four diagnoses and associated therapies

To the extent that the second problem – increasingly *distorted* rather than *declining* participation – is recognized as a 'problem', there are four broad categories of conceivable answers. The *first* response is to solve problem (2) in indirect ways by solving problem (1). As noted before, solving the overall turnout problem would offer an (approximate) solution to the distorted participation problem, but not vice versa. If this is so, there seems to be a strong prima facie suggestion for making voting mandatory for all citizens (as influentially advocated by Lijphart 1997), thus imitating arrangements as they are in use, for instance, in Belgium and Australia, where as a consequence turnout rates range in the upper nineties and electoral disproportionalities are effectively neutralized. Lijphart suggests an *institutional* theory as to why people don't vote and why some vote less than others: that we get the outcome we observe because the institutional rules in which acts of voting are embedded are insufficiently and unevenly inviting and encouraging. Yet Lijphart's proposal (which he combines with other participation-facilitating institutional rules such as 'voter-friendly registration rules, proportional representation, infrequent elections, weekend voting, and holding less salient elections concurrently with the most important national elections' [1997: 1]) meets with a number of objections, partly normative and partly empirical.

One normative objection is that it must be considered *illiberal* to make voting compulsory, as it would deprive citizens of their *negative* voting freedom, the right to abstain. Compulsory voting would also, it might be argued, illegitimately and undeservedly protect political elites from the embarrassing evidence of their candidates and programmes being considered unappealing by large and slowly increasing parts of the population.[4] Empirically, compulsory voting seems to be on the decline (as is one of the other duties of citizenship, compulsory military service), both as a statutory duty (or even constitutionally enshrined, as in Greece) and in terms of the sanctions applied in case the duty is violated.[5] Yet, even if enforced by strong sanctions, voting cannot *really* be made compulsory, only the presence of people at the voting booth; they still remain free to cast invalid or empty ballots (Quintelier et al. 2011). In the present context, however, the main objection is this: even if the participatory distortion in *voting* could be eliminated through making it compulsory, this would take care only of the evidently smallest (and hence arguably least urgent) part of the overall problem of participatory distortion or inequality. For, among all forms of political participation, voting is by far the *least* unequally distributed (Verba et al. 1995; Gallego 2007; Schäfer 2010; Marien et al. 2010). So Lijphart's proposed solution would help to tackle the overall problem, but only marginally.

A *second* way to remedy the problem of participatory inequality is to resolve the problem by providing for the *random composition* of decision-making bodies, including electorates themselves. This amounts to solving problem (2) *without* solving problem (1). While such random procedures are recommended in much of the recent literature on deliberative democracy and deliberative polls (Fishkin 1995; Offe 2011: 467–9) – i.e., as democratic innovations that are being proposed as *supplements* to the procedures of majoritarian and representative democracy – it is hard to imagine that randomization could serve any meaningful and legitimate purpose beyond such a supplementary function. Randomization would involve a massive *dis*enfranchisement of all those who have *not* 'won' the lottery, and an element of non-random (self-) selection cannot possibly be fully excluded (whereas the other desirable function of randomization, that of neutralizing the influence of organized stakeholders and interested corporate actors, can be well fulfilled). In the absence of a strictly enforced equivalent of the institutions of jury duty (which itself allows for a number of opportunities for 'opting out'), the social selectivity would just be pushed one step back, from the question who actually *casts a ballot* to the question of who *enters the pool* of those among whom random selection then takes place, and who, if selected, *agrees to perform* as decision-maker or deliberator. Greater diversity of decision-making bodies (such as legislatures and party lists) could also be achieved through mandatory quotas, as is the case in many countries with gender quotas. Yet this would provoke, among other problems, the issue of 'second-order-quotas': how many seats should be allocated according to a gender quota (incidentally, a less significant determinant of participatory distortion) and how many according to the (overlapping) dimensions of minority or migrant status, income, education, class, age, etc.? While all referendums and similar forms of direct democracy operate on the basis of a quorum (a minimum limit which, if not surpassed, makes the poll invalid), one could think here of a combination of quotas and quorums: for instance, a referendum could be valid only with a turnout of at least 50 per cent – not of the *overall* constituency, but of those belonging to certain categories by age, gender, ethnicity or other possible attributes.

A *third* possible solution to the problem of participatory distortion is to try to 'activate' the non-participants. This is an approach that is based on an implicit *behavioural* theory that associates outcomes with individuals' characteristics: some people lack the skills, motivations, knowledge and other personal features that are conducive to participation, and these deficiencies must be overcome through countervailing incentives – material, cognitive and normative ones. As far as voting is concerned (remember: voting is the *least* dramatic of our distortion problems), turnout could be increased through material incentives: after casting his or her ballot, each voter would automatically participate in a lottery in which a significant amount of cash, or a luxury car, could be won. Others would prefer an educational approach: civics curricula in secondary schools, for example, could familiarize students with the full range of the portfolio of rights and organizational means with which citizens in a democracy are endowed and encourage the use of these rights as a matter of civic virtue. Or targeted information and mobilization campaigns could be launched (e.g., by public electronic media) to make it understood, even to the politically least enlightened and least interested, what is at stake for them, specifically, in upcoming elections and other political decisions, and who is likely to eventually benefit if they *fail* to participate. All of this is meant to strengthen the 'voice' of those who tend to keep silent and to encourage them to make demands.[6]

The truth, however, seems to be that all of these solutions (except for the lottery for voters) are *already* being undertaken by schools, media, civil society organizations, trade unions, religious communities, social movements and political parties themselves. In the absence of these efforts, the situation might be much worse than it actually is, but that does not mean that additional efforts of this sort will achieve significant improvements in a situation that for a long time has been deteriorating in terms of participatory inequalities. Beyond that, there must be something wrong with the behavioural theory in the first place.[7] The democratic motive for mobilizing non-participants into participation is, of course, the concern that those who do not vote (or who do not use other forms of civic participation) will be neglected by policy-making elites because the latter have nothing to *fear* from the former. Yet 'it is by no means obvious that politicians *would* pay much heed to the views of the poor if they *did* vote. It may be ... unfair to push the blame for unresponsiveness, at least implicitly, onto poor nonvoters' (Bartels 2008: 275). Perhaps non-participants do understand this 'unresponsiveness' of elites, implying that the former have little anyway to expect and hope for that can be delivered by the latter.

Which leaves us with the *fourth* and last of my stylized options of how we should understand – and, if possible, act upon – the condition of unevenly distributed political participation in all of its forms. The argument that I shall explore and defend for the rest of this chapter is a 'supply-side' argument. Its implicit theory is one that could be called *interpretive political economy*, meaning an understanding of social action and its cognitive foundations that starts with people's 'lived experience' of the interplay of economic and political forces in contemporary capitalist democracies. Those who do not, or do not fully, participate in political life fail to do so because they perceive the state, governments and political parties as lacking both the necessary *means* and the credible *intent* to 'make a difference' on matters (such as employment, equality, education, the labour market, social security and financial market regulation) that form the core concerns of those who do not participate; they fail to participate *because* they have come to understand that lack perfectly well. Roughly speaking, their 'lived experience' is that of living in a disempowered state, or in one that is overpowered by the *poderes fácticos* of corporate market actors. Their negative response is proportionate to their perception of the state's disempowerment (cf. Makszin and Schneider 2010). They do not join the game of democratic politics because they are unconvinced that doing so would yield results that are worth their effort and worthy of their recognition, nor do they trust that making such efforts could succeed in changing the agenda and priorities ruling the overall political economy. To be sure, the only practical implication that this perspective has to offer is the appeal, addressed to political parties and elites as the suppliers of public policies, to restore, reassert and consistently demonstrate some of their trust-engendering governing capacity.[8]

4 Non-participation: a challenge for democratic theory

How do we then account, in normative terms, for our two issues of (1) a percentage of *all* relevant social categories failing to make full use of the political resources accorded to them by law in the form of '*voluntary*' abstention and, even more difficult, (2) the pattern of an empirically *uneven* under-utilization of citizens' political resources? As we have seen, the first of these two cases is much easier to cope with than the second, at least if we consider voting alone. Whatever its social causation, and given that every freedom includes the freedom to abstain from its use (among family rights is chosen childlessness, among property rights is the right voluntarily to donate or destroy what one owns), *random* non-utilization of political resources can arguably be accommodated within the liberal (if not the (neo)republican; cf. Schäfer 2011b) version of democratic theory.

To do so, we would have to rely on a rule of thumb that some people will always, independently of their social status, freely develop a taste for forfeiting some of their freedoms. In contrast, problem (2) describes a situation in which the 'waste' of political resources is empirically correlated to indicators of individuals' life chances (such as education, income, labour-market status, age). Here, non-participation is evidently not 'freely chosen', or it is freely chosen in a different sense, as the conditions that are statistically correlated with this choice are themselves not freely chosen but consist of circumstances that are 'given' in a way that, at any moment, is beyond the control of those affected by them. Findings to this effect give rise to the suspicion that *social* and *economic* factors operating beyond the system of *legal* rights can bring about discriminatory and exclusionary effects that are normatively problematic from the point of view of democratic citizenship and civic equality. Even worse, the normative problem for democratic theory is not just distortion itself, but the plausible possibility that distortion breeds on itself and leads to more distortion, or becomes permanent: as people are conditioned to 'waste' their rights and political resources, and as competing political elites and political parties *come to understand* that parts of the electorate are less likely than others to make use of their political resources, those elites will concentrate their platforms, campaigns and mobilization strategies upon those segments of the citizenry who actually 'count' and neglect others, launching a negative and exclusionary learning cycle of mutual alienation between elites and underprivileged citizens.

Moreover, these concerns relating to the quality of democracy cannot be put to rest with the argument that the preferences of those who vote and those who do not differ so greatly that, even under strong distortions, the overall outcome of elections would be roughly the same as if participation across social categories had been more even. What is dubious about this argument is the fact that elections (and, even more, other forms of participation) are not just an opportunity to *express* given preferences; they are, at the same time and in anticipation of such expression, a challenge for citizens to *find out* about and *form* those preferences by learning and deliberating about their own choices, as well as discussing them with others. People whose circumstances make voting more difficult miss this kind of opportunity and challenge for preference formation, one which arguably would lead them to form preferences that *would* differ from those who do vote (Offe 2011). Here another vicious circle suggests itself: the more that people of certain status categories are (self-)excluded from voting and other forms of political participation, the more ill-considered and unreflective their political preferences and opinions are likely to remain or become, as they forgo learning opportunities to form judgements on public affairs. In this sense, undistorted political participation is desirable because it equalizes the challenge for individual citizens to practise and refine their capacity for judgement on those affairs.

Yet this is not the only reason why political participation should be undistorted. Indeed, those *least* endowed with education, income and security are clearly the ones who lack the *individual* means and resources to improve their condition (by spending income or making use of labour-market opportunities, for example). Given this lack of individual resources, they would likely turn to the *collective* resource of democratic state power as the only instrumental means available to them to improve their condition, through state-provided services and transfers. In doing so and succeeding, they would benefit from the fruits of such collective efforts more strongly and more directly than the middle class. The opportunity costs of non-participation can be safely assumed to be greater for the resource-poor than for the resource-rich.[9] This would lead us to expect that, the poorer, less educated or more insecure people are about their socio-economic status, the more eagerly they should seek to put their political rights to use, and the more readily should vote-seeking left-of-centre elites focus on mobilizing and educating them to this effect. Yet this is not the case – arguably not just because of a lack of information, but also because of a lack of confidence that political involvement is worth the effort.

People lack what in the older literature used to be termed a 'sense of subjective political efficacy':[10] they live in a highly and increasingly unequal society in which the government is evidently not in control of the resources needed for redistributive measures. Isn't it conceivable that large parts of the population, rather than lacking the intellectual skills and energies to engage in democratic politics, have come to understand quite well that they live, for all practical purposes, in a kind of 'post-democracy', while the rest of the population lives and partakes in a 'two-thirds democracy' (to quote the strangely oxymoronic term coined by Merkel and Petring [2011: 19])?

4.1 Revisiting Schattschneider

The classic formulation of the puzzle of voluntary non-participation of less privileged strata is from Schattschneider (1960). He observes the 'massive self-disfranchisement' (1960: 102) of American voters that occurs through extra-legal means, as it is not coerced but voluntary. He tries to understand the 'invisible' (ibid.: 98) and 'imperceptible' (ibid.: 108) forces that bring about the counter-intuitive self-disfranchisement of exactly the less privileged strata within the electorate who would often benefit most from actually making their voices heard. As I read it, Schattschneider's puzzle goes something like this: starting with a Schumpeterian model of the democratic political process, we must distinguish between elite *suppliers* in the political market (i.e., competing political parties) and *buyers* in that market (mass constituencies of voters and 'policy-takers'). The ballot is the equivalent of money, through the spending of which buyers purchase what competing elites (promise to) supply.[11] The interest of suppliers is twofold: first, and as a *common* interest of all suppliers, the author suggests, elites will do all they can to endow their (potential) constituency with political purchasing power (or 'exchange value'), namely the right to vote. 'The expansion of the electorate was largely a by-product of the system of party conflict . . .. One of the best ways to win a fight is to widen the scope of the conflict, and the effort to widen the involvement of . . . bystanders produced universal suffrage' (ibid.: 100–1). Seen this way, political parties would have had a strong incentive to have voting rights granted to hitherto disenfranchised social categories.[12]

Once any of those elites have attracted sufficient voter support to put themselves in the possession of political power, however, even if only for the time being, they must now start to design the products – bundles of programmatic policy proposals, candidates – that are likely to appeal to buyers (or rather creditors) in the political market – the 'use value' of public policies. At this point, the managerial (as opposed to entrepreneurial) logic of cautious economizing takes over, which means the priority of risk and blame avoidance and of keeping the core segments of a party's constituency reasonably happy. The key organizational objective is to defend one's market share (i.e., to remain in power after the *next* election); this must not be jeopardized by ill-advised ambitions, risks or confrontational moves beyond one's powers to cope. There are important but potentially dangerous issues that parties will wisely keep off their platforms and agendas; otherwise, they would run the risk of being denounced by opponents for their lack of 'realism'.

Such reasoning seems to underlie Schattschneider's analysis when he emphasizes the contradiction that 'the right to vote is now [in place] for a generation, but the *use* of the ballot as an effective instrument of democratic politics is something else altogether' (1960: 101). *After* its party-driven universalization, political parties 'attempt to make the vote meaningless' (ibid.: 103). It is this sense of meaninglessness that in turn leads to selective mass abstention caused by the 'agenda of politics' chosen (ibid.: 104): 'Abstention reflects the suppression of the options and alternatives that reflect the needs of the non-participants', who consist of 'the poorest, the least well-established, least educated stratum of the community' (ibid.: 105). The strategy of risk avoidance by competing (and often also colluding) political parties means that 'large areas of need and interest are excluded from the political system' (ibid.: 106). Absent the perception of such use value, increasing segments of constituencies simply drop out of political life, following the simple logic of 'if you fail to deliver, we refuse to pay'.[13] The key theorem here is that the political agenda set up by supply-side strategies in the political market selects 'the submerged millions [who] have found it difficult to get interested in the game' (ibid.: 109) and who, as 'a body of dissociated people', come to conclude 'that politics is simply not a game worth playing' (Solt 2008: 58). 'The root of the problem of nonvoting is to be found ... above all by *what* issues are developed' (Schattschneider 1960: 110). A political agenda is more than just a list of what to do and which problems to address; it is also, implicitly, a scheme of *whom* to appeal to, protect, rely upon, address – and whom *not*. 'Whoever decides what the game is about decides also who can get into the game' (ibid.: 105). This interaction between the substantive and the social selectivity of strategically established agendas can serve to solve the puzzle of voluntary, non-coerced self-exclusion by major parts of the citizenry: 'The exclusion of people by extralegal processes ... may be far more effective than the law' (ibid.: 111). The root of this exclusionary process is the silent complicity of strategic non-decision-making by actors on the supply side of the policy transaction (Bachrach and Baratz 1970) – i.e., of leaving 'touchy' issues and agents untouched.

4.2 Political versus social equality

In the normative literature, there does not seem to be much disagreement that political equality is the core principle of a democratic political order. Most authors would also agree that political equality must not only be legally (*de jure*) provided for, but socially and politically implemented (*de facto*).[14] Political equality is not antagonistic to the other (and arguably *only* ultimate; cf. Honneth 2011) principle of a political order, namely freedom; to the contrary, equality is *instrumental* for the achievement of the latter. 'Political equality is not ... an end we can obtain only at the expense of freedom ... it is instead an essential means to a just distribution of freedom and to fair opportunities for self-development' (Dahl 1989: 322).

According to Dahl, there are three social conditions that can stand in the way of the achievement of *de facto* political equality – i.e., the fair distribution of what he calls 'political resources' (1989: 130). These inequalities are (1) 'differences in resources and opportunities for employing violent coercion'; (2) differences 'in economic positions, resources, and opportunities'; and (3) differences 'in knowledge, information, and cognitive skills' (ibid.: 323–4). Yet these differences are more than just hindrances to a democratic political process: they also distort (according to any conceivable standard of a *fair* distribution of political resources) the *'inputs'* that citizens make into that process.

Such distributional patterns of coercive, economic and cognitive powers must also be seen as the *'outputs'* of previous rounds of policy-making in which those patterns of unequal distribution of political resources were brought into being – whether through political acts of commission or of omission. Since political inequality must thus be understood as a *consequence* (and not just a *premise*) of the making of public policy, Dahl goes on to argue that the principle of political equality requires that rulers in 'an advanced democratic country would actively seek to reduce great inequalities in the capacities and opportunities for citizens to participate effectively in political life that are caused . . . by the distribution of economic resources, positions . . . and by the distribution of knowledge, information, and cognitive skills' (1989: 324). In other words: participatory inequality must be understood not just as an unpleasant and (for democrats) somewhat embarrassing fact of life 'out there', but as a condition that is inherently produced and reproduced by the conduct of public policy and its supply (or lack) of policies that would create an approximate *de facto* equalization of political resources (Schäfer, chapter 7 in this volume).

What Dahl proposes here is a dualist model of how democratic citizenship relates to public policy. The first and most familiar side of that model is that *citizens* of a democracy, endowed with their political rights and by means of various procedures of aggregation, representation, coalition-building, etc., *shape public policies*. The second and more striking side is this: public policies, by 'actively seeking to reduce great inequalities', *or by failing to do so*, conversely *shape citizens* and the actual use they make of their political rights. More specifically, if governments allow *and thereby cause* income gaps to widen, educational opportunities to become massively unequal, precariousness of labour market status to spread, and the integration of migrants and their descendants often to fail, they thereby *create* strata of citizens who are 'objectively' ill-disposed to make use of the political rights and resources with which they are nominally endowed as citizens (Solt 2008; Makszin and Schneider 2010). They also create, among people affected by these conditions, a 'subjective' life-world of meanings, lived experience, expectations, fears and denied recognition, along with accumulated diffuse aggressiveness that alienates them from the supposedly normal practices of political organization and participation. On the basis of these emotional dispositions and cognitive frames, they come to consider their political rights largely useless – and act (or rather fail to act) accordingly. Taken together, these two ways in which citizens are shaped through policies of omission or commission act to create groups that are marginalized and as economically hopeless as they are politically and culturally homeless (Walter 2010: 203–19).

It is thus not the case that a high level of inequality and social insecurity will in any way automatically lead to popular demands for policies that provide for redistribution, as Markoff (2011) suggests. It can also be the case that the perceived inability and/or unwillingness of any governing coalition to respond to inequalities through the adoption of redistributive measures have become so evident (given the extent and persistence of problems of poverty, inequality of opportunity, and insecurity) that citizens affected by these conditions have given up on raising their voice and demanding such measures. (Once you learn that the trains are not running any more, it makes no sense to wait on the platform any longer.) 'The evidence indicates, however, that higher levels of inequality are not associated with more redistributive spending', or even with more loudly voiced demands for such spending. In this way, 'economic inequality undermines political equality' (Solt 2008: 57).

The first of the two loops in the democratic model (from needs to demands to remedial policies) presupposes the presence not just of democratic political rights but also of the *confidence* that democratic government is a reasonably responsive agency, and hence the appropriate address to which demands can be directed. Absent this confidence, demands will be neither voiced nor responded to, in spite of the largely unadulterated presence of these rights. While authoritarian rulers focus on demolishing these democratic rights, 'post-democratic' rulers adopt the far less conspicuous strategy of frustrating the confidence that these rights are of much use, thus activating a negative version of the second loop: from failed policies to silenced demands to unaddressed needs.

5 Two and a half theories about the operation of democratic capitalism

In this concluding section I shall describe in a stylized fashion and contrast three theoretical approaches to both *understanding* and *justifying* the realities of democratic capitalism and its (desired) mode of operation. Each of these theories specifies in a consistent and empirically validated way how the state, policy-makers, market actors in the economy, and citizens act and should act. The three theories are the social democratic-cum-social market economy theory, the market-liberal theory and a theory (as yet incomplete) that, for want of a better name, will here be sketched out under the clumsy title of 'global financial market-driven post-democracy'. This last is incomplete because it is well able to describe the 'logic' that governs the realities of contemporary markets and politics but lacks the normative argument to demonstrate why these realities are justified, universally beneficial or even sustainable.

5.1 Social-democratic and social-market economy

At the legal and constitutional level, democratic political rights guarantee *civic* equality – not, of course, the equality of socio-economic *outcomes*. Civic equality is normatively premised upon a strict separation and disjunction of (unequally distributed) socio-economic resources and (equal) political rights according to the principle of *non-convertibility* of the former into the latter. Ownership of economic assets should not be allowed to translate into privilege, political power or a shortcut to access either. Correspondingly, inferior socio-economic status should not be allowed to deprive citizens of their political voice and its effectiveness. At the same time, it can trivially be observed that the actual use of political resources (*rights* such as the right to vote, the right to form associations, freedom of opinion and assembly, all determining the content of law-making by representative legislatures) can (and is actually intended to) *have a major impact upon the relative socio-economic status and status security of citizens*, as any democratically legislated tax law can serve to illustrate. This is the *asymmetrical* linkage between economic and political resources, or spheres of action, with the former being to some extent (e.g., through the regulation of party and campaign finance, etc.) *banned* from being converted into the latter, yet the latter being *allowed*, in fact *intended*, to have an impact on the former.

This formula is the normative bedrock of the 'social-democratic' or 'social-market economy' normative theory of capitalist democracy: political power, reflecting prevailing conceptions of social justice and claiming *primacy* over the dynamics of markets, can legitimately shape the distribution of economic resources, *but not the other way around*. More specifically, whenever a point on the trade-off curve of efficiency versus equity is to be determined, the choice is to be made by democratically accountable political agents rather than by economic ones. This normative theory seeks to secure the primacy of the social over the economic, or of the political over the market (Streeck 2011a: 8).

The social-democratic theory shares two assumptions with the precepts of the 'social market' (the latter of which have their roots in the Roman Catholic social doctrine). First, the economic process is one that is entirely shaped by and embedded in institutional arrangements and political decisions that have been framed at the political and constitutional levels. These arrangements can be made to operate smoothly because of the ongoing bargaining among corporatist collective actors, statutory co-determination rights, taxation and political regulation. It is public policies that set into motion, license, regulate and thus provide an institutional framework for market forces, such that the democratic state can then steer the economic process in ways that reliably avoid the twin dangers of devastating economic crises and disruptive social conflict. The second assumption of the social-democratic theory amounts to a theory of worker-citizens' participation and 'voice', one which claims that, given this confidence in the state's supervisory and steering capacities, and given the uneven distribution of life chances that characterizes capitalist social structures, there will be a 'natural' tendency in all segments of the population, and in particular the less privileged ones, to make active use of the political resources that are granted to them as political rights. In such an institutional arrangement, there is a built-in incentive for citizens to make full use of their rights, as such use offers the prospect of cumulatively limiting socio-economic inequalities on the 'output' side of state policies. More specifically, and in line with the slogan 'millions against millionaires' that was popular on the political left in the Weimar Republic, the less privileged strata of the population will have good reason, and thus feel encouraged, *actually to voice* their complaints and demands for redistributive policies and greater (job and social) security. This is meant to result in a self-correcting dynamic that generates policies to reduce inequality and thus provide for political stability. The combined effect of what is suggested by these two social-democratic assumptions is a peaceful, non-violent and non-disruptive process in which political institutions of both territorial representation (parties and parliaments) and functional representation (trade unions and other major interest associations) allow for the ongoing accommodation of conflicting interests. This process will be especially successful if economic policies are adopted by the government that promote growth and hence set the stage for ongoing positive-sum games, as fiscal growth dividends are continuously generated and spent on social investment and transfers.

5.2 The market-liberal theory of democratic capitalism

An alternative theory of capitalist democracy, the 'market-liberal' theory, describes and prescribes a strictly symmetrical separation of markets and politics. As market power should not translate into political decision-making power, neither should the state and politics be allowed to intervene (more than marginally) into the market-generated distribution of resources. All liberal theories, particularly if combined with 'pluralist' political theory, assume that, under such symmetrical differentiation of political and economic spheres, neither of the two will have legitimate reasons – or indeed the opportunity or prospect – to claim primacy over the other. While neither the state nor the market is fully autonomous, the mutual relations and inputs required cannot possibly amount to any relationship of dependency or robust prevalence. This theory, which found its most sophisticated elaboration in the work of sociological theorists such as Talcott Parsons and Niklas Luhmann, describes a relationship between the democratic state and the capitalist economy as one of interdependence without primacy. The input that the political system provides to the economic systems is the legal guarantee of property rights, the enforcement of contracts, and the provision of infrastructural facilities and services. Conversely, the inputs coming from the economy are taxes, on the one hand, and pluralist group pressures, on the other. Given a highly diversified socio-economic structure, none of the organized groups can mobilize political pressure strong enough to impose binding demands on the political system; pressures also generate ('countervailing') counter-pressures so as to cancel each other out, leaving the government free to give in and cater to this or that group.

Moreover, not all citizens in a 'mass society' will actually belong to or identify with *any* particular group; yet many will belong to *more* than one group, however loosely (e.g., a trade union and the Roman Catholic church) – a situation that gives rise to the healthy phenomenon of 'cross-pressure' at the micro-level of voters and serves to mitigate the intensity of societal conflict. Nor does the pressure that one particular group can generate pertain to *all* policy areas equally, which further increases the freedom of discretion enjoyed by the governments of pluralist societies.

What does this stylized liberal theory have to say about patterns of political participation and its motives? Here the prevailing concern is with the systemic dangers of 'excessive' mobilization and participation, which according the social-science doctrines of the 1950s and 1960s was suspected as a source of instability, if not of 'totalitarian' dangers (Huntington 1975). A political culture that leads people to stay passive or indifferent to most issues most of the time, combined with a sense of diffuse loyalty and support for the political system as a whole, is widely considered to be desirable for the sake of stability. At any rate, widespread political apathy is normatively unproblematic and can even be considered an asset, as *voluntary* non-participation is to be read (wrongly, as Kohler 2006 demonstrates) as a sign of basic *satisfaction* with policies and political institutions on the part of all those who decide to refrain from raising their voice in spite of their right to do so. The multiplicity of opportunities to *join* groups that is present in a pluralistic society and the multiplicity of opportunities to *vote* in local, state and federal elections of a highly decentralized political system are both welcomed as buffer mechanisms that serve to hinder excesses of mobilization, which could jeopardize political stability.

A further reassuring feature of liberal-pluralist political theorizing is the axiomatic assumption, derived from Schumpeter, of a deep divide between political elites and non-elites that is modelled on the market transaction. Just as there is the hiatus between producers and consumers in markets, there is a divide between elite suppliers and non-elite consumers in politics. As dissatisfied consumers would never in their right mind consider invading the place of production in order to make their dissatisfaction heard, but would instead rationally switch to a competing supplier who catered better to their needs and tastes, so the democratic citizen is categorically assumed to be able to 'exit' by changing to another supplier rather than engaging in verbal (or other) types of conflict with an unsatisfactory supplier/political elite. Thus, in both economy and politics, the market (or its political equivalent, driven by the ballot rather than cash payments) makes for the smooth and inconspicuous accommodation of divergent tastes and interests. Moreover, and given that the politically unrestrained market economy lets its output trickle down even to the least prosperous parts of the population, apolitical attitudes of 'privatism' (Peterson 1984), 'family-centredness' and consumerism become so widespread as lifestyles that they effectively marginalize both the motives and time resources for political participation.[15]

5.3 Post-democratic capitalism?

Both the social-democratic and the liberal-pluralist theories, as well as their implications concerning levels, kinds and social distribution of participatory practices, are now a largely obsolete matter of the past in both their analytical and normative aspects. They reached their expiration dates following the historical turning points that democratic capitalism experienced in the second half of the 1970s and again after 1989. What we are entirely lacking, however, is a theory or normative justification of the current realities, when economic resources do determine the agenda and decision-making of the political process, while the owners of those resources themselves, and the distributional outcomes caused by markets, are not being significantly constrained by social rights and political interventions. To the contrary, the latter are to a large extent put at the disposition of economic 'imperatives'. Note that, compared to the social-democratic model, the present condition of globalized financial market capitalism-cum-endemic fiscal crisis is tantamount to an *inverted* asymmetry: *markets* set the agenda and (fiscal) constraints of public policies, but there is little that *public policies* in their turn can do in terms of constraining the realm and dynamics of the ever-expanding market –

unless, that is, political elites are suicidally prepared to expose themselves to the second-strike capabilities of the 'markets'. Yet it is this logic of a pervasive preponderance of accumulation, profit, efficiency, competitiveness, austerity and the market over the sphere of social rights, political redistribution and sustainability, as well as the defencelessness of the latter sphere against the former, that governs the contemporary version of capitalist democracy (or rather 'post-democracy'; Crouch 2004), and will probably do so for many years to come (Streeck 2011a). This logic, as it unfolds before our eyes and on a global scale, is sufficiently powerful and uncontested, it seems, to prevail through its sheer facticity and in the absence of any supporting normative theory – as a stark reality, naked of any shred of justification.

In brief, the operation of this logic begins with the categorical denial of any tension between the rights of people and the rights of property owners, of social justice versus property and market justice. To the extent the governments of nation-states are in charge of the former and the addressee of respective demands and complaints – i.e., of 'voice' – they are largely deafened by the overpowering and ubiquitous 'noise' of the austerity imperative. The urgency of this imperative, and at the same time the difficulty to comply with it, is determined by three factors. First, there is a need to bail out failed (or potentially failing) financial institutions who count governments among their preferred clients.[16] Second, governments cannot manage their financial troubles by raising taxes, because that would constitute a burden on private investors in the 'real' economy and would disincentivize their continued (domestic) investment. Third, expenses cannot be cut because increasing parts of the social security system, so far covered mostly by the 'para-fiscal' mechanism of contributions, need to be covered out of general revenues (to the extent that transfers cannot be cut) in order to decrease the burden on employers. Cornered in this triangle of constraints (and visible to the public as such), the state is no longer a plausible supplier of what all kinds of demand-side actors may desire it to provide. To gain any room for manoeuvre at all, it is undergoing a creeping permutation from a classical (Schumpeterian) 'tax state' into a 'borrowing state'. That is, expenditures are being covered not out of present revenues, but out of (anticipated) *future* revenues – the prospective tax base of which, however, is itself being decimated by the increasing parts of state budgets that are spent on servicing debt (rather than on providing services and infrastructure). With Streeck (2007: 32, 34), we can speak of 'emaciated state capacity' and the 'attrition of its disposable resources'. The endemic fiscal crisis 'preempts democratic choice' (Streeck 2010: 5); citizens simply have to get used to the fact that a fiscally starved state is the wrong interlocutor when it comes to demands concerning 'costly' policies.

This configuration of constraints leaves little space for the processes and institutions that supposedly make up the core decision-making site of democracy, namely party competition, elections and parliamentary representation[17] and legislation. After all, if decision-making on taxing and spending is off the agenda, a core function of parliamentary government is largely suspended. Instead, policy-making moves to other sites that are typically out of reach of the participant agents of normal democratic politics. All kinds of government-appointed commissions and fiduciary institutions (including central banks) are being endowed with *de facto* policy-making competencies, often of a supranational kind, as has occurred in ad hoc peak meetings of European (or G-20) heads of governments. These bodies, among them the European Commission, are non-partisan in their composition and are involved in transactions behind closed doors that put them by and large outside of the democratic loop of transparency and accountability, as is the case for other instances of multi-level and multi-actor governance that tend systematically to obscure and anonymize the locus of political responsibility (Offe 2009).

Public authorities are seen as having lost their grip on key issues of fiscal and budgetary policy, driven instead by rating agencies and other forces of the financial markets. Since the neoliberal turn of the 1980s (when symptoms of participatory distortion began to show up in the data), they have also lost much of their control over the quality, price and distribution of public services in the name of efficiency, austerity, privatization, deregulation, private–public partnership, new public management, artificial voucher-driven markets, etc. As a result, growing numbers of the citizenry (particularly those who are interested in and depend on government social spending and services) have come to understand that participating in democratic politics is largely a pointless activity. We might speak of a *dual control gap*: governments lose control over taxation and the financial sector, and in response citizens lose their confidence that the idea of democratic control over government policies is a credible one. Not only does the new political economy of globalized financial capitalism have a diminished space for elected parliaments and their democratic role, it can also do without active citizens who find themselves cut off from meaningful opportunities for participation. 'Citizens increasingly perceive their governments, not as *their* agents, but as those of other states or of international organizations, such as the IMF or the European Union' (Streeck 2011a: 26). As the arenas in which policies are actually made move ever further away from citizens, the latter respond to both the form and the substantive content of policies made 'elsewhere' by moving away from the official yet evidently blocked channels of political communication and influence. If 'there is no alternative' anyway, why should citizens bother to find out or decide which alternative to opt for?

The obvious question that worries political elites as well as social scientists today is what citizens are likely to do *instead*. Obviously, it would be risky to expect that citizens' retreat from politics into a mental state of alienated silence could be a steady state, although the media market does its utmost to make it so. Alternatively, there are four conceivable developments, which commentators and analysts have been debating on the basis of recent political phenomena that can be read as early symptoms.

The first is what I call non-institutional 'DIY politics' within civil society. Symptoms range from individuals engaging in critical consumption and consumer boycotts, to protest movements such as the Mediterranean *indignados*, to initiatives of civic engagement that organize through movements, donations and foundations, self-help, and private charity, in part as substitutes for inadequate public services. These forms of political participation, while highly selective in their (largely educated, urban, middle-class) social base, can achieve a great deal of sympathetic public attention and even the rhetorical support of political and economic elites.

The second is ephemeral eruptions of mass violence in metropolitan cities, as we have seen in the early part of this century, originating from (mostly) poor urban areas of London, Paris, Athens and elsewhere. In contrast to the rebellions of 2011 in Cairo and other Middle Eastern and North African cities, these eruptions are politically entirely unfocused and have provided partial cover for the unleashing of acquisitive and aggressive mass instincts (interpreted by some commentators as mirroring the acquisitive *elite* instincts of today's stock-exchange brokers). They also meet with a great deal of public attention, if of a strongly and rightly unsympathetic, as well as fearful, nature. Recent events have put the 'return of the violent mob' (Walter 2010: 214) on the social-science agenda. Wolfgang Streeck (2011b) warns that, 'where legitimate outlets of political expression are shut down, illegitimate ones may take their place, at potentially very high social and economic cost'.

A third alternative is further growth of the right-wing populism that has strongholds in the countries of South-Eastern Europe (Austria, Hungary, Bulgaria, Romania, Greece; cf. Berezin, chapter 10 in this volume) and has surfaced, to a somewhat lesser extent, in France, the Netherlands and the Scandinavian countries. Key elements of the formula that has been used with remarkable success by rightist populist movements and parties are the *strengthening of borders* (against foreign goods, foreign migrants and foreign political influence, e.g., from the EU) as a means to protect the 'weak'; the intolerant and often aggressive *denial of difference* (from ethnic difference to differences of political views and opinions) in the name of ethno-national homogeneity; and the strong reliance on charismatic leaders and successful political entrepreneurs. These parties and movements have become successful by organizing a game of losers against other (namely 'foreign') losers. They are the only political agents in the decades since 1990 who have managed to broaden their political base and enhance participation, if not the kind of participation envisaged by liberal democratic theory.

Finally, there is the intense, sometimes even desperate search, both in the social sciences (Smith 2005, 2009) and among various political parties (across almost the entire spectrum), to deepen and enhance political participation through the introduction of new institutional and procedural opportunities that allow and commit people to raise their 'voice' more directly, more often, and on more matters than representative institutions and political party competition have so far allowed them to do. While such projects of making democracies more democratic clearly deserve great social scientific attention and imaginative experimentation, political theorists should also look into the social conditions under which interest and political preferences are *formed* before they are voiced. After all, new procedures may not be sufficient to increase and broaden participation by citizens unless the *supply* of public policies and its 'possibility space', as perceived by citizens, is prevented from becoming ever more restricted, as in Lindblom's (1982) 'prison'.

References

Bachrach, P., and Baratz, M. S. (1970) *Power and Poverty: Theory and Practice.* New York: Oxford University Press.

Bartels, L. M. (2008) *Unequal Democracy: The Political Economy of the New Gilded Age.* Princeton, NJ: Princeton University Press.

Berger, B. (2011) *Attention Deficit Democracy.* Princeton, NJ: Princeton University Press.

Crouch, C. (2004) *Post-Democracy.* Cambridge: Polity.

Dahl, R. A. (1989) *Democracy and its Critics.* New Haven, CT: Yale University Press.

Fishkin, J. S. (1995) *The Voice of the People: Public Opinion and Democracy.* New Haven, CT: Yale University Press.

Gallego, A. (2007) Unequal participation in Europe, *International Journal of Sociology* 37: 10–25.

Honneth, A. (2011) *Das Recht der Freiheit: Grundriß einer demokratischen Sittlichkeit.* Berlin: Suhrkamp.

Huntington, S. P. (1975) The United States, in M. Crozier, S. P. Huntington and J. Watanuki (eds), *The Crisis of Democracy: Report on the Governability of Democracies to the Trilateral Commission.* New York: New York University Press, pp. 59–118.

Kohler, U. (2006) Die soziale Ungleichheit der Wahlabstinenz in Europa, in W. Merkel and J. Alber (eds), *Europas Osterweiterung: Das Ende der Vertiefung?* WZB Jahrbuch 2005. Berlin: Sigma, pp. 159–79.

Lane, R. E. (1962) *Political Ideology: Why the American Common Man Believes What He Does*. New York: Free Press of Glencoe.

Lijphart, A. (1997) Unequal participation: democracy's unresolved dilemma, *American Political Science Review* 91(1): 1–14.

Lijphart, A. (1998) *The Problem of Low and Unequal Voter Turnout – and What We Can Do About It*, Working paper, Political Science Series, no. 54. Vienna: Institute for Advanced Studies; available at: www.ihs.ac.at/vienna/IHS-Departments-2/Political-Science-1/Publications-18/Political-Science-Series-2/Publications-19/publication-page:8.htm (accessed 29 February 2012).

Lindblom, C. E. (1982) The market as prison, *Journal of Politics* 44(2): 324–36.

Madsen, D. (1978) A structural approach to the explanation of political efficacy levels under democratic regimes, *American Journal of Political Science* 22(4): 867–83.

Mair, P. (2006) Ruling the void? The hollowing of Western democracy, *New Left Review* 42: 25–51.

Makszin, K., and Schneider, C. Q. (2010) *Education and Participatory Inequalities in Real Existing Democracies: Probing the Effect of Labor Markets on the Qualities of Democracies*, CES Papers, Open Forum 2. Cambridge, MA: Minda de Gunzburg Center for European Studies, Harvard University.

Marien, S., Hooghe, M., and Quintelier, E. (2010) Inequalities in non-institutionalised forms of political participation: a multi-level analysis of 25 countries, *Political Studies* 58: 187–213.

Markoff, J. (2011) A moving target: democracy, *Archives européennes de sociologie* 2: 239–76.

Merkel, W., and Petring, A. (2011) Partizipation und Inklusion, in Friedrich Ebert Stiftung (ed.), *Demokratie in Deutschland 2011*. Berlin: Friedrich Ebert Stiftung; available at: www.demokratie-deutschland-2011.de/common/pdf/Partizipation_und_Inklusion.pdf (accessed 1 March 2012).

Offe, C. (2009) Governance: an 'empty signifier'?, *Constellations* 16(4): 550–62.

Offe, C. (2011) Crisis and innovation in liberal democracy: can deliberation be institutionalized?, *Czech Sociological Review* 47(3): 447–72.

Peterson, S. A. (1984) Privatism and politics: a research note, *Political Research Quarterly* 37: 483–9.

Petring, A., and Merkel, W. (2011) *Auf dem Weg zur Zweidrittel-Demokratie: Wege aus der Partizipationskrise*, WZB Mitteilungen no. 134. Berlin: WZB.

Piven, F. F., and Cloward, R. A. (1988) *Why Americans Don't Vote*. New York: Pantheon.

Quintelier, E., Hooghe, M., and Marien, S. (2011) The effect of compulsory voting on turnout stratification patterns: a cross-national analysis, *International Political Science Review* 32(4): 396–416.

Römmele, A., and Schober, H. (2010) Warum die Primarschule in Hamburg gescheitert ist, *Die Zeit online*, 19 July, http://blog.zeit.de/zweitstimme/2010/07/19/warum-die-primarschule-in-hamburg-gescheitert-ist/ (accessed 1 March 2012).

Saunders, B. (2011) The democratic turnout 'problem', *Political Studies* 60(2): 306–20 [article first published online 5 December 2011].

Schäfer, A. (2010) Die Folgen sozialer Ungleichheit für die Demokratie in Westeuropa, *Zeitschrift für vergleichende Politikwissenschaft* 4(1): 131–56.

Schäfer, A. (2011a) Der Nichtwähler als Durchschnittsbürger: Ist die sinkende Wahlbeteiligung eine Gefahr für die Demokratie?, in E. Bytzek and S. Rossteutscher (eds), *Der unbekannte Wähler? Mythen und Fakten über das Wahlverhalten der Deutschen*. Frankfurt am Main: Campus, pp. 133–54.

Schäfer, A. (2011b) *Republican Liberty and Compulsory Voting*, MPIfG Discussion Paper 11/17. Cologne: Max Planck Institute for the Study of Societies.

Schäfer, A. (2011c) Wahlen und politische Gleichheit: Warum eine sinkende Wahlbeteiligung der Demokratie schadet, paper presented at the joint conferences of the DVPW, SVWP and ÖVPW, Basel, 13–15 January.

Schattschneider, E. E. (1960) *The Semi-Sovereign People: A Realist's View of Democracy in America*. New York: Holt, Rinehart & Winston.

Smith, G. (2005) *Beyond the Ballot: 57 Democratic Innovations from around the World: A Report for the Power Inquiry*. London: Power Inquiry.

Smith, G. (2009) *Democratic Innovations: Designing Institutions for Citizen Participation*. Cambridge: Cambridge University Press.

Solt, F. (2008) Economic inequality and democratic political engagement, *American Journal of Political Science* 52(1): 48–60.

Solt, F. (2010) Does economic inequality depress electoral participation? Testing the Schattschneider hypothesis, *Political Behavior* 32(2): 285–301.

Streeck, W. (2007) *Endgame? The Fiscal Crisis of the German State*, MPIfG Discussion Paper 07/7. Cologne: Max Planck Institute for the Study of Societies.

Streeck, W. (2010) Noch so ein Sieg, und wir sind verloren: Der Nationalstaat nach der Finanzkrise, *Leviathan* 38(2): 159–73.

Streeck, W. (2011a) The crisis of democratic capitalism, *New Left Review* 71: 5–29.

Streeck, W. (2011b) Public sociology as a return to political economy, available at: http://publicsphere.ssrc.org/streeck-public-sociology-as-a-return-to-political-economy/ (accessed 18 September 2012).

Van Biezen, I., Mair, P., and Poguntke, T. (2012) Going, going, . . . gone? The decline of party membership in contemporary Europe, *European Journal of Political Research* 51: 24–56.

Verba, S., Schlozman, K. L., and Brady, H. E. (1995) *Voice and Equality: Civic Voluntarism in American Politics*. Cambridge, MA: Harvard University Press.

Walter, F. (2010) *Vom Milieu zum Parteienstaat: Lebenswelten, Leitfiguren und Politik im historischen Wandel*. Wiesbaden: VS Verlag für Sozialwissenschaften.

9

From Markets versus States to Corporations versus Civil Society?

Colin Crouch

In most areas of public policy debate, both political and academic participants focus on a confrontation between states and markets. This is particularly true of controversies over the welfare state, since the so-called marketization of previous state monopolies over health services, other aspects of social care, pensions, education and several other fields has dominated policy for up to twenty years. It is part of the more general phenomenon of the triumph of ostensibly market-oriented neoliberal policy approaches over state-centred social democratic ones. However, as I have argued elsewhere (Crouch 2011), actually existing, as opposed to ideologically pure, neoliberalism is nothing like as devoted to free markets as is claimed. It is, rather, devoted to the dominance of public life by the giant corporation. The confrontation between the market and the state that seems to dominate political conflict in many societies conceals the existence of this third force, which is more potent than either and transforms the workings of both. The polarity is in fact a triangle. The politics of the early twenty-first century, continuing a trend started in the previous one and accentuated rather than weakened by the crisis, has ceased to be a confrontation at all, but a series of comfortable accommodations among all three forces. There is a challenge to democracy here, as political processes and decision-making retreat from public gaze into a realm where only economic and political elites operate. Democracy and the market may therefore sometimes even appear together as victims.

Particularly important is the way in which giant corporations go far further than being the powerful lobbies that they are generally recognized to be, and become major insider participants in the policy-making process. In this chapter I shall discuss why and how in general this has happened. I shall illustrate the general argument with examples, taken mainly from recent UK experience. Finally I shall consider the reshaped form of politics that emerges from the process. This is something that no economic or political theory defends or advocates in any way, but it is a central reality of our public life.

If neoliberalism stands for anything, it is for a strong separation of state power from commercial markets. If it can be shown that in fact neoliberalism has brought about a dense and opaque entanglement of private corporations with government, the dominant political ideology of our day emerges damaged below its waterline. It is of course routine for ideologies to be hypocritical. State socialism did not rescue workers from subordination to economic exploitation but rather put them further into it. And Christian democracy has little to do with the teachings of Jesus of Nazareth. Ideologies survive such problems, but it is useful to display hypocrisies, as they indicate vulnerabilities that are the starting point for the discussion of alternatives.

1 How corporations become policy-making insiders

In the neoclassical economic theory on which neoliberalism claims to be based, markets have to be kept free from state intervention, because this distorts their operation. By the same token, states need to be protected from opaque influence by corporate interests, as this influence is likely to be used to push governments to act precisely in the kind of distorting way that offends neoclassical theory. Contemporary neoliberalism, however, focuses overwhelmingly on the former and ignores the latter, as a result turning a blind eye to the distorting interventions that can take place when governments respond to corporate influence. I limit influence to 'opaque' influence here, because transparent influence is more vulnerable to challenge, including democratic challenge, particularly if it seeks privileges that either other corporations or other social interests cannot contest. Neoliberalism concentrates its criticism on government interventions of a welfare-state kind – that is, those that seek to address negative market externalities or economic inequalities. It tends to be silent about those that disregard externalities or strengthen inequalities by catering to the interests of large corporations.

The most obvious examples concern the use of large cash payments as part of corporate lobbying. This has long been central to political life in many countries, most notably the United States, as Jeffrey Sachs (2011) has recently explored in detail. In 2010 the International Monetary Fund (IMF) claimed that, during the previous four-year electoral cycle, US firms spent \$4.2 billion on political activities, particularly prominent among them being firms in the high-risk end of the financial sector (IMF 2010).

In a number of advanced economies, particularly but by no means only in the US, lobbying has probably grown in scale as inequalities in wealth have risen. This makes it easier for large corporations, rather than small businesses or non-business interests, to lobby. But in this chapter we are concerned mainly with corporate activities that go beyond lobbying. In principle the 'lobby' is a place outside the decision-making chamber, where those not involved in the formal governmental process can make their case to those who are. In important respects corporations are today 'inside the chamber'. We can detect four processes whereby this happens: the power accorded to transnational corporations (TNCs) by their ability to transcend national jurisdictions; economic theories of competition that place the idea of consumer welfare above that of consumer choice; the new public management doctrine that government organizations should model themselves on private firms; and the contracting out of public services to private providers.

1.1 The power of transnational corporations

The first of these is the most obvious, but also perhaps the one whose importance has often been exaggerated. It has two aspects. First, global firms have some capacity to 'regime shop' – that is, to direct their investments to countries where they find the most favourable rules. Second, the global economy itself constitutes a space where governmental actors (compared to the national level within stable nation-states) are relatively weak and corporations therefore have more autonomy. A clear and unusually public example of this occurred in the UK in 2011, when the global bank HSBC threatened to move its headquarters to the Far East if the government persisted with a particular item of bank reregulation following the financial crisis. Government rapidly and equally publicly revised its proposals.

The first argument seems straightforward: if firms have a choice between two countries for maintaining their investments, they should be predicted to choose that which presents better opportunities for profit maximization, which will mean lower costs, and therefore lower levels of corporate taxation, of labour protection and social standards, and of environmental and other regulation. In the short run we should therefore expect a shift of investments from the more costly to the cheaper country. In the longer run the former should be expected to adjust its own standards downwards in order to be able to compete for investments with the cheaper country. The result would be a general lowering of standards to meet the preferences of multinational enterprises – a process often known as 'the race to the bottom' (Oates 1972).

In reality, matters are not always as clear-cut as this (Basinger and Hallenberg 2004). Existing investments in plant, distribution and supplier networks, as well as social links, are not so easily moved. Firms have sunk costs in their existing locations, and in order to move existing investments from one jurisdiction to another they need confidence that profits in the new location will be sufficient to outweigh these costs (Sutton 1991). The more likely threat is not a transfer of existing investments but a preference for the cheaper country for future new investments. Even here, there is not necessarily a consistent preference for the cheapest locations. Firms, especially those that are capable of strategy, choose in which market niches to locate themselves, and this does not always mean the lowest costs. The high quality of the goods or services being produced is often a criterion, and this may require highly paid staff with good working conditions, or a strong social infrastructure requiring high taxation. It is therefore not the case that high-wage, high-tax economies have always lost out in competition for direct inward investment.

However, the pressure still exists, as Genschel and Schwarz (chapter 3 in this volume) show. In any case, this argument still places the initiative with the firms: it is their market strategy that determines (or at least strongly affects) whether or not particular government policies will be 'rewarded' with investment and whether these are policies for making available a population to work at low wages or one with high skills and secure lives. Globalization does not necessarily mean a race to the bottom, but it does increase the power of global firms in setting the rules of the race.

The second argument maintains that, there being no government at global level, TNCs are left fairly free to make what rules they like there, including deals they make with other TNCs for setting standards or rules of trade. Since this is the level at which there is currently the most economic dynamism, this regulation determined by global firms feeds back into national levels, undermining government authority. A particularly important component of this shift from the historical position of private interests being the regulated rather than the regulators is the role of credit-ratings agencies. These comprise a small oligopoly of about three firms, all American, which rate the creditworthiness of both individual corporations and national governments. The ratings-agency model is prized by neoliberals as a form of market-driven regulation that they deem to be *a priori* superior to government regulation. In a market for regulation, the argument runs, agencies that provided guidance that proved to be inaccurate would be forced out of business, so they have a strong incentive to get things right. However, in the late 1990s they failed to notice anything amiss with the accounts of Enron, and the subsequent exposure of the scandal surrounding that company seemed to do nothing to dent their reputation (Hill 2003). Then in 2008 the agencies were all spectacularly wrong in not realizing that many, mainly Anglo-American banks had taken on excessive risks, but none of them has been driven from the market (Goodhart 2008). Instead they went on to take up strong and controversial positions undermining the credit ratings of European governments. In fact the market for ratings agencies is a very imperfect one, since there are only three major agencies that are all based in the US and share US perspectives. Their failures do not demonstrate that one could not have a market in regulation, but they do show that, at present, such a market does not exist in the financial sector.

The argument about the power of this kind of corporate regulation is also exaggerated, though not as much as that about an alleged 'race to the bottom'. Alongside the growth of the global economy has come an increase in regulatory activity by international agencies whose members comprise national governments and which therefore constitute delegated governmental authority. Since the postwar period, some (but not much) of the work of the United Nations and the activities of the World Bank and the IMF have had some authority of this kind. In recent years these bodies have interacted more with global civil-society movements to produce something resembling a pluralistic, if not democratic, global polity (Scholte 2011). The Organization for Economic Cooperation and Development (OECD), long mainly a source of data and statistics on national economies, has gradually acquired more of an international policy-coordinating role – for example, in the field of corruption in governments' business deals with TNCs. Most recently, the World Trade Organization (WTO) has begun to regulate terms of international trade – though its authority extends more over governments than over corporations, and its regulation is directed overwhelmingly at reducing barriers to trade. Its potential positive regulation to abate abuses such as child labour has not been used. Finally, between the nation-state level and the global level, there has been growth in intergovernmental organizations regulating economic affairs in a more detailed way across world regions, though only the European Union (EU) has developed extensive policies across a wide range of fields. Global economic space is therefore not entirely without public regulation, but individual giant firms clearly occupy a more directly regulatory role at this level than at national levels.

Even after we have put both these processes into perspective, we are left with a situation where the dominance of the economic over the political takes the form not of a dominance of markets but of corporations, often indeed using their power to limit markets – as occurs where a TNC uses its market dominance to develop standards that exclude its competitors.

1.2 Competition and consumer welfare

This last point brings us to an important argument in contemporary neoliberal thinking: that market competition means a process whereby the most successful firms either acquire their less successful rivals or drive them out of business. In other words, the end point of the competitive process is the abolition of competition. This contrasts with an earlier neoclassical view in economic and legal thought, that market competition meant the maintenance of market conditions in which a large number of firms was able to survive – that is, the end point of competition was the continuation of competition. The more recent view, which is associated with the law and economics school of the University of Chicago, contends that the pure neoclassical approach produces a less efficient economy, as firms that would have been taken over or wiped out through market forces are artificially kept alive (Bork 1993 [1978]; Posner 2001; for a critical overview of the whole debate, see Amato 1997). True, consumer choice is weakened through this reduction in competition, but, it is contended, it cannot be in consumers' interests to have a less efficient economy. Consumer welfare may therefore conflict with consumer choice, and in such a case the former is more important. Probably of more interest to contemporary neoliberals is that the strict neoclassical approach requires increasing state regulation to sustain competition; the primary concern of neoliberalism is the reduction of regulation, even at the expense of the market. The earlier approach, which is associated with both traditional US antitrust law and modern European competition law, both insisted on the importance of consumer choice and stressed the importance of limiting concentrations of economic power in the interests of democracy and pluralism. Chicago theory tends to ignore the latter argument, except to contend that, if the state disengages from the economy, it does not matter if corporations are politically powerful, as they cannot do anything with their power.

1.3 New public management

Systems of public management that developed under the influence of nineteenth-century liberal concepts insisted on rules that governed and limited relations between ministers and senior civil servants, on the one hand, and businesspeople, on the other. The rationale for this was to avoid the corruption that might occur if individual businesspeople or firms tried to gain favours from the state. This was partly to protect the autonomy of the capitalist economy and its markets, and partly to protect the state from corruption. In many countries the rules did not at all prevent corruption, but the concept certainly existed that such separations were necessary. This approach was reinforced by twentieth-century social democracy, which was suspicious of the mutual entanglements of business and politics. The desire of liberals to protect the market from politicians, and the desire of social democrats to protect the polity from businessmen, produced an unusual but powerful alliance. Late twentieth- and early twenty-first-century neoliberalism departs radically from this consensus, as it criticizes the division between business and politics for having produced a political and public administrative class that has become remote from private business and out of touch with its market-driven incentives, and therefore unlikely to innovate or achieve efficiencies.

This criticism has been part of the doctrine of new public management (NPM), a branch of neoliberalism that concentrates on remedying alleged inefficiencies of government organizations by modelling them more closely on corporations (Hood 1991; Christensen and Lægreid 2002; Osborne 2006). As part of this doctrine, governments have been encouraged to employ private-sector consultants, to appoint senior managers from private business, and to allow easier passage into senior positions with private firms by ministers and civil servants when they leave public life, even into firms connected with areas where they had earlier had responsibilities. This has opened up important opportunities to corporations to influence governments. Some of the strongest examples come from the US, where many of the key public officials engaged in the deregulation of investment banking – a deregulation that was directly responsible for the financial crash of 2008 – either had worked for investment banks before moving into government or moved from government to banks after office, or did both. Some of these individuals became important figures in the Obama administration (Sachs 2011).

A related development is the employment by government of private-sector consultants and seconded staff from corporations within the government machinery, working to advise governments on public policy within areas where they were conducting business and seeking contracts.

A curious example of a private firm being enabled to penetrate deeply into government and the police force, as well as both the country's main political parties, has taken place in recent years in the UK. Throughout the summer of 2011 there were revelations of illegal telephone hacking by at least one of the newspapers owned by News International, the British branch of News Corp, the US media corporation owned by the former Australian – and now US – magnate Rupert Murdoch. At the time of writing the revelations have not yet ended, and the full facts of the case are not known. We do, however, know that journalists from the news-paper the *News of the World* were hacking the phones of a wide range of celebrities, politicians and other newsworthy people. Since this was an illegal activity, it necessitated collaboration with 'private detectives' with criminal links. Phone-hacking could reveal secrets about individuals' private lives that could provide material for newspaper stories, but there was also the possibility of blackmail. While this story had been develop-ing for several years, two coincidental events brought it to a crisis in July 2011. First, during that month it was expected that the Conservative–Liberal Democrat coalition government would grant News International a highly controversial monopoly control over the UK's major satellite television service. Second, it was discovered that among the mobile phones that had been hacked by *News of the World* journalists were one belonging to a murdered girl and others belonging to the families of British soldiers killed in Iraq and Afghanistan. There was a widespread expression of public disgust at this behaviour, especially in the case of the murdered girl, as the activity on her phone produced by the hacking had led her parents to believe she was still alive.

It became impossible (at least temporarily) for the government to grant the satellite television monopoly to News International, but the earlier government support for it rendered the whole issue of the firm's behaviour of central political interest. Newspapers and politicians began to devote serious resources to the case. It was already known that the prime minister had appointed a former editor of the *News of the World* to be the government's senior communications officer; this official had already had to resign. But it now became clear that both major political parties, Conservative and Labour, had several former employees of News International in senior positions in their press offices. More surpris-ing, the corporation had developed similar links with the Metropolitan Police, the UK's main police force. Following inquiries five years before the phone-hacking scandal, the Metropolitan Police had declared that very few instances of hacking had occurred. This was now known to be untrue. During the summer of 2011 the head of the police force and one other senior officer were required to resign their posts.

What exactly News International has been doing in British public life is difficult to determine, but even if we set the phone-hacking aside we still have a major example of a corporation embedding itself in govern-ment, political parties and the police through the placement of personnel. It may be in part related to contract-winning, as in the satellite television case. It was surprising that a government in principle devoted to market competition wanted to grant an unnecessary monopoly over satellite tel-evision to a corporation that already owned several national newspapers.

A second example concerns the UK government's current proposed changes to British planning laws to make it easier for developers to erect new buildings in rural areas and towns considered to have landscape or architectural value, areas currently protected by planning legislation. Several major property companies bought land at low prices – low because the sites were protected by existing legislation – in anticipation that the planning laws would be changed, enabling them to build. A number of these firms had made large donations to the Conservative Party. It also emerged that personnel from house-building firms had drafted some of the legislation that would introduce the changes.

The News International and planning law cases may simply be examples of old-fashioned graft rather than the product of NPM. However, NPM has helped to create a climate in which this behaviour was considered reasonable. If neoliberalism meant an exposure to market forces and the clear separation of government from economic interests, as required by market economics, then a neoliberal government should have been particularly averse to such conduct. In fact it willingly embraced it. The plan to grant satellite television monopoly to News International was disrupted not by devotion to the competitive market, but only through the coincidental revelations about phone-hacking in a separate part of the firm's holdings. The relationship between property companies and the UK planning law changes came to light mainly because certain other interests close to the Conservative Party were offended. This aspect will be pursued further below.

These have all been cases where 'making government more like business' has not meant what economists understand as a true introduction of markets, but rather has been their possible distortion, and certainly a growing political power for firms.

1.4 Contracting out public services

Finally, in the welfare state a compromise between a drive for privatization of services and a continuing commitment to provision of services on the basis of need and not ability to pay has had some similar effects. What happens here is a privatization of supply but not of demand and a separation of the user from the purchaser (Crouch 2011). Typically, a public authority offers contracts to provide a public service, possibly in certain geographical areas. It is therefore the purchaser, because it pays for the service through taxation revenues rather than requiring service users to pay, except on a token basis. This latter case is consistent with social democratic welfare-state principles. The users continue to be the members of the public who avail themselves of the service, but they have no customer or user relationship with the firms that win the contracts.

Therefore, in these contracts there is no market on the demand side;

there is a monopoly purchaser, or possibly a small number of purchasers among different public authorities. The supply side potentially has a market, but in practice the contracting business is dominated by a small number of contractors. Interestingly, these are often firms who engage in public-service contracts across a wide range of activities. A road-construction firm might provide local government back-office services; a defence contractor might provide school education. Road construction and defence have long been almost entirely areas of public contract work; from there firms have extended to other areas of public service as the welfare state has been opened up to private contractors. The core business of these firms is not therefore the substantive activity; providing defence equipment does not have much to do with educating children. This is entirely logical. The core business is the art of winning government contracts. The government is the customer, not the service users, and government is not directly buying the substance of a service but a contract to provide it. The process of winning contracts from government is clearly a specialized business, or more firms would engage in it; the techniques it requires are not identical to those of winning a contract in the market.

The number of providers is made smaller by the fact that in many of these welfare-state areas there has been no history of mass private provision. Before it can offer contracts, government therefore has to engage in what is called 'market making', which is essentially the process of persuading firms to let government be their customers. The 'markets' that result are usually small, and relations between purchaser and provider do not follow economists' rules.

This process overlaps with the previous discussion both of private consultants and staff seconded from firms to work in government and of the passage of individuals between government and corporations. The work of these persons is often to enable their firms to help 'make a market'. Once again, what they in fact make are corporate insiders to government rather than markets. As we know from the literature on contract performance within the private sector itself, the abstract distinction between principals and agents does not really work (Williamson 1975; Williamson and Masten 1995). In theory, the principal decides policy and the agent merely implements. But this is unrealistic for any complex contract performance; the agent becomes involved in proposing ways of working or even objectives that are more suited to its preferences or which reflect its expert assessment. When this happens in the contracting out of public services, corporations start to share in determining public policy. This is happening across a range of activities, from care to military services.

It is notable that the countries with the largest welfare states, the

Nordics and especially Sweden, have moved a long way towards this form of contracting out (Tritter 2011). Such contracting played a major role in the eventual negotiation of health-care reform by the Obama administration in the US; the president was able to achieve an increase in public funding of health care, provided that private firms gained a major share of the delivery. This may be the emerging new social contract of the twenty-first century: populations can keep their welfare states, provided they become an arena for corporate profit-making. As Freedland has argued (1998), there is a distinct democratic deficit in the process, as the relationship between government and citizens is replaced by that between government and contractor, while the citizens' only relation to the contractor is that of user – a more passive one than that of customer. If the European Union policy of opening up public services provision to international competition becomes generalized, the service providers will become international firms even further beyond citizens' reach.

2 Corporate social responsibility

As more areas of life are brought within the scope of neoliberal reasoning, there is a strong trend towards amorality in public life. Fields such as health and education, which in the past were seen as having their own sets of values, have been brought within the market. Not only is profit maximization the sole goal of corporations as such, but it seems that nothing else in society should try to establish alternative goals. Meanwhile globalization has increasingly been separating corporate activity from the values of specific human communities.

We see this process particularly clearly in the growing dominance in corporate law of the Anglo-American model of the firm. This presents the firm with a single goal: the maximization of shareholder value. This focuses managers' attention on making their activities as efficient as possible, maximizing profits and therefore making society richer. It should be noted that there is a claimed general good here: in principle shareholder maximization is not an appeal to selfishness *tout court*, but the usual claim on behalf of the market that it turns selfish motivations into benign pursuit of general welfare. But this rules out any criticisms of the intermediate consequences of maximizing behaviour and argues that ultimate ends justify both means and intermediate implications. This Anglo-American approach to the firm is contrasted favourably by economists with traditional German corporate law, which saw a firm as having several stakeholders in addition to shareholders, including employees, whose interests must be reconciled with one another. It is argued that the traditional German system results in a confusion of goals, in lower profits, and therefore in lower wealth creation. The justification of this 'demoralization' of social life is that, in the market, people are free to choose. But, as we have seen, many contemporary markets are dominated by large corporations, where judgements are made by lawyers in commercial courts as to what constitutes consumer welfare, rather than the ideologically promoted concept of 'freedom of choice'.

There is, however, an important twist to this story. The years during which the Anglo-American concept was coming to dominate the world were also the years when the idea of corporate social responsibility (CSR), which meant having regard for goals other than profit, was being strongly promoted – and proclaimed by some major enterprises, including Anglo-American ones. The CSR movement has been asserting that corporations cannot escape having a moral personality – and at a level short of the general argument that profit maximization automatically guarantees the public interest. The case for CSR has been developed as a response to increasingly intense criticism of the morality of many aspects of corporate behaviour. Arguments about the total priority of shareholder value have completely failed to put an end to controversies over a mass of issues, ranging from the treatment of labour in global supply chains, to the responsibility of Western firms in Africa for the spread of HIV/AIDS, to the conduct of investment banks in derivative markets, to very many questions around pollution and environmental damage (Crouch and Maclean 2011). Many corporate leaders have found it necessary to declare that their businesses pursue goals in these areas, alongside profit maximization.

Much of this may be just public-relations talk without much substance. Also, there are arguments that CSR can be reconciled with profit maximization. (In their most sophisticated form, these arguments claim that firms that listen to changing public moods in their CSR practices are also likely to be sensitive to new market opportunities.) But neither of these very different objections to seeing CSR as a challenge to profit maximization can refute the main point: some firms are being required to respond to important ethical challenges. This new emphasis on CSR works mainly with firms to whom brand names and reputation in mass markets matter, above all to fashion-sensitive industries such as clothing, domestic petroleum products and food. Firms whose customers are mainly other corporations, such as investment banks, are less likely to be challenged.

But something happens as we slip from ethical practices embedded in law (as was the most likely outcome of such challenges in the recent past) to those chosen by business leaders themselves. The initiative in formulating a moral agenda has passed from political and legal elites to corporate ones, and from a broadly democratic arena to a private and often secretive one. There is an interesting dialectic at work: the price of the triumph of the corporation over the state – and, as we have seen, to some extent over the market – as society's leading institution has been an end to the claim that firms just need to pursue private profit and ignore public issues. The process resembles that whereby medieval monarchs had to start providing some public goods (such as a system of law courts) once they had made strong claims to sovereignty.

Both politico-legal and corporate elites can claim some democratic legitimacy, and both of these claims are vulnerable. Politics has all formal democratic legitimacy on its side, but can be accused of manipulating the people's voice through the tricks of the political trade. Corporate leaders can make no formal democratic claims, but they can argue that they are in touch with the preferences of masses of consumers through the market. It can then be counter-argued that consumers have no voice with which they can articulate their demands; they can simply purchase or not; control over marketing strategy, including any CSR components of it, rests with corporate leaders.

These debates over CSR, and the wider debates over the ethics of corporate behaviour to which it relates, enable us to reach two important conclusions. First, despite globalization, despite the dominance of the profit-maximization model, disputes over the ethical quality of the economic system have not gone away. If anything, they are stronger and more diverse now than at many times in the past. Second, the very triumph of neoliberal arguments over the earlier model of the active state has landed corporations in the middle of the controversy. Corporate leaders find it increasingly difficult to argue that their job is just to maximize profits and that, if we want limits imposed on them, we should look to politics and the state. This has become difficult precisely because neoliberalism has taught us that states are inefficient and that we should look to corporations for effective action. The very ideology that proclaimed the autonomy and superiority of economic motivations has produced complications for those same motivations.

3 Enter civil society

As I have argued elsewhere (Crouch 2011), once corporations have accepted, and sometimes indeed boasted of, a commitment to pursue social responsibility, they are vulnerable to criticism and challenge if they seek to keep this activity at the level of PR exercises. Thanks partly to the unmanageable communications possibilities of the Internet, almost every major corporation now has attached to it a critical campaigning group that draws attention to any negative externalities associated with its activities and any perceived hypocrisy in its CSR claims. This has not resulted from the uncoordinated responses of millions of consumers. As John Campbell (2007) has argued, pressure comes from several elements in a firm's social and political context. At one level, it has had to be organized. Groups campaigning around environmental issues, fair trade with developing countries and labour conditions in supply chains have worked hard to mobilize customers, drawing attention to unethical and environmentally damaging – and occasionally to good – behaviour. This marks a shift from CSR as an agenda framed and controlled by firms themselves to corporate social accountability framed by groups of citizens. As Néron (2010) and Vogel (2008) have both pointed out, this in turn creates a genuinely new political arena. Critics of corporate behaviour target firms directly, as well as indirectly via parties and governments – though the existence of laws and regulations often provides a vital springboard for campaigning action. As the corporation operates in both markets and politics, so its critics operate through market pressure as well as through direct political action.

It is even possible that – only sometimes and in only some cases – firms may be more responsive than governments to pressures of this kind. There are two reasons for this. First, governments may become so obsessed with ensuring they provide no impediments to enterprise that they establish a general strategy of leaving firms alone as much as possible. Meanwhile, some firms are becoming sensitive to the market opportunities offered by subtle nuances of taste changes among consumers.

A further advantage of campaigns directed at giant corporations rather than at governments is that these usually have an important built-in international component, as the firms themselves are transnational. Consumers and campaigners can organize internationally, and the objects of concern are often in a number of developing countries. These campaigns therefore constitute the early germination of the seeds of a transnational civil society (Brix et al. 2010). Meanwhile, governments, parties and political systems remain doggedly national; they are defined by the nation-state and are dedicated to pursuing the interests of that nation-state, any solidary action being of very marginal importance and existing mainly at very formal diplomatic levels, remote from civil society.

The role of corporations in politics can be seen as part of the non-democratic component of the constitution of modern societies. So too is the oppositional politics around the corporation. The vitality of campaigns and cause groups is evidence of a lively, pluralistic civil society, but it is not democracy in the formal sense of electoral processes within which all adults have a right to participate. At the outset of this chapter I said that political discussion should replace its polarity of state and market by the triangle of state, market and corporation. But the political rise of the corporation and the often comfortable accommodation among all members of the triangle has stimulated a fourth force in the shape of this non-parliamentary, non-party but clearly political activity by campaigning groups, or what in German have long been known as *Bürgerinitiativen* – citizens' initiatives. In general, it is what is often called 'civil society'. The politics of advanced societies therefore sometimes takes the form of a quadrilateral of forces rather than a triangle, though one where the fourth limb is clearly weaker than the others.

I have written elsewhere about this phenomenon and have depicted civil-society activity as comprising relatively small groups – politically important but demographically probably limited (Crouch 2011; see also Della Porta 2003). There may, however, be a further twist still to this unfolding of a new politics.

The rise of neoliberalism, the emergence of a global financial sector rooted in derivatives markets, and the general rise of corporate oligopolies have been accompanied by the growth in inequality referred to above. One aspect of this inequality is often discussed: a growing gap between the great majority of the population and the bottom 10 to 15 per cent of the income distribution. But the gap at the other end also merits consideration. The top 1 per cent is moving away from everyone else, and within that an even smaller group further extends a lead. The gap that separates the bottom 10 to 15 per cent brings major social problems; the gap at the top brings political ones, in the form of the concentration of political influence in large corporations under consideration here. This influence is restricted to the most powerful transnational corporations. There is little here for small and medium-sized firms. There is also little here for interests outside the corporate sector. This growing inequality of power creates uneasiness across large sections of the public, social tensions that are not the same as those of the now declining class divisions on which our party systems are still largely based.

The two British cases – News International and proposed changes in the planning laws – discussed above illustrate the point. The News International incident produced a profound sense of unease in the British public. At its heart was apprehensiveness over the use of economic power, including its morality. Values were involved here, not just economic interests. In responding to criticisms of hacking the phones of a murdered girl and relatives of dead soldiers, News International did not dare to use the usual defence of dubious media activities – that its actions might bring a story that would sell newspapers and make more profits.

They simply apologized. Profit maximization had for once lost its ability to be the trump card.

The planning law case raised very different substantive issues from News International, but it also attracted criticism for its attack on values other than those of profit maximization – criticism from defenders of the countryside and of historic urban centres. The national newspaper the *Daily Telegraph*, which would normally be totally reliably sympathetic to a Conservative-led government, gave prominent attention to the role played by party donations and the insider role of property companies in drafting policy. Several of the groups that campaign for Britain's rural heritage and traditions, and which opposed the change in the law, are also groups that would normally share many values with the Conservative Party. As in the News International case, a small but economically powerful set of corporate interests used its resources successfully at the level of the political elite, but found itself opposed by large sections of public opinion – including many of those that would normally ally themselves politically with the economically powerful.

Historically, in the UK and elsewhere, wealthy interests and corporate elites have been able to persuade large numbers of middle-income or middle-class groups to share a political identity with them, against the perceived threat of the organized manual working class. Their ability to do this was originally a condition of these elites' participation in democracy: when and where they felt themselves to be isolated against the potentially combined ranks of middle and working classes, they opposed democracy; when and where they succeeded in building that link to the middle class, they participated in a general democratic conservative bloc that has, around the advanced world, been extraordinarily successful.

There may be some change to that pattern today, in response to several factors. On the one hand, wealthy and corporate elites have become 'denationalized'; wealthy individuals have holdings all around the world, the big corporations are global enterprises. These elites are not particularly interested in the internal politics of any country, except perhaps the US. Their lobbying power is largely independent of electoral politics and generally more powerful; alliances with any particular national *Mittelstand* are not important to them. On the other hand, the old threat to middle-class interests presented by organized labour has considerably diminished as the workforce of manufacturing industry has declined in size, while the lower-income groups of the services economy have not yet created a political identity.

The dominant, largely financial elite has little need for the support of the middle class, while the latter has little need to fear the working class. This can create considerable tension between the elite and the middle class, when the conduct of the former undermines the values and interests of the latter. It is unlikely that this will lead, at least in the short term, to a party-political realignment of classes. Modern parties do not have strong identities; they try to avoid them and appeal to as many voters as possible. Therefore party allegiances have decreasing meaning, except as historical cultural symbols, which are fairly proof against disturbance by events. But outside the formal and increasingly ritual arena of electoral competition, new patterns of shifting alliances are forming for specific campaigns. One cannot really say that politics is becoming fluid and increasingly pluralistic, as the dominance of wealthy elites is rather stable; with the financial sector at their heart, they can still define the general interest of our societies. But there are interesting changes. Depending on the issue, the fourth limb of the quadrilateral may not be so weak as first appears, and it may have wider implications than challenging disconnected elements in the behaviour of individual corporations. It is unlikely that the politics of post-industrial societies will form the large blocs of alliances typical of industrialism and the world of mass parties. More fluid structures and fragmented organizations, overlapping boundaries between polity, economy and society may well be characteristic. One must not, however, be carried away by images of fluidity. The concentrations of capital typical of this kind of society may be fluid in that the financial markets on which they concentrate are fast-moving and unstable, but the concentrations of wealth themselves are very solid.

4 Conclusions

Along with some others, I have described contemporary advanced societies as being on a path towards 'post-democracy', which I define as a polity within which, while all democratic institutions continue to function, the energy of political action has moved elsewhere, in particular into a small, combined political and economic elite (Crouch 2004). The trends towards corporate political dominance discussed above constitute the major evidence for such a claim. The decline in democratic capacity described is not what neoliberals could see as a necessary withdrawal of the polity into its 'real' terrain as it stops trying to overreach itself in the regulatory, Keynesian and welfare state. The decline that we perceive is one that should have been anathema to neoliberals themselves: the use of strong corporate power within politics. The tendency will not be easily reversed, because the two major forces behind it – the growing scale of corporations in several major sectors and economic globalization – are too important to economic growth for any serious political movement to seek their reversal. The two counter-trends considered here – civil society and CSR – are far too weak to impose any major change of direction. Indeed, to the extent that the latter represents a disappearance of public policy into the private chambers of giant firms, it is more part of the problem of democratic decline than part of its solution.

In the above discussion, the state has been depicted as increasingly the close ally of corporate power. It remains, however, the main channel for challenging that power. CSR and corporate philanthropy are the nearest that firms can get to dealing with their own negative externalities, and these are both minor aspects of corporate life and removed from democratic reach. Charitable, religious and other bodies making primarily moral claims to authority can act in relation to externalities, but except in societies united by strong moral integration – which is not the case of contemporary advanced societies – these are weak. Even if civil-society actions often target corporations, or act directly to tackle a problem, they still address many, perhaps most, of their demands to political authorities, whether national or transnational. This cannot change, as only such authorities can tackle fully the issues raised by market externalities. Meanwhile, market externalities necessarily increase precisely as profit-making and market-making activities expand into further areas of life as neoliberalism enables and requires them to do. In this way, neoliberalism creates a need for the very market-limiting measures to which it is opposed.

Only the body that monopolizes the legitimate means of collective violence – the Weberian state – has the capacity fully to tackle major negative market externalities, though this does not mean that the possibilities of using civil-society actions as supplementary forces should be neglected. When the state's reach is inadequate (for example, because it is trapped at the level of historical nations) or it is thoroughly penetrated by corporate power anxious to evade regulation, then the damage caused by those externalities will go largely unchecked. This will probably be the fate of measures to arrest man-made climate change.

Climate change and other aspects of environmental damage demonstrate particularly strongly the inadequacies of geographically based entities like nation-states, especially when such entities need to confront deterritorialized private economic power. The idea of state 'sovereignty' is predicated on the assumption that the state is the most powerful institution operating over its geographical space. So long as democracy has its primary expression at this level, it will be unable to check corporate power. The idea of the state, including very prominently the welfare state, has to reach out to more inclusive levels. For Europeans the major first steps in this process are the construction of stronger European institutions, including citizenship. Both here and more obviously in any attempts to strengthen global governance, democracy has to take some steps back in order to take others forward. Clearly, democracy and citizenship weaken in quality as they try to operate across large numbers of people, even more so when they operate through bodies that are only indirectly democratic – as must be the case with any global governance (Scholte 2011). But if the national level is simply unable to tackle issues, it is better to have a diluted democracy with reach than a stronger one that is ineffective. In practice, this means, for example, surrendering some elements of socially embedded and valued national welfare states and regulatory regimes to a weaker European social policy. But without that step there will only be an overall and unresolvable weakening.

References

Amato, G. (1997) *Antitrust and the Bounds of Power: The Dilemma of Liberal Democracy in the History of the Market.* Oxford: Hart.

Basinger, S. J., and Hallenberg, M. (2004) Remodeling the competition for capital: how democratic politics erases the race to the bottom, *American Political Science Review* 98(2): 261–76.

Bork, R. H. (1993 [1978]) *The Antitrust Paradox: A Policy at War with Itself.* 2nd edn, New York: Free Press.

Brix, E., Nautz, J., Trattnigg, R., and Wutscher, W. (eds) (2010) *State and Civil Society.* Vienna: Passagen.

Campbell, J. (2007) Why would corporations behave in socially responsible ways? An institutional theory of corporate social responsibility, *Academy of Management Review* 32(3): 946–67.

Christensen, T., and Lægreid, P. (2002) *New Public Management: The Transformation of Ideas and Practice.* Aldershot: Ashgate.

Crouch, C. (2004) *Post-Democracy.* Cambridge: Polity.

Crouch, C. (2011) *The Strange Non-Death of Neoliberalism.* Cambridge: Polity.

Crouch, C., and Maclean, M. (eds) (2011) *The Responsible Corporation in a Global Economy.* Oxford: Oxford University Press.

Della Porta, D. (2003) *I new global.* Bologna: Il Mulino.

Freedland, M. (1998) Law, public services, and citizenship – new domains, new regimes?, in M. Freedland and S. Sciarra (eds), *Public Services and Citizenship in European Law: Public and Labour Law Perspectives.* Oxford: Clarendon Press, pp. 1–35.

Goodhart, C. A. E. (2008) The background to the 2007 financial crisis, *International Economics and Economic Policy* 4(4): 331–46.

Hill, C. A. (2003) Ratings agencies behaving badly: the case of Enron, *Connecticut Law Review* 35(3): 1145–56.

Hood, C. (1991) A public management for all seasons?, *Public Administration* 69(1): 3–19.

IMF (International Monetary Fund) (2010) *A Fistful of Dollars: Lobbying and the Financial Crisis.* Washington, DC: IMF.

Néron, P.-Y. (2010) Business and the polis: what does it mean to see corporations as political actors?, *Journal of Business Ethics* 94(3): 333–52.

Oates, W. (1972) *Fiscal Federalism*. New York: Harcourt, Brace, Jovanovich.

Osborne, S. (2006) The new public governance?, *Public Management Review* 8(3): 377–87.

Posner, R. A. (2001) *Antitrust Law*. 2nd edn, Chicago: University of Chicago Press.

Sachs, J. (2011) *The Price of Civilization: Economics and Ethics after the Fall*. London: Bodley Head.

Scholte, J. A. (ed.) (2011) *Building Global Democracy? Civil Society and Accountable Global Governance*. Cambridge: Cambridge University Press.

Sutton, J. (1991) *Sunk Costs and Market Structure*. Cambridge, MA: MIT Press.

Tritter, J. (2011) Trouble in paradise: the erosion of the Nordic social welfare state, unpublished paper presented at the conference 'Beyond the Public Realm?', University of Warwick.

Vogel, D. (2008) Private global business regulation, *Annual Review of Political Science* 11: 261–82.

Williamson, O. E. (1975) *Markets and Hierarchies: Analysis and Antitrust Implications: A Study in the Economics of Internal Organization*. New York: Free Press.

Williamson, O. E., and Masten, S. E. (1995) *Transaction Cost Economics*. Aldershot: Edward Elgar.

10

The Normalization of the Right in Post-Security Europe[1]

Mabel Berezin

1 What is normalization?

European right-wing parties and right-wing ideas have gained increased political traction in recent years. As the global financial crisis unfolded in the autumn of 2008 and a fully fledged European sovereign debt crisis hit in spring 2010, parties on the right began to accumulate significant electoral successes. Parties such as the Sweden Democrats that were marginal political players in their respective nation-states have won seats in parliaments, and in some instances have become part of governing coalitions. In the April 2011 Finnish legislative elections, the right-nationalist True Finn Party came in third place and achieved the same percentage of votes as the Finnish Social Democrats.

During this period, nationalist rhetoric and policy proposals that are usually the purview of the European populist right have become part of the centre-right and, in some instances, left political discourse. For example, in October 2010 the German chancellor, Angela Merkel, told a gathering of young members of the Christian Democratic Union Party that Germany's attempt to build a multicultural society had 'failed, utterly failed'. Although Merkel went on to say that immigrants were still welcome in Germany, the phrase 'failed, utterly failed' resonated in Germany and across Europe. David Cameron, the British prime minister, seconded Merkel's assessment of multiculturalism in a lecture on Islamist extremism delivered at the Munich Security Conference in early February 2011. A week later, the French president, Nicolas Sarkozy, declared during a television interview that 'clearly, yes' – multiculturalism was a failure. Nationalist appeals to identities and practices are not new, but for the most part they have remained in the interstices of the European project. Whereas cultural conflict in the past arose from below, it now appears to be descending from above. Until recently, heads of state, especially heads of state that are committed to the European project, have not led the national identity charge. The events of 9/11 in the United States and subsequent terrorist activities in Europe have rendered it legitimate to argue that unassimilated immigrants, and specifically Muslims, are dangerous.

The economic events that began in the United States in autumn 2008 and soon travelled to Europe also made it legitimate to argue that Europe was a dangerous economic and political project. The European financial crisis trailed that in the United States by a few months. The struggle between national interest and the plans to preserve the European Monetary Union (EMU) began in spring 2009 with the Hungarian debt crisis. The conflict between national and European interests continues to plague attempts to adjudicate the full-blown European sovereign debt crisis that emerged in 2010, when Greece began to head towards default. In the spring of 2009, pundits and politicians spoke of a weakening European project and a potential failure of the eurozone. Editorials with titles such as 'Europe's gone missing' (Ash 2009), 'Eastern crisis that could wreck the eurozone' (Munchau 2009) and 'A continent adrift' (Krugman 2009) were common in major international newspapers. As early as January 2009, the French supply-side economist Éloi Laurent (2009) warned that the euro could not be allowed to fail and that member states needed to take action soon.

In spring 2009, policy-makers and politicians did not view the eurozone as being in danger. Public commentary had little effect upon them. The democratic deficit and the lack of accountability to ordinary citizens of EU institutions had long been a subject of discussion in EU academic debates. Yet no one seriously thought that the EU challenged democracy.[2] When faced with fiscal deficits and potential defaults, neither politicians nor commentators saw a serious challenge to European democratic practices or sentiments. Ideas that were inconceivable in spring 2009 are conceivable today.

When, a week before the summit in Brussels on 21 July 2011, the news emerged that Italy was on the verge of default, the cover of *The Economist* (16–22 July 2011) captured the shift in public perception. A gold 1 euro coin teetered on the edge of a black cliff, the edge shaped as the Italian boot against a background of bold red. The caption read: 'On the edge: why the euro crisis has just got a lot worse'. A week later, in *The Guardian*, Nobel Prize-winning economist Amartya Sen (2011) linked the preservation of the eurozone to the preservation of European democracy, and argued: 'It is . . . worrying that the dangers to democratic governance today, coming through the back door of financial priority, are not receiving the attention they should.' Two weeks after the Brussels summit, with global equity markets crashing, politicians as well as pundits began to view Europe as a threat not only to itself but also to others. Robert Samuelson (2011), writing in the *Washington Post*, warned: 'The big danger is Europe'. Walter Russell Mead (2011), in the *Wall Street Journal*, argued that maybe it was time for Europe to consider downsizing back to the national level. A recent *New York Times* (2011) 'Room for debate' feature, devoted to 'A Europe divided?', revealed that even some 'experts' remain divided on the future of Europe.

The *normalization of the right* is the analytical term that I developed to capture the twin phenomena of the electoral surge of the European right and the mainstreaming of nationalist ideas and practices. The *normalization of the right* has evolved in tandem with two global processes – the diffusion of terrorism and the onset of financial crisis. In *Illiberal Politics in Neoliberal Times* (Berezin 2009), I argued that the accelerated pace of Europeanization, including the creation of the EMU, fostered the emergence of a revitalized European right and ultimately promoted centre-right political coalitions. But *Illiberal Politics* did not anticipate the 2008 financial crisis, which by spring 2010 had become a full-blown European sovereign debt crisis. Since 2008, visions of a united, economically competitive and socially cosmopolitan Europe have blurred in the wake of the financial crisis. The sovereign debt crisis underscores the connection between the *normalization of the right* and the European project and also points to the fragility of that project.

Building upon Berezin (2009), this chapter argues that the global financial crisis has exacerbated economic fissures and cultural fault lines in the European project and has brought institutional problems into focus that were formerly adjudicated by nations. The sovereign debt crisis is forcing Europe to recalibrate itself as a *post-security polity*. Nation-states, the bedrock of pre-EU Europe, institutionalized a form of 'practical security' that lent collective emotional security to citizens. Political security was located in citizenship laws and internal and external defence ministries. National social welfare systems produced economic security and social solidarity as a by-product. Linguistic, educational and even religious policies created cultural security because they enforced assumptions, if not realities, of similarity and identity. In contrast to the 'old' Europe, where security, solidarity and identity were guaranteed, the *post-security polity* privileges markets, fosters austerity that threatens solidarity, and supports multicultural inclusion at the expense of nationalist exclusion.

This chapter develops a historical approach to the study of the right and argues that the breakdown of the institutions of 'practical security', driven by expanding European integration and exacerbated by the financial crisis, has provided a political climate in which right-wing solutions to political issues appear *normal*. It explores the relation between the rise of the nationalist right and the weakening, if not outright imploding, of the European project. It describes and theorizes the effect of the financial crisis and the ensuing austerity measures on the flourishing of non-democratic political sentiments in contemporary Europe. Sentiments, rather than practices, more accurately capture events in contemporary Europe, since all European nation-states, with the exception of the European Union, are procedurally democratic.

The analysis in this chapter is two-pronged. First, it explores the developing political salience of the European right that began in the early 1990s. The political trajectory of the French National Front (*Front National*) – one of the oldest and most continually relevant European right-wing parties – is a core component of this story. The chapter then situates the French right and the right more generally within the current European context.

2 Analysing the right

Extremist political parties and movements have been a constituent feature of European politics since the early twentieth century. With the exception of the 1920s and 1930s, these parties and movements have remained for the most part extreme and at the margins of normal politics. The spectacular disaster of the Second World War overshadowed the fact that, even in the 1920s and 1930s, the Italian fascist regime was tepid. Mussolini met his downfall through his alliance with Hitler; and in Spain Franco prudently avoided war and alliances (Berezin 2009: 17–22). The right was outlawed in various European countries after the war, but it did not disappear. Former fascist parties regrouped, changed their names and generally existed in the interstices of European political life. In 1988, the journal *West European Politics* published a special issue devoted to 'Right-wing extremism in Western Europe'. With the exception of the French National Front, the parties and movements that it discussed were not meaningful political actors even as few as ten years after its publication.

Social scientists developed an analytical response to the right that emerged in the 1990s. Political scientists (for example, Eatwell 2003; Mudde 2007; Rydgren 2007) tend to divide the available literature on the contemporary right along the analytical axes of *supply* and *demand*. *Supply* variables describe the availability of a right-wing party, and *demand* variables speak to voter characteristics and preferences. Berezin (2009: 40–5) develops an alternative framework that uses *institutions* and *culture* as analytical axes. This framework captures nuances and contextual complexities that *supply* and *demand* tend to miss. Institutional approaches assume rational calculation. The legal system underlies institutional approaches. The cultural classification encompasses meaning in the broadest sense. *Organizations*, *agenda setting* and *labour markets* provide further specification of the institutional category. In contrast to institutional approaches, cultural approaches to the right assume non-rationality – that is, to borrow from Max Weber, actions oriented towards values and beliefs – and include theories based upon *post-materialist values*, *ressentiment* and *legacies*.

Organization theories have an implicit notion of efficiency built into them because they prioritize party strategy. The choice theoretic versions of these theories assume that marginality is a mark of strength and not weakness (Givens 2005; Norris 2005; Meguid 2008). Political scientists examine the logic of right-wing party coalitions and focus upon the right's ability to become a strategic player in electoral politics. *Organization* theories do a good job of explaining the regional success of right-wing parties because they can point to the intersection of local-level bargaining and political strategy. They are less able to explain right-wing success and failure in national elections.

Agenda-setting approaches assume political rationality and posit that the right garners political legitimacy by bringing marginal issues into the electoral arena ahead of mainstream political parties (Schain 1987). They confuse issues of perception and timing and conflate causes with effects. For example, the French state placed immigration on its agenda before the National Front identified it as a political issue (Schor 1985).

Labour-market explanations of the rise of the right assume that inefficiencies in the post-industrial labour market and subsequent unemployment due to structural obsolescence lead to the propensity to vote for a right-wing party. Kitschelt's (1995) influential political economy model of right-wing success argues that the new occupational structure of post-industrial society has pushed traditional left/right parties towards an undifferentiated centre and has left an ideological void that 'extremists' fill. He assumes that the right is a proponent of free-market capitalism – an assumption that, as Ivarsflaten (2005) has pointed out, does not fit the French case.[3]

Labour-market theories assume economic rationality; *ressentiment* theories assume emotional rationality – i.e., a fear of immigrants leads to support for the right (Betz 1993). *Ressentiment* posits that losers in the competition over scarce social goods and material resources respond in frustration with diffuse emotions of anger, fear and, in the extreme case, hatred. While *labour-market* theories are structural and *ressentiment* theories are psychological and emotional, they share the assumption that an observed correlation between unemployment and immigration is causal with respect to right-wing ascendance.

The relation between xenophobia and immigration policy has dominated *labour-market* and *ressentiment* approaches to the European right (for example, Schain 1996). The riots in the *banlieues* of Paris in autumn 2005 and 2007 demonstrated that increased numbers of unemployed and disenfranchised second- and third-generation immigrants are genuinely problematic (Mucchielli 2009). Xenophobia is a contingent but not a necessary response to the social problems that immigrants pose. *Labour-market* theories establish a correlation between the presence of the right and unemployment. They fail to account for why a hypernationalist movement should be the outcome of the fear of unemployment. Widespread unemployment could as easily trigger a reinvigorated European left as an emergent European right.

Cultural approaches draw inspiration from Inglehardt's (1977) concept of 'post-materialist values' and from new social movements theory. These theories describe the right as comprised of protest parties and movements with anti-system goals that are not easily identified as left or right (for example, Kriesi 1999). Cultural theories sometimes echo mass society theory from the 1940s, since they focus on persons who, because of the dislocation of advanced capitalism, have become anomic and now feel an attraction to political parties and movements that offer certainty.

Organization and *agenda-setting* approaches, based on different forms of means/end rationality, are formal theories that fail to capture the content of politics as they are equally applicable to left, right or centre parties. *Labour-market* and *ressentiment* approaches identify correlations among social phenomena but fall short of explaining the social mechanisms behind those correlations. Post-materialism describes the instability of political preferences but does not account for left/right variation or answer well for extreme nationalism.

3 Legacies that matter: situating the right in the new Europe

Legacy theories that suggest that the past will repeat itself are empirically weak, as contemporary right-wing parties and movements do not map neatly onto interwar right-wing parties and movements.[4] Yet legacies do have analytical power if properly deployed. A robust account of the *normalization of the right* requires a historical approach – meaning an account that situates the right in broad patterns of social, economic and political change. The legacy that matters is not the legacy of whether a country had a fascist party or regime in the past but the legacy of the particular national iteration of the relation between people and polity. The institutional matrix that embeds a people in a national polity includes the legal system, the structure of the welfare state, citizenship prerequisites, education, the labour market and even the location of religion. Institutional configurations vary from nation-state to nation-state across the European continent, but they share an important similarity: European nation-states in the postwar period were secure states, in that the relation between people and polity, although different across Europe, was stable within national states (Eichengreen 2007).

The social science literature on the contemporary European right is party-centric and assumes deep party commitment. Analysts focus on variables, defined either as actor preferences or as structural factors, and pay less attention to national and international context. For this reason, the social science literature illuminates only partially the transient commitments that drove the right in the 1990s and does not account well for the current *normalization of the right*.

Illiberal Politics in Neoliberal Times (Berezin 2009) located the emergence of right-wing populism in the accelerated process of Europeanization that included political, economic and cultural integration and failed to account for the conflict between culture and institutional realignment. Market liberalism – the Archimedean principle of the new European project – challenged the social safety nets that had been firmly put in place during the postwar period. This social and political fact is behind the cultural strife and broad-based national yearnings that are emerging across contemporary Europe. If right-wing populism was simply a response to economic liberalization in various national states, then Europeanization should have provided an opening to the left. The opposite has occurred: the traditional European left has weakened in the years since 1992.[5]

Theories that overlook the historical legacy of postwar trans-European security miss the relation between Europeanization and the right of the 1990s. If analysts fail to grasp this prior relation, the current normalization of the right appears puzzling. Yet the normalization process is an extension of what preceded it in the period between 1990 and the current financial crisis.

Right-wing populism, its more respectable cousin national affirmation, and European integration gained momentum during the 1990s – a temporal coincidence that matters. The accelerated pace of European integration disequilibrated the existing mix of national cultures and legal norms that governed nation-states. An unintended consequence of disequilibration was a weakening of national social contracts, which threatened to make the national space unfamiliar to many of its citizens. Unfamiliarity has practical consequences: it produces insecurity in feeling and in fact. Right-wing populist parties and movements – a label of classificatory convenience rather than strict analytic precision, as these parties and movements have as many differences as commonalities – thrived in the European climate of insecurity. Until the European financial crisis began, the right had been singularly effective in foregrounding fear in the political discourse.

4 France and the National Front: a paradigmatic case of the normalization of the right

4.1 Winning the battle of ideas

The political trajectory of the French National Front provides insight into the current ethnocentric turn in European politics and political rhetoric. In the years between 1997 and 2007, the period during which the National Front appeared to be a political threat, its political positions and those of its leader, Jean-Marie Le Pen, often intersected with public opinion and mainstream policy. Events of that period provide context for the current French attitudes towards Islam, national identity and globalization. They also suggest a model of how social scientists might view other national iterations of similar processes.

In the early 1980s, when the French media establishment was vociferously criticizing Le Pen for his anti-immigration positions, the French state was quietly designing laws that restricted immigration. The right publicized the issue of immigration, but the immigration policy practices in France, and in European states more generally, did not map onto whether a government was left or right. In June 1993, the French state revised the French Code of Nationality to rescind automatic citizenship for the French-born children of immigrants and to require new citizens to assimilate to French culture (Weil 2002). In March 1998, Jean-Marie Le Pen's National Front shocked the French public and political establishment when it gained 15 per cent of the votes in the French regional elections (Perrineau and Reynié 1999).

A year later, the National Front split in two and analysts predicted the end of the party. The downward trajectory applied only to the National Front's electoral possibilities – not to its ideas, which were gaining wide acceptance. The National Front's issues were becoming increasingly French issues even though the party appeared to be in decline.

Europeanization as an iteration of the globalization that Le Pen had once labelled the 'new slavery of today' became a particularly salient French issue during this period.

The first round of the 2002 French presidential elections temporarily revived Le Pen, who came in second place, with 16.86 per cent of the vote. His presence on the ballot shocked the nation and returned Jacques Chirac, the sitting president, to office, with 82 per cent of the vote. Just about everyone who took note of such things in France – the media, the political science community and the candidates themselves – failed to observe in 2002 that Le Pen's ideas, if not his person, had been gaining strength, particularly his attacks on Europeanization and globalization and his defence of social solidarity and increased public security. The events of 21 April 2002 showed that his ideas and problems were French issues, not National Front issues – because ordinary citizens, and not only cadres of party militants, voted for him in the first round of the presidential election.

The French fears and anxieties around the issues of Europeanization and globalization that Le Pen had articulated reached their climactic moment on 29 May 2005, when French citizens rejected the European constitution. Between the 2002 and 2007 presidential elections in France, Le Pen's ideas on crime, immigration and national identity, as well as Europe, became a normal component of French public discussion. In 2003, the then minister of the interior, Nicolas Sarkozy, pushed a domestic security law through the National Assembly that vastly increased the powers of the French police. Sarkozy would reinforce this tough image during the 2005 riots in the poor suburbs on the outskirts of Paris, when he called the rioters 'thugs' and threatened to 'clean the neighbourhoods with a Kärcher' (a high-speed German water hose). Later in 2003, the Stasi Commission published a report recommending that the wearing of religious symbols be banned in public, which for all practical purposes meant the Islamic headscarf.

Sarkozy continued to capitalize on Le Pen's narrative in his 2007 presidential campaign. On 22 April, Le Pen received only 11 per cent of the vote in the first round of the presidential election. This was the lowest percentage he had received since he first ran for president in 1974. Once again, Le Pen and the National Front's political efficacy seemed to have evaporated. But Le Pen's issues (globalization, Europe, and the need to develop viable policies that integrate second- and sometimes third-generation immigrants into French society) did not disappear. As he proclaimed on the evening of his defeat, 'We have won the battle of ideas: nation and patriotism, immigration and insecurity were put at the heart of the campaign of my adversaries.' In the French case, the ramifications of European integration moved the right's issues into the mainstream of French politics and diminished the political capacity of the extreme right.

4.2 Looking towards 2012: a post-crisis presidential election

In June 2007, as the newly elected president of France, Sarkozy went to Brussels to renegotiate the European constitution that his party had supported in 2005. Upon his return to France, he proclaimed that he had succeeded in eliminating a clause in the new treaty that supported 'free and undistorted competition' and that this signalled 'the end of competition as an ideology and dogma' (*The Economist* 2007: 59). Sarkozy's comments, uttered from a place of political expediency rather than conviction, reflected the ambivalence towards Europe and globalization that characterizes all segments of French society.

In anticipation of his presidency of the EU in the second half of 2008, Sarkozy commissioned Laurent Cohen-Tanugi, a lawyer specializing in international mergers and acquisitions, to draw up a plan that would 'convey our vision of a Europe that is capable of combining economic growth, innovation and a high level of social protection and employment' (Cohen-Tanugi 2008: 205). Cohen-Tanugi's *Euromonde 2015: une stratégie européene pour la mondialisation* (published in English in 2008 as *Beyond Lisbon: A European Strategy for Globalisation*) included a survey on 'Perceptions of globalisation and France's relative specificity'. Respondents were asked whether they viewed globalization as a 'good opportunity' or as a 'threat to employment and companies in (OUR COUNTRY) [*sic*]'. Sixty-four per cent of the French respondents viewed globalization as a threat – the highest percentage among all of the national respondents sampled. French attitudes have shifted little since then. In a recent survey (Fondapol 2011) on European sentiment among the French (*Le sentiment européen chez les Français*), 52 per cent of respondents viewed 'globalization as a menace'. In the same poll, 62 per cent of respondents associated 'unemployment' with Europe, as opposed to 40 per cent who associated 'prosperity' with Europe.

The 2007 presidential election was the high point of Sarkozy's popularity in France. Support for his presidency among French citizens began a downward slide less than four months after he took office and did not rise above 41 per cent after 2008. In response to his growing unpopularity, he initiated a conversation on French national identity. In a joint address to Parliament and Congress, Sarkozy (2009) began with the financial crisis and government response to it, but then quickly moved on to France's favourite *bête noire*: globalization. He was soon peppering the speech with phrases such as 'our common values' and 'our common heritage', and eventually arrived at the importance of upholding *laïcité*

– the French version of the separation of church and state. The national identity debate had no appreciable effect on Sarkozy's approval ratings and unleashed a barrage of criticism from the left.[6] Critics from the left and within his own party accused him of fanning the flames of cultural conflict and of providing an opportunity for the National Front to re-emerge as a force in French politics.[7]

In preparation for the spring 2010 regional elections, the National Front launched a 'No to Islamification!' campaign that echoed the government discussion. The Socialist Party was the big winner in the regional elections, but the National Front did better than expected. In the second round, the Socialist Party came in first, with 49 per cent of the vote, and Sarkozy's Union for a Popular Movement party (Union pour un Movement Populaire, or UMP) came in second, with 33 per cent of the vote. The National Front came in third, with 9 per cent of the vote. The Socialist Party's position was somewhat weaker than its numbers suggested because its voting share came not only from socialists but also from members of Europe Écologie, a coalition of Greens and environmentalists. The National Front's position was somewhat stronger than its numbers suggested.

National identity was not the foremost preoccupation among the French in 2010. According to a TNS Sofres (2011b) poll (see table 10.1) that mapped the concerns of the French in 2010, 74 per cent of the respondents listed 'unemployment' as their principal worry. The figure remains constant even when the data is disaggregated for gender and age. The second concern was 'retirement', and the third was 'health'. Gender and age did affect what came in second and third place, with women placing health ahead of retirement and men placing 'buying power'. From age eighteen to thirty-four, 'buying power', 'school' and the 'environment' figured in the list. Among those aged thirty-five and older, 'health' and 'retirement' remained in second or third place, depending

Table 10.1: Preoccupations of the French in rank order for 2010

	All	Gender		Age				
		Men	Women	18–24	25–34	35–49	50–64	>65
Unemployment	1	1	1	1	1	1	1	1
Retirement	2	2	3	–	–	3	2	2
Health	3	–	2	–	–	2	3	3
Buying power	–	3	–	–	2	–	–	–
Environment	–	–	–	2	–	–	–	–
School	–	–	–	3	3	–	–	–

Source: TNS Sofres (2011b).

on birth cohort. In July 2011, the Ministry of Labour announced that unemployment in France had reached a high of 9.5 per cent (S. Laurent 2011). Both the Socialist Party and the National Front immediately and publicly blamed Sarkozy's failed policies for the rise in unemployment.

The unemployment statistics suggest that Sarkozy miscalculated the current priorities of the French (TNS Sofres 2011c). In addition to the unemployment rate, Sarkozy's role in negotiating the European sovereign debt crisis combined with his long-standing association with European Union politics and globalization contributed to his weakening political position. In the five years between the 2002 and 2007 presidential elections, events occurred in France, Europe and the world to move the National Front's positions closer to mainstream public opinion and official politics than they had been in the past. While this benefited Sarkozy in 2007, it worked against him in the 2012 French presidential election.

4.3 Marine Le Pen: seizing the economic moment

In January 2011, the French National Front elected Marine Le Pen to replace her father, Jean-Marie Le Pen, as head of the party. A lawyer who has held several local elected offices, Marine Le Pen is articulate and a frequent commentator on French national television. In December 2010, she set off a fury in the French and international media when she claimed that Muslims who knelt to say their daily prayers on the street in certain neighbourhoods of Paris evoked a 'state of occupation'. The word 'occupation' used in the political sphere always suggests the German occupation of France during the Second World War. The press and public officials widely accused Marine Le Pen of equating French Muslims to Nazis. Accusations aside, Marine Le Pen's goal is to make the National Front sufficiently respectable so as to attain national, rather than simply local, offices. She made this objective clear in her inaugural speech on 16 January 2011 (my translation): 'Dear friends, this is the moment that will date the irresistible rise to power of our movement. From this Congress [forward] will begin an unprecedented effort to transform the National Front.'

Marine Le Pen's inaugural speech focused squarely on economic issues. She argued that 'the Europe of Brussels ... bypasses or goes against the will of the people' and was unleashing the 'destructive principles of ultraliberalism and free exchange' that made France's miserable economic growth, the worst in twenty years, seem less extreme given current economic realities. Instead of more Europe, Le Pen advocated 'economic patriotism and social patrimony'. She posed a 'grand alternative' for 2012, rather than the 'monitoring and patching of a system that is collapsing before our eyes': 'For the French, the choice in 2012 will be simple, clear and even binary: the choice will be globalization that is deregulation, alignment with the lowest social bidder, demographic submersion, the dilution of the values of our civilization . . . [or] the choice will be the nation.'

Current European financial realities lend cogency to Marine Le Pen's economic ideas. Even politicians on the left acknowledge that 'economic protectionism' is popular among the French and that the euro is not (Schwartz 2011). On 10 March 2011, Angela Merkel and Nicolas Sarkozy outlined a 'Euro pact' (quickly retitled from its original designation, the 'competitiveness pact') that was one of their proposed long-term solutions to the European debt crisis. Marine Le Pen responded to their proposal immediately on her website. She advocated replacing the Euro pact with the 'People's Pact' and argued that her proposal had two 'simple objectives': first, that 'the people and social politics should not be sacrificed on the altar of the euro'; and, second, that the economy would be relaunched with an effective monetary policy – which for Le Pen meant leaving the EMU. The Euro pact that Merkel and Sarkozy had proposed in February advocated the abolition of wage indexation and the adjustment of the pension system to account for changing demographics. In another political world, it would be the classic left, and not the classic right, that would be arguing against this pact.

As of yet, no analyst or politician, and perhaps not even Marine Le Pen herself, believes that France can exit the eurozone and revert to the franc, but the political resonance of her arguments is apparent. In April 2011, the National Front posted its 'economic project' on its website (Front National 2011). The core proposal of this project is 'free money' in the face of the 'failure of the euro'. The document begins by invoking Martin Feldstein, an economics professor at Harvard who as early as 1999 described the euro as a 'risk'. The National Front ascribes many economic ills to the euro, from unemployment to national debt to declining purchasing power. It argues that Sarkozy's decision to save the euro 'at all costs' is ideological and represents nothing more than 'social rampage'. In contrast, the National Front's position on the euro is 'pragmatic' and requires a 'gradual exit' from the EMU.

On 21 July 2011, Sarkozy went to Brussels for a European summit and entered into a pact to save the euro. This meant a second bailout for Greece. Upon his return, he wrote a public letter to members of the French Parliament to explain his decision (Sarkozy 2011). The letter reminded French deputies and citizens that the European Union was born out of the wars and disasters of 'old Europe' and that France, as a founding member of Europe, should view Europe as one of its children. Sarkozy argued that he was certain that the Europe that would emerge from the financial crisis would carry on 'the dream of those who, after surviving the totalitarian nightmare of the last century, wanted to leave us [the French] a heritage of peace and prosperity'. Sarkozy called the prospect of a Greek bailout 'our common responsibility in the face of History [capitalization in original]'. Marine Le Pen denounced Sarkozy's letter immediately on the National Front website.

The current National Front party slogan is 'With Marine, it is the moment!' Sarkozy's personal unpopularity, his association with the European bailouts and his neoliberalism, coupled with the vagueness of the French left, provided Marine Le Pen and the National Front with a political opening. But this is an excessively parsimonious explanation of a broader and deeper political and social phenomenon. The fault lines that make Marine Le Pen a viable political candidate were present in 2005, when French citizens voted against the European constitutional referendum (Berezin 2006). The significance of the 2005 referendum was not lost on Le Pen, who commemorated its fifth anniversary on her website in a post entitled 'The spirit of 29 May'. Sarkozy and his UMP party were not celebrating, nor was any other French political party. Commemoration was a savvy political move on Le Pen's part. In May 2010, the bailout of Greece was foremost in the French mind: at that moment, the 2005 vote against the European constitution could hardly have seemed like a bad idea.

4.4 Financial crisis and austerity across the French political spectrum

In 1985 the Socialist prime minister Laurent Fabius made the frequently cited remark 'M. [Jean-Marie] Le Pen raises real problems, but gives bad answers'. The polling firm TNS Sofres regularly tests public opinion on the National Front. A poll in 2011 (TNS Sofres 2011a) revealed several trends that are favourable to the National Front, suggesting that the valence between the 'real problems' and 'bad answers' was shifting. Between January 2010 and 2011, there was an upward trend in popular agreement with several classic positions of the right, including the defence of traditional values, the presence of too many immigrants in France, the fact that Islam was being granted too many rights in France, and that the police did not have enough power.

When respondents were asked if they agreed with the National Front's social criticisms but not the solutions that they proposed, 32 per cent of the sample agreed, while 55 per cent supported neither the NF's criticisms nor its solutions (TNS Sofres 2011a; table 10.2). The more disturbing figure emerges when the polling sample is disaggregated. Among 'right sympathizers' the agreement rate was 45 per cent, and this figure jumped to 48 per cent among members of Sarkozy's party, the UMP. Public perception of Marine Le Pen follows a similar trajectory (TNS Sofres 2011a;

Table 10.2: Attitudes towards the French National Front (percentages)

Question: Regarding the National Front, do you agree with:

	All	*Right*	*UMP*	*FN*
1) **neither** their social criticism **nor** their solutions	55	34	45	16
2) their social criticism **and** their solutions	7	16	6	58
3) their social criticism **but not** their solutions	32	45	48	32

Source: TNS Sofres (2011a).

Table 10.3: Attitudes towards the French National Front leader (percentages)

Question: How do you perceive Marine Le Pen today?

	All	Left	Right	UMP	FN
1) as an extreme-right xenophobe and nationalist	46	61	32	39	3
2) as a patriot of the right attached to traditional values	37	28	56	46	94
3) no opinion	17	11	12	15	3

Source: TNS Sofres (2011a).

table 10.3): when asked whether she is a 'patriot of the right attached to traditional values' or an 'extremist nationalist xenophobe', 37 per cent of the entire sample chose the 'patriot' option. When the sample is disaggregated, the figures changed in ways that favoured Le Pen: 56 per cent of the right and 46 per cent of the UMP saw her as a 'patriot'.

Even a cursory perusal of the National Front's website reveals that the majority of their recent political tracts and posters emphasize economic issues. A sampling of poster and brochure titles demonstrate this point: 'France in permanent insecurity!'; 'With Sarkozy, it is a new tax every month!'; 'Euro: the winning countries are those that leave'. A flyer entitled 'Financial crisis: the French victims of globalization!' attributes increased unemployment, precarious employment, housing shortages, increased national debt and the tightening of credit to Sarkozy's failure to abandon the 'ideological straightjacket' of globalization. The 2012 presidential election was the first major French election since the financial crisis and the sovereign debt crisis. During the campaign and the months leading up to it, Marine Le Pen seized the economic moment. The National Front shifted the focus of its public discourse from cultural issues to economic issues just as national leaders were discussing multiculturalism while negotiating trans-European austerity measures.

During the first day of the October 2010 strikes to protest the raising of the retirement age, the French Socialist Party organized a grand march through the centre of Paris. The official party organizers gave out stickers with sayings such as 'Retirement is life, not survival' and '60 years is freedom'. Plastered through the streets of central Paris were posters designed and distributed by a group calling itself the New Anticapitalist Party. The poster displayed a picture of Sarkozy and François Hollande, the Socialist Party candidate for president, on a €500 note. Referring to the politicians and the banknote, the poster proclaimed in bold letters 'GET OUT! [Dehors!]: Because they are worth nothing'. While many political analysts speak of an electoral alliance among parties of the right, Marine Le Pen's future may include co-opting fringe parties of the left. The National Front has always been popular among the French working classes (Viard 1997). Marine Le Pen is increasingly the preferred presidential candidate among French workers who feel abandoned by the Socialists and the centre-right (Piquard 2011), though it is unlikely that she would actually win a presidential election. In the months before the election in spring 2012, analysts began to talk about a repeat of 2002, when her father, Jean-Marie Le Pen, was runner up to Jacques Chirac in the first round (Fressoz and Wider 2011). On 22 April 2012, Marine Le Pen won by losing: she came in third place behind Sarkozy, with 17.9 per cent of the first-round vote, receiving a higher percentage of votes than her father did in 2002. The future is before her.

5 Timing matters: France in the European context

Animus towards Europe became a National Front issue in the late 1990s. The vote to reject the European constitution in 2005 made it apparent that antipathy towards Europe at worst, or ambivalence at best, was widespread among the French. The European sovereign debt crisis confirmed that anti-Europe sentiment was more widespread than public opinion polls suggested (Berezin 2011). When national leaders asked European citizens to support bailouts of financially troubled euro-zone members, collective popular resistance emerged. Euro enthusiasm was restricted to the governing elite – and even the elite are far from united in this project. The first stage of the European crisis occurred in March 2009, when Hungary seemed on the verge of financial collapse. Politicians discussed the resistance to bailing out Hungary as an issue of national 'protectionism'. The more severe and ongoing debt crisis began in May 2010, when Spain, Ireland and Portugal followed in Greece's footsteps. Angela Merkel baulked at bailing out less solvent EMU members, and the German public supported her decision. PIGS was the unfortunate acronym used to describe Portugal, Italy, Greece and Spain – all of which were getting dangerously close to state bankruptcy.

The European sovereign debt crisis fanned the flames of cultural conflict, legitimizing nationalism by making it appear to be a rational response to potential economic disaster. The European Parliament election in spring 2009 was an important harbinger of political direction. The centre-right dominated, the left did extremely poorly and far-right politicians won seats.

The extreme right is not the only political faction now questioning a commitment to a neoliberal Europe and urging a retreat into the nation. Between July 2009 and April 2011, there were fourteen parliamentary elections and one presidential election in EMU member states.[8] There were identifiable trends in the results across Europe. First, voters tended to desert parties that had previously led in voting. For example, in Ireland, the Fine Gael party overturned the dominance of Fianna Fáil, a long-standing conservative party. The left performed better in countries such as Greece and Portugal, which had required bailouts and austerity measures and had been sites of mass protest. The trends present in these elections suggest that France is not alone in its retreat into national identity and in the presence of a revitalized right. The two most salient features of European elections since the spring of 2009 have been a tendency to overthrow parties that had been in power for some time, and a gain in electoral spoils for the nationalist right.

On 9 June 2010, Geert Wilder's Party of Freedom came in third place in the Dutch parliamentary elections. Much of Wilder's agenda focuses upon free-market liberalism – as long as it remains Dutch and not European. Wilders and his party were, until September 2012, minority partners in the Dutch coalition government. Four days after the Dutch election, a Flemish nationalist party that wanted to secede from French-speaking Belgium captured the largest share of the votes in a parliamentary election there. On 19 September 2010, the Swedish right-wing populist party the Sweden Democrats received 5.7 per cent of the vote, which made the party eligible for a seat in Congress. The party's leader, 31-year-old Jimmie Åkesson, is now a member of the Sweden Parliament. The Sweden Democrats decorated their campaign mailings with blue and yellow flowers – the colours of the Swedish flag. 'Safety and tradition' was their motto. 'Give us Sweden back!' was their *cri de coeur*.

The Finnish election of April 2011 is perhaps the most startling: here a nationalist right-wing party replaced an entrenched socialist party.[9] The populist party True Finns received 19 per cent of the vote in the parliamentary election. This percentage provides a sharp contrast to the 4.1 per cent that they received in the 2007 election. In 2011, the True

Finns received the same percentage of votes as the Social Democrats (19 per cent) and 1 percentage point less than the Liberal Conservatives (20 per cent). Writing in the *Wall Street Journal*, Timo Soini (2011), head of the True Finns, explained why he did not support bailing out Europe:

> At the risk of being accused of populism, we'll begin with the obvious: it is not the little guy who benefits. He is being milked and lied to in order to keep the insolvent system running . . . . I was raised to know that genocidal war must never again be visited on our continent and I came to understand the values and principles that originally motivated the establishment of what became the European Union. This Europe, this vision, was one that offered the people of Finland and all of Europe the gift of peace founded on democracy, freedom and justice. This is a Europe worth having, so it is with great distress that I see this project being put in jeopardy by a political elite who would sacrifice the interests of Europe's ordinary people in order to protect certain corporate interests.

6 The political power of exogenous events: scarcity and insecurity

Since the Maastricht Treaty became operational in 1992, two visions of Europe have dominated social science analysis, European policy initiatives and public discussion. The first vision is primarily institutional: that Europe and its expansion encompassing ever more countries is a technical solution to competition from global markets.[10] In practice, this vision captures the neoliberal dimension of the European project. The second vision is primarily cultural: it focuses upon the creation of a European identity.[11] Public opinion polls such as the Eurobarometer continually attempt to measure European identity. Much empirical research has suggested that ordinary Europeans tend to think in national rather than European terms (for example, Díez-Medrano 2003; Favell 2008; Fligstein 2008).

The European sovereign debt crisis and the European public's response to it challenge both visions of Europe. If the European project was perceived simply as an improved set of institutional arrangements, then the bailouts of member nations would not be problematic. If the citizens of EU member states identified themselves as European, then one would expect a willingness to bail out fellow Europeans in financial difficulty. But exactly the opposite has occurred. Even in nation-states such as Finland, which formally agreed to the bailouts, the nationalist opposition is strong. National attachment and sentiment has never been absent from European public opinion, but analysts and policy-makers have chosen not to emphasize it or have argued that it was not consequential. Nationalist sentiment was behind the widespread resistance to a European constitution. In contrast to national elections, voter turnout for European Parliament elections is historically low and declines at every election period.

The European Union, as conceived in the early 1990s, was a project of plenty – more nations, more people, more money, more regulations – not a project of scarcity. This current global crisis, especially in European iterations, is a crisis of scarcity and contraction. The potential consequences of scarcity are multiple, but they highlight one of the central contradictions in the European project as it expanded in the last twenty years – a contradiction for which theories and practices of Europeanization, globalization, post-nationalism and 'new world order' ideas have failed to account.

The European right was the first to label immigrants, market liberalism and Europeanization as security threats. In the presence of plenty, the right seemed recidivist at best and racist at worse. But exogenous security shocks made it possible for even mainstream politicians to resort to language and policies that previously had been the exclusive domain of the right. The combined shocks of the 2008–9 financial crisis and the 2010 sovereign debt crisis made it easier to argue that some nations were less virtuous than others and undeserving of financial aid. It also made it possible for the right plausibly to argue, as Marine Le Pen does in France and Timo Soini does in Finland, that Europe as a concept *and* the European Union as an institution are dangerous.

The European sovereign debt crisis expedited the *normalization of the right* that had begun to gain ground in the late 1990s. It pushed mainstream politicians to the centre right, as opposed to being comfortably in the centre. Politicians, to borrow from Mair (chapter 6 in this volume), were 'responsive' rather than 'responsible'. It is difficult to imagine that the EU as a political institution will disappear. Yet its future trajectory, particularly monetary union, is uncertain. Instead of the optimistic dream of a multicultural, united Europe, we can expect nostalgia politics and cultural conflict coupled improbably with enthusiasm for the free market. If the familiar sources of social, economic and cultural security not only seem tenuous but actually become so, fear and pessimism will become dominant political emotions. A collective sense of insecurity weakens the social largesse and empathy that lie at the core of democratic sentiment and normalizes ideas that many Europeans previously viewed as unacceptable and right-wing. How this will play out politically remains to be seen.

References

Art, D. (2006) *The Politics of the Nazi Past in Germany and Austria*. Cambridge: Cambridge University Press.

Arter, D. (2010) The breakthrough of another West European populist radical right party? The case of the True Finns, *Government and Opposition* 45(4): 484–504.

Arter, D. (2011) Taking the gilt off the conservatives' gingerbread: the April 2011 Finnish general election, *West European Politics* 34(6): 1284–95.

Ash, T. G. (2009) Europe's gone missing, *Los Angeles Times*, 26 March; available at: http://articles.latimes.com/2009/mar/26/opinion/oe-gartonash26 (accessed 29 March 2009).

Berezin, M. (2006) Appropriating the 'no': the French National Front, the vote on the constitution, and the 'new' April 21. *PS: Political Science and Politics* 39(2): 269–72.

Berezin, M. (2009) *Illiberal Politics in Neoliberal Times: Culture, Security, and Populism in the New Europe*. Cambridge: Cambridge University Press.

Berezin, M. (2011) Europe was yesterday, *Harvard International Review*, 7 January; available at: http://hir.harvard.edu/europe-was-yesterday?page=0 per cent2C2 (accessed 29 February 2012).

Betz, H.-G. (1993) The new politics of ressentiment: radical right-wing populist parties in Western Europe, *Comparative Politics* 25(4): 413–26.

Bowyer, B. T., and Vail, M. I. (2011) Economic insecurity, the social market economy and support for the German left, *West European Politics* 34(4): 683–705.

Capoccia, G. (2005) *Defending Democracy: Reactions to Extremism in Interwar Europe*. Baltimore: John Hopkins University Press.

Checkel, J. T., and Katzenstein, P. J. (eds) (2009) *European Identity*. New York: Cambridge University Press.

Cohen-Tanugi, L. (2008) *Beyond Lisbon: A European Strategy for Globalisation*. Brussels: Peter Lang.

Cronin, J., Ross, G., and Shoch, J. (eds) (2011) *What's Left of the Left: Democrats and Social Democrats in Challenging Times*. Durham, NC: Duke University Press.

Díez-Medrano, J. (2003) *Framing Europe: Attitudes to European Integration in Germany, Spain, and the United Kingdom*. Princeton, NJ: Princeton University Press.

Eatwell, R. (2003) Ten theories of the extreme right, in P. H. Merkl and L. Weinberg (eds), *Right Wing Extremism in the Twenty-First Century*. London: Frank Cass, pp. 47–73.

The Economist (2007) The Sarko show, *The Economist*, 30 June.

Eichengreen, B. J. (2007) *The European Economy since 1945: Coordinated Capitalism and Beyond*. Princeton, NJ: Princeton University Press.

Erlanger, S. (2009) Europe's socialists suffering even in downturn, *New York Times*, 29 September; available at: www.nytimes.com/2009/09/29/world/europe/29socialism.html (accessed 29 September 2009).

Favell, A. (2008) *Eurostars and Eurocities: Free Movement and Mobility in an Integrating Europe*. Oxford: Blackwell.

Fligstein, N. (2008) *Euroclash: The EU, European Identity, and the Future of Europe*. New York: Oxford University Press.

Fondapol (Fondation pour L'innnovation Politique) (2011) *Le sentiment européen chez les Français*. Paris: TNS Sofres.

Fressoz, F., and Wider, T. (2011) Pour la présidentielle, 'un scénario de type 2002 ne peut être exclu'. *Le Monde*, 2 November.

Front National (2011) Projet économique du Front National: les grandes orientations, available at : www.frontnational.com/pdf/projet-eco-fn-orientations.pdf (accessed April 2011).

Givens, T. E. (2005) *Voting Radical Right in Western Europe*. New York: Cambridge University Press.

Holmes, D. R. (2000) *Integral Europe: Fast-Capitalism, Multiculturalism, Neofascism*. Princeton, NJ: Princeton University Press.

Inglehart, R. (1977) *The Silent Revolution: Changing Values and Political Styles among Western Publics*. Princeton, NJ: Princeton University Press.

Ivarsflaten, E. (2005) The vulnerable populist right parties: no economic realignment fuelling their electoral success, *European Journal of Political Research* 44: 465–92.

Kitschelt, H. (1995) *The Radical Right in Western Europe: A Comparative Analysis*. Ann Arbor: University of Michigan Press.

Kriesi, H. (1999) Movements of the left, movements of the right: putting the mobilization of two new types of social movements into political context, in H. Kitschelt, P. Lange, G. Marks and J. D. Stephens (eds), *Continuity and Change in Contemporary Capitalism*. Cambridge: Cambridge University Press, pp. 398–423.

Krugman, P. (2009) A continent adrift, *New York Times*, 16 March; available at: www.nytimes.com/2009/03/16/opinion/16krugman.html (accessed 18 April 2011).

Laurent, É. (2009) Eurozone: the high cost of complacency, *Economists' Voice* 6(1): 1–4.

Laurent, S. (2011) Chômage: cinq ans d'annonces, cinq ans d'insuccès, *Le Monde*, 28 July.

Mead, W. R. (2011) Europe's less than perfect union, *Wall Street Journal*, 9 August; available at: http://online.wsj.com/article/SB10001424053111903454 50457648856380933 1544.html (accessed 2 November 2011).

Meguid, B. M. (2008) *Party Competition between Unequals: Strategies and Electoral Fortunes in Western Europe*. New York: Cambridge University Press.

Moravcsik, A. (2005) Europe works well without the grand illusions, *Financial Times*, 14 June; available at: www.ft.com/cms/s/0/12e2b18a-dc71-11d9-819f-00000e2511c8.html#axzz2454nn8jr (accessed 29 February 2012).

Moravcsik, A. (2006) What can we learn from the collapse of the European constitutional project?, *Politische Vierteljahresschrift* 47(2): 219–41.

Mucchielli, L. (2009) Autumn 2005: a review of the most important riot in the history of French contemporary society, *Journal of Ethnic and Migration Studies* 35(5): 731–51.

Mudde, C. (2007) *Populist Radical Right Parties in Europe*. Cambridge: Cambridge University Press.

Mudge, S. L. (2011) What's left of leftism? Neoliberal politics in Western party systems, 1945–2004, *Social Science History* 35(3): 337–80.

Munchau, W. (2009) Eastern crisis that could wreck the Eurozone, *Financial Times*, 22 February; available at: www.ft.com/cms/s/0/06a45f2a-0118-11de-8f6e-000077b07658.html#axzz2454nn8jr (accessed 24 February 2009).

New York Times (2011) Room for debate: a Europe divided?, *New York Times*, 12 September; available at: www.nytimes.com/roomforde-bate/2011/09/12/will-culture-clash-splinter-the-european-union (accessed 28 February 2012).

Norris, P. (2005) *Radical Right: Voters and Parties in the Electoral Market*. New York: Cambridge University Press.

Nunes, E. (2011) Ce que Nicolas Sarkozy a fait du discourse de Grenoble, *Le Monde*, 7 July.

Perrineau, P., and Reynié, P. (eds) (1999) *Le Vote incertain: les élections région-ales de 1998*. Paris: Presses de Sciences Po.

Piquard, A. (2011) Marine Le Pen, candidate préférée des ouvriers, *Le Monde*, 4 April.

Rydgren, J. (2007) The sociology of the radical right, *Annual Review of Sociology* 33: 241–362.

Samuelson, R. (2011) The big danger is Europe, *Washington Post*, 9 August; availa-ble at: www.washingtonpost.com/opinions/the-big-danger-is-europe/2011/08/08/gIQABzq02I_story.html (accessed 10 August 2011).

Sarkozy, N. (2009) Déclaration de M. le président de la République devant le Parlement réuni en Congrès, *L'Année Politique 2009*. Paris: Editions Evenements et Tendances.

Sarkozy, N. (2011) La lettre de Sarkozy aux parlementaires, *Le Monde*, 26 July.

Schain, M. A. (1987) The National Front and the construction of political legiti-macy, *West European Politics* 10(2): 229–52.

Schain, M. A. (1996) The immigration debate and the National Front, in M. A. Schain and J. T. S. Keeler (eds), *Chirac's Challenge: Liberalization, Europeanization and Malaise in France*. New York: St Martin's Press, pp. 169–97.

Schmitter, P. C. (2000) *How to Democratize the European Union . . . and Why Bother?* New York: Rowman & Littlefield.

Schor, R. (1985) *L'Opinion française et les estrangers en France, 1919–1939*. Paris: Publications de la Sorbonne.

Schwartz, A. (2011) Le gauche française bute sur l'Europe, *Le Monde Diplomatique* 667: 1.

Sen, A. (2011) It isn't just the euro: Europe's democracy itself is at stake, *The Guardian*, 22 June; available at: www.guardian.co.uk/commentisfree/2011/jun/22/euro-europes-democracy-rating-agencies (accessed 15 July 2011).

Soini, T. (2011) Why I don't support Europe's bailouts, *Wall Street Journal*, 9 May; available at: http://online.wsj.com/article/SB10001424052748703864204576310851503980120.html (accessed 4 August 2011).

TNS Sofres (2011a) *Baromètre d'image du Front National*, January. Paris: Sofres.

TNS Sofres (2011b) *Baromètre des préoccupations des Français-bilan 2010*, February. Paris: Sofres.

TNS Sofres (2011c) *Les Français et l'urgence économique et sociale*, September. Paris: Sofres.

Viard, J. (1997) *Pourquoi des travailleurs votent FN et comment les reconquérir*. Paris: Seuil.

Weil, P. (2002) *Qu'est-ce qu'un Français? Histoire de la nationalité française depuis la Révolution*. Paris: Grasset.

11

The Crisis in Context: Democratic Capitalism and its Contradictions[1]

Wolfgang Streeck

What can a social scientist contribute to our understanding of that world-shaking event, the collapse of the American financial system, that occurred in 2008 and has since turned into an economic and political crisis of global dimensions? Nobody expects us to offer practical advice on to how to repair the damage and prevent similar disasters in the future: what 'stress tests' to apply to banks; what capital reserves to require them to hold; or whether to create and how to design a bailout mechanism for bankrupt states belonging to a currency union. In one sense, of course, this is unfortunate, as there are obviously no consulting fees to collect here. On the other hand, however, regrettable as this may be, it may actually be an advantage, as it makes it unnecessary for sociologists or political scientists to believe, or to pretend to believe, that, in principle at least, there does exist a fix for the problem and that one needs only to find it.

Unlike the economic mainstream, sociology in particular, unless it has given in to fashionable pressures to convert to a 'rational choice' model of social order, or alternatively has failed to leave behind the Parsonian functionalism of the 1950s, is in no way compelled to conceive of society as governed by a general tendency towards equilibrium, where crises and change are no more than temporary deviations from what is for most of the time the steady state of a normally well-integrated social system. Rather than having to construe our present affliction as a singular disturbance to a fundamental condition of stability, a sociological – i.e., not an efficiency-theoretical – approach to political economy can afford to try out a historical perspective relating today's crisis to earlier, similar events and explore the possibility of their being systematically related, by both historical sequence and common causes. In fact this is what I will do in this chapter, in which I will suggest considering the Great Contraction (Reinhart and Rogoff 2009) and the subsequent near collapse of the modern tax state's public finances as a manifestation of an underlying basic tension in the political-economic configuration of advanced capitalist societies, a tension that makes disequilibrium and instability the rule rather than the exception, and that has found expression in a historical succession of different but cognate disturbances of the socio-economic order.

More specifically, I will argue that the present crisis can be fully understood only when considered as one more stage in an ongoing, inherently conflictual evolution and transformation of that very particular social formation that we call *democratic capitalism*. Democratic capitalism came to be more or less safely established only after the Second World War, and only in the Western part of the world. There it functioned extraordinarily well for the next two to three decades – so well in fact that this period, which was one of uninterrupted economic growth, still dominates our ideas and expectations of what modern capitalism (Shonfield 1965) is or should and could be. This is true in spite of the fact that, looked at with hindsight and in the light of the turbulences that followed, the quarter century immediately after the war should without difficulty be recognizable as truly exceptional. Indeed, I suggest that it is not the *trente glorieuses* (Judt 2005) but the series of crises that followed that is representative of the normal condition of democratic capitalism. That condition, I maintain, is ruled by an endemic and essentially irreconcilable conflict between capitalist markets and democratic politics that, having been temporarily suspended for the historically short period immediately following the war, forcefully reasserted itself when high economic growth came to an end in the 1970s. I will now in general terms discuss the nature of that conflict before I turn to the sequence of political-economic disturbances produced by it that preceded as well as shaped the present global crisis.

1

Suspicions that capitalism and democracy may not easily go together are far from new. Beginning in the nineteenth and continuing well into the twentieth century, the bourgeoisie and the political right were afraid that majority rule, being inevitably the rule of the poor over the rich, would ultimately do away with private property and free markets. The rising working class and the political left, for their part, were fearful of capitalists allying themselves with the forces of reaction to abolish democracy, in a search for protection from being governed by a permanent majority dedicated to the redistribution of economic advantage and social status. I will not discuss here the relative merits of the two positions, although I believe that, unfortunately, at least in the industrialized world, the left had more reason to fear the right overthrowing democracy in order to save capitalism than the right had to fear the left abolishing capitalism for the sake of democracy. However that may be, in the years immediately after the Second World War it was a widely shared assumption that, for capitalism to be compatible with democracy, it had to be subjected to extensive political control[2] so as to protect democracy from having to be restrained in the name of free markets. While Keynes and, to an extent, Kalecki and Polanyi carried the day, Hayek had to withdraw into temporary exile.

This was not to remain so, however. Today's political economy literature, to the extent that it comes out of mainstream economics, is obsessed with the figure of the opportunistic or myopic, in any event irresponsible, politician who caters to an economically uneducated electorate by fiddling with otherwise efficient markets, thereby preventing them from achieving equilibrium – all in pursuit of objectives, such as full employment and social justice, that truly free markets would in the long run deliver anyway but must fail to deliver when distorted by politics. Economic crises, according to standard economic theories of 'public choice' (Buchanan and Tullock 1962), stem essentially from political intervention, in particular from market-distorting intervention for 'social' objectives. While the right kind of intervention is one that sets markets free from political interference, market-distorting intervention derives from an excess of democracy or, more precisely, from democracy being carried over, by irresponsible politicians, into the economy where it has no business.

Today, not many go as far as the formidable Friedrich von Hayek, who in his later years advocated abolishing democracy as we know it in defence of economic freedom and civil liberty. Still, the *cantus firmus* of current neo-institutionalist economic theory sounds very Hayekian indeed. For capitalism to work, it requires a rule-bound economic policy; constitutionally enshrined protection of markets and property rights from discretionary political interference; independent regulatory authorities; central banks firmly protected from electoral pressures; and international institutions such as the European Commission or the European Court of Justice that do not have to worry about popular re-election. Ideal, of course, would be some sort of assurance that government will always be in the hands of the likes of a Thatcher or Reagan – leaders with the courage and the muscle to shield the economy from the immodest demands of short-sighted citizens for protection and redistribution. It is not by chance, however, that such theories studiously avoid the crucial question of how to get from here to there, very likely because they have no answer, or at least none that can be made public.

There are various ways to conceive of what is at the bottom of the friction between capitalism and democracy. For present purposes, I will characterize democratic capitalism as a political economy ruled by two conflicting principles, or regimes, of resource allocation: one operating according to marginal productivity, or what is revealed as *merit* by a 'free play of market forces', and the other following social need, or *entitlement*, as certified by the collective choices of democratic politics. Governments under democratic capitalism are under pressure to honour both principles simultaneously, although substantively the two almost never agree – and they can afford to neglect one in favour of the other only for a short time until they are punished by the consequences, political in the one case and economic in the other. Governments that fail to attend to democratic claims for protection and redistribution risk losing their majority, while governments that disregard the claims for compensation from the owners of productive resources, as expressed in the language of marginal productivity, cause economic dysfunctions and distortions that will be increasingly unsustainable and will thereby also undermine political support.

In the liberal utopia of standard economic theory, the tension in democratic capitalism between its two principles of allocation is overcome by the theory turning into what Marx had expected *his* theory to become: a material force (*materielle Gewalt*). Economics as a 'science' instructs citizens and politicians that markets are better for them than politics, and that *real* justice is *market* justice under which everybody is rewarded according to contribution rather than to needs redefined as rights. To the extent that *economic* theory became in this sense accepted as a *social* theory, it also *would come true* in the sense of becoming *performative* – which reveals its essentially rhetorical nature as an instrument of *social construction by persuasion*. In the real world, however, it is not all that easy to talk people out of their 'irrational' beliefs in social and political rights, as distinguished from the law of the market and the right of property. Up to now, at least, non-market notions of social justice have resisted all efforts at economic rationalization, forceful as these may have become, especially in the *bleierne Zeit* of advancing neoliberalism. Apparently people stubbornly refuse to give up on the idea of a moral economy (Thompson 1971; Scott 1976) under which they have rights as people or as citizens that take precedence over the outcomes of market exchanges.[3] In fact where they have a chance, as they inevitably do as long as there is democracy, they tend in one way or another to insist on the primacy of the social over the economic; on social commitments and obligations being protected from market pressures for 'flexibility'; and on society honouring human expectations of a life outside of the dictatorship of ever fluctuating 'market signals'.[4]

In the economic mainstream, that there should be a conflict in a market economy between rivalling principles of allocation can be explained only by a deplorable lack of economic education of citizens or by demagoguery on the part of irresponsible politicians. Economic disorders, such as inflation, public deficits and excessive private or public debt, result from insufficient knowledge of the economic laws that govern the functioning of the economy as a wealth-creation machine or from a frivolous disregard of such laws in selfish pursuit of political power. This is quite different in theories of *political economy*, to the extent that they take the political seriously.[5] Such theories recognize market allocation as one political-economic regime among others, one that is governed by the special interests of those owning scarce productive resources that put them in a strong position, while its alternative, political allocation is preferred by those with little economic but potentially high political power. From this perspective, standard economics is basically the theoretical exaltation of a political-economic social order that serves the interests of those well endowed with market power, in that it equates *their* interests with the *general* interest and represents the *distributional claims* of the owners of productive capital as *technical imperatives* of good, in the sense of scientifically sound, economic management. In fact, for political economy, if standard economists account for economic dysfunctions by a cleavage between *traditionalist* principles of *moral* economy and *rational-modern* principles of *economic* economy, this amounts to a tendentious misrepresentation of the nature of the problem, as it hides the fact that the economic economy is *also* a moral economy – namely, that of those commanding strong power in markets for indispensible productive resources.

In the language of mainstream economics, economic disturbances, as caused by market allocation being interfered with by politics, arise as punishment for governments failing to respect the natural laws that are the true governors of 'the economy'. By contrast, a theory of political economy worth its name accounts for crises as manifestations of what one could call the *Kaleckian reactions*[6] of the owners of productive resources to democratic politics penetrating into what they consider their exclusive domain, preventing them from exploiting their market power to the fullest and thereby violating their expectations of being justly rewarded for their astute risk-taking.[7] Unlike political economy, standard economic theory treats social structure and the distribution of interests and power vested in it as exogenous, holding them constant and thereby making them both invisible and, for the purposes of economic 'science', naturally given. The only politics such a theory can envisage are the inevitably counter-productive efforts by opportunistic or, at best, incompetent politicians to bend economic laws. Good economic policy is non-political by definition. This view is, of course, not shared by the many for whom politics is a much needed recourse against markets whose unfettered operation interferes with what they happen to feel is right. Unless they are somehow persuaded to adopt neoclassical economics as a self-evident model of what social life is and should be – unless, in other words, they are turned into practising life-world economizers – their political demands as democratically expressed will differ from the prescriptions of standard economic theory. The implication is that, while an *economy*, if sufficiently conceptually disembedded, may be modelled as tending towards equilibrium, a *political* economy may not, unless it is one devoid of democracy and run by a Platonic dictatorship of economist-kings.

As long as capitalist politics fails to lead democratic societies out of the desert of corrupt democratic opportunism into the promised land of self-regulating markets, governments must fear their societies being torn apart by conflicts over distributional claims the sum total of which considerably exceeds what is at any point in time available for distribution. Outside of the, as we now know, exceptional and short periods when strong economic growth makes it possible for all parties to improve their positions simultaneously, democratic governments find themselves under pressure to convert, by whatever means, zero-sum into positive-sum distributional games. In democratic capitalism after the end of postwar growth, this was done essentially by moving additional, in particular not yet existing resources into the pool out of which current distributional claims were settled. As we will see, different methods were successively employed to pull forward resources that were still to be produced for present distribution and consumption. None of these methods lasted long as all of them were bound ultimately to result in economic crisis by provoking the resistance – the Kaleckian reactions – of those insisting on an allocation of rewards according to the laws of the market.

2

Postwar democratic capitalism underwent its first crisis in the decade following the late 1960s, when inflation rates began to rise rapidly throughout the Western world. Accelerating inflation resulted when declining economic growth made it difficult to sustain the political-economic peace formula between capital and labour that had ended domestic strife after the devastations of the Second World War. Essentially that formula entailed the organized working class accepting capitalist markets and property rights in exchange for political democracy enabling them to achieve social security and a steadily rising standard of living. When the 1960s came to a close, more than two decades of uninterrupted economic growth had resulted in deeply rooted popular perceptions of continuous economic progress as a right of democratic citizenship – perceptions that translated into political expectations that governments felt constrained but were increasingly unable to honour when growth began to slow down.

The structure of the 'postwar settlement' between labour and capital was fundamentally the same across those otherwise widely different countries where democratic capitalism had come to be instituted. In addition to an expanding welfare state, it included a right of workers to free collective bargaining through independent trade unions, together with a political guarantee of full employment underwritten by governments liberally applying the toolkit of Keynesian economic policy. When growth began to falter, however, the latter two in particular became difficult to maintain alongside each other. While free collective bargaining enabled workers through their unions to act effectively on what had meanwhile become firmly ingrained expectations of regular yearly wage increases, governments' commitment to full employment, together with a growing welfare state, protected unions from potential employment losses caused by wage settlements in excess of productivity growth. Government economic policy thus increased the bargaining power of trade unions far beyond what a free labour market would have sustained. In the late 1960s this found expression in a worldwide wave of labour militancy fuelled by a strong sense of political entitlement to a continuously rising standard of living unchecked by fears of unemployment.

In subsequent years governments all over the Western world faced the question of how to make trade unions moderate their members' wage demands without having to rescind the Keynesian promise of secure full employment. In the numerous countries where the institutional structure of the collective bargaining system was not conducive to the negotiation of tripartite 'social pacts', governments remained convinced throughout the 1970s that allowing unemployment to rise in order to contain real wage increases was too risky for their own survival, if not for the stability of capitalist democracy as such. Their only way out was an accommodating monetary policy that allowed free collective bargaining and politically provided full employment to continue to coexist at the expense of raising the going rate of inflation, with the risk of inflation accelerating over time.

For a limited period, inflation is not much of a problem for workers represented by trade unions strong and politically powerful enough to achieve *de jure* or *de facto* wage indexation. Inflation comes at the expense primarily of holders of financial assets and of creditors – groups that do not as a rule include workers, or at least did not do so in the 1960s and 1970s. This is why inflation can be, and has been, described as a monetary reflection of distributional conflict between a working class demanding both employment security and a higher share in their country's income and a capitalist class striving to maximize the return on its capital. As the two sides act on mutually incompatible ideas of what is theirs by right, one emphasizing the entitlements of citizenship and the other those of property and productive achievement, inflation may also be considered an expression of anomie in a society which for structural reasons cannot agree on common criteria of social justice. It was in this sense that the eminent British sociologist John Goldthorpe, in the late 1970s, suggested that high and indeed accelerating inflation was ineradicable in a democratic-capitalist market economy that allowed workers and citizens to organize politically to correct market outcomes through collective action (Goldthorpe 1978; Hirsch and Goldthorpe 1978).

For governments facing conflicting demands from workers and capital owners in a world of declining growth rates, an accommodating monetary policy was a convenient *ersatz* method for avoiding zero-sum social conflict. In the immediate postwar years it had been economic growth that had provided governments, then as now struggling with incompatible concepts of economic justice, with additional *goods and services* by which to defuse class antagonisms. Now governments had to make do with additional *money*, as yet uncovered by the real economy, as a means of pulling forward future resources into present consumption and distribution. This mode of conflict pacification, effective as it at first was, could not, however, continue indefinitely. As Friedrich von Hayek (1967 [1950]) never tired of pointing out, sustained inflation that is in all likelihood accelerating over time is bound to give rise to all sorts of ultimately unmanageable economic distortions: among other things, in relative prices, in the relation between contingent and fixed incomes, and especially in what economists refer to as *economic incentives*. In the end, by calling forth Kaleckian reactions from increasingly suspicious capital owners, inflation will even produce unemployment, punishing the very workers whose interests it may initially have served. At this point at the latest, governments under democratic capitalism will be pressured to cease accommodating redistributive wage settlements and restore monetary stability.

3

Inflation was conquered in the early 1980s (figure 11.1), when the Federal Reserve Bank of the United States under its new chairman, Paul Volker, who had been appointed in 1979, still during the Carter presidency, raised interest rates to an unprecedented height, causing unemployment to jump to levels not seen since the Great Depression.[8] The Volcker revolution, or one might also speak of the Volcker putsch, was sealed when President Reagan, who is said initially to have been afraid of the political fallout of Volcker's aggressive disinflation policies, was re-elected in 1984. Before him, Margaret Thatcher, who had followed the American lead, had won a second term in June 1983, also in spite of high unemployment and rapid de-industrialization caused, among other things, by a restrictive monetary policy. In both the US and the UK, disinflation was accompanied by fierce and in the end highly successful attacks by governments and employers on trade unions, epitomized by Reagan's victory over the

Figure 11.1: Inflation rates, seven countries, 1970–2010

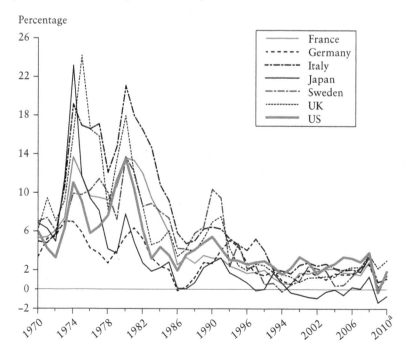

Note: ᵃEstimate.

Source: OECD Economic Outlook Database No. 87.

Figure 11.2: Unemployment rates, seven countries, 1970–2010

Percentage

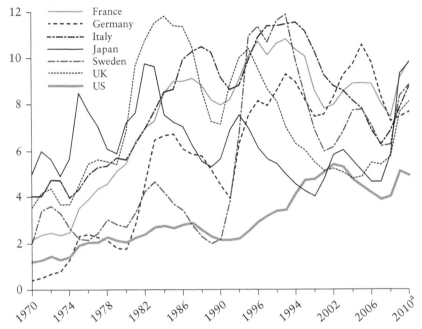

Note: ªEstimate.
Source: OECD Economic Outlook Database No. 87.

air traffic controllers and Thatcher's breaking of the National Union of Mineworkers. In subsequent years, inflation rates throughout the capitalist world remained continuously low while unemployment went more or less steadily up (figure 11.2). In parallel, unionization declined almost everywhere, and strikes became so infrequent that some countries ceased to keep strike statistics (figure 11.3).

The neoliberal era began with Anglo-American governments casting aside the political orthodoxy of postwar democratic capitalism. It was founded on the belief that inflation was always preferable to unemployment, as unemployment would be certain to undermine political support, not just for the government of the day but also for the democratic-capitalist political-economic regime. The experiments conducted by Reagan and Thatcher on their electorates were observed closely by policy-makers worldwide. Those, however, who may have hoped that the end of inflation would mean an end to economic disorder were soon to be disappointed. As inflation receded, public debt began to increase,

Figure 11.3: Strike volume, seven countries, 1971–2007[a]

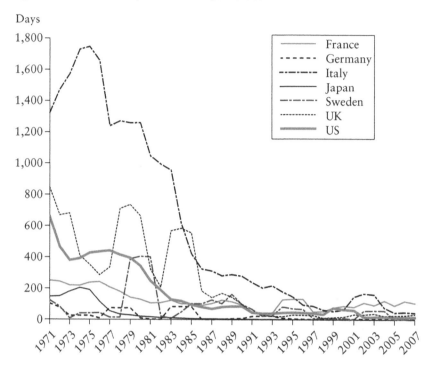

Days

Note: [a]Days not worked per 1,000 employees, three-year moving averages.

Source: ILO Labour Statistics Database; OECD Labour Force Statistics; author's own calculations.

and not entirely unexpectedly so. Already in the 1950s Anthony Downs (see, for example, Downs 1960) had claimed that in a democracy the demands from citizens for public services tended to exceed the supply of resources available to government, and as early as the late 1960s the Marxist scholar James O'Connor, sympathetically commented upon by none other than Daniel Bell (1976), had seen emerging on the horizon of contemporary capitalism an endemic 'fiscal crisis of the state' (O'Connor 1970a, 1970b, 1972, 1973).

Rising public debt in the 1980s had many causes. Stagnant growth had made taxpayers more averse than ever to taxation, and, with the end of inflation, automatic tax increases through what was called 'bracket creep' also came to an end. The same held for the continuous devaluation of public debt in the course of the devaluation of national currencies, a process that had first complemented economic growth, and then increasingly substituted for it in reducing a country's accumulated debt relative to its nominal income. On the expenditure side, rising unemployment, caused by monetary stabilization, required rising expenditures on social assistance. Also the various social entitlements created in the 1970s in return for trade union wage moderation – as it were, deferred wages from the neocorporatist era – began to mature and became due, increasingly burdening public households.

With inflation no longer available for closing the gap between the demands of citizens, on the one hand, and of 'the markets', on the other, the burden of securing social peace fell on the state and on public finance. Public debt turned out, for a while, to be a convenient functional equivalent of inflation. Like inflation, public debt made it possible to introduce resources into the distributional conflicts of the time that had not yet in fact been produced, enabling governments to draw on future resources in addition to those already on hand. What had changed was the method by which resources were pulled forward to satisfy politically irresistible or economically irrefutable demands that could not be simultaneously satisfied with existing economic resources alone. As the struggle between market and social distribution moved from the labour market to the political arena, electoral pressure took the place of trade union pressure. Governments, instead of inflating the currency, began to borrow on an increasing scale to accommodate demands for benefits and services as a citizen's right, while accepting competing claims simultaneously to reflect as closely as possible the judgement of the market and thereby to provide opportunities for a maximally profitable use of productive resources. Low inflation was helpful in this, since it assured creditors that government bonds would keep their value, even over the long haul; and so were the low interest rates that had resulted when inflation had been stamped out.

Just like inflation, however, accumulation of public debt cannot go on forever. Economists have always warned of public deficit spending 'crowding out' private investment, causing high interest rates and low growth. But they were never able to specify where exactly the critical threshold was. In actual practice, it turned out to be possible, at least for a time, to keep interest rates low by deregulating financial markets (Krippner 2011) while containing inflation through continued union-busting. Still, the US in particular, with its exceptionally low national savings rate, soon had to sell its government bonds not just to citizens but also to foreign investors, including sovereign wealth funds of various sorts (Spiro 1999). Moreover, as debt burdens rose, a growing share of public spending had to be devoted to debt service, even with interest rates remaining low – which could, however, not forever be taken for granted. Above all, there had to be a point, although apparently unknowable beforehand, at which creditors, foreign and domestic alike, would begin to worry about getting their money back eventually. By then at the latest, pressures would begin to mount from 'financial markets' for consolidation of public budgets and a return to fiscal discipline.

4

The dominant theme of the 1992 presidential election in the United States was the two deficits, the one of the federal government and the other of the country in foreign trade. The victory of Bill Clinton, who had campaigned above all on the 'double deficit', set off worldwide attempts at fiscal consolidation, aggressively promoted under American leadership by international organizations such as the OECD and the IMF. Initially the Clinton administration seems to have envisaged closing the public deficit by accelerated economic growth brought about by social reform, such as increased public investment in education (Reich 1997). However, when in the mid-term elections of 1994 the Democrats lost their majority in both houses of Congress, Clinton soon turned to a policy of austerity involving deep cuts in public spending, including changes in social policy which, in the words of the president, were to put an end to 'welfare as we know it'.[9] Indeed, in the three final years of the Clinton presidency, from 1998 to 2000, the US federal government for the first time in decades was running a budget surplus.

This is not to say, however, that the Clinton administration had somehow found a way of pacifying a democratic-capitalist political economy without recourse to additional economic resources that were yet to be produced. The Clinton strategy of social conflict management drew heavily on the deregulation of the financial sector that had already started under Reagan and was now driven further than ever before (Stiglitz 2003). Rapidly rising income inequality caused by continuing de-unionization and sharp cuts in social spending, as well as the reduction in aggregate demand caused by fiscal consolidation, were counter-balanced by unprecedented new opportunities for citizens and firms to indebt themselves. It was Colin Crouch (2009) who coined the fortuitous term 'privatized Keynesianism' for what was in effect the replacement of public with private debt. What this amounted to was that, rather than the government borrowing money to fund equal access to decent housing or the formation of marketable work skills, it was now individual citizens who, under a debt regime of extreme generosity, were allowed, and in fact compelled, to take out loans at their own risk with which to pay for their education or their advancement to a less destitute urban neighbourhood.

The Clinton policy of fiscal consolidation and economic revitalization through financial deregulation had many beneficiaries. The rich were spared higher taxes, while those among them – a fast-growing number – who had been wise enough to move their interests into the financial sector were making huge profits on the ever more complicated so-called financial services that they now had an almost unlimited licence to sell. But the poor also prospered, at least some of them and for a while. Subprime mortgages became a substitute, however illusory in the end, for the social policy that was simultaneously being scrapped, as well as for the wage increases that were no longer forthcoming at the lower end of a more and more flexible labour market. For African Americans in particular, owning their home was not just the 'American dream' come true but also a much-needed substitute for the old-age pensions that they were unable to earn in the labour markets of the day and that they had no reason to expect from a government pledged to a policy of permanent austerity.

In fact, for a time home ownership offered the middle class and even some of the poor an attractive opportunity to participate in the speculative craze that was making the rich so much richer in the 1990s and early 2000s, treacherous as that opportunity would later turn out to have been. As property prices escalated under rising demand from people who would in normal circumstances have never been able to buy a house, it became common practice to use the new financial instruments to extract part or all of one's home equity to finance the – rapidly rising – costs of the next generation's college education, or simply for personal consumption to offset stagnant or declining wages. Nor was it entirely uncommon for home owners to use their new credit to buy a second or third house, in the hope of cashing in on what was somehow expected to be an open-ended increase in the market value of real estate. In this way, unlike the era of public debt when future resources were procured for present use by government borrowing, such resources were now made available by a myriad of individuals selling in liberalized financial markets more or less solemn commitments to pay a significant share of their expected future earnings to creditors, who in return provided them with the instant power to purchase whatever they needed or liked. Financial liberalization thus compensated for social policy being cut in an era of fiscal consolidation and public austerity. Individual debt replaced public debt, and individual demand, constructed for high fees by a rapidly growing money-making industry, took the place of collective demand governed by the state in supporting employment and profits in industries far beyond 'financial services', such as construction (figure 11.4).

Especially after 2001, when the Federal Reserve switched to very low interest rates to prevent an economic slump, and with the return of high employment this implied, the new financial freedoms that had made the privatization of Keynesianism possible sustained, in addition to unprecedented profits in the financial sector, a booming economy that

Figure 11.4: Fiscal consolidation and private debt in percent of GDP, three countries, 1995–2008

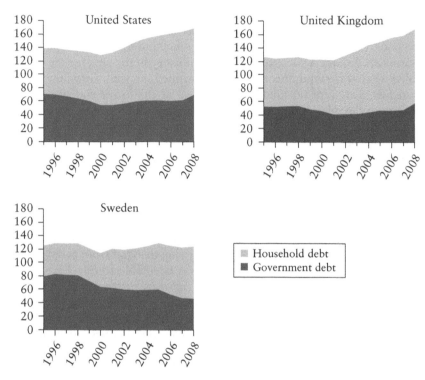

Source: OECD Economic Outlook Database No. 87; OECD National Accounts Database.

became the envy not least of the European left. In fact Alan Greenspan's policy of easy money supporting the rapidly growing indebtedness of American society was held up as a model by European trade unions, which never tired of noting that, unlike the European Central Bank, the Federal Reserve was bound by law to provide not just monetary stability but also high levels of employment. All of this, of course, ended when in 2008 the international credit pyramid on which the prosperity of the late 1990s and early 2000s had rested suddenly collapsed.

5

With the crash of privatized Keynesianism, the crisis of postwar democratic capitalism entered its fourth and, up to now, latest stage, after

Figure 11.5: The United States: Four crises of democratic capitalism, 1970–2010

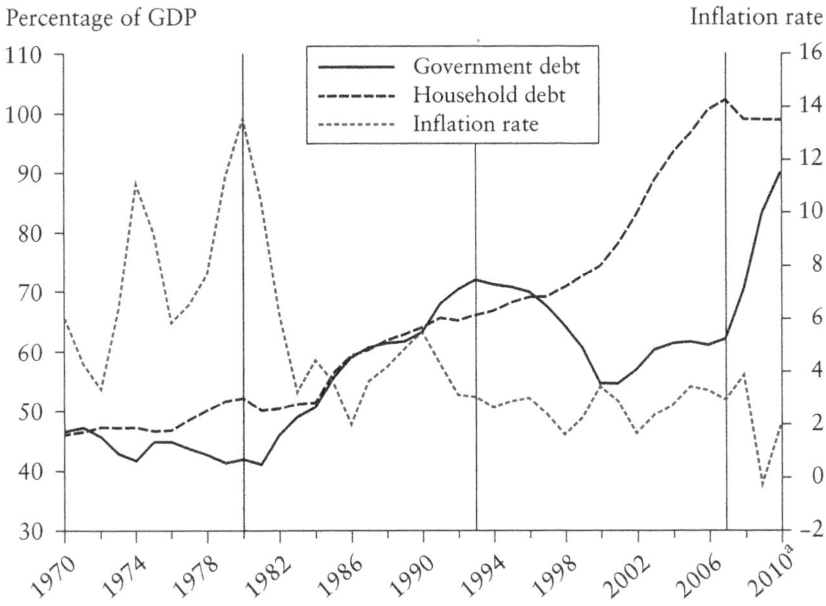

Percentage of GDP   Inflation rate

Note: ᵃEstimate.

Source: OECD Economic Outlook Database No. 87.

the successive eras of inflation, public deficits and private indebtedness (figure 11.5).[10] As the global financial system was about to disintegrate, nation-states had to restore economic confidence by socializing the bad loans licensed in compensation for fiscal consolidation. Together with the fiscal expansion necessary to prevent a breakdown of what the Germans call the *Realökonomie*, this resulted in a dramatic new increase in public deficits and public debt – a development that, it may be noted, was not at all due to frivolous overspending by opportunistic politicians, as implied by public-choice theories, or to misconceived public institutions, as suggested by a broad institutional economics literature produced in the 1990s under the auspices of, among others, the World Bank and the IMF (for a representative collection, see Poterba and von Hagen 1999).

The quantum leap in public indebtedness after 2008, which completely undid whatever fiscal consolidation might have been achieved in the preceding decade, reflected the fact that no democratic state could have dared to impose on its society another economic crisis of the dimension of the Great Depression of the 1930s as punishment for the excesses of a deregulated global money industry. Once again, political power was deployed to make future resources available for securing present social peace, in that states more or less voluntarily took upon themselves a significant share of the new debt, originally created in the private sector, so as to reassure creditors. But while this effectively rescued the financial industry's money factories, reinstating in very short time their extraordinary profits, salaries and bonuses, it did not and could not prevent rising suspicions, on the part of the very same 'financial markets' that had just been saved by national governments from the consequences of their own indiscretion, that in the process governments might have overextended themselves. Even with the global economic crisis far from over, creditors began vociferously to demand a return to sound money through fiscal austerity, in search for reassurance that their vastly increased investment in government debt will not be lost.

In the years after 2008, distributional conflict under democratic capitalism has turned into a complicated tug-of-war between global financial investors and sovereign national states. Where in the past workers struggled with employers, citizens with finance ministers, and private debtors with private banks, it is now financial institutions wrestling with the same states that they had only recently successfully blackmailed into saving them from themselves. While this is what we see on the surface, the underlying configuration of power and interests is, however, far more complex and still awaits systematic exploration. For example, financial markets have since the crisis returned to charging different states widely different interest rates, thereby differentiating the pressure they apply on governments to make their citizens acquiesce with unprecedented spending cuts in line, again, with a basically unmodified market logic of distribution. In fact, given the amount of debt carried by most states today, even minor increases in the rate of interest on government bonds could cause fiscal disaster.[11] At the same time, markets must avoid states declaring sovereign bankruptcy, which states can always do if market pressures become too strong. This is why other states have to be found that are willing to bail out those most at risk, in order to protect themselves from a general increase in interest rates on government bonds once the first state has defaulted. Solidarity, if one can call it this, between states in the interest of investors is also fostered where sovereign default would hit banks located outside the defaulting country, which might force the banks' home countries once again to nationalize huge amounts of bad debt in order to stabilize their economies.

There are still more facets to the way in which the tension in democratic capitalism between demands for social rights and the workings of free markets currently expresses itself today. Some governments, foremost among them the Obama administration, are making desperate attempts to generate renewed economic growth through even more debt – in the hope of future consolidation policies, should they become inevitable, being assisted by a sizeable growth dividend. Others may be secretly hoping for a return to inflation melting down accumulated debt by softly expropriating creditors – which would, like economic growth, mitigate the political tensions to be expected from austerity. At the same time, financial markets as well as academic economists may be looking forward, given the nature of the new battlefield, to a more than ever promising fight against political interference once and for all reinstating market discipline and putting an end to all political attempts to subvert it.

Further complications arise from the fact that financial 'markets', whoever they may be, need government debt for safe investment, and pressing too hard for balanced budgets may deprive them of highly desirable investment opportunities. The middle classes of the rich countries in particular have put a good part of their savings into government bonds, not to mention workers now heavily invested in supplementary pensions. Balanced budgets might mean that states would have to take from their middle classes, in the form of higher taxes, what these can now save and invest, among other things in public debt. Not only would citizens no longer collect interest, but they would also cease to be able to pass sizeable savings on to their children. However, while this should make them interested in states being, if not debt-free, then reliably able to fulfil their obligations to their creditors, they might have to pay for their government's liquidity by deep cuts in public benefits and services on which they also, in part, depend.

At the end of the day, however complicated the cross-cutting cleavages between the various interests in the emerging new field of the international politics of public debt may be, the price for financial stabilization is unlikely to be paid by the owners of money, or at least of real money. For example, public pension reform will be accelerated by fiscal pressures at home and abroad, to the extent that governments default anywhere in the world, private pensions will be hit as well. The average citizen will pay – for the consolidation of public finances, for the bankruptcy of foreign states, for the rising rates of interest on the public debt and, if eventually necessary and still possible, for another rescue of national and international banks – with his or her private savings, with cuts in public entitlements, with reduced public services and, one way or other, with higher taxes.

6

In the four decades since the end of postwar growth, the epicentre of the tectonic tension inside the political economy of democratic capitalism has migrated from one institutional location to the next, in the course giving rise to a sequence of different but systematically related economic disturbances. In the 1970s the conflict between democratic claims for social justice and capitalist demands for distribution by marginal productivity played itself out primarily in national labour markets, where trade union wage pressure under politically guaranteed full employment caused accelerating inflation. When what was in effect redistribution by debasement of the currency became economically unsustainable, forcing governments under high political risks to put an end to it, the conflict re-emerged in the electoral arena. Here it gave rise to growing disparity between public spending and public revenues and, as a consequence, to rapidly rising public debt, in response to voter demands for benefits and services in excess of what a democratic-capitalist economy could be made to hand over to its 'tax state' (Schumpeter 1991 [1918]).

Just like inflation, conflict management by deficit spending could not continue forever. When efforts to rein in public debt became unavoidable, however, they had to be accompanied, for the sake of social peace, by financial deregulation easing access to private credit as an alternative route to accommodating normatively popular and politically powerful demands of citizens for security and prosperity. This, too, lasted not much longer than a decade, until the global economy almost faltered under the burden of unrealistic promises of future payment for present consumption and investment, licensed by governments in compensation for fiscal austerity. Since then, the clash between popular ideas of *social justice* and economic insistence on *market justice* has once again changed sites, re-emerging this time in international capital markets and the complex contests currently taking place there between financial institutions and electorates, governments, states and international organizations. Now the issue is how far states can and must go in enforcing on their citizens the property rights and profit expectations of those that call themselves 'the markets', so as to avoid having to declare bankruptcy while protecting as best they can what may still remain of their democratic legitimacy.

Toleration of inflation, acceptance of public debt and deregulation of private credit were no more than temporary stopgaps for governments confronted with an apparently irrepressible conflict between the two contradictory principles of allocation under democratic capitalism: social rights, on the one hand, and marginal productivity, as determined by the relationship between supply and demand, on the other. Each of the three worked for a while until they began to cause more problems than they solved, indicating that a lasting reconciliation of social and economic stability in capitalist democracies is no more than a utopian project. Eventually, all that governments were able to achieve in dealing with the crises of their day was to move them to new arenas, where they reappeared in new forms. There is no reason to believe that the successive manifestation of the contradictions inherent in democratic capitalism in ever new varieties of economic disorder should today be at an end.

7

The capacity of the social sciences to make predictions, if it exists at all, is limited. Like evolutionary biology, social science may, if it does its work well, provide plausible interpretations of the past in the form of systematically comparable historical reconstructions of chains of events that at first glance may appear nothing but chaotic. Looking forward, however, the social scientist faces the same open future as anybody else. Nevertheless, it appears to me that one can say with some certainty that the political manageability of democratic capitalism has in recent years sharply declined, obviously in some countries more than in others, but also and more importantly overall in the emerging global political-economic system. As a result the risks seem to be growing, both for democracy and for the economy.

Beginning with the economy, it would seem that economic policy-makers since the Great Depression have rarely, if ever, been faced with as much uncertainty as today. One example among many is that 'the markets' expect not just fiscal consolidation but also, and at the same time, a reasonable prospect of future economic growth. How the two may be combined, however, is not at all clear. Although the risk premium on Irish government debt fell when the country pledged itself to aggressive deficit reduction, a few weeks later it rose again, allegedly because the country's consolidation programme suddenly appeared so strict that it would make economic recovery impossible.[12] Moreover, among those who must know, one finds a widely shared conviction that the next bubble is already building somewhere in a world that is more than ever flooded with cheap money. Subprime mortgages may no longer offer themselves for investment, at least not for the time being. But there are the markets for raw materials or the new Internet economy. Nothing prevents financial firms from using the surplus of money provided by the central banks to enter whatever appear to be the new growth sectors, on behalf of their favourite clients and, of course, of themselves. After all, with regulatory reform in the financial sector having failed in almost all respects, capital requirements are still as low as they were, and the banks that were too big to fail in 2008 can count on being so also in 2012 or 2013. This leaves them with the same capacity for blackmailing the public that they were able to deploy so skilfully back then. But now the public bailout of private capitalism on the model of 2008 may be impossible to repeat, if only because public finances are already stretched beyond their limit.

As I said, it is not for the social scientist to make predictions – for example, on where the next bubble may burst; on whether the United States will continue to find creditors willing to finance its apparently ineradicable double deficit; whether it will be possible or not to impose the costs of consolidation entirely on pensioners and public-sector workers, so as to spare 'the markets' from economic hardship; or to what extent economic growth or inflation will be forthcoming to ease countries' debt burdens. What we do know, however, is that democracy is as much at risk in the current crisis as the economy. Using concepts developed long ago by the British sociologist David Lockwood (1964), it is not only the *system integration* of contemporary societies – that is, the efficient functioning of their capitalist economies – that has become precarious, but also their *social integration*. With the arrival of a new age of austerity, the capacity of nation-states to mediate between what in the past were the rights of citizens, on the one hand, and the evolving requirements of capital accumulation, on the other, has suffered profoundly. For example, governments everywhere face stronger resistance to tax increases than ever, in particular in highly indebted countries, where fresh public money would have to be spent for many years to pay for goods that have long been consumed. Even more importantly, with continuously increasing global interdependence, the times are over when it was still possible to pretend that the tensions between economy and society, and indeed between capitalism and democracy, could be handled inside national political communities. No government can govern today without paying very close attention to international constraints and obligations, in particular to obligations in financial markets forcing it to impose sacrifices on its population. The crises and contradictions of democratic capitalism have finally become internationalized, playing themselves out not just within states but also between them, and simultaneously at both levels in as yet unexplored combinations and permutations.

As we read in the papers almost every day in summer 2011, 'the markets' have begun in unprecedented ways to dictate what presumably sovereign and democratic states may still do for their citizens and what they must refuse them. Moreover, the very same ratings agencies that were instrumental in bringing about the disaster of the global money industry are now threatening to downgrade the bonds of the very same states that had to accept a previously unimaginable level of new debt to rescue that industry and the capitalist economy as a whole. Politics still contains and distorts markets, but only, it seems, at a level remote from the daily experience and the political and organizational capacities of normal people: the US, armed to its teeth not just with aircraft carriers but also with an unlimited supply of credit cards for the most militant shoppers in human history, still gets China to buy its mounting debt and manages to muscle the three global ratings firms, all based at the southern tip of Manhattan, into awarding its government bonds the triple A to which it feels forever entitled. All others, however, have to listen to what 'the markets' tell them. As a result citizens increasingly perceive their national governments not as *their* agents, but as those of other states or of international organizations, such as the IMF or the European Union, organizations that are immeasurably more insulated from electoral pressure than was the traditional nation-state. In countries such as Greece and Ireland in particular, anything resembling democracy will be effectively suspended for many years, as national governments of whatever political colour, forced to behave *responsibly* as defined by international markets, will have to impose strict austerity on their societies, at the price of becoming increasingly *unresponsive* to their citizens (Mair 2009).

Democracy is being pre-empted not just in those countries, however, that are currently under attack. Germany, which is still doing relatively well economically, is doing so not least because it has committed itself to decades of public expenditure cuts. In addition, the German government had, and will again have, to get its citizens to provide liquidity to countries at risk of defaulting, not just to save German banks but also to stabilize the common European currency and prevent a general increase in the rate of interest on public debt, as is likely to occur in the case of the first country collapsing. The high political cost of this is documented by the progressive decay of the electoral capital of the Merkel government, culminating up to April 2011 in two crushing defeats in major regional elections. Populist rhetoric to the effect that perhaps creditors should also pay a share of the costs, as vented by the chancellor in early 2010, was quickly abandoned when 'the markets' expressed shock by slightly raising the rate of interest on new public debt. Now the talk is about the need to shift, in the words of the German finance minister, from old-fashioned 'government', which is supposed to be no longer up to the new challenges of globalization, to 'governance', meaning in particular a lasting curtailment of the budgetary authority of the Bundestag.[13]

In several ways, the political expectations democratic states are today facing from their new principals are such that they may be impossible to meet. International markets and organizations require that not just governments but also citizens credibly commit themselves to fiscal consolidation. Political parties that oppose austerity must be resoundingly defeated in national elections, and both government and opposition must be equally pledged to 'sound finance', or else the cost of debt service will inexorably rise. Elections in which voters have no effective choice, however, may be perceived by them as inauthentic, which may cause all sorts of political disorder, from declining turnout to a rise of populist parties to riots in the streets. What may at first sight help is that the arenas of distributional conflict have with time become ever more remote from popular politics. Compared to the fiscal diplomacy and the international capital markets of today, the national labour markets of the 1970s, with the manifold opportunities they offered for corporatist political mobilization and inter-class coalitions, and the politics of public spending of the 1980s were not necessarily beyond either the grasp or the strategic reach of the 'man in the street'. Since then, the battlefields on which the contradictions of democratic capitalism are fought out have become ever more complex, making it exceedingly difficult for anyone outside of the political and financial elites to recognize the underlying interests and identify their own.[14] While this may generate apathy at the mass level and thereby make life easier at the elite level, there is, however, no relying on it in a world in which blind compliance with the demands of financial investors is made to appear the only institutionally rational and responsible behaviour. To those who refuse to be talked out of other, social rationalities and responsibilities, such a world may at some point seem nothing but absurd, making it the only rational and responsible conduct to throw as many wrenches as possible into the works of *haute finance*. Where democracy as we know it is effectively suspended, as it already is in countries such as Greece, Ireland and Portugal, street riots and popular insurrection could be the last remaining mode of political expression for those devoid of market power. Should we hope in the name of democracy that we will soon have the opportunity to observe a few examples?

Social science can do little, if anything, to help resolve the structural tensions and contradictions underlying the economic and social disorders of the day. What it can do, however, is bring them to light and identify the historical continuities of which present crises are only the latest expression. It also can – and indeed I believe it must – point out the drama of democratic states being turned into debt-collecting agencies on behalf of a global oligarchy of investors compared to which C. Wright Mills's 'power elite' (1956) must appear like a shining example of liberal pluralism. More than ever, economic power seems today to have become political power, while citizens appear to be stripped almost entirely of their democratic defences and their capacity to impress on the political economy interests and demands incommensurable with those of capital owners. In fact, looking back at the democratic-capitalist crisis sequence since the 1970s, one cannot but be afraid of the possibility of a new, however temporary, settlement of social conflict in advanced capitalism, this time entirely in favour of the propertied classes now firmly entrenched in their politically unconquerable institutional stronghold, the international financial industry.

References

Bell, D. (1976) The public household: on 'fiscal sociology' and the liberal society, in D. Bell (ed.) *The Cultural Contradictions of Capitalism*. New York: Basic Books, pp. 220–82.

Buchanan, J., and Tullock, G. (1962) *The Calculus of Consent: Logical Foundations of Constitutional Democracy*. Ann Arbor: University of Michigan Press.

Crouch, C. (2009) Privatised Keynesianism: an unacknowledged policy regime, *British Journal of Politics and International Relations* 11(3): 382–99.

Downs, A. (1960) Why the government budget is too small in a democracy, *World Politics* 12(4): 541–63.

Goldthorpe, J. (1978) The current inflation: towards a sociological account, in F. Hirsch and J. Goldthorpe (eds), *The Political Economy of Inflation*. Cambridge, MA: Harvard University Press, pp. 186–216.

Hayek, F. A. von (1967 [1950]) Full employment, planning and inflation, in *Studies in Philosophy, Politics, and Economics*. Chicago: University of Chicago Press, pp. 270–9.

Hirsch, F., and Goldthorpe, J. (eds) (1978) *The Political Economy of Inflation*. London: Martin Robertson.

Judt, T. (2005) *Postwar: A History of Europe since 1945*. London: Penguin.

Kalecki, M. (1943) Political aspects of full employment, *Political Quarterly* 14(4): 322–31.

Krippner, G. R. (2011) *Capitalizing on Crisis: The Political Origins of the Rise of Finance*. Cambridge, MA: Harvard University Press.

Lockwood, D. (1964) Social integration and system integration, in G. K. Zollschan and W. Hirsch (eds), *Explorations in Social Change*. London: Houghton Mifflin, pp. 244–57.

Mair, P. (2009) *Representative versus Responsible Government*, MPIfG Working Paper 09/8. Cologne: Max Planck Institute for the Study of Societies; available at: www.mpifg.de/pu/workpap/wp09-8.pdf (accessed 1 March 2012).

Mills, C. W. (1956) *The Power Elite*. New York: Oxford University Press.

O'Connor, J. (1970a) The fiscal crisis of the state: part I, *Socialist Revolution* 1(1): 13–54.

O'Connor, J. (1970b) The fiscal crisis of the state: part II, *Socialist Revolution* 1(2): 34–94.

O'Connor, J. (1972) Inflation, fiscal crisis, and the American working class, *Socialist Revolution* 2(2): 9–46.

O'Connor, J. (1973) *The Fiscal Crisis of the State*. New York: St Martin's Press.

Polanyi, K. (1957 [1944]) *The Great Transformation: The Political and Economic Origins of Our Time*. Boston: Beacon Press.

Poterba, J. M., and Hagen, J. von (eds) (1999) *Institutions, Politics and Fiscal Policy*. Chicago: University of Chicago Press.

Reich, R. B. (1997) *Locked in the Cabinet*. New York: Knopf.

Reinhart, C. M., and Rogoff, K. S. (2009) *This Time Is Different: Eight Centuries of Financial Folly*. Princeton, NJ: Princeton University Press.

Samuelson, R. J. (2010) *The Great Inflation and its Aftermath: The Past and Future of American Influence*. New York: Random House.

Scharpf, F. W. (1991) *Crisis and Choice in European Social Democracy*. Ithaca, NY: Cornell University Press.

Schumpeter, J. A. (1991 [1918]) The crisis of the tax state, in R. Swedberg (ed.), *The Economics and Sociology of Capitalism*. Princeton, NJ: Princeton University Press, pp. 99–141.

Scott, J. C. (1976) *The Moral Economy of the Peasant: Rebellion and Subsistence in Southeast Asia*. New Haven, CT: Yale University Press.

Shonfield, A. (1965) *Modern Capitalism: The Changing Balance of Public and Private Power*. New York: Oxford University Press.

Spiro, D. E. (1999) *The Hidden Hand of American Hegemony: Petrodollar Recycling and International Markets*. Ithaca, NY: Cornell University Press.

Stiglitz, J. E. (2003) *The Roaring Nineties: A New History of the World's Most Prosperous Decade*. London: W. W. Norton.

Streeck, W. (2009) *Re-Forming Capitalism: Institutional Change in the German Political Economy*. Oxford: Oxford University Press.

Thompson, E. P. (1971) The moral economy of the English crowd in the eighteenth century, *Past and Present* 50(1): 76–136.

Notes

Chapter 1 Introduction

1 The full impact of debt on public budgets has not yet been felt, since long-term interest rates on government bonds have been at comparatively low levels throughout the last two decades. As a result, net interest payments as a percentage of GDP declined in the 2000s despite rising debt. If interest rates on government bonds increase only slightly – which has been the case recently in most countries – this will have a substantial impact on national budgets.

2 Unlike his bourgeois counterparts, of course, Marx expected the increasingly social nature of capitalist production eventually to collide with private property, leading to capitalist relations of production being overthrown by the development of (increasingly collectivized) means of production.

3 How the perspective changed is documented by the fact that, in 1960, Anthony Downs, one of the most prominent proponents of 'public choice', was still writing about 'why the government budget is too small in a democracy' (Downs 1960), rather than too large.

4 The concluding chapter of this book will suggest how the increase in public debt over the past three or four decades may be related to the general evolution of democratic capitalism after the postwar growth period, and to the progress of liberalization in particular.

5 Taxing, for example, the Onassis or Niarchos families to lower the deficit of the Greek state is obviously considered by political realists to be so illusory that it is not even mentioned as a possibility. All that remains if revenue is to be increased, then, are higher taxes on electricity or petrol. The ability of the very rich to evade taxation in their home countries by moving their assets abroad is another and highly significant indicator of a lack of power on the part of democracy. Liberalization has added vastly to that capacity, and thereby severely weakened democratic governance, in that it has removed almost all limitations on international movements of capital.

6 Excluding countries with compulsory voting (Australia, Belgium and Luxembourg) pushes the average well below 70 per cent for the latest elections.

7 The underlying image is similar to that of the clash between a 'logic of membership' and a 'logic of influence' in intermediary organizations such as trade unions and business associations (Schmitter and Streeck 1999).

Chapter 2 Public Finance and the Decline of State Capacity in Democratic Capitalism

1 It is interesting to note that, originally, someone like Anthony Downs (1960) did not account for 'why the government budget is too small in a democracy' by finding fault with the opportunism of democratic politicians or the greed of distributional coalitions (Olson 1982, 1983), but by noticing voters' resistance to pay for the public services and investments that they required in a complex society. Later the notion of social need was dropped, and what had been underfinancing of public goods caused by voter unwillingness to pay turned into overprovision of private or club goods driven by the egoistic interests of democratic politicians.

2 For a concise formulation of the problem, see Stiglitz's account of the policies of the first Clinton administration, which began in January 1993: 'That the deficits were not sustainable in the long run was clear . . . . With a growing debt, the federal government had to pay higher and higher interest rates, and with higher interest rates and more debt, more and more money simply went to pay interest on the national debt. These interest payments would eventually crowd out other forms of expenditure' (Stiglitz 2003: 35f.).

3 On self-undermining institutions, see Greif (2006) and Greif and Laitin (2004).

4 See also Steuerle and Rennane (2010).

5 Of course, since government debt is sovereign debt, it can in principle be unilaterally revoked or 'restructured', in the sense of forcing creditors to accept so-called haircuts. We will leave this possibility aside for the time being.

6 The formula for the index, then, is '1 − [(mandatory spending + interest)/revenues], multiplied by 100 for conversion to a percentage'. The index 'falls when revenues are reduced without cutting mandatory spending, and it is reduced when mandatory spending is increased without increasing revenues' and is therefore 'neutral on the size of government' (personal communication from Eugene C. Steuerle, 11 February 2010).

7 Meaning that, in the year after the beginning of the current 'financial crisis', mandatory expenses including interest payments exceeded total government income. This was caused by a simultaneous decline in revenue and a rapid increase in mandatory spending. As a result, all discretionary spending, including military expenditure, had to be debt-financed.

8 Another conceptual problem when comparing Germany and the United States results from the different ways the two countries finance their social security systems. In the US, social security contributions are collected as payroll taxes

by the federal government, whereas in Germany they do not appear in the federal budget at all. Although German social security contributions are taxes for all practical purposes, they are paid into and administered by four para-fiscal funds that together collect contributions amounting to about 40 per cent of the real wage, up to an indexed cut-off point beyond which individuals are exempt from paying. To increase comparability with the United States, one may add social security contributions to federal government revenues, as though not only the latter but also the former were collected by the state and included in the state budget. The sum of the two, representing the sum total of public revenues at the national level, would then be the denominator of a revised index, while the numerator would include the total expenditure of the social security system in addition to the federal government's mandatory expenditure. The effect would be a decline in the absolute value of the index. This is as it should be, given the fact that social security contributions are dedicated entirely to a pre-established purpose. Over time, the revised index follows basically the same path as the index based on the revenues of the federal government alone, apart from the fact that a relative increase in social security contributions compared to federal taxes during the period in question makes the decline in overall fiscal discretion (even) steeper.

9 The exact definition of public investment was always contested. We rely here on the OECD (2009: 44).

10 It is increasingly acknowledged that there is more to public investment than material infrastructure, and that a wider conceptualization of the term is thus required. For example, the revised System of National Accounts of 2008 discusses the need to incorporate spending on R&D and education into GFCF (United Nations 2009: 8, 206). The concept of 'social investment' we take from Morel et al. (2012), where it refers, in our reading, to a supply-side-oriented social policy aimed not at the decommodification of labour but at the improvement of its employability.

11 According to an authoritative International Labour Office source, active labour market policies (ALMPs) 'contribute to an improvement in the participants' employability and thus increase their re-employment prospects. ALMPs can also be used to achieve greater equity by favouring more disadvantaged labour market groups. In addition to these functions, they are also one of the imperative measures that help create more income and employability security in times of multiple labour market changes' (Auer et al. 2008).

12 In Germany this was the case only in five years and in the United States only in four.

13 Breunig and Busemeyer (2010) use the measure to explore trade-offs and interdependencies between budgetary categories.

14 Details on sources and definitions for the components of social investment and for fiscal stress may be found in Streeck and Mertens (2011).

15 Economic growth rates and public investment spending were negatively correlated in the observed period, ranging from r = −0.52 for the US to r = −0.63 for Germany.

16 To control for policy demand, one may divide ALMP spending as a percentage of GDP by a country's unemployment rate. This reveals a flat and low spending curve in the US throughout the observed period, whereas German spending had upswings in the late 1980s and late 1990s but eventually returned to the modest levels of the mid-1980s. Sweden's adjusted spending dropped dramatically in the early 1990s from very high levels and moved closer to the German level.

17 The clearest results come from the Swedish case, where the four investment variables are correlated at coefficients between 0.29 (education and R&D) and 0.54 (R&D and family support). Germany and the US show a more mixed picture, with highly positive but also a few negative correlations.

18 GFCF is technically defined according to the nature of the assets in question (OECD 2009: 44), whereas our data on social investment are defined functionally with respect to policy areas.

19 As a result of reduced public support for education, together with the rising costs of tuition in the private college market, the total college loan debt of American households is now equal to the total American debt on credit cards (Lewin 2011).

Chapter 3 Tax Competition and Fiscal Democracy

1 The OECD-22 countries are Austria, Australia, Belgium, Canada, Denmark, Finland, France, Germany, Greece, Ireland, Italy, Japan, Luxembourg, the Netherlands, New Zealand, Norway, Portugal, Spain, Sweden, Switzerland, the United Kingdom and the United States of America.

2 We use tax harmonization here as a catch-all term for cooperative measures to curb tax competition.

3 Cross-national differences in wealth, location and domestic institutions can also create asymmetric effects under tax competition (see Baldwin and Krugman 2002; Basinger and Hallerberg 2004; Plümper et al. 2009; Hays 2009).

4 The tax wedge refers to the sum of personal income tax and employee social security contributions together with any payroll tax, expressed as a percentage of labour costs.

5 Following standard practice, we operationalize country size as the logarithm of population size in order to dampen the impact of very small and very large countries on the correlation.

6 What happened to public deficits after 2007 is, of course, a different story entirely.

7 Not shown in figure 3.2a is the rapid decline in corporate tax revenues following the financial crisis in 2008.

8 Unfortunately, data on the share of non-resident capital income in total domestic capital income are not easily available. Thus we present no evidence of the international distribution of the mobile personal capital income tax base.

Chapter 4 Governing as an Engineering Problem

1 Clearly Sweden has been deeply affected by the economic crisis, and in 2008 it witnessed one of the darkest moments it has seen in nearly twenty years – but just two years later the OECD reported that, in 2010, it had *lowered* its budget debt and posted GDP growth of 5.2 per cent.

2 There are a number of good studies showing how this model of social corporatism worked in practice. For a general overview, see Hancock (1972) and Lewin (1970). For some more recent work analysing this system and its political/economic consequences, see Katzenstein (1984) and Rothstein (1986).

3 Most important among these was the establishment of the Ghent unemployment insurance system, which effectively gave the unions control over unemployment insurance; see Rothstein (1992). But other pro-union public policies were also set up, and certainly the anti-union incentives common throughout the capitalist world were eliminated.

4 See Leif Lewin's (1970) masterful treatise on the evolution of this policy-making system, *Planhushållningsdebatten* (The Planning Debate).

5 This model is discussed further on in the chapter; the major point to note here is that those who lose their jobs are retrained and even relocated if necessary so that the individual worker does not bear the costs of economic change.

6 The government also invested in a massive building programme in which 100,000 apartments per year were constructed on the outskirts of major cities and industrial centres. One million apartments designed for the mobile workforce were built during this ten-year programme. Today, forty years later, the new working class of Sweden – the immigrants – dominates these apartment complexes.

7 Interview with this author, Gunnar Sträng. Sträng recalled that convincing the Social Democrats of these policies was one of the most difficult tasks in his long tenure as minister of finance.

8 Several changes were introduced in the new constitution. The most significant, however, was the elimination of the upper house of the Riksdag (von Sydow 1989). This reform transformed Swedish governance, in that now a relatively small change in election outcomes could actually change who held the reins of government. The Social Democrats finally lost power in 1976.

9 The 1982 devaluation of the Swedish krona by 16 per cent was particularly traumatic for the government.

10 The extent of the Swedish social welfare system's generosity also became legend. See Ministry of Health, *Välfärd vid vägskäl* [Welfare at the Crossroads], vol. 3 (SOU, 2000) for a more complete analysis of the Swedish welfare system and its benefits.

11 Among the economic analyses were Agell (1996); Lars Bertmar, 'Företagsbeskattning – behovs den? [Capital taxation: do we need it?]', in *Hur klarar vi 1990?* [How do we make it in 1990?], ed. A. Lindquist and S. Stigmark (Stockholm: Riksbankens Jubileumsfond, 1983); Klas Eklund, 'Vad göra med skatterna? [What should we do with taxes?]', *Affärsvarlden*

29(2) (1984): 7–17; Sven-Olof Lodin et al., *Beskattning av inkomst och förmögenhet, del 1 och del 2* [The taxation of income and wealth, parts 1 and 2] (Studentlitteratur, 1978); Muten (1988).

12 See Myrdal (1982) and Muten (1988) for influential arguments presented in public debate that contributed to the change of views both inside and outside government.

13 Though these tax reforms were passed after the centre-right government had come to office, the decisions surrounding them were made and agreed to by the commission that had been appointed and supported by the Social Democrats.

14 I have examined the tax reform in detail elsewhere (Steinmo 2002). That analysis follows a pattern that is very similar to the banking and social security reforms discussed here.

15 The commission was chaired by Bo Könberg (Liberal Party/Folkpartiet), who was meant to represent the whole centre-right coalition government (with Carl Bildt as prime minister). The Social Democrats also had two representatives – Ingela Thalén and Anna Hedborg. Each of the other parties had one representative: Margit Gennser (Conservatives), Åke Pettersson (Centre Party), Pontus Wiklund (Christian Democrats) and Barbro Westerholm (Liberal Party). Importantly, no labour-union members or business representatives were appointed to the commission – though of course they were allowed to present arguments and data. Ulla Hoffman (Left Party/Vänsterpartiet) and Leif Bergdahl (Ny Demokrati) were also on the commission, but these latter two did not support the reform package that was eventually passed.

16 For a solid introduction to these changes, see Palme (2003) and Thakur et al. (2003).

17 This reform also increased the retirement age for most workers.

18 See, for example, Bundesregierung (2003), OECD (2002), Palme (2003) and Bayram et al. (2012).

19 Soon after the problems in the financial system became apparent, the government swiftly seized control of several of the most troubled institutions, injecting them with capital and providing blanket guarantees to those holding debt. Importantly, however, they did not attempt to bail out the investors or the financial institutions' stockholders. Bo Lundgren, minister for economic and fiscal affairs, put the issue quite simply: 'I'd rather get equity so that there is some upside for the taxpayer . . . . For every krona we put into the bank, we wanted the same influence. That ensured that we did not have to go into certain banks at all.' Urban Backstrom, another senior official in the Ministry of Finance at the time, recalled similarly that the thinking in the government was that it would be a political and economic mistake to '[put] taxpayers on the hook without [giving them] anything in return . . . . The public will not support a plan if you leave the former shareholders with anything' (Dougherty 2008).

20 Interview with the author, 2010.

21 The result was that the budget deficit increased to 13 per cent of GDP. At one point, international confidence in the krona had sunk so low that the central

bank was forced to increase the overnight lending rate to 500 per cent in a vain effort to protect the currency.

22 Tax as a percentage of GDP went up to 60 per cent during the crisis (and Moderate Party tenure) and has now been eased back to approximately 54 per cent. But note that tax *revenues* increased in absolute terms as a result of the tax changes imposed by the Social Democrats after they returned to office (Ministry of Finance 1995: 402).

23 For example, employees were no longer eligible for up to seven days of full sick pay without a doctor's note. A number of other reforms introduced similar reductions. Some of these, of course, caused considerable financial hardship in specific public bureaucracies. The health-care sector appears to have been particularly hard hit.

24 Quotations taken from Moderaterna's English-language website, www. moderat.se/web/In_English.aspx (4 December 2011). While tax cuts for workers have been introduced, specific exemptions for paying for household help and other deductions make it very difficult to calculate whether lower- or upper-income earners have benefited the most from the new government's tax-cutting programme.

25 Although these were increased again in 2009, they are no longer anywhere near the internationally high levels they reached in the 1980s.

26 The actual changes in structure, administration and fees for different unemployment schemes are in fact quite complicated. For a detailed analysis of these changes and their consequences, see Kjellberg (2010).

27 Indeed, in a rather embarrassing speech after the electoral defeat in 2010, outgoing party leader Mona Sahlin revealed that she didn't actually believe in many of the party positions that she had been defending during the election campaign.

28 In a recent report on Swedish Radio, a reporter remarked on what he called 'the Svallfors Paradox': that Swedish voters overwhelmingly support high taxes but vote for parties that lower taxes (personal communication from Joakim Palme, 3 December 2011).

29 Wolfgang Streeck, personal communication, 29 October 2011.

30 See also the *Financial Times*, which on 13 October 2011 titled a lead article 'European bailout needs Swedish model'.

Chapter 5 Monetary Union, Fiscal Crisis and the Disabling of Democratic Accountability

1 Since citizens cannot be obliged to perform sophisticated causal analyses or to act fairly, sanctions are likely to be suffered by those levels of government that can in fact be punished by voters.

2 These concerns relate to both the perceived problem-solving effectiveness and the perceived normative appropriateness, or justice, of policy outcomes.

3 In David Marsh's (2011) magisterial history of the run-up to the euro there are numerous accounts of the Bundesbank's resistance to requests begging it to consider the impact of its policies on other member states, even when these requests were presented at the highest political level.

4 EMU pessimists in Germany differed in their predictions of failure. On the one hand, the inclusion of former soft-currency economies was expected to generate uncontrollable inflationary spillover into the eurozone as a whole. On the other hand, uncontrollable wage dynamics were expected to undermine competitiveness and to generate mass unemployment in former soft-currency economies (Scharpf 1991: 263–9). Initially, however, both expectations turned out to be wrong.

5 They were right in predicting that (1) monetary union would increase trade flows and capital flows and that (2) increasing trade flows under a common currency would tend to equalize the prices of tradable goods and services. It was wrong to expect, however, that (3) prices in the non-traded sector would also be equalized. Thus differences in inflation rates could persist even though differences in consumer prices were reduced by price convergence in the traded sector.

6 Initially, German fiscal policy had indeed been expansionary. And when the deficit limit was exceeded, the German and French governments blocked the Commission's sanctioning initiative in the Council. But the Red–Green government did not openly challenge the counterproductive logic of the Stability Pact designed by its predecessor. Instead it switched to fiscal consolidation in order to comply with a misconceived rule that required retrenchment in a recession and in the economy with the lowest rate of inflation.

7 For households in the GIPS economies, very low real interest rates would decrease the attractiveness of saving and increase the attractiveness of credit financing, consumption and investment in non-productive assets. For foreign creditors, however, what mattered were not these low real interest rates but the uniform nominal interest rates in the eurozone.

8 In the history of economic theory, the need for differentiated solutions had been postulated by the renowned Swedish economist Erik Lindahl (1930). In his view, the central bank of a monetary union of independent states would need to correct diverging business cycles and inflation rates in member economies by differentiating the supply of central-bank money that national central banks could offer to national banks – which would in turn lead to nationally differing interest rates. It has recently been argued, albeit by heterodox economists, that such options could also be realized in the EMU (Spethmann and Steiger 2005).

9 In contrast to currently popular narratives, external indebtedness even in Greece and Portugal was mainly, and in Spain and Ireland exclusively, due to private-sector rather than public-sector borrowing. Thus in 2007, the year before the financial crisis began, Greece's external balance had amounted to −14.67 per cent of GDP, to which public-sector borrowing contributed only −5.3 per cent. The respective figures for Portugal were −9.78 per cent and −2.65 per cent. In Spain (−10.02 per cent and +1.09 per cent) and Ireland (−5.34 per cent and +0.14 per cent), public-sector surpluses had actually reduced the external imbalance (Eurostat data).

10 In hindsight it seems obvious that the Irish and Spanish (or American and British) governments should have intervened against real-estate bubbles

through legislation tightening the availability of housing credit (Fitz Gerald 2006).

11 It should also be noted, however, that, according to a recent OECD report (2008), income inequality and poverty increased more in Germany after 2000 than in any other OECD country.

12 Council Regulations (EU) nos. 1173–7 and Council Directive 2011/85/EU, 8 November 2011.

13 A contributing motive may have been doubts about the legal viability of 'six-pack' sanctioning rules under the existing treaty (Ohler 2010; Häde 2011; Fischer-Lescano and Kommer 2011).

14 Regulation (EU) no. 1176/2011, at §(3).

15 In the meantime, the Commission has issued a staff working paper specifying that 'external imbalances' include current account balance, net international investment position, real effective exchange rate, export market shares and nominal unit labour cost. 'Internal imbalances' include deflated house prices, private-sector credit flow, private-sector debt and general government debt (SEC 2011: 1361 final, 8 November 2011, table 1).

16 For current accounts, the Commission's staff paper has adopted a deficit threshold of 4 per cent of GDP and, under German pressure, a surplus threshold of 6 per cent – which has provoked protests in the European Parliament (Giegold 2011).

17 Instead of manifesting distrust in the people, the imposition of hierarchical controls might also imply distrust in the competence and integrity of the national government. In either case, the purpose is to disable the mechanisms of democratic self-government in national polities.

18 Empirically and theoretically, this is an overly simplistic summary. But I have neither the capacity nor the space to explore the variety of pragmatic and moral problems, dilemmas and aporias of democratic governments resisting, or collaborating with, the injunctions of hostile or paternalistic external or occupying powers.

Chapter 6 Smaghi versus the Parties

1 The authors have not updated this chapter, which remains as the author left it at his death.

2 See Mair (2009). Section 3 below draws extensively from this paper.

3 For reasons of space, this latter aspect is not treated here. But see Farrell et al. (2011).

4 The details of the story are drawn from the lengthy account by Simon Carswell (2010).

5 For a recent insightful assessment, see Dellepiane and Hardiman (2010).

6 See O'Brien (2011).

7 See Willis (2011), Cahill (2011) and McDermott (2010). I would like to thank Conor Little for guiding me to some of these sources and discussions.

8 There were also minor parties and independent candidates who were campaigning on the pledge of tearing up the agreement in its entirety and reneging

on the overall guarantee to the banks. According to Sinn Féin president Gerry Adams, for example, the party's policy remained to tell the IMF 'to go home and take their money with them' (O'Regan 2011). Speaking in the Dáil on the last day of business before the election, the Sinn Féin parliamentary leader stated: 'I call on all parties in this general election to make clear to the European Union, the IMF and the wider international community that this deal is not acceptable, not affordable and ruinous to the Irish economy and the Irish people. It was negotiated and imposed by a discredited Government and it must be set aside' (Dáil Debates 2011).

9 Transcript of a conference call on the Extended Fund Facility Arrangement for Ireland (www.imf.org/external/np/tr/2010/tr121710.htm). See also McDermott (2010).

10 On the last day of Dáil business before the election, for example, the Labour leader Eamon Gilmore stated that 'this election is a three-way contest. Those who want more of the same can vote for the Fianna Fáil party that brought down the country, that tied the State to the sinking and stinking misfortunes of the banks and that sold us out in the deal with the EU and IMF' (Dáil Debates 2011). Later, launching his party's economic programme for the election, he stated that the choice facing the electorate was to have the budget decided by the ECB or by the Irish government, and the voters could either accept the rescue deal or trust Labour to change its terms: 'It's Frankfurt's way or Labour's way' (McGee 2011).

11 See also the comments by Olli Rehn, EU Economics Commissioner: 'I'm of course following the Irish debate closely and I'm aware that in democratic politics we have freedom of speech and freedom of positions. At the same time, it is clear that the EU has signed the Memorandum of Understanding with the State, with the Republic of Ireland and we expect continuity and respect of the memorandum . . . . If there will be any changes to the pricing policy, which I personally support and the Commission supports, it will take place for the overall European reasons not specifically because of electoral statements in Ireland' (Beesley et al., 2011).

12 See Cowen (2010).

13 For an extensive discussion of these cumulating problems in application to the German case, see Streeck (2006, 2007).

Chapter 7 Liberalization, Inequality and Democracy's Discontent

1 I would like to thank Martin Höpner, Julian Garritzmann and Jonas Pontusson for their helpful comments and suggestions.

2 Hayek (1980: 271) considers this to be Keynes's 'most dangerous legacy'.

3 One of Olson's aims is to answer the question 'Why are some modern societies to some degree *ungovernable*?' (Olson 1982: 8; emphasis added).

4 Unless indicated otherwise, averages are based on data for the set of twenty-three countries listed in table 7.1.

5 The underlying judgements about what constitutes economic freedom are of course highly normative and disputable. For example, in this index, higher

collective bargaining coverage rates indicate less freedom, as do higher levels of government expenditure. I use the index to track empirical changes without subscribing to its normative intentions.

6 Union density has the strongest impact on the distribution of incomes. The influence of unions is probably twofold: strong unions can compress market incomes and put pressure on (left-wing) parties to take measures to decommodify labour. As trade unions lose members, however, they may become less able to achieve either goal.

7 This assessment is based on the inspection of a conditional plot that shows how social expenditure moderates the effect of employment protection. The graph has not been included here.

8 This set-up roughly follows Solt (2008), but with different indicators and a larger number of elections. See table 7.7 for the list of elections and surveys.

9 Substituting education for income in the analyses does not alter the results, as was the case for turnout.

Chapter 8 Participatory Inequality in the Austerity State

1 Note that the interest of political parties in the *overall* turnout in elections is at best qualified. Party A, while interested in mobilizing its own constituency as much as possible, will also be interested in Party B's failure to mobilize *its* constituency, as the abstention of (potential) B-voters is bound to benefit A. Neither can parties be unequivocally interested in *maximizing* the number of those who join them as members, since, depending on how active these members are, they may exacerbate the party's problems of internal conflict management. In cases where citizens turn from voting and party membership to less formal modes of political expression (civil society associations, movements, protests), such moves could be considered by political party elites to be positively unwelcome.

2 In most countries, however, party membership has been declining considerably since the 1970s. See van Biezen et al. (2012).

3 Nor is the problem of participatory distortion of a self-healing nature, as several authors seem to imply. There is nothing 'paradoxical' (Schäfer 2011c: 4) or a 'puzzle' (as Solt 2008: 57 explains) about the fact that (a) high rates of non-participation are statistically correlated with low levels of individual income, education and security and the fact that (b) the average *increase* in educational standards and prosperity coincides with growing levels of participatory distortion and patterned political disaffection. To argue otherwise is to do so based on a fallacy of composition and on disregard for the possibility that growing overall inequality, which discourages participation, could trump the effect of growing *average* income and education on participation.

4 To be sure, this deficiency could be fixed if voters were provided with the option to tick an additional box on the ballot that would allow them to vote NOTA (meaning 'none of the above').

5 This apparent trend (with only five EU member states maintaining the duty, sometimes without any sanctions: Cyprus, Greece, Italy, Luxembourg and

Belgium) has, however, a counter-trend in the Andean states of Chile, Peru, Ecuador and (with positively draconian sanctions attached) Bolivia. In these latter countries, sanctions can take the form of monetary fines that in most cases are quite moderate; voters may also conceivably be excluded from the next election if they fail to show up for the present one.

6 One example is the registration campaigns for African Americans of the 1980s. Cf. Piven and Cloward (1988).

7 Only if one were to adopt the perspective of making individual 'deficiencies' causally responsible for distortions could one find it 'especially disturbing' that the decline in turnout persists even though 'levels of education and pros-perity (factors that can be expected to increase turnout) have been going up dramatically in Europe, as they have in the United States' (Lijphart 1998: 5).

8 This is also the conclusion that Petring and Merkel (2011: 33) draw in a postscript to a summary of their earlier paper (Merkel and Petring 2011). In that postscript they write: 'Instead of engaging in a hopeless struggle against symptoms, the causes should be addressed. Such a causal approach should consist primarily of new educational, social, tax, and economic poli-cies. Demonstrating that public policies are still able to reduce inequalities, tame markets, and subject them to democratic control . . . could motivate participation by those parts of the citizenry who now have turned away from it [political participation] in frustration' [my translation]. Interestingly and perhaps symptomatically, this key thought is deleted from the 'official' version of their paper (ibid.) as published by the Social Democratic Friedrich Ebert Foundation, which had commissioned it.

9 One striking illustration of this is a referendum on a school-reform proposal in the city-state of Hamburg that was backed by all political parties. The turnout of the intended beneficiaries of this reform was much lower than that of its middle-class opponents, and the latter defeated the reform. This result can be explained by the combined effect of the losers being poorly informed by the media and the winners having much greater resources to invest in the campaign. Cf. Römmele and Schober (2010).

10 Conveniently operationalized as the percentage of those surveyed who *disa-greed* with the statement 'People like me don't have any say about what the government does' (Madsen 1978).

11 In contrast to real money, however, there is no saving or hoarding with politi-cal money, which should provide a built-in incentive actually to spend it at the only time when it has value, namely on election day.

12 This logic could still be seen at work when the Red–Green coalition govern-ment in Germany liberalized the German Citizenship Act (effective 2000), which facilitated the access to full citizenship (including voting rights) to long-term resident foreign workers and their spouses and descendants.

13 The obvious problem with this response is that, in a dynamic analysis, we can expect a second-order effect where political parties thus rejected will decide even more consistently to drop the interests of the less privileged from their agenda, since the latter do not vote for them anyway and therefore the former will face no loss by ignoring their interests. This dynamic can explain

the change, away from vote-maximizing, catch-all parties and their broad bases of support, to clientelistic parties who cater only to special interests and specific segments of the constituency, while their agendas ignore the interests of all those who are unlikely to support them in the first place.

14 See recent challenges to these assumptions, however: Berger (2011); Saunders (2011)

15 'Most Americans are much more concerned with the business of buying and selling, earning and disposing of things, than they are with the "idle" chatter of politics' (Lane 1962: 25).

16 States are preferred clients because so-called sovereign debtors have a number of advantages that are absent from ordinary borrowers of financial means: they have the authority to extract revenues from citizens, they can print money, and they have no choice but to bail out 'systemic' financial institutions if they fail.

17 Had it not been for an intervention of the German Constitutional Court, an ad hoc installed special committee of the Bundestag consisting of just nine members would have been allowed exclusive decision-making rights on urgent European Financial Stability Facility (EFSF) affairs, thereby pre-empting the right of Parliament as a whole to approve of international treaties that could cost taxpayers dozens of billions of euros or more. Another initiative to bypass elected legislatures (this time the European Parliament) occurred when not even the EP president was allowed to be present (in contrast to representatives of 'systemic banks') when eurozone heads of government negotiated a 'Fiscal Pact' on 31 January 2012. The role of parliaments is evidently in danger of being suspended in favour of the rating agencies.

Chapter 10 The Normalization of the Right in Post-Security Europe

1 I wish to thank Armin Schäfer and Wolfgang Streeck for their thoughtful comments on the first version of this chapter, as well as for their invitation to the conference on 'Democracy in Straightjackets' held in Schloss Ringberg, Germany, on 24–5 March 2011. Their comments and the discussion of conference participants helped shape my revisions. In addition, I thank Richard Swedberg for his reading of my draft chapter, Alexa Yesukevich for her assistance in manuscript preparation and Jenny Todd for designing the tables.

2 Schmitter (2000) captures the irony of this position.

3 In contrast, Holmes (2000) argues that the 'fast capitalism' of globalization has given rise to right-wing impulses across the European continent.

4 Art's (2006) study of how German and Austrian politicians used national memory to influence public debate displays a sophisticated use of legacy theory. Analysts tend to invoke legacy only to dismiss it (Capoccia 2005: 83–107).

5 This perception has been a standard feature of accounts by journalists such as Steven Erlanger (2009) and is working its way into the academic literature.

See, for example, the essays in Bowyer and Vail (2011); Cronin et al. (2011); and Mudge (2011).

6 Sarkozy's popularity experienced a small upturn in April 2011 because of his support for Libya.

7 Results from a variety of public opinion polls converge on the point that Sarkozy's national identity campaigns, coupled with his attack on the Roma, further weakened him politically (Nunes 2011).

8 The data for this section come from the following websites: www.nsd.uib.no/european_election_database/country/france/presidential_elections.html and www.parties-and-elections.de/.

9 Arter (2010, 2011) describes this party and election in the context of Finnish electoral politics.

10 Moravcsik (2005, 2006) is a leading proponent of this position.

11 The essays in Checkel and Katzenstein (2009) introduce this topic, which has been over-theorized and under-empiricized.

Chapter 11 The Crisis in Context

1 Sections of this chapter appeared in *New Left Review*, 71 (2011).

2 For example, through nationalization of key firms and sectors or, as in Germany, through 'economic democracy' in the form of worker rights of 'co-determination' in large companies.

3 The exact content of such rights may change and obviously differs between social and geographical locations. But certain elements seem universal – for example, that someone who puts in a 'good day's work' should not be poor, meaning that his income should enable him and his family to participate fully in the life of his community. Other common principles of moral economy include the insistence on attributions of social worth different from economic worth and on values and entitlements that cannot be expressed in terms of market prices.

4 This, to me, is the essence of what Polanyi (1957 [1944]) means when he writes of a 'counter-movement' against the commodification of labour (Streeck 2009: 246ff.).

5 That is, that they are not just functionalist efficiency theories.

6 In a seminal essay, Michal Kalecki identified the 'confidence' of investors as a crucial factor determining economic performance (Kalecki 1943). Investor confidence, according to Kalecki, depends on the extent to which current profit expectations of capital owners are reliably sanctioned by the distribution of political power and the policies to which it gives rise. Economic dysfunctions, such as unemployment, – ensue when business sees its profit expectations threatened by political interference. 'Wrong' policies that cause a loss of business confidence may result in turn in what would amount to an investment strike by capital owners. Kalecki's perspective makes it possible to model a capitalist economy as an interactive game, as distinguished from a natural or machine-like mechanism. If the economy is in this way conceived as interactive, the point at which capitalists react adversely to

non-market allocation by withdrawing investment need not be seen as once and for all fixed and mathematically predictable but may be negotiable. For example, it may be set by a historically evolved and historically changeable level of aspiration or by strategic calculation on the part of capitalists. This is why predictions based on universalistic – i.e., historically and culturally indifferent – economic models so often fail: they assume fixed parameters where in reality these are socially and historically flexible.

7   In other words, standard economic accounts of economic crises are essentially representations, in the form of sets of simultaneous equations, of the strategic reactions of the owners of productive resources, making what are the particularistic claims of a social group appear like the laws of gravity driving the motions of the stars in a Newtonian universe.

8   On the following, see Samuelson (2010), among others.

9   With the Personal Responsibility and Work Opportunity Reconciliation Act of 1996.

10 Figure 11.5 shows the development in the lead capitalist country, the United States, where the four stages unfold in ideal-typical fashion. For other countries it is necessary to make allowances reflecting their particular circumstances, including their position in the global political economy. In Germany, for example, public debt began to rise sharply in the 1970s. This corresponds to the fact that German inflation was low long before Volcker, as a result of the independence of the Bundesbank and the monetarist policies it adopted as early as 1974 (Scharpf 1991).

11 For a state with public debt equaling 100 per cent of GDP, an increase by 2 percentage points in the average rate of interest it has to pay to its creditors would raise its yearly deficit by the same amount. A current budget deficit of 4 per cent of GDP would as a result increase by half.

12 In other words, not even 'the markets' are willing to put their money on the supply-side mantra according to which growth is stimulated by cuts in public spending. On the other hand, who can say how much new debt is enough, and how much too much, for a country to outgrow its old debt.

13 Wolfgang Schäuble, in an interview with the *Financial Times* (5 December 2010): 'We need new forms of international governance, global governance and European governance.' As summarized by the *FT*: 'If the German parliament were asked for a vote today on giving up national budgetary authority, "you would not get a Yes vote", he added. But "if you would give us some months to work on this, and if you give us the hope that other member states will agree as well, I would see a chance."' Schäuble was, fittingly, 'speaking as winner of the FT competition for European finance minister of the year'.

14 For example, political appeals for redistributive 'solidarity' are now directed at entire nations asked by international organizations to support other entire nations, such as Slovenia being urged to help Ireland, Greece and Portugal. This hides the fact that those being supported by this sort of 'international solidarity' are not the people in the streets but the banks, domestic and foreign, that would otherwise have to accept losses or lower profits. It also neglects differences in national income. While Germans are on average

richer than Greeks (although some Greeks are much richer than almost all Germans), Slovenians are on average much poorer than the Irish, who have statistically a higher per capita income than nearly all euro countries, including Germany. Essentially the new conflict alignment translates class conflicts into international conflicts, pitting against one another nations that are all subject to the same financial market pressures for public austerity. Rather than from those who have long resumed collecting their 'bonuses', ordinary people 'on the streets' are told to demand 'sacrifices' from other ordinary people, who happen to be citizens of other states, somehow to make less painful the 'sacrifices' they themselves are asked to make.

Index